1994

Pocket Guide to the

WINES

OF AUSTRALIA and NEW ZEALAND

James Halliday

Angus&Robertson
An imprint of HarperCollins*Publishers*

An Angus & Robertson Publication

Angus & Robertson, an imprint of
HarperCollins*Publishers*
25 Ryde Road, Pymble, Sydney NSW 2073, Australia
31 View Road, Glenfield, Auckland 10, New Zealand
77–85 Fulham Palace Road, London W6 8JB, United Kingdom
10 East 53rd Street, New York NY 10022, USA

First published in Australia in 1992
This revised edition published in October 1993

ISBN 0 207 179158
Cover photograph by Oliver Strewe
Printed in Hong Kong

9 8 7 6 5 4 3 2 1
96 95 94 93

CONTENTS

HOW TO USE THIS GUIDE

In an endeavour to keep the *Pocket Guide* as compact as possible, a number of abbreviations have been used. A full list of the abbreviations is provided on page 9. Hopefully, you will quickly become used to the abbreviations and will not need to constantly cross-refer to them. I will now walk you through the information for each entry in the order in which it occurs in the entry.

HENSCHKE A–A Est 1868 $11–35 R 102, 119, 147, 169, 170, 264 ADELAIDE HILLS Moculta Road, Keyneton, SA 5353 (085) 64 8223 fax (085) 64 8294
Open Mon–Fri 9–4.30, Sat 9–12 **Production** 35 000 cases
Winemaker Stephen Henschke
Principal Wines Chard, Chenin, Gewurz, Ries, Sauv Bl, Sem, Cab Sauv, Hill of Grace, Mount Edelstone and Cyril Henschke are the great red wine labels; Lenswood (Adelaide Hills) the new addition.
Best Vintages W '82, '85, '87, '89, '90 R '82, '84, '86, '88, '90
Summary Unchallenged as one of the top half dozen wineries in Australia, and has gone from strength to strength over the past 13 years or so under the guidance of Stephen and Prue Henschke. The red wines fully capitalise on the very old, low-yielding, high quality vines, and are superbly made with sensitive but positive use of new small oak; the same skills are evident in the white wine making.
Recommended Wines 1992 Semillon (lovely wine with complex fruit flavours, peachy and almost Chardonnay-like, with excellent oak integration; to 1998). 1992 Lenswood Giles Pinot Noir (stylish, aromatic plum and spice aroma, very tangy, complex Burgundian palate with spice and sappiness; drink now). 1990 Mount Edelstone (strong dark fruit, plum and liquorice aroma; structured, rich palate with dark red fruits, a hint of gaminess and soft tannins; to 2010). 1990 Hill of Grace (wonderfully smooth yet deep; powerful, classic velvet fist in iron glove; hints of berry, earth and dark chocolate; to 2020). Also strongly recommended: 1990 Cyril Henschke Cabernet Sauvignon, 1991 Lenswood Croft Chardonnay, 1990 Lenswood Abbotts Prayer Merlot Cabernet.

WINERY NAME   **HENSCHKE**

This may seem straightforward, but is not necessarily so. Wherever possible, I have used the name which appears most prominently on the label, and have not made reference to an associated trading name. Likewise, the label frequently abbreviates the winery name (dropping off such words as 'Wines', 'Estate', 'Pty Ltd', and so on), and I have used that abbreviated name. Where a ' • ' appears before the winery name, it indicates that the winery is a new entry for 1994.

RATINGS   **A–A**

Quality   **Price**
A   Very good to outstanding   A   Very well priced
B   Good   B   Fairly priced

C	Adequate commercial wine	**C**	Borderline value
D	Variable or poor	**D**	Over-priced for quality
NR	Not rated		

eg an **A–A** rating indicates very good to outstanding wines which are very well priced.

Two letters linked in a rating (eg **CA**) means one of two things: either that there is some real variation in the quality or value from wine to wine (within the terms of reference of each), or simply that the average falls somewhere between the levels ascribed to each single letter rating. To try to avoid this ambiguity would have led to an impossibly complex rating scheme, and at the end of the day one has to accept the ratings as subjective and arbitrary, and as an imprecise guide at best.

In the manner of wine shows — notwithstanding that the real difference between a gold and a silver medal can be one-third of a point (out of 20), with gold, silver or bronze medals commonly given at different shows to the same wine — all of the attention will be given to the gold medals, in other words, the **A–A** ratings. But I urge you to realise there is only the finest distinction between a **BA–A** rating (or an **A–AB** rating) and an **A–A** rating — and so on down the scale. And please remember, too, that a **B–B** rating indicates the winery is producing good wines offered at a fair price.

In the case of the major producers, I have had to take a flexible approach in relation to the quality ratings; had I not done so, none of the medium to large-sized companies could have possibly achieved an **A** rating simply because they have such a wide range of products. What the **A** rating means in this circumstance is that across the board, the wines (relative to their station in life) are very good to outstanding.

Finally, quality ratings are like vintage ratings in any event. They represent a gut-feel at a given point of time. They will not be valid for every wine which the maker produces from every vintage. Individual wines may be distinctly better or distinctly worse than the ratings would indicate.

NR means the winery is not rated, usually because I have not recently tasted its wines, or because it is too recent on the scene. In this (1994) edition I have increased the number of **NR** ratings for newer wineries simply because I have come to realise it is dangerous to assess a winery on the evidence of only one or two vintages.

YEAR OF ESTABLISHMENT   **EST 1868**

A more or less self-explanatory item, but you should be aware that some makers choose the year in which they purchased the land, others the year in which they first planted grapes, others the year they first made wine, others the year they first offered wine for sale . . . and so on. There may also be minor complications where there has been a change of ownership or a break in production; varying practices exist here, and I have not attempted to arbitrate or adjudicate between them.

PRICE   **$11–35 R**

PRICES GIVEN ARE FOR PURCHASE IN AUSTRALIA, IN AUSTRALIAN DOLLARS; THOSE FOR NEW ZEALAND ARE IN NEW ZEALAND DOLLARS AND FOR PURCHASE THERE.

1. In each instance I have indicated whether the price is cellar door or retail; by and large the choice has been determined by which of the two methods of sale is most important to the winery, ie it will reflect the way you will most probably purchase the wine. In this day and age it is hazardous in the extreme to try and predict the difference between the retail price and the cellar door price, but most wineries would seek to offer the wine cellar door (or by mailing list — the price will be one and the same except for freight) at about 15% less than the normal single bottle retail price.

2. The concept of normal retail price was once a simple matter, but is no longer so. Whether or not encouraged by the winery (some do, some don't) discounting is a way of life, so much so that there are three or four different retail prices for any given wine. The first is the recommended retail price, arrived at by applying a full margin (according to various formulae). Some wine is sold at that price these days, but not much. The next price (lower than the recommended) is sometimes called the real retail price; it does not assume any special promotional deal, but does in all probability reflect a less than full margin being obtained by the retailer.

The third price is the so-called promotional price, a price arrived at by virtue of the wholesaler/distributor (or the winery where it deals direct with retailers) giving a percentage reduction in the case price, usually for a multi-case purchase, matched by a reduced retailer margin.

These three levels of price all exist, and may give rise to a $5 variation in the price of a $15 bottle of wine.

Fourthly and finally, there is the super discount price, which bears little or no relationship to the recommended price, and little or no relationship to the price which prevailed when the wine was first released. It may reflect a retailer quitting stock at or below cost as a loss leader, or as a means of getting cash flow, or it may represent a special incentive from the wine company or distributor anxious to get rid of the last remaining stocks of a particular wine. In almost all instances, the retail prices quoted are the recommended retail prices, and it should not take a great deal of ingenuity on your part for you to find wines at lower prices.

3. The price range is simply for the cheapest and most expensive table wine being sold by the winery in mid 1991. The letter 'R' of course means that it is the retail price, 'ML' or 'CD' indicates that it is the cellar door price. In almost all instances I have not reflected the cost of fortified wines or sparkling wines, simply because these tend to distort the relative pricing as between those wineries which do sell fortified wines (which are more expensive) and those which do not. The only exception is in respect to the producers in North East Victoria who specialise in fortifieds, Muscats and Tokays, and the top prices of these are quoted. There the maximum will be for fortified wines, the minimum for table wines.

4. Space does not permit a wine-by-wine pricing, and the span of prices is there simply for an approximate indication of the pricing structure of each winery.

PRICING NOTES FOR UNITED KINGDOM READERS*

1. The price of wine in the United Kingdom is affected by a number of factors, including excise and customs duty rates, VAT, and the level of mark-up applied at the various stages of distribution.

At present, a bottle of Australian wine entering the United

Kingdom attracts approximately £1 (£2 for sparkling wines) in duties and 17.5% VAT on its retail price. The importer of the wine will mark up the price by up to 25% before selling to the retailer, who in turn will add 30–35%. Any additional links in the distribution chain will add further to the eventual cost of the wine. Importers selling direct to the public cut out at least one of these margins.

The tax system in Australia is different from that in the United Kingdom: normally 10% of the purchase price of a bottle is passed to the government as tax on the alcohol. Therefore, the tax on wines selling for under $20 is less than it would be if they were sold in the United Kingdom for an equivalent price. The tax on wines selling for over $20 is more.

2. As a general rule the above holds true and most prices in the United Kingdom are comparable with the full retail, ie non-discounted, price in Australia once the tax differential has been removed. Some wines are less expensive in the United Kingdom; for example, Penfolds' Grange Hermitage can be 20% cheaper. Certainly Australian wines represent very good value in the United Kingdom, compared not only with other regional and varietal wines but even with those in Australia. New Zealand wines also offer good value at present, due to the weakness of the New Zealand dollar.

As a result of heavy discounting/loss leading in Australia and the very high duty rates on sparkling wines in the United Kingdom, these wines appear to be very much more expensive in the United Kingdom than in Australia.

3. The very high fixed costs associated with wine in the United Kingdom make it virtually impossible to retail wine for less than £2. However, major buyers, dealing direct with the producer in Australia, bottling under their own label and retailing the wine through their own outlets, have been able to offer sound Australian wine for under £3 per bottle. As a rule, though, the general starting price for wine from a known producer is closer to £3.50.

* Information by courtesy of Philip Reedman, The Australian Wine Centre.

METHODS OF DISTRIBUTION	102, 119, 147, 169, 170, 264

One of the changes (and hopefully improvements) to this edition of the Guide has been the incorporation of a distributor index. On pages 226–40 you will find distributor lists for Australia, New Zealand, the United Kingdom and Canada. Each distributor is given a number, and that distributor number appears as indicated in the sample entry. Alternatively, you will find SD, which means that the winery sells all of its wine direct, even if to resellers such as restaurants and retailers.

REGION	ADELAIDE HILLS

At the end of the first line or on the second line, I give the region of the winery, often abbreviated for space reasons, but hopefully decipherable without the need of any special key.

ADDRESS AND PHONE NUMBER
Moculta Road, Keyneton, SA 5353 (085) 64 8223

Largely self-explanatory; the address is that of the winery and cellar door; in a few instances it is simply of the vineyard — this occurs when the wine is made at another winery under contract, and is sold only through retail.

CELLAR DOOR SALES HOURS	OPEN MON–FRI 9–4.30, SAT 9–12

These appear after the words 'Open' in the third or fourth line of the text. Where the winery is either shown as not open, or (for example) only open on weekends, a telephone call will quickly tell you whether it is in fact prepared to open by appointment. Many will, some won't. Also, virtually every winery which is shown as being open only for weekends is in fact open for public holidays. Once again, a phone call will put that matter beyond doubt.

PRODUCTION	35 000 CASES

The figure is given merely to give you an indication of the size of the operation. Some wineries (principally but not exclusively the large companies) regard the information as confidential, and in that event 'NFP' (not for publication) will appear.

WINEMAKER	STEPHEN HENSCHKE

In the large companies, the winemaker is simply the head of a team; there may be many executive winemakers actually responsible for specific wines.

PRINCIPAL WINES

Chard, Chenin, Gewurz, Ries, Sauv Bl, Sem, Cab Sauv, Hill of Grace, Mount Edelstone and Cyril Henschke are the great red wine labels; Lenswood (Adelaide Hills) the new addition.

Abbreviations once again raise their ugly head, but hopefully you will quickly become familiar with them. Particularly with the larger companies, it is not possible to give a complete list of the wines; the saving grace is that these days most of the wines are simply identified on their label by their varietal composition.

BEST VINTAGES	W '82, '85, '87, '89, '90 R '82, '84, '86, '88, '90

This is the only area in which I defer to the winemaker's judgment. While I may well have tasted many of the wines from a given winery over the years, I do not have the opportunity that the maker does of constantly undertaking vertical tastings (ie tastings of successive vintages) — when I say constantly, I mean once or twice a year. There really is no option but to defer to the winemaker's view of such matters. It should also be realised that these judgments are a generalisation within themselves: if a winery has three white wines and three red wines, there might well be a different vintage rating for each wine if space permitted. The problem becomes acute for some producers who, for example, produce both Pinot Noir and Cabernet Sauvignon, or Rhine Riesling and Chardonnay.

SUMMARY

Unchallenged as one of the top half dozen wineries in Australia, and has gone from strength to strength over the past 13 years or so under the guidance of Stephen and Prue Henschke. The red wines fully capitalise on the very old, low-yielding, high quality vines, and are superbly made with sensitive but positive use of new small oak; the same skills are evident in the white wine making.

My summary of the winery; little needs to be said, except that I have tried to mix up the subjects I have touched on.

RECOMMENDED WINES

Those wines appearing in red are of very high quality, typically of gold medal or trophy winning standard. Those appearing in black are wines of well above average quality, roughly corresponding to silver medal standard in national wine shows. Obviously enough, I have tasted many more wines in the course of the last year, many specifically for the purposes of this Guide. Partly for reasons of space, I have elected only to give notes of those which really are of excellent quality. Frustratingly, not all of these will still be available for sale either through retail outlets or at cellar door, particularly as 1994 runs by. However, the notes will hopefully be of interest to those who have the wines in their cellar, and by rights should give some guide to the style of wine you might expect from succeeding vintages. The other indicator here is the overall winery quality rating, which I have already explained.

KEY TO ABBREVIATIONS

CD	Cellar door/Cellar door price	NFP	Not for publication
LR	Limited Retail	R	Retail
ML	Mailing List	SD	Self-distributor
Ausl	Auslese	Meth Champ	Methode Champenoise
Burg	Burgundy		
Cab Franc	Cabernet Franc	Mos	Moselle
Cab Mer	Cabernet Merlot	Muller	Muller Thurgau
Cab Sauv	Cabernet Sauvignon	P Gris	Pinot Gris
		Pinot	Pinot Noir
Cab Malb	Cabernet Malbec	Ries	Riesling
Cab Shir	Cabernet Shiraz	Saut	Sauternes
Chab	Chablis	Sauv Bl	Sauvignon Blanc
Champ	Champagne	Sem	Semillon
Chard	Chardonnay	Shir	Shiraz
Chenin	Chenin Blanc	Sparkl	Sparkling
Colomb	Colombard	Spat Lex	Spatese Lexia
Fronti	Frontignac	Sylv	Sylvaner
Fumé	Fumé Blanc	Tram Ries	Traminer Riesling
Gewurz	Gewurztraminer		
Gren	Grenache	Verd	Verdelho
Herm	Hermitage	Viog	Viognier
LH	Late Harvest	Wh	White
LP	Late Picked	Wh Burg	White Burgundy
Mer	Merlot	Zin	Zinfandel

1993 VINTAGE

AUSTRALIA

The year 1993 will be remembered by vignerons as 'the year we got out of gaol'. Abnormally wet and cool weather prevailed through spring and summer, causing widespread mildew and botrytis. March was better, and the warmest and sunniest April on record transformed the year. 583 000 tonnes were harvested, 7.4% down on the 1992 crush, with overall quality far better than expected. In NEW SOUTH WALES, all districts experienced a very late vintage. In the Lower Hunter some Cabernet Sauvignon was not harvested until mid April, a month later than any previous vintage; yields, sugar levels and flavours were modest. The Murrumbidgee Irrigation Area fared better, with above average yields of eagerly sought grapes. SOUTH AUSTRALIA broke records set in 1992 for low temperatures and high rainfall, with yields reduced by poor fruit set and fungal diseases — although losses varied widely from one vineyard to the next: in Coonawarra, from nil to 90%. Quality was very good, helped by the reduced crop levels, and by a vintage that was only slightly delayed. Padthaway yields were down by 10%, but whites and reds have exceptional character and flavour. The Southern Vales and Adelaide Hills produced superb white wines, thanks to cool ripening conditions and crop down 20–30%. The Barossa Valley vintage started very late, but the April sunshine meant the later-ripening varieties caught up, with all wineries stretched to the limit. Reduced yields resulted in intense flavours and strong colours in the reds. The Clare Valley experienced the most difficult year: some vineyards were devastated, and vintage was a month late. The Riverlands largely recovered from an indifferent start; yields were down 10–15%, but white wine quality was well above average. VICTORIA followed the national pattern: April completely turned the year around, and although vintage started and finished very late, fully ripe grapes were harvested. The Yarra Valley fared better than the Mornington Peninsula, and although Pinot Noir will not have the remarkable colour intensity of 1991 and 1992, flavour is good. The same late vintage ran all the way to the North East, with some great Muscats and Tokays. WESTERN AUSTRALIA'S southern regions experienced a wild start with hail (and even snow) causing early season losses, but the white wines of the Margaret River are magnificent; those of the Swan Valley are very good. Conditions during harvest in the Great Southern partially replicated those of spring, but varieties such as Rhine Riesling and Cabernet Sauvignon rose above the vicissitudes of the year.

NEW ZEALAND

The southern Australian weather systems carry across the Tasman, and New Zealand — with the notable exceptions of AUCKLAND and CENTRAL OTAGO — had an exceptionally difficult year, with the overall yield down by a devastating 40%. GISBORNE had a poor vintage, with Chardonnay particularly affected (as it was in much of the country). HAWKE'S BAY fared somewhat better, as did MARTINBOROUGH, with a late but satisfactory harvest. MARLBOROUGH, too, was nail-bitingly late, and yields down, a situation repeated in CANTERBURY. While the loss of crop could not have come at a worse time given the demand for grapes, most vignerons agree that a normal crop would not have ripened in the central and southern regions, so the winds (and rains) were not all ill.

•ABBEY VALE VINEYARD NR EST 1988 $10–13 CD 94 MARGARET R
Wildwood Road, Margaret River, WA 6282 phone and
fax (097) 55 2286
Open 7 days 10–5 **Production** 8000 cases
Winemaker K McKay, Houghton (Contract)
Principal Wines Sem, Sem Verd, Verd, LP Verd, Chen Bl, Cab
Sauv; also Moonshine Ale brewed on the premises.
Summary With 25 hectares of vineyard, planted predominantly to
semillon and verdelho, this vineyard (formerly Kidepo Valley) sells most
of its grapes to Houghton. The wine is made under contract at
Houghton, and is sold through an attractive colonial-style mudbrick
cellar door facility at highly competitive prices. A small restaurant open
every day for lunch overlooks the omnipresent Margaret River dam.

AFFLECK C–CB Est 1976 $8.50–17 SD CANBERRA
RMB 244 Gundaroo Road, Bungendore, ACT 2621 (06) 236 9276
Open By appointment **Production** 200 cases
Winemaker Ian Hendry
Principal Wines Chard, Pinot, LH Sauv Bl, Cab Shir, Muscat.
Summary A strictly weekend and holiday interest for busy
professionals Ian and Sue Hendry; a firm, herbaceous 1990 Chardonnay
showed competent winery skills. No more recent tastings.

ALKOOMI BA–BA Est 1971 $11–19.95 R 20, 31, 69, 81, 145,
165, 167, 208, 220 GRT SOUTHERN
Wingeballup Road, Frankland, WA 6396 (098) 55 2229
fax (098) 55 2284
Open 7 days 10.30–5 **Production** 15 000 cases
Winemaker Kim Hart
Principal Wines Ries, Chard, Sauv Bl, Classic DW, Shir, Cab
Sauv, Malb, Classic Red, Sparkl Burg.
Best Vintages W '82, '84, '85, '90, '91 R '83, '84, '86, '89, '89,
'90
Summary One of the senior and most important wineries of the far-
flung district, remote, but well worth seeking out. A high degree of
skill and dedication in both vineyard and winery pays handsome
dividends.
Recommended Wines 1992 Chardonnay (complex, toasty barrel
ferment oak with citrus and melon fruit; tight, ageworthy). 1990
Cabernet Sauvignon (briary, earthy concentrated bouquet, dark berry
cassis fruit, very well structured, silky tannins; to 2010). 1992 Rhine
Riesling (richer, more forward style than usual with full lime fruit,
touch of herbaceousness).

ALLANDALE B–B Est 1977 $12.50–18 CD 61, 157, 178, 226
HUNTER V
Lovedale Road, Pokolbin via Maitland, NSW 2321 (049) 90 4526
fax (049) 90 1714
Open Mon–Sat 9–5, Sun 10–5 **Production** 15 000 cases
Winemaker Bill Sneddon
Principal Wines Meth Champ, Sauv Bl, Sem, Chard, Tram, Pinot,
Shir, Cab Sauv.

Best Vintages W '84, '85, '86, '87, '91 R '83, '85, '86, '87, '91
Summary Unostentatious, medium-sized winery which has been under the control of winemaker Bill Sneddon for well over a decade. Harpers Hill is second label; watch for the occasional special release Chardonnays.
Recommended Wines 1992 Semillon (crisp, nicely balanced, well made wine which should blossom by 1998). 1991 Chardonnay (rich, buttery, toasty regional aromas and flavours; drink now). 1991 Matthew Shiraz (moderately ripe, hint of spicy oak, clean regional style not overripe or over extracted).

ALLANMERE BA–BA Est 1984 $12.50–20 CD 11 HUNTER V
Allandale Road, Allandale via Pokolbin, NSW 2321 (049) 30 7387
Open Mon–Fri 11–4, w'ends 9.30–5 **Production** 4000 cases
Winemaker Newton Potter, Geoff Broadfield
Principal Wines Chard, Sem, Trinity (Chard, Sem, Sauv Bl blend), Cab Sauv, Trinity Red (Cab blend); Durham is top of range Chard.
Best Vintages W '85, '86, '88, '90, '91 R '85, '86, '87, '89, '90
Summary For the time being at least, Newton Potter, assisted by long-term part-time winemaker Geoff Broadfield (who also officiates at Wandin Valley Estate), continues to own and run Allanmere, producing beautifully crafted white and red wines.
Recommended Wines 1992 Chardonnay (elegant, well balanced, well made wine with soft peach and melon fruit, and an echo of oak; to 1995). 1991 Durham Chardonnay (extremely rich, buttery, viscous peaches and cream style, now at its peak). 1991 Trinity White (smooth, honeyed buttery fruit with some toasty aromas and flavours; soft finish). 1989 Trinity Red (clean, pleasant wine not varietally distinct, but with good texture and weight; faintly leafy; drink now).

ALL SAINTS NR Est 1864 $6.85–35 R 81 NE VIC
All Saints Road, Wahgunyah, Vic 3687 (060) 33 1922
Open Mon–Sat 9–5, Sun 11–5 **Production** 30 000 cases
Winemaker Neil Jericho
Principal Wines Chard, Tram Ries, Chenin, Ries, Shir, Cab Mer, Muscat, Tokay, Port.
Summary The purchase of All Saints by Brown Brothers in 1991 was an almost fairytale ending to what promised to be a disaster. It makes great sense, and should ensure the future of the historic All Saints Winery as a major cellar door and tourist attraction — as well as giving Brown Brothers some fabulous fortified wine stocks.

AMBERLEY ESTATE NR Est 1987 $11.60–18.65 R 33, 34, 55, 220 MARGARET R
Wildwood and Thornton Road, Yallingup, WA 6282 (097) 55 2288
fax (097) 55 2171
Open 7 days 10–4.30 **Production** 24 000 cases
Winemaker Eddie Price
Principal Wines Wh Burg, Sauv Bl, Chenin, Sem, Sauv Blanc Sem, Cab Sauv, Mer, Nouveau.
Summary An ambitious venture owned by South African-born Albert Haak with ex-Brown Bros winemaker Eddie Price in charge of production. Still early days, but the first white wines were very light bodied with the exception of the tangy, lively top-of-the-range Sauvignon Blanc Semillon. The Chenin Blanc has been — and remains

— a runaway success in the market, with its soft, easy fruit and slightly sweet finish.

•ANDERSON WINERY NR Est 1983 $9–16.50 CD SD NE VIC

Lot 12 Chiltern Road, Rutherglen, Vic 3685 (060) 32 9111
fax (060) 32 9028
Open Mon–Sat 9–5, Sun 10–5 **Production** 1500 cases
Winemaker Howard Anderson
Principal Wines Ries, Sem, Pinot, Soft Cab, Port, Muscat, Tokay, Sparkl.
Summary With a winemaking career spanning 30 years, including a stint at Seppelt Great Western, Howard Anderson and family have started their own winery, ultimately intending to specialise in sparkling wine made entirely on site. Most recently, Howard Anderson was a partner in Cofield Wines, but each has gone its own way.

ANDREW GARRETT B–B Est 1983 $8.95–19.90 R 34, 48, 113, 119, 153, 154, 163 STHN VALES

Kangarilla Road, McLaren Vale, SA 5171 (08) 323 8853
fax (08) 323 8550
Open 7 days 10–5 **Production** 95 000 cases
Winemaker Warren Randall
Principal Wines Chard, Ries, Fumé, Sem, Gewurz, Pinot, Cab Mer, Shir, Sparkl.
Best Vintages W '85, '87, '90, '91, '92 R '86, '87, '90, '91, '92
Summary Now controlled by Suntory of Japan, this high-flying winery was a major conversation topic in the late 1980s as production soared and aggressive purchasing helped push grape prices to unsustainable heights. It has since adopted a lower profile. Well-crafted wines are sourced from all the major South Australian regions.
Recommended Wines 1992 Padthaway Rhine Riesling (fragrant, flowery high-toned bouquet with very clean, high-toned lime juice flavours and a long finish). 1991 Cabernet Merlot (powerful, dark berry fruit with spicy oak; robust palate with lots of flavour, although a touch of astringency does run right through the wine; to 1998). 1990 Bold Style Shiraz (as the name suggests, abundant, ripe sweet berry fruit aroma and flavour, with a firm finish; to 1998).

•ANGELSEY ESTATE See Minton Grove

ANGOVE'S CB–A Est 1886 $3.95–15.50 R 5–10, 181, 191, 200, 213, 243 RIVERLANDS

Bookmark Avenue, Renmark, SA 5341 (085) 85 1311
fax (085) 85 1583
Open Mon–Fri 9–5, Sat 9–1 **Production** 800 000 cases
Winemaker Frank J. Newman
Principal Wines Four ranges: at the top, Limited Edition Chard and Cab Sauv; then a complete range of white and red varietal wines; next the export-oriented Butterfly Ridge wines and at the bottom the Misty Vineyards generic range. Also Premium Brandy St Agnes and Stones Ginger Wine.
Best Vintages W '80, '88, '90, '91, '92 R '85, '87, '89, '90, '92
Summary Exemplifies the economies of scale achievable in the Australian Riverlands without compromising potential quality. Very good technology provides wines which are never poor and which can

sometimes exceed their theoretical station in life. The white varietals are best.

• **ANTCLIFFE'S CHASE** NR Est 1982 $9–15 CD SD CENTRAL GOULBURN
RMB 4510, Caveat via Seymour, Vic 3660 (057) 90 4333
Open W'ends 10–5 **Production** 800 cases
Winemaker Chris Bennett, Ian Leamon
Principal Wines Ries, Chard, Pinot, Cabernet.
Summary A small family enterprise which commenced planting the vineyards at an elevation of 600 metres in the Strathbogie Ranges in 1982, but which has only recently commenced wine production from the 10 acre vineyard. As the scarecrow label indicates, birds are a major problem for remote vineyards such as this.

• **ARLEWOOD ESTATE** NR Est 1988 $10.50–12.30 ML SD MARGARET R
Harmans Road South, Willyabrup, WA 6285 (097) 55 6267
Open By appointment **Production** 700 cases
Winemaker Mike Davies (Contract)
Principal Wines Sem, Sem Sauv Bl, Cab Sauv.
Summary Liz and John Wojturski have established their 2.5 hectare vineyard between Ashbrook and Vasse Felix, with contract winemaking by Mike Davies. Production is projected to peak at 2000 cases in the medium term. The initial release of 1991 Semillon was well reviewed, being described by Ray Jordan (in the *West Australian*) as 'terrific stuff'; the 1992 Semillon is full flavoured, if a fraction tough on the finish.

ARROWFIELD CB–B Est 1969 $9.90–37 13, 204, 311 UPPER HUNTER V
Highway 213, Jerrys Plains, NSW 2330 (065) 76 4041
fax (065) 76 4144
Open 7 days 10–4 **Production** 160 000 cases
Winemaker Simon Gilbert
Principal Wines Top-of-the-range Show Reserve Chard, Shir, Cab Sauv; Cowra Chard, Sauv Bl, Pinot; Arrowfield varietals Chard, Sem Chard, Sem Sauv Bl, Traminer, Shir Cab, Cab Mer; Sparkl and fortifieds.
Best Vintages W '85, '86, '87, '91 R '85, '86, '87, '91
Summary After largely dropping the Arrowfield name in favour of Mountarrow and a plethora of other brands, this Japanese-owned company has come full circle in once again marketing the wines solely under the Arrowfield label. Its principal grape sources are Cowra and the Upper Hunter, but it does venture further afield from time to time.
Recommended Wines 1992 Cowra Sauvignon Blanc (clean, crisp wine showing remarkably good varietal character with herbal/gooseberry fruit; drink now). 1991 Cowra Chardonnay (clean, pleasant wine with soft oak and smooth, gently honeyed melon fruit; drink now).

ASHBROOK ESTATE BA–A Est 1975 $15–20 R 3, 147, 164, 171, 179, 191, 200, 275 MARGARET R
Harman's South Road, Willyabrup, WA 6284 (097) 55 6262
fax (09) 481 3836

Open W'ends 11–5 **Production** 6000 cases
Winemakers T. & B. Devitt
Principal Wines Sem, Sauv Bl, Ries, Chard, Verd, Cab Sauv.
Best Vintages W '87, '89, '90, '91 R '82, '84, '85, '86, '90
Summary A fastidious maker of outstanding table wines but which shuns publicity and the wine show system alike, and is less well known than it deserves to be. Richly tropical 1991 Verdelho and ripe, gooseberry flavoured and sculptured Sauvignon Blanc are especially good. The 1992 vintage wines not tasted, but 1989, 1990 and 1991 white wines all of uniformly outstanding quality.

ASHTON HILLS BA–B Est 1982 $12–16 CD 55, 168, 186, 280
ADELAIDE HILLS
Tregarthen Road, Ashton, SA 5137 phone and fax (08) 390 1243
Open Fri/Sat/Sun 10–5 **Production** 1200 cases
Winemaker Stephen George
Principal Wines Chard, Ries, Pinot, Obliqua, Mer Cab, Cab Mer.
Best Vintages W '90, '91, '92 R '88, '90, '91, '92
Summary The southern end of the Adelaide Hills region is one of immense potential, but the cool springs and summers have led to many problems for the pioneer viticulturists. The style is as far removed from that of the Clare Valley, where Stephen George makes the wines for Wendouree, as one could conceive. Slowly but surely the wines of Ashton Hills are taking shape and definition.
Recommended Wines 1991 Riesling (fragrant, crisp and toasty with excellent length and balance; to 1997). 1990 Cabernet Merlot (elegant, briary/woodsy aromas, dark fruit flavours and fine tannins; to 2000). 1990 Merlot Cabernet (a little more aromatic and softer in the mouth, but with similar style and weight; to 1997).

AUGUSTINE NR Est 1918 $5.95–9.95 CD SD 228 MUDGEE
George Campbell Drive, Mudgee, NSW 2850 (063) 72 3880
Open 7 days 10–4 **Production** 7000 cases
Winemaker Jon Reynolds
Principal Wines Chard, Sem, Tram Ries, Pinot, Cab Sauv, Aleatico.
Summary The moribund fortunes of this long-established winery were revived under the stewardship of Sydney wine identity Dr Ray Healey, but its future direction was in a state of uncertainty in mid 1993. No recent tastings.

AULDSTONE NR Est 1989 $8–12 CD SD NE VIC
Booth's Road, Taminick via Glenrowan, Vic 3675 (057) 66 2237
Open Thurs–Sun 9–5 **Production** 1600 cases
Winemaker Contract
Principal Wines Taminick Dry, Ries, Chard, Cab Sauv, Port, Muscat.
Summary Michael and Nancy Reid have restored a century old stone winery and are replanting the largely abandoned vineyard around it. No recent tastings.

AUSTIN'S BARRABOOL WINES NR Est 1982 $10–16 CD
SD GEELONG
50 Lemins Road, Waurn Ponds, Vic 3221 (052) 41 8114
Open By appointment **Production** 750 cases
Winemaker John Ellis (Contract)

Principal Wines Ries, Chard, Cab Sauv.
Summary A tiny winery which has made its mark with a gold medal winning, full-flavoured, intense 1990 Rhine Riesling and a trophy winning Chardonnay, a quite superb wine with tangy, barrel ferment fruit. The Austin family intends to progressively establish 15 hectares of vineyard on their 300 hectare farm, with a great deal of additional suitable land available for future expansion.

AVALON VINEYARD NR Est 1981 $8–11 CD SD NE VIC
RMB 9556 Whitfield Road, Wangaratta, Vic 3678 (057) 29 3629
Open 7 days 9–5 **Production** 650 cases
Winemaker Doug Groom
Principal Wines Chard, Sem, Cab Sauv, Pinot.
Summary Despite winemaker Doug Groom's Roseworthy training and degree, wine quality — particularly white wine quality — has been extremely variable.

AVALON WINES NR Est 1986 $10–14 CD SD PERTH HILLS
Lot 156 Bailey Road, Glen Forrest, WA 6071 (09) 298 8049
Open By appointment **Production** 400 cases
Winemaker Candy Johnsson (Contract)
Principal Wines Chard, Sem, Cab Sauv.
Summary One of the newest wineries in the Perth Hills; the appointment of Candy Johnsson (of Jane Brook Winery) as contract winemaker should lift quality.

BAILEYS CA–BA Est 1870 $7.95–47 CD 48, 86–90, 171, 227 NE VIC
Cnr Taminick Gap Road and Upper Taminick Road, Glenrowan, Vic 3675 (057) 66 2392 fax (057) 66 2596
Open Mon–Fri 9–5, w'ends 10–5 **Production** 35 000 cases
Winemaker Steve Goodwin
Principal Wines Colomb, Ries, Sauv Bl, Chab, Chard, Chasselas, Cab Sauv, Shir, Classic Herm, Muscat, Tokay, Port.
Best Vintages W '88, '89, '90, '91, '92 R '85, '86, '88, '89, '90, '92
Summary One of the great names of North East Victoria, justifiably famous for its textured, opulent Muscats and Tokays; the ferruginous red table wines have a devoted following but, while better than the white table wines, are not in the same class as the fortifieds. Became part of the Rothbury Estate group in 1992.
Recommended Wines Winemakers Selection Tokay (dark brown colour with olive green rim; tremendously concentrated, but showing classic tea leaf varietal aroma and flavour; intensely luscious mid palate, but finishes appropriately dry; great wine). Founders Liqueur Muscat (very fruity style of moderate age with sweet raisiny muscat varietal character from younger material used in the blend, balanced by older, rancio-driven material).

BALDIVIS ESTATE B–B Est 1982 $8.95–14.95 CD 113 SW COASTAL
Lot 165 River Road, Baldivis, WA 6171 (09) 525 2066 fax (09) 525 2411
Open Mon–Sun 10–4 **Production** 5500 cases
Winemaker John Smith
Principal Wines Chard, Sem, Sauv Bl, Cab Mer, Nouveau Rouge.

Summary The 8 hectare Baldivis estate vineyard is but a tiny part of a $5 million, 120 hectare mixed horticultural farm which also boasts 62 hectares of avocados, as well as mangoes, Tahitian limes and table grapes. It is owned by Peter Kailis, whose family has played a leading role in the West Australian fishing industry. Viticultural input is provided by leading consultant Di Davidson, who has the unique qualities of the Tuart Sands upon which the vines are established to deal with, and which tend to produce rather soft, light-bodied wines.

Recommended Wines 1992 Semillon (smoky, grassy and crisp, showing distinctive varietal character; to 1994). 1992 Vintage Selection Chardonnay (smooth, gently ripe melon and fig fruit; a simple, but well made wine with a hint of sweetness; drink now).

BALD MOUNTAIN CB–BA Est 1985 $9.90–12.90 CD 57, 175
GRANITE BELT
Old Wallangarra Road, Wallangarra, Qld 4383 (076) 84 3186
fax (076) 84 3433
Open 7 days 10–4 **Production** 3200 cases
Winemaker Simon Gilbert (Contract)
Principal Wines Sauv Bl, Chard, Shir.
Summary Denis Parsons is a self-taught but exceptionally competent vigneron who, in a few short years, has turned Bald Mountain into the viticultural showpiece of the Granite Belt. Wine quality has yet to consistently reflect that success, but changed contract winemaking arrangements may well see the potential of the vineyard realised.
Recommended Wine 1989 Shiraz Cabernet (firm clean berry fruit with minimal oak on the bouquet, followed by interesting earthy/briary/stemmy flavours on the palate which work quite well; to 1995).

• BALD SPUR ESTATE NR Est 1983 SD YARRA VALLEY
c/o 40 Grand Bud, Montmerency, Vic 3094 (03) 439 8241
Open Not **Production** 1500 cases
Winemaker Lindsay Belbin
Principal Wines Cab Sauv; also Meads under the Miruvore label.
Summary A new venture situated in the Eltham shire, part of the Yarra Valley viticultural region; owner Lindsay Belbin commenced making Meads in 1985, and the first Cabernet Sauvignon in 1988.

BALGOWNIE ESTATE CB–CB Est 1969 $11–19.50 R 110
BENDIGO
Hermitage Road, Maiden Gully, Vic 3551 (054) 49 6222
fax (054) 49 6506
Open Mon–Sat 9–5 **Production** 13 000 cases
Winemaker Lindsay Ross
Principal Wines Estate produced Herm and Cab Sauv; Premier Cuvee (second non estate label) Chard and Cab Herm.
Best Vintages R '80, '85, '86, '90, '91
Summary Once in a class on its own, Balgownie has come back into the pack in recent years, in part living on the long-term record of its intense, long-lived Cabernet Sauvignon. Recent tastings (especially '89) show distressing toughness and astringency in the estate wines.

BALLANDEAN ESTATE CB–B Est 1970 $8–15 CD 169, 170
GRANITE BELT
Sundown Road, Ballandean, Qld 4382 (076) 84 1226
fax (076) 84 1288

Open 7 days 9–5 **Production** 10 000 cases
Winemakers Angelo Puglisi, Adam Chapman
Principal Wines Chard, Sem Sauv Bl, Ausl Sylv, Shir, Cab Sauv.
Best Vintages W '83, '86, '89, '90 R '83, '87, '89, '90
Summary The senior winery of the Granite Belt, and by far the largest. The white wines are of diverse but interesting styles, the red wines smooth and usually well made.

BALNARRING VINEYARD B–B Est 1982 $11–15 CD SD MORNINGTON P

Bittern-Dromana Road, Balnarring, Vic 3926 (059) 83 5258
Open 7 days 10–4 **Production** 1200 cases
Winemaker Bruce Paul
Principal Wines Chard, Ries, Gewurz, Pinot, Mer, Cab Mer, Cab Sauv.
Best Vintages W '86, '87, '90, '91, '92 R '85, '86, '87, '90, '91
Summary Over the years, the wines of Balnarring have been made at various wineries under contract, but have shown a consistent vineyard style, with the red wines in particular possessing exceptional colour and depth of flavour.
Recommended Wines 1990 Cabernet Merlot (unusually elegant for Balnarring, with fine briary/berry/blackcurrant fruit and finely balanced tannins; almost Bordeaux-like; to 1995). 1991 Chardonnay (citrus and honeysuckle tinged, slightly hard finish; may develop with bottle age).

BALNAVES OF COONAWARRA BA–BA Est 1975

$14.20–15.75 SD COONAWARRA
Main Road, Coonawarra, SA 5263 (087) 37 2946
fax (087) 37 2945
Open 7 days 9–5 **Production** 2000 cases
Winemaker Ralph Fowler (Contract)
Principal Wines Chard, Shir, Cab Sauv, Cab Mer, Sparkl Burg.
Summary Former Hungerford Hill vineyard manager and now viticultural consultant-cum-grape grower Doug Balnaves established his vineyard in 1975, but did not launch into winemaking until 1990, with colleague Ralph Fowler as contract maker. Only a small part of the production from the 25 hectare vineyard is vinified under the Balnaves label, but the wines have been of consistently excellent quality.
Recommended Wines 1991 Cabernet Sauvignon (solid, ripe dark fruit and dark chocolate bouquet; attractive, sweet blackcurrant fruit and warm American oak flavours, with soft tannins; to 2005). 1991 Cabernet Merlot (complex, stylish wine with quite pronounced leafy merlot varietal overtones balanced by sweet cabernet fruit and again some American oak; to 2000). 1990 Cabernet Sauvignon (a complete cabernet, with lots of dark berry fruit and excellent tannin structure and balance; to 2010). 1992 Chardonnay (highly scented, almost lemon sherbet aroma, with high-toned citrus and melon fruit on the palate, finishing with a hint of alcohol-derived sweetness; early developing).

BANNOCKBURN A–AB Est 1974 $12–28 R 65, 147, 169, 170, 182, 251 GEELONG

Midland Hwy, Bannockburn, Vic 3331 (052) 81 1363
fax (052) 81 1349

Open By appointment **Production** 6000 cases
Winemaker Gary Farr
Principal Wines Sauv Bl, Ries, Chard, Pinot, Saignee (Rosé), Shir, Cab Sauv.
Best Vintages R and W '88, '89, '90, '91, '92
Summary One of Australia's foremost producers of Pinot Noir, made in an uncompromising style which owes much to Gary Farr's extensive Burgundian winemaking experience gained at Domaine Dujac; the viticulture, too, is strongly French-influenced. The white wines are frequently outstanding.
Recommended Wines 1992 Sauvignon Blanc (intense, superbly balanced and structured, leaning more towards White Bordeaux than Loire Valley in style; food rather than terrace style; to 1994). 1991 Chardonnay (complex, textured, tightly structured with powerful fruit and long finish; to 2000). 1991 Pinot Noir (supremely idiosyncratic, with strong whole-bunch/carbonic influences giving stalky/leafy overtones; the fruit is there; needs time; to 1995).

BARONGVALE NR Est 1988 $8–10 CD SD GEELONG
East West Road, Barongarook, Vic 3249 (052) 33 8324
Open By appointment **Production** NFP
Winemaker Stuart Walker
Principal Wines Chard, Colomb, Sem, Ries, Cab Sauv, Pinot Cab.
Summary One of the most remote wineries in the West Geelong region, making a surprisingly wide range of wines of (to me) unknown quality.

BAROSSA SETTLERS CB–B Est 1983 $7.50–19.50 CD SD BAROSSA V
Trial Hill Road, Lyndoch, SA 5351 (085) 24 4017
Open Mon–Sat 10–4, Sun 1–4 **Production** Nil (1993)
Winemaker Howard Haese
Principal Wines Champ, Chard, Ries, Ausl Ries, Shir Claret, Cab Sauv, Port.
Best Vintages W '83, '84, '85, '89, '90 R '80, '83, '84, '86, '87, '89
Summary A superbly located cellar door is the only outlet (other than mail order) for the wines from this excellent vineyard owned by the Haese family. Contract winemaking by Doug Lehmann has produced some attractive Rhine Rieslings and Cabernets. Production has slowed in recent years, with the grapes from the 31 hectare vineyard being sold to others.
Recommended Wine 1990 Late Harvest Rhine Riesling (traditional late harvest Riesling with plenty of fruit weight, but no botrytis; well balanced; to 1997).

BAROSSA VALLEY ESTATES CB–B Est 1985 $6.95–19.95 R 22–26 ADELAIDE PLAINS
Heaslip Road, Angle Vale, SA 5117 (08) 284 7000
fax (08) 284 7219
Open Mon–Fri 9–5, Sat 11–5, Sun 1–5 **Production** 55 000 cases
Winemaker Colin Glaetzer
Principal Wines Chard, Herm, Cab Sauv; top-of-the-range E & E Black Pepper Shir and E & E Sparkl Burg.
Best Vintages W '85, '89, '90, '91, '92 R '85, '86, '88, '90, '91

Summary A stand-alone brand of the Berri Renmano group, using the best grapes from grower members in the Barossa Valley, but made at Lauriston winery. Quality is reliably sound; watch for the special E & E Black Pepper Shiraz, even if it is oak dominated.

BARRETTS NR Est 1983 $9–14 CD SD SW VIC
Portland-Nelson Highway, Portland, Vic 3305 (055) 26 5257
Open 7 days 10–6 **Production** 1000 cases
Winemakers Rod Barrett, Simon Clayfield (Contract)
Principal Wines Ries, Tram Ries, Pinot, Cab Sauv.
Summary The second (and newer) winery in the Portland region. The initial releases were made at Best's, but since 1992 all wines have been made on the property by Rod Barrett with consultant advice from Best's winemaker Simon Clayfield. The 1990 and 1991 vintage wines all showed good varietal character, clean winemaking, and elegant, cool climate style.

BASEDOW B–B Est 1896 $5.45–15 CD 86–90, 231 BAROSSA V
161–165 Murray Street, Tanunda, SA 5352 (085) 63 2060
fax (085) 633 3597
Open Mon–Fri 9–5, Sat 10–5, Sun 12–4 **Production** 32 000 cases
Winemaker Roger Harbord
Principal Wines Front Spatlese, Chard, Wh Burg, Ries, Herm, Cab Sauv, Port.
Best Vintages W '86, '87, '88, '89, '90 R '81, '82, '84, '89, '90
Summary Part of the troubled MS McLeod Group, and being offered for sale in 1993 independently of its sister winery Peter Lehmann Wines. Over the years it has been a rock of Gibraltar with its wooded white wines, especially the Wood Matured Semillon alias White Burgundy. The quality seemed to slip a little in 1992, although the wines have pleasant, full flavour.

BASKET RANGE WINES NR Est 1980 $12 ML SD ADELAIDE HILLS
Blockers Road, Basket Range, SA 5138 (vineyard only); postal PO Basket Range, SA 5138
Open Not **Production** 300 cases
Winemaker Phillip Broderick
Principal Wines A single Bordeaux-blend of Cab Sauv Cab Franc Mer Mal.
Summary A tiny operation known to very few; the '89 Basket Range is the most recently tasted, with pleasant red berry plum and spice fruit.

BASS PHILLIP BA–BA Est 1979 $18–24 R SD STH GIPPSLAND
Tosch's Road, Leongatha Sth, Vic 3953 (056) 64 3341
Open By appointment summer **Production** 1000 cases
Winemaker Phillip Jones
Principal Wines Pinot, sold in three grades, headed by Premium.
Best Vintages R '84, '86, '88, '89, '91
Summary The Pinots of Bass Phillip have attracted much deserved publicity; at their best they are quite superb, but a now-discontinued policy of individual cask bottling led to disconcerting variability with the initial releases. The potential is exceptional, particularly for the Premium bottlings.

Recommended Wine 1989 Premium Pinot Noir (extremely stylish and aromatic bouquet with sappy, tobacco overtones strongly reminiscent of Burgundy; the palate is lighter than the bouquet suggests, with lifted fruit and moderate length).

BELBOURIE NR Est 1963 $12–20 CD SD HUNTER V
Branxton Road, Rothbury, NSW 2330 (049) 38 1556
Open Sat–Mon 9–5 **Production** 1100 cases
Winemaker John Roberts
Principal Wines Tram, Sem Chard, Cab Malb.
Summary Not rated simply because the idiosyncratic wines of Belbourie cannot be judged by conventional yardsticks. Try them for yourself.

BELLINGHAM NR Est 1984 $10 ML 173 PIPERS BROOK
Pipers Brook, Tas 7254 (003) 82 7149
Open By appointment **Production** 1000 cases
Winemaker Greg O'Keefe (Contract)
Principal Wines Ries, Chard, Cab Sauv.
Summary Dallas Targett sells most of the grapes from his substantial vineyard to Greg O'Keefe; a small part has been made for the Bellingham label.
Recommended Wine 1991 Rhine Riesling (intense, lime juice aroma and flavour, and good length; to 1995).

BELUBULA VALLEY VINEYARDS NR Est 1986 SD
CENTRAL HIGHLANDS
Golden Gully, Mandurama, NSW 2798 (063) 67 5236 or (02) 258 6024
Open Not **Production** 100 cases
Winemaker D. R. Somervaille
Principal Wines Chard, Sem, Cab Sauv.
Summary Belubula Valley is a foundation member of the Central Highlands Grapegrowers Association, centred on Orange; the vineyard is located on the Belubula River, near Carcoar, and the small amounts of wine made to date have not yet been commercially released.

BENFIELD ESTATE CB–B Est 1985 $7–12 CD SD CANBERRA
DISTRICT
Fairy Hole Road, Yass, NSW 2582 (06) 226 2427
Open W'ends, pub hols 10–5 **Production** 850 cases
Winemaker David Featherstone
Principal Wines Ries, Chard, Sem, Mer, Cab Sauv.
Summary After a hiatus, Benfield Estate returned to active winemaking and marketing with a most attractive soft, minty/berry 1990 Merlot and a light, elegant and faintly limey 1991 Rhine Riesling leading the way. No 1992 vintage wines tasted.

BERESFORD C–B Est 1985 $10 R 41, 242 STHN VALES
Old Heritage Horndale Winery, Fraser Avenue, Happy Valley, SA 5067 (08) 322 3611 fax (08) 322 3610
Open 7 days 9–5 **Production** NFP
Winemaker Robert Dundon
Principal Wines For the Australian market Sauv Bl, Chard, Pinot, Cab Mer under the Beresford label; then a range of other labels, most

export oriented, including Beacon Hill, Echo Point, Crystal Brook, all offering a range of varietal wines.

Best Vintages W '87, '88, '89, '90, '91 R '82, '86, '88, '90, '91

Summary The Chardonnays have been the most consistent performers showing good oak handling and complexity. Rob Dundon prefers light, understated red wines, although his carbonic maceration Pinot Noir has positive flavour and attracts a loyal following.

BERRI ESTATES C–B Est 1916 $3.95–17.95 R 22–26, 194, 256 RIVERLAND
Sturt Highway, Glossop, SA 5344 (085) 83 2303 fax (085) 83 2224
Open Mon–Sat 9–5 **Production** 4.5 million cases
Winemaker Reg Wilkinson
Principal Wines Brentwood Ries, Chab, Moselle, Spat Lexia, Nouveau, Claret; Berri Estates 5 litre wine casks, table and fortified.
Summary The Brentwood label is a very modest tip of the vast iceberg; much of the production is sold in bulk in export markets, and in five litre casks on the local market. The premium wines appear under the Renmano banner.

✓ **BEST'S** BA–A Est 1866 $8.20–20 CD 72, 134, 157, 239 GRT WESTERN
2km off Western Highway, Great Western, Vic 3377 (053) 56 2250 fax (053) 56 2430
Also at Lake Boga, off Murray Valley Highway (follow brown tourist signs).
Open Mon–Fri 9–5, Sat 9–4, Sun 12–4 on long w'ends & sch hols
Production 12 000 cases
Winemakers Viv Thomson, Simon Clayfield
Principal Wines Chard, Ries, Gewurz, Shir, Cab Sauv, Sparkl, fortifieds.
Best Vintages W '84, '87, '89, '91 R '84, '87, '88, '89, '91
Summary An historic winery, owning some priceless vineyards planted as long ago as 1867 (other plantings are, of course, much more recent) that has consistently produced elegant, supple wines which deserve far greater recognition than they in fact receive.
Recommended Wines 1990 Chardonnay (outstanding bottle developed aroma with classy oak and smooth peach and melon flavours). 1990 Cabernet Sauvignon (spotlessly clean and sweet dark cherry/blackcurrant fruit with supple tannins and great balance; to 2003). 1990 Shiraz (strong, spicy nutmeg fruit and oak aromas, wonderfully rich dark berry/plum palate with soft, lingering tannins; to 2010). 1991 Chenin Blanc (from Lake Boga, with tropical fruit salad and a hint of toasty oak; exceptionally well made).

BETHANY B–B Est 1977 $8.20–16.40 CD 3, 33, 145, 173, 184 BAROSSA V
Bethany Road, Bethany via Tanunda, SA 5352 (085) 63 2086 fax (085) 63 0046
Open Mon–Sat 10–5, Sun 1–5 **Production** 10 000 cases
Winemakers Geoff & Robert Schrapel
Principal Wines Ries (Dry, Spat, LH), Chard, Sem (Wood Mat), Cab Mer, Shir, Grenache, Port, Sparkl.
Best Vintages W '87, '88, '90, '91, '92 R '86, '88, '89, '90, '92
Summary Once known principally for its full-flavoured, sometimes

sweet Rhine Rieslings but has since also shown a deft hand with buttery, honeyed, oaky Chardonnay and a fresh, modern-style Cabernet Merlot. The winery nestles in an old hillside quarry, with panoramic views of the Barossa Valley.

Recommended Wine 1992 Oak-aged Semillon (strongly scented lemon and vanilla American oak dominates both bouquet and palate; made in a particular style which certainly does appeal to some; drink now before the oak phenolics overtake the wine).

BIANCHET CB–B Est 1976 $10–18 CD SD YARRA V

Lot 3 Victoria Road, Lilydale, Vic 3140 (03) 739 1779
Open W'ends 10–6 **Production** 2000 cases
Winemaker Lou Bianchet
Principal Wines Chard, Gewurz, Verduzzo, Sem, Pinot, Shir, Cab Sauv, Mer.
Best Vintages W & R '85, '86, '88, '90, '92
Summary Makes invariably full flavoured wines in a traditional and at times rustic style, with little or no reliance on oak. Verduzzo, an Italian white grape, is an interesting winery specialty.

BIRDWOOD ESTATE NR Est 1990 $9–13 CD SD ADELAIDE HILLS

Narcoonah Road, Birdwood, SA 5234 (08) 263 0986
Open Not **Production** 900 cases
Winemaker Oli Cucchiarelli
Principal Wines Chard, Ries, Cab Sauv.
Summary Italian-born Oli Cucchiarelli, an engineer by trade, graduated from Charles Sturt University in Wine Science in 1986, and now pursues a part-time career as vigneron. The initial releases from 1990 showed promising fruit flavour but were marred by rather raw, splintery oak.

BLACKWOOD CREST C–B Est 1976 $12–17.50 R SD GRT SOUTHERN

RMB 404A Boyup Brook, WA 6244 (097) 67 3029
fax (097) 62 3029
Open 7 days 10–6 **Production** 1250 cases
Winemakers Kim Hart, Max Fairbrass
Principal Wines Ries, Sem Sauv Bl, Shir, Cab Sauv.
Summary A remote and small winery which has produced one or two striking red wines full of flavour and character; worth watching.

BLANCHE BARKLY NR Est 1972 SD BENDIGO

Rheola Road, Kingower, Vic 3517 (054) 43 3664
Open 7 days 10–5; please phone **Production** NFP
Winemaker David Reimers
Principal Wines Mary Eileen Shir, Alexander Cab Sauv, George Henry Cab Sauv.
Summary Sporadic but small production and variable quality seem to be the order of the day; the potential has always been there. No recent tastings.

BLEASDALE C–B Est 1850 $7–10.50 CD 32, 181 LANGHORNE CREEK

Wellington Road, Langhorne Creek, SA 5255 (085) 37 3001

Open Mon–Sat 9–5, Sun 11–5 **Production** 40 000 cases
Winemaker Michael Potts
Principal Wines Ries, Chard, Verd, Colomb, Cab Sauv, Cab Malb Mer, Shir Cab.
Best Vintages R and W '86, '88, '90, '91, '92
Summary Supremely honest, soft, bottle-aged red wines are the winery specialty, usually with a particular gamey edge which may or may not appeal. Now also making soft, pleasant Chardonnay and Verdelho.

BLEWITT SPRINGS B–B Est 1987 $8–14 R 42 STHN VALES
Fraser Avenue, Happy Valley, SA 5159 (08) 322 3611
fax (08) 322 3610
Open Not **Production** 4000 cases
Winemaker Brett Howard
Principal Wines Chard, Sem, Shir, Cab Sauv.
Summary A relative newcomer to the scene which has attracted much attention and praise for its voluptuous Chardonnays, crammed full of peachy, buttery fruit and vanillin American oak. Oak also plays a major role in the Semillon and the red wines; a lighter touch might please some critics.

BLOODWOOD ESTATE NR Est 1983 $12.95–16 CD SD CENTRAL TABLELANDS
4 Griffith Road, Orange, NSW 2800 (063) 62 5631
Open By appointment **Production** 2000 cases
Winemaker Stephen Doyle
Principal Wines Chard, Ries, Rosé, Cab Mer.
Summary A relative newcomer from an extremely interesting region. The strikingly labelled early releases promise a great deal, none more than the 1992 Chardonnay.
Recommended Wines 1992 Chardonnay (reasonably pronounced but very well handled oak in the bouquet; full flavoured peachy wine on the palate, again showing sophisticated oak handling, with very good mouthfeel, balance and acidity; to 1995). 1992 Rosé of Malbec (fresh, clean, well made with hints of cherry and a touch of sweetness).

BONNEYVIEW WINES NR Est 1975 $6–9 CD SD RIVERLAND
Sturt Highway, Barmera, SA 5345 (085) 88 2279
Open 7 days 9–5.30 **Production** 2000 cases
Winemaker Robert Minns
Principal Wines Tram Ries, Front, Chard, Shir, Cab Mer, fortifieds.
Summary The smallest Riverland winery selling exclusively cellar door, with an ex-Kent cricketer and Oxford University graduate as its owner/winemaker.

BOOTH'S TAMINICK CELLARS C–CB Est 1900 $5–12 CD SD NE VIC
Taminick via Glenrowan, Vic 3675 (057) 66 2282
Open Mon–Sat 9–5, Sun 10–5 **Production** NFP
Winemaker Cliff Booth
Principal Wines Chard, Shir, Cab Sauv, Cab Mer, Port, Muscat.
Summary Ultra-conservative producer of massively flavoured and

concentrated red wines, usually with more than a few rough edges which time may or may not smooth over.

BOROKA NR Est 1974 $6.50–10 CD SD GRT WESTERN
Pomonal Road, Halls Gap, Vic 3381 (053) 56 4252
Open Mon–Sat 9–5 **Production** 1500 cases
Winemaker Bernard Breen
Principal Wines Chab & Ries blends, Rosé, Shir, Cab Sauv.
Summary Out of the mainstream in terms of both wine quality and location, but does offer light lunches or picnic takeaways, and the views are spectacular.

BOSANQUET ESTATE C–B Est 1989 $7 R 127, 242 STHN VALES
Old Heritage Horndale Winery, Fraser Avenue, Happy Valley, SA 5067 (08) 322 3611 fax (08) 322 3610
Open 7 days 9–5 **Production** NFP
Winemaker Robert Dundon
Principal Wines Sem, Sem Sauv Bl, Ries, Sem Chard, Cab Shir.
Summary The strikingly labelled wines compete against the major wine companies in the most competitive sector of an overly competitive market; the quality is all one could reasonably hope for, the softly fruity style being precisely aimed at the target market. This is in fact one of the arms of Beresford Wines.

BOSTON BAY B–B Est 1986 $9.90–12.90 CD 14, 33 PORT LINCOLN
Lincoln Highway, Port Lincoln, SA 5606 (086) 84 3600
fax (086) 84 3600
Open W'ends/sch/pub hols 11.30–4.30 **Production** 2500 cases
Winemaker Roger Harbord
Principal Wines Ries, Spat Ries, Cab Mer, Chard.
Summary While strongly tourist oriented, wine quality is good by any standards, thanks to competent contract winemaking by Basedow's Roger Harbord.
Recommended Wines 1992 Rhine Riesling (rich, lime-accented aroma with gentle lime and toast flavours, good length and balance; to 1997). 1991 Cabernet Sauvignon (soft, gently ripe fruit, and strong American oak influence on both bouquet and palate; to 1995).

BOTOBOLAR B–B Est 1971 $4.50–11.50 CD 69, 115, 316 MUDGEE
Botobolar Lane, Mudgee, NSW 2850 (063) 73 3840
Open 7 days 10–5 **Production** 8000 cases
Winemaker Gil Wahlquist
Principal Wines Crouchen, Ries Tram, Mars, Chard, Ries, Shir, Cab Sauv, St Gilbert.
Best Vintages W '82, '88, '89, '90, '91 R '82, '84, '85, '87, '89.
Summary Gil Wahlquist was one of the original proponents of organic viticulture in Australia, and the vineyards have a Grade A classification by the National Association for Sustainable Agriculture. This direction has been carried through in the winery with two wines, a preservative-free dry white and dry red, both of which sell out rapidly. The other wines in the portfolio are made using conventional techniques, albeit from organically grown grapes.

BOWEN ESTATE BA–BA Est 1972 $9–12 CD 17, 48, 147, 169, 170 COONAWARRA

Main Penola-Naracoorte Road, Penola, SA 5277 (087) 37 2229

Open Mon–Sat 9–5, Sun, long w'end **Production** 7000 cases

Winemaker Doug Bowen

Principal Wines Ries, Chard, Shir, Cab Sauv.

Best Vintages W '82, '84, '86, '90 R '80, '84, '89, '90

Summary For long regarded as the best of the small wineries in Coonawarra, with its often peppery, rich Shiraz and classically restrained Cabernet Sauvignon vying against each other for supremacy.

Recommended Wine 1990 Shiraz (full, sweet berry fruit, little spice, but lots of weight and depth; to 2005).

BOYNTON'S OF BRIGHT CA–B Est 1987 $8–14 CD SD NE VIC

Ovens Valley Highway, Bright, Vic 3747 (057) 56 2356

fax (057) 56 2610

Open 7 days 10–5 **Production** 4000 cases

Winemaker Kel Boynton

Principal Wines Chard, Ries, Sauv Bl, Cab Sauv, Shir, Mataro.

Summary Boynton's 1989 and 1990 red wines had spectacular success at some wine shows; American oak aroma and flavour is pronounced and may not appeal to all, but there is no doubting the strength and depth of flavour.

Recommended Wines 1990 Shiraz (strong vanillin American oak, sweetly ripe and minty fruit on the palate, with oak again obvious, but balanced by the fruit). 1990 Cabernet Sauvignon (very clean with well balanced and integrated sweet vanillin oak on the bouquet; palate oaky but rich; to 1997).

BRAHAMS CREEK WINERY NR Est 1990 $not fixed SD YARRA V

Woods Point Road, East Warburton, Vic 3799 (059) 66 2802 Postal PO Box 105, Oakleigh, Vic 3166

Open W'ends 10–5 **Production** 800 cases

Winemaker Geoffrey Richardson

Principal Wines Pinot, Cab Sauv.

Summary No wines have been released at the time of writing, although they are due for release in 1993.

BRANDS LAIRA BA–B Est 1965 $12.05–20 R 107, 145, 202 COONAWARRA

Penola-Naracoorte Highway, Coonawarra, SA 5263 (087) 36 3260 fax (087) 36 3208

Open 7 days 8–5 **Production** 16 000 cases

Winemaker Jim Brand

Principal Wines Chard, Ries, Shir, Cab Sauv, Cab Franc, Cab Mer; limited release of Original Vineyard Shir.

Best Vintages W '85, '86, '90, '91, '92 R '81, '84, '86, '90, '91

Summary Now 50% owned by McWilliams, the technical input of which has seen a sharp lift in quality right across the range, but particularly with the white wines.

Recommended Wine 1991 Chardonnay (charred oak aromas, with tight fruit on the bouquet, moving to a particularly rich and complex palate with great depth and length to the flavour; to 1994).

BREAM CREEK NR Est 1975 $12–14 R 181 EAST COAST TAS
Marion Bay Road, Bream Creek, Tas 7175 (vineyard only); postal
655 Main Road, Berriedale, Tas 7011 (002) 492 2949
Open Not **Production** 2200 cases
Winemaker Julian Alcorso (Contract)
Principal Wines Ries, Chard, Cab Sauv (light and wooded), Pinot.
Summary Fred Peacock, long-time vineyard manager of Moorilla
Estate, purchased the Bream Creek vineyard (which had hitherto
sold its grapes to Moorilla) in 1990 and in that year had the first wines
made for him by Julian Alcorso at Moorilla. Since then, every wine
made has won at least one medal at the Royal Hobart Wine Show; the
best to date is the 1991 Rhine Riesling with lime aromas and flavours,
and appreciable sweetness giving the wine weight and flesh.

BRIAGOLONG ESTATE CB–CB Est 1979 $18 ML SD
GIPPSLAND
Valencia-Briagolong Road, Briagolong, Vic 3860 (051) 47 2322
fax (051) 47 2400
Open Not **Production** 400 cases
Winemaker Gordon McIntosh
Principal Wines Chard, Pinot.
Best Vintages W '83, '84, '89, '90, '91 R '86, '87, '89, '90, '91
Summary This is very much a weekend hobby for medical
practitioner Gordon McIntosh, who nonetheless tries hard to invest
his wines with Burgundian complexity, with mixed success; the
stylish, tangy 1991 Pinot Noir is the best yet tasted, and the 1991
Chardonnay is marvellously concentrated and balanced.

BRIAR RIDGE B–B Est 1972 $12.50–15 CD 55, 65, 126
HUNTER V
Mount View Road, Mount View, NSW 2325 (049) 90 3670
Open Mon–Fri 9–5, w'ends 10–5 **Production** 7000 cases
Winemaker Kees Van De Scheur, Karl Stockhausen (Consultant)
Principal Wines Sem, Chard, Herm, Cab Sauv, Sparkl.
Best Vintages W '84, '87, '89, '91 R '85, '86, '87, '91
Summary Originally the Robson Vineyard, Briar Ridge has
gradually assumed its own identity, with winemaking and style
continuity provided by Kees Van De Scheur.
Recommended Wines 1991 Hermitage (very clean wine with
smooth, ripe red fruit flavours, soft tannins and good acidity giving an
almost silky palate; to 2000). 1992 Traditional Semillon (smooth, well
made wine with solid, honeyed, full flavoured fruit in an early
developing but attractive style).

BRIARS, THE NR Est 1989 $14.50 CD SD MORNINGTON P
Nepean Highway, Mount Martha, Vic 3934 (059) 74 3686
Open W'ends 11–4.30 **Production** 1000 cases
Winemaker Brian Fletcher (Contract)
Principal Wines Chard, Pinot, Cab Sauv.
Summary An enterprising venture of the Mornington Shire
Council, with grapes grown at and sold from the historic Briars
Homestead, marketed cellar door, through a few Mornington
Peninsula restaurants and through The Briars Wine Club mailing list.
The wine is not exported, and has no connection with the former
Dromana Estate export brand also called The Briars.

BRIDGEWATER MILL BA–A Est 1986 $10.70–15.50 R 147, 169, 251 ADELAIDE HILLS
Mount Barker Road, Bridgewater, SA 5155 (08) 339 3422
fax (08) 339 5253
Open Mon–Fri 9.30–5, w'ends 10–5 **Production** 25 000 cases
Winemaker Brian Croser
Principal Wines Chard, Ries, Sauv Bl, Shir, Cab Malb.
Best Vintages W '87, '88, '90, '92, '93 R '86, '88, '90, '91, '92
Summary The second label of Petaluma, which consistently provides wines most makers would love to have as their top label. The fruit sources are diverse, with the majority of the Sauvignon blanc and Chardonnay coming from Petaluma-owned or managed vineyards, while the Shiraz is made from purchased grapes.
Recommended Wines 1993 Sauvignon Blanc (bright, fresh, crisp and tangy with a mix of herbal and gooseberry fruit aromas and flavours; well balanced, with good mouthfeel; drink now). 1991 Millstone Shiraz (a massive, dense, chewy, ripe wine, with dark cherry and plum flavours intermingling with earthy notes; to 2005). 1991 Chardonnay (shows good fruit intensity with fig and melon flavours; quite long, but not particularly complex; minimal oak influence; to 1997).

BRINDABELLA HILLS BA–BA Est 1989 $9–14 CD 120 CANBERRA
Woodgrove Close via Hall, ACT 2618 (06) 230 2583
Open W'ends & public hols 10–5 **Production** 2000 cases
Winemaker Dr Roger Harris
Principal Wines Ries, Chard, Sauv Bl, Sem, Pinot, Cab Mer.
Summary The three hectare Brindabella Hills vineyard has been planted on a granite ridge above the Murrumbidgee River, 20 km north of Canberra. Distinguished research scientist Roger Harris has a PhD in Chemistry from Adelaide University and a Bachelor of Wine Science degree from Charles Sturt University, and it is hardly surprising that he is making some of the best wines to come from the Canberra district, with a wholly admirable consistency of quality across the range.
Recommended Wines 1992 Rhine Riesling (rich, clean, strong lime juice aromas with lots of fleshy, limey fruit on the palate; a highly expressive, well made wine). 1992 Semillon Sauvignon Blanc (faintly herbal aromas, with lively, lemony fruit with length and acidity; good mouthfeel). 1991 Cabernets (fresh, bright red berry fruit aromas; similarly clean, firm palate with fruit flavours in the mid range; fine tannins and good length; to 1998).

•BRITANNIA CREEK ESTATE NR Est 1982 $not fixed SD YARRA V
Lot 234 Britannia Creek Road, Wesburn, Vic 3799 (03) 484 3607
Open By appointment **Production** 400 cases
Winemaker Charlie Brydon
Principal Wines Sauv Bl, Sem, Cabernet.
Summary Owner/winemaker Charlie Brydon has progressively established the four and a half hectare vineyard, which is still coming into bearing. It is planned to open a cellar door facility in late 1993.

BROKE ESTATE NR Est 1989 $15–17.50 CD SD HUNTER V
Wollombi Road, Broke, NSW 2330 phone and fax (065) 79 1065
Open Not **Production** 3000 cases

Winemaker Simon Gilbert (Contract)
Principal Wines Chard, Sauv Bl, Cabernets.
Summary Viticultural consultancy advice from Dr Richard Smart and contract winemaking by Simon Gilbert got Broke Estate away to a flying start with its 1991 vintage. Only part of the production of the 16 hectare vineyard is vinified for the Broke Estate label; the rest of the grapes are sold.
Recommended Wines 1991 Cabernet (an excellent wine with purple-red colour, abundant redcurrant fruit on both bouquet and palate, with a subtle touch of spicy oak, and soft tannins; to 2005).

BROKEN RIVER WINES NR Est 1984 $8–11 CD 175 NTH GOULBURN R
Cosgrove Road, Lemnos, Vic 3631 (058) 29 9486
Open Thur–Sun 10–5 **Production** 1500 cases
Winemaker David Traeger
Principal Wines Meth Champ, Chenin, Ries, Cab Franc, Cab Sauv.
Summary Frank and Helen Dawson are dedicated vignerons and wine lovers; given the experience of contract winemaker David Traeger the frankly disappointing quality of the initial releases will surely be remedied in due course. No recent tastings.

BROKENWOOD A–A Est 1970 $14–22 CD 34, 139, 147, 169, 171, 193, 226 HUNTER V
McDonalds Road, Pokolbin, NSW 2321 (049) 98 7559
fax (049) 98 7893
Open 7 days 10–5 **Production** 22 000 cases
Winemakers Iain Riggs, Fiona Purnell
Principal Wines Sem (unwooded and oak-matured) Chard, Pinot, Herm, Cab Sauv, 'Graveyard' top of the range release.
Best Vintages W '83, '85, '86, '87, '91 R '83, '86, '87, '89, '91
Summary Deservedly fashionable winery producing consistently excellent wines. Unwooded Sauvignon Blanc Semillon has an especially strong following, as has Cabernet Sauvignon; the three Graveyard releases are well worth the extra money, the red wines being exceptionally long lived. The Graveyard Hermitage is one of the best Hunter reds available today.
Recommended Wines 1992 Yarra Valley Pinot Noir (while of light to medium weight, has stylish cherry and plum varietal aroma with subtle oak leading into a fresh, well balanced palate; early maturing style). 1991 Graveyard Hermitage (very rich, dark berry fruit with spicy oak; tremendously complex and rich palate with masses of soft tannins; headed towards Grange Hermitage in style; to 2005). 1992 Chardonnay (stylish, elegant melon/fig aromas with subtle oak supporting the fruit on both bouquet and palate; the best Chardonnay from Brokenwood for some years; to 1996).

BROOKLAND VALLEY VINEYARD B–CB Est 1984
$13.50–15.90 CD 72, 109, 125 MARGARET R
Caves Road, Willyabrup, WA 6284 (097) 55 6250
fax (097) 55 6214
Open Tues–Sun 11–4.30 **Production** 6000 cases
Winemakers John Durham, Gary Baldwin (Consultant)
Principal Wines Chard, Sauv Bl, Cab Sauv, Cab Franc.

Summary Malcolm and Diedre Jones have made every post a winner at Brookland Valley, with the on-site Flutes Cafe and wine arts gallery a major Margaret River drawcard; the restaurant seats up to 100 people at a time. The wines are technically very well made, but — but perhaps due to young vines — are not especially rich or concentrated.

Recommended Wines 1991 Chardonnay (complex barrel ferment oak aromas and flavours, with light but pleasant fruit). 1992 Sauvignon Blanc (light, aromatic passionfruit aromas and similar fresh, clean but light palate).

BROOKS CREEK WINES NR Est 1973 $10–15 CD SD CANBERRA

RMB 209 Brooks Road, Bungendore, NSW 2621 (06) 236 9221
Open W'ends 9–5 **Production** 2000 cases
Winemaker Lawrie Brownbill
Principal Wines Gewurz, Bot Ries, Mataro, Cab Sauv.
Summary The Brownbill family purchased what was then known as Shingle House from Max and Yvonne Blake in early 1990, and have re-named it Brooks Creek Vineyard. Production varies, as the vineyard can be prone to frost, but one of the continuing specialties is the Mataro, which in 1991 produced a light-bodied wine but one that is crammed with vibrant pepper and spice. The same year produced a pleasant botrytis-affected Rhine Riesling.

BROUSSARDS CHUM CREEK WINERY NR Est 1977 $16 CD SD YARRA V

Cunninghams Road, Chum Creek via Healesville, Vic 3777
(059) 62 5551
Open W'ends & public hols 10–6 **Production** 250 cases
Winemaker Contract made
Principal Wines Chard, Pinot, Cab Sauv.
Summary One of the more remote and smallest of the Yarra Valley wineries, quietly selling all of its wine through the cellar door.

BROWN BROS B–BA Est 1885 $8–25 R 181, 189, 206, 272 NE VIC

Snow Road, Milawa, Vic 3678 (057) 20 5500 fax (057) 20 5511
Open Mon–Sat 9–5, Sun 10–6 **Production** 300 000 cases
Winemaker John Brown, Roland Walquist
Principal Wines An immense range of varietal wines in various price categories; at the bottom Victorian range, then Limited Production, then Regional Releases including Koombahla, Meadow Creek and Whitlands, next Family Reserve and, finally, Classic Vintage Releases.
Best Vintages W '86, '88, '90, '91, '92 R '80, '82, '86, '91, '92
Summary The parallels with Tyrrells abound; each has enjoyed tremendous growth since 1960, providing absolutely reliable wines at big company prices but with a small company image. Each company enjoys tremendously strong markets in its home state but each has also prospered in export markets; here in fact Brown Bros has led the way, particularly in the United Kingdom. Brown Bros has also showed great enterprise in developing new varietal styles, new high-country vineyards and in establishing a commercial-scale experimental high-tech winery adjacent to the main winery.

Recommended Wines 1992 Rhine Riesling (beautifully made wine with crisp, clean pure fruit with light lime flavours, a hint of toast and good acidity; now to 1997). Pinot Chardonnay Brut NV (fine, reserved elegant style with hints of spice and citrus; citrus flavours again evident on a long, crisp, clean palate). Show Liqueur Muscat (extremely concentrated and aged with plum pudding bouquet; very complex palate showing obvious aged rancio characters, and again those plum pudding flavours). 1992 Chardonnay (stylish wine, even if somewhat dominated by pronounced lemony oak; redeemed by the length of flavour; to 1996).

BUCHANAN CB–CB Est 1985 $14–17.90 CD 48, 167, 168 TAMAR V
Glendale Road, Loira, West Tamar, Tas 7275 phone and fax (003) 94 7488
Open 7 days 10–4 **Production** 4550 cases
Winemaker Don Buchanan
Principal Wines Chard, Ries, Pinot, Cab Sauv.
Summary Don Buchanan has considerable experience in both winemaking and viticulture, and there is no reason why he should not leave his mark on Tasmanian winemaking. These days, however, other very successful business interests occupy much of his time.
Recommended Wine 1988 Cabernet Sauvignon (masses of sweet red berry fruit, hints of chocolate, concentrated tannins and sweet American oak; Tamar Valley at its lush best; to 2000).

BULLERS BEVERFORD DC–CB Est 1952 $7–13 CD 80 MURRAY R
Murray Valley Highway, Beverford, Vic 3590 (050) 37 6305
Open Mon–Sat 9–5 **Production** 26 000 cases
Winemaker Richard Buller (Jnr)
Principal Wines Wh Fronti, Ries, Chenin, Chab, Sem, Chard, Cab Sauv, Shir, Cab Mer.
Summary Traditional wines, principally white, which in the final analysis reflect both their Riverland origin and a fairly low-key approach to style in the winery.

BULLERS CALLIOPE CB–B Est 1921 $6.50–12.50 CD 80 NE VIC
Three Chain Road, Rutherglen, Vic 3685 (060) 32 9660
Open Mon–Sat 9–5, Sun 10–5 **Production** 10 000 cases
Winemaker Andrew Buller
Principal Wines Shir, Cab Sauv, Tawny Port, Vintage Port, Muscat, Tokay, Madeira.
Summary The dry red table wines and the range of fortifieds are well priced; the Vintage Port has a style all of its own, but the fresh, medium-weight Tokay and Muscat are particularly easy to drink.

BUNGAWARRA NR Est 1975 $14–17 CD SD GRANITE BELT
Bents Road, Ballandean, Qld 4382 (076) 84 1128
Open 7 days 9–5 **Production** 600 cases
Winemaker Philip Christensen
Principal Wines Chard, Shir, Cab Sauv.
Summary Was offered for sale in March 1993, and with future direction uncertain.

BURGE FAMILY BA–BA Est 1928 $7.80–12.50 CD SD
BAROSSA V
Barossa Way, Lyndoch, SA 5351 (085) 24 4644 fax (085) 24 4444
Open 7 days 10–5 **Production** 3300 cases
Winemaker Rick Burge
Principal Wines Sem, Chard, Ries, Draycott Herm, Grenache,
Clochmerle Pinot-Herm, Draycott Homestead Cab blend, Tawny
Port.
Best Vintages W '86, '90, '91, '92 R '84, '88, '90, '91, '92
Summary Rick Burge came back to the family winery after a
number of years successfully running St Leonards; there was a lot of
work to be done, but he has achieved much, using the base of very
good fortified wines and markedly improving table wine quality.
Recommended Wines 1991 Old Vines Grenache (attractive, full
sweet berry fruit, clean and ripe but not overblown; that silky/satiny
texture of old vines; to 1997). 1991 Draycott Hermitage (full, dense
and ripe aroma, slightly gamey and with touches of dark chocolate;
soft red berry fruit on a deep, structured palate; to 1998). 1989
Homestead Cabernets (round, gently ripe sweet fruit with no off
flavours whatsoever; very good mouthfeel and finish; to 1995). 1991
Jollytown Semillon (pronounced but not excessive lemony firm oak
on both bouquet and palate; clean, well flavoured).

BURNBRAE DB–CB Est 1976 $8–14 CD SD MUDGEE
The Hargraves Road, Erudgere via Mudgee, NSW 2850
(063) 73 3504
Open 7 days 9.30–5 **Production** 1800 cases
Winemaker Robert Bassel Mace
Principal Wines Chard, Wh Burg, Tram Ries, Gren Rosé, Shir,
Shir Cab Malb, Port, Muscat.
Summary Wine style is both erratic and idiosyncratic, exemplified
by the monumental 1990 Cabernet Sauvignon, with 15.5° of alcohol;
the still massive 1990 Shiraz Grenache works rather better.
Recommended Wines 1992 Sauvignon Blanc (a startling style
contrast, light, fresh and crisp; hints of passionfruit; light bodied).
1989 Vintage Port (dark chocolate, spice and blackberry aromas and
flavours; good spirit; well balanced).

CALAIS ESTATES CB–CB Est 1987 $9–15 CD SD HUNTER V
Palmers Lane, Pokolbin, NSW 2321 (049) 98 7654
Open Mon–Fri 9–5, w'ends 10–5 **Production** 11 000 cases
Winemaker Colin Peterson
Principal Wines Sem, Chard, Chard Sem, Tram Ries, Pinot, Shir,
Cab Sauv.
Best Vintages W '88, '89, '90, '91 R '87, '88, '90, '91
Summary The former Wollundry vineyards are now fully mature
and are among the best in the Hunter Valley; a little more
sophistication in the winemaking could see outstanding wines under
the Calais label. Colin Peterson, incidentally, is the son of Ian and
Shirley Peterson of Petersons.

CAMDEN ESTATE CB–B Est 1980 $15 R SD SYDNEY DISTRICT
Lot 32 Macarthur Road, Camden, NSW 2570 (046) 58 1237
Open 11–4 by appointment **Production** 11 000 cases
Winemaker Norman Hanckel

Principal Wines Chard, Cab Sauv, Pinot Noir Methode Champenoise.
Best Vintages W '83, '86, '87, '88, '91
Summary Situated on the banks of the Nepean River opposite one of the birthplaces of Australian wine, and has produced some attractive buttery, mouthfilling Chardonnays. The other wines are not in the same class, reflecting a humid and often rather wet autumn.

CAMPBELLS CA–B Est 1870 $6.80–50 CD 86–90, 317 NE VIC

Murray Valley Hwy, Rutherglen, Vic 3685 (060) 32 9458
fax (060) 32 9870
Open Mon–Sat 9–5, Sun 10–5 **Production** 36 000 cases
Winemaker Colin Campbell
Principal Wines Chard Sem, Ries, Fronti, Shir, Durif, Malb, Cab Sauv, Muscat, Tokay, Port; Quarry Hill range (cellar door only).
Best Vintages W '86, '88, '90, '91, '92 R '86, '88, '90, '91, '92
Summary A wide range of table and fortified wines of ascending quality and price, which are always honest; as so often happens in this part of the world, the fortified wines are by far the best, with the extremely elegant Isabella Tokay and Merchant Prince Muscat at the top of the tree.
Recommended Wine 1990 Shiraz (sweet, almost essency fruit, ripe but not jammy; in traditional Campbell style, which favours high alcohol and high pH, giving tremendous softness and sweetness in the mouth; to 2000).

CANOBLAS-SMITH NR Est 1986 SD CENTRAL TABLELANDS

Boree Lane, off Cargo Road, Lidster via Orange, NSW 2800
(063) 65 6113
Open By appointment **Production** 300 cases
Winemaker Murray Smith
Principal Wines Chard, Cab Sauv.
Summary Due to be open for cellar door sales in 1993.

CAPE CLAIRAULT B–B Est 1976 $12–19 CD 21, 63, 92, 149 MARGARET R

Henry Road, Willyabrup, WA 6284 (097) 55 6225
fax (097) 55 6229
Open 7 days 10–5 **Production** 3500 cases
Winemaker Ian Lewis
Principal Wines Sauv Bl, Sem Sauv Bl, Ries, Cab Sauv.
Best Vintages W '85, '86, '88, '90, '92 R '85, '86, '89, '90, '91
Summary Ian and Arni Lewis have the great gift of not taking themselves (or their wines) too seriously. They were still committed to quality however, always seeking to improve on the impressive record of crisp, herbaceous Sauvignon Blanc and finely structured, berry-flavoured Cabernet Sauvignon. However, they had put Cape Clairault on the market in mid 1993.

CAPE MENTELLE A–A Est 1970 $14.95–24 R 30, 66, 158, 169, 170, 182, 198, 284 MARGARET R

Off Wallcliffe Road, Margaret River, WA 6285 (097) 57 2070 fax (097) 57 3233
Open 7 days 10–4.30 **Production** 25 000 cases

Winemaker John Durham

Principal Wines Chard, Sem Sauv Bl, Cab Sauv, Shir, Zin, Cab Mer.

Best Vintages W '82, '86, '88, '90, '91 **R** '82, '87, '88, '90, '92

Summary Majority owned by Veuve Clicquot, but still very much under the management control of founder David Hohnen. Its red wines are legends in their own lifetime; the white wines deserve no less recognition.

Recommended Wines 1991 Chardonnay (exceptionally complex, structured wine showing some malolactic fermentation influence, melon/fig fruit and subtle oak; to 1997). 1992 Semillon Sauvignon Blanc (pungent, lively and crisp with gooseberry/herbal/passionfruit aromas and flavours; just a hint of nutmeg oak). 1991 Zinfandel (extremely rich and ripe, chocolate and stewed prune; classic mid to heavyweight Zinfandel; to 1994). 1990 Shiraz (violets, red berry and spice aromas; incredibly intense pepper spice on the palate with balancing tannins; to 1996).

CAPEL VALE BA–BA Est 1979 $12.50–16 CD 20, 31, 69, 81, 119, 163, 181, 204 SW COASTAL
Lot 5 Capel North West Road, Stirling Estate, Capel, WA 6271
(097) 27 2439 fax (097) 91 2452

Open 7 days 10–4 **Production** 28 000 cases

Winemaker Rob Bowen

Principal Wines Ries, Sem Sauv Bl, Chard, Pinot, Shir, Cab Sauv, Baudin; also CV range Red (Cab Sauv), Chenin, Classic White.

Best Vintages W '86, '87, '88, '91, '92 **R** '87, '88, '89, '91, '92

Summary Always an outstanding maker of pungent and intense white wines, Capel Vale has now lifted its red wines (with the '88 and '90 vintages, the latter in particular) into the same high class. The arrival of Rob Bowen as winemaker should see even greater things, if this is indeed possible.

Recommended Wines 1990 Baudin (fine, elegant, cedary, with fine-grained tannins). 1992 Riesling (toasty rich and full with hints of honey; relatively soft and forward; to 1996). 1992 Chardonnay (smooth, softly fruity fig, melon and peach accented wine).

CAPOGRECO NR Est 1976 $7–10 CD SD MURRAY R
Riverside Avenue, Mildura, Vic 3500 (050) 23 3060

Open Mon–Sat 10–6 **Production** NFP

Winemaker Bruno Capogreco

Principal Wines Ries, Mos, Cab Sauv, Claret, Rosé, fortified and flavoured.

Summary Italian-owned and run, the wines are a blend of Italian and Australian Riverland influences; the herb infused Rosso Dolce is a particularly good example of its kind.

CAROSA NR Est 1986 $9.70–14 CD 77 PERTH HILLS
Lot 3 Houston Street, Mount Helena, WA 6555 (09) 572 1603

Open W'ends 10–5 **Production** 350 cases

Winemaker James Elson

Principal Wines Sem, Chard, Cab Mer, Pinot.

Summary Barrel samples tasted early in the piece were not in proper condition for judging, but winemaker (and consultant) Jim Elson has extensive Eastern states experience, so should succeed.

CASELLA WINES C–B Est 1969 SD MIA
Farm 1471 Yenda, NSW 2681 (069) 68 1346
Open Not **Production** 40 000 cases
Winemaker Filippo Casella
Principal Wines Sem, Chard, Sem Chard, Shir, Shir Cab, Cab
Sauv, Sparkl.
Summary Filippo Casella makes lush, soft, early maturing and full-
flavoured white wines, and surprised with a highly toned, ripe, spicy
berry 1990 Cabernet Sauvignon.

CASSEGRAIN CA–B Est 1980 $8.95–23.95 CD 102, 131, 253
HASTINGS V
Hastings Valley Winery, Pacific Highway, Port Macquarie, NSW
2444 (065) 83 7777 fax (065) 84 0353
Open 7 days 9–5 **Production** 45 000 cases
Winemakers John Cassegrain, Drew Noon
Principal Wines Wines sold in three tiers: Hastings Valley
Individual Vineyard Fromentau Chard, Morrillon Pinot and First
Ridge Sem; Vintage Selection Chard, Sem, Gewurz, Pinot, Cab Sauv
and Shir; and budget-priced Foundation range blended white and red
wines including Chambourcin, Shir and Pinot.
Best Vintages W '85, '86, '89, '91, '93 **R** '85, '86, '87, '91, '92
Summary Highly sophisticated viticulture together with the
planting of varieties such as Chambourcin and Chardonnay help meet
the challenges of a very wet and humid growing and harvest season in
the north coast of New South Wales. Overall wine quality (some
grapes are bought from the Hunter Valley) is excitingly variable.
Recommended Wine 1992 Vintage Selection Chardonnay (fresh,
lifted citrus fruit in crisp, direct style).

CASTLE ROCK ESTATE B–B Est 1983 $11.80–14.80 CD 33,
155, 179 GRT SOUTHERN
Porongurup Road, Porongurup, WA 6324 (098) 41 1037
fax (098) 53 1010
Open Wed–Fri 10–4, w'ends 10–5 **Production** 1500 cases
Winemaker Kim Hart (Contract)
Principal Wines Ries, LH Ries, Chard, Pinot, Cab Sauv, Liqueur
Muscat.
Summary A beautifully sited vineyard and cellar door sale area with
sweeping vistas from the Porongurups, operated by the Diletti family.
Recommended Wines 1990 Chardonnay (crisp, citric/melon fruit
with good mouthfeel and balance; to 1995). 1992 Chardonnay (light
and crisp, but already showing some interesting Burgundian aromas;
should develop well; to 1996).

CATHCART RIDGE NR Est 1977 $10–17 R 132 GRT WESTERN
Byron Road, Cathcart via Ararat, Vic 3377 (053) 52 1997
fax (053) 52 1558
Open 7 days 10–5 **Production** 2500 cases
Winemaker David Farnhill
Principal Wines Chard, Shir, Cab Sauv, Mer.
Best Vintages W '85, '86, '88, '90, '91 **R** '85, '88, '89, '90, '91
Summary Now owned and operated by the Farnhill family; it
remains to be seen whether the high reputation which Cathcart
Ridge enjoyed in the early 1980s can be restored.

K HILL WINES NR Est 1973 $5.90–9 CD SD STHN

... Hill Road, McLaren Vale, SA 5171 (08) 323 8815
Open 7 days 1–5 **Production** Nil 1991
Winemaker Nancy Benko
Principal Wines Ries, Rosé, Shir, Cab Sauv, Port.
Summary The retirement hobby of distinguished research scientist Dr Nancy Benko; wines from numerous vintages back to 1978 are still available at very low prices.

CHAPEL HILL A–A Est 1979 $10.50–28 CD 177, 178 STHN VALES

Chapel Hill Road, McLaren Vale, SA 5171 (08) 323 8429
fax (08) 323 9245
Open Mon–Fri 9–5, w'ends 11–5 **Production** 20 000 cases
Winemaker Pam Dunsford
Principal Wines Ries, Chard, Shir, Cab, Cab Sauv, Port
Best Vintages W '90, '91, '92 R '89, '90, '91, '92
Summary With new owners, and Pamela Dunsford in charge of winemaking, the once sleepy Chapel Hill has sprung into top gear, winning trophies and gold medals with near monotonous regularity.
Recommended Wines 1991 Chardonnay (complex toasty aroma with tangy, stylish long and intense flavour). 1990 Shiraz (concentrated, rich, ripe cassis aroma, with a touch of charred oak; powerfully structured dark currant, briary palate; to 2010). 1991 Cabernet Sauvignon (voluptuously sweet cassis berry fruit aroma and flavour, and a lusciously complex palate; to 2005).

CHARLES CIMICKY B–B Est 1972 $9–15.50 CD 33, 115 BAROSSA V

Gomersal Road, Lyndoch, SA 5351 (085) 24 4025
Open 7 days 10–4 **Production** 2500 cases
Winemaker Charles Cimicky
Principal Wines Sauv Bl, Ries, Colomb, Cab Mer, Shir, Port.
Best Vintages W '81, '82, '85, '89, '91 R '81, '84, '87, '88, '91
Summary These wines are of very good quality, thanks to the lavish (but sophisticated) use of new French oak in tandem with high quality grapes. The intense, long-flavoured Sauvignon Blanc has been a particularly consistent performer.

CHARLES MELTON BA–BA Est 1984 $7.90–14 CD SD 226 BAROSSA V

Krondorf Road, Tanunda, SA 5352 (085) 63 3606
fax (085) 63 3422
Open 7 days 11–5 **Production** 4500 cases
Winemaker Charlie Melton
Principal Wines Rosé, Shir, Pinot Herm, Nine Popes (Shir Grenache Mourvedre), Shir, Cab Mer Franc, Cab Sauv, Sparkl.
Best Vintages R '86, '89, '90, '91, '92
Summary Graeme (Charlie) Melton is one of the great characters of the Barossa Valley, one of the small group determined to preserve its heritage in every way possible, including the encouragement of growers to retain very old dryland vineyards. Situated within a stone's throw of Rockford and St Hallett, and sharing similar philosophies and (to a degree) wine styles.

Recommended Wines 1992 Nine Popes (dark coloured, concentrated and complex bouquet with aromas of liquorice and prunes; dark fruits interwoven with hints of bitter chocolate; fine tannins and wonderful mouthfeel; now to 2000+). 1993 Rose of Virginia (fresh, crisp and lively with cherry and fresh citrus fruits; has good acidity and is not too sweet; drink now). 1991 Shiraz (complex fruit bouquet with red berry, earth and mint aromas; concentrated, rich and chewy on the palate, with extremely ripe fruit; to 2005). 1991 Cabernet Merlot (another extremely concentrated and ripe wine loaded with fruit and extract; certainly needs time, and might have benefited from a slightly lighter hand; to 2005).

CHARLES STURT UNI B–B Est 1977 $10.95–14.95 CD 4, 73 HILLTOPS
Boorooma Street, North Wagga Wagga, NSW 2650 (069) 22 2435 fax (069) 22 2107
Open Mon–Fri 10–4, w'ends 11–4 **Production** 10 000 cases
Winemaker Rodney Hooper
Principal Wines Chard, Traminer, Ries, Sem, Meth Champ, Sauv Bl, Cab Shir, Port, Muscat.
Best Vintages W '80, '88, '90, '91, '92 **R** '87, '88, '90, '91, '92
Summary With the highly talented Rodney Hooper now in charge of winemaking the erratic wines of the past are no more, and the regionally based styles are worthy of this tertiary wine-teaching institution.
Recommended Wines 1992 Chardonnay (crisp, citric/herbaceous aromas; fresh and lively on the palate with a hint of sweetness to balance the citrus flavours; drink now). 1990 Limited Release Cabernet Sauvignon (complex, sweet earthy aromas; palate gently developed sweet red berry fruit and soft tannins; to 1996).

CHATEAU DORRIEN NR Est 1983 $7.90–9.90 CD SD BAROSSA V
Cnr Seppeltsfield Road and Barossa Valley Way, Dorrien, SA 5352 (085) 62 2850
Open 7 days 10–5 **Production** 1000 cases
Winemaker Fernando Martin
Principal Wines Ries, Chab, Chard, Sem, Ausl Ries, Herm, Cab Sauv, fortified.
Summary Unashamedly and successfully directed at the tourist trade.

CHATEAU FRANCOIS CB–B Est 1969 $9–10 CD SD HUNTER V
Off Broke Road, Pokolbin, NSW 2321 (049) 98 7548
Open W'ends 10–5 or by appointment **Production** 1000 cases
Winemaker Don Francois
Principal Wines Sem, Chard, Shir Pinot.
Summary Soft flavoured and structured wines which frequently show regional characters, but which are very modestly priced and are all sold through the cellar door and mailing list to a loyal following.
Recommended Wine 1992 Mallee Semillon (has what is a distinctive regional edge to the bouquet, vaguely medicinal; rich, round and mouthfilling palate with good balance; to 1996).

CHATEAU LEAMON NR Est 1973 $10–16 CD SD BENDIGO
140 km post, Calder Highway, Bendigo, Vic 3550 (054) 47 7995 fax (054) 47 0855

Open Wed–Mon 10–5 **Production** 2000 cases
Winemaker Ian Leamon
Principal Wines Sem, Ries, Chard, Shir, Cab Sauv.
Best Vintages W '82, '83, '89, '90 **R** '83, '84, '86, '87, '88
Summary Produces ever-interesting red wines, sometimes showing spicy characters, sometimes minty, but always with balance and length. However, it is a long time since I have tasted any of the wines.

CHATEAU PATO C–B Est 1978 $6–12 CD SD HUNTER V

Thompson's Road, Pokolbin, NSW 2321 (049) 98 7634
Open By appointment **Production** 300 cases (120 cases in 1992)
Principal Wines Gewurz, Herm.
Summary All-night ABC radio announcer David Patterson died prematurely after a short illness during the 1993 vintage. The future of the tiny winery remains uncertain.

CHATEAU REMY B–B Est 1963 $7–30 R 102, 131, 295 PYRENEES

Vinoca Road, Avoca, Vic 3467 (054) 65 3202 fax (054) 65 3529
Open 7 days 10–4.30 **Production** 53 000 cases
Winemaker Vincent Gere
Principal Wines Meth Champ, Sem, Blue Pyrenees (Cabernet blend); Fiddlers Creek is a recently introduced second label extending the table wine range.
Best Vintages W '82, '86, '89, '90, '92 **R** '80, '82, '88, '90, '91
Summary Owned by Remy Martin of France and making determined efforts to lift the quality (and style) of its Methode Champenoise wines. It is having some success in so doing, however much the climate may be seen as more suited to making full flavoured red table wine, exemplified by the wholly seductive 1989 Blue Pyrenees Estate dry red.
Recommended Wines 1989 Fiddlers Creek Semillon (rich, toasty oak with honeyed fruit; a bargain at its price). 1989 Blue Pyrenees (clean, firm faintly herbaceous aromas, but riper and more solid on the palate; with firm red berry fruit and lingering tannins; to 1998).

CHATEAU REYNELLA BA–B Est 1838 $6.95–19.95 R 22–26, 85, 203, 321 STHN VALES

Reynella Road, Reynella, SA 5161 (08) 381 2266 fax (08) 381 1968
Open Mon–Fri 10–5, w'ends 10–4.15 **Production** 12 500 cases (table wine)
Winemaker David O'Leary
Principal Wines Chard, Cab Sauv, Cab Mer, Shir under the Stony Hill label; also sparkling and Vintage Port.
Best Vintages W '86, '87, '88, '90, '91 **R** '82, '88, '89, '90, '91
Summary Now restricted to a severely pruned range of good table wines and one of the two truly great Australian vintage ports. The Reynella winery and homestead complex is both historic and extremely beautiful, one of the priceless treasures of the industry, and is the headquarters of the BRL Hardy group.
Recommended Wines 1975 Vintage Port (very complex, complex earth, chocolate and sweet spirit aromas with that peculiarly distinctive spicy/peppery/tangy (almost lantana-like) palate). 1991 Stony Hill Chardonnay (complex oak-driven style with nutty/spicy flavours predominating; drink now).

CHATEAU TAHBILK BA–A Est 1860 $8–29.95 R 147, 17
201, 289 GOULBURN V
Off Goulburn Valley Highway, Tahbilk, Vic 3607 (057) 94 2555
fax (057) 94 2360
Open Mon–Sat 9–5, Sun 11–5 **Production** 95 000 cases
Winemaker Alister Purbrick
Principal Wines Chard, Ries, Mars, Shir, Cab Sauv, Private Bin
and Original V'yd.
Best Vintages R '81, '86, '87, '88, '90
Summary A winery steeped in tradition (with high National Trust
classification) which should be visited at least once by every wine-
conscious Australian, and which makes wines — particularly red
wines — utterly in keeping with that tradition. There are no modern,
trendy wines for immediate consumption made here, just wines for
real men (and women) to be cellared for decades.
Recommended Wines 1991 Chardonnay (potent, rich and striking
wine showing both bottle development and its generous alcohol of
14.5%; carries its oak with ease, and does not finish 'hot'; excellent full
bodied food style; drink now). 1990 Shiraz (firm, earthy with hints of
spice; solid, strongly structured, long lived; to 2005). 1991 Marsanne
(classic chalky/honeysuckle aroma with crisp, firm fruit flavour and
structure). 1990 Cabernet Sauvignon (red berry fruit aromas with
cedary overtones; similar cedary flavours, with a hint of spice, and soft
tannins; to 2007).

CHATEAU XANADU CA–B Est 1977 $12–28.50 CD 12, 18,
20, 102, 115 MARGARET R
Railway Terrace off Wallcliffe Rd, Margaret River, WA 6285
(097) 57 2581 fax (097) 57 3389
Open 7 days 10–5 **Production** 10 000 cases
Winemaker Jürg Muggli
Principal Wines Sem, Sem Res, Noble Sem, Sauv Bl, Chard,
Rosé, Cab Sauv, Cab Sauv Reserve.
Best Vintages W '85, '87, '89, '91, '92 R '83, '86, '90, '92
Summary There has always been a degree of variability and
unpredictability in the Chateau Xanadu wines. So much so it is not
easy to tell whether it is the vineyard or the winery which sometimes
plays tricks, the end result being a certain bitterness and astringency
in the less successful wines.
Recommended Wines 1992 Semillon (youthful, crisp, faintly
herbaceous in typical Margaret River style; will develop to 1998).
1990 Cabernet Sauvignon (oak still needing to integrate, but has
length and elegance on the palate; to 1998).

CHATEAU YALDARA CB–BA Est 1947 $3.50–21.90 R 36, 37,
38, 215, 303 BAROSSA V
Gomersal Road, Lyndoch, SA 5351 (085) 24 4200
fax (085) 24 4678
Open 7 days 9–5 **Production** 700 000 cases
Winemaker Herman Thumm (Ch Yaldara, H & R Thumm), Jim
Irvine (Lakewood, Acacia Hill)
Principal Wines A large range of table wines under four labels:
Lakewood, Acacia Hill, Robert Thumm and Chateau Yaldara, the
first three effectively being the premium wines. The Chateau Yaldara
range also extends to fortified, sparkling and non-alcoholic wines.

Best Vintages R & W '86, '88, '90, '92

Summary A thriving operation with a turnover in excess of $15 million and which employs 145 people nationally, now successfully entering the export market with the Lakewood and Acacia Hill brands. The wines are all carefully styled for their market niches, and are made with a high degree of technical and production expertise. The white wines are almost invariably a little sweet, with highly scented oak where oak is used. The red wines are likewise very soft and distinctly fruity. To be hypercritical, they are apt to cloy slightly and tend towards confection tastes, but this is an advantage, rather than a disadvantage, given the positioning of the brands.

CHATSFIELD BA–BA Est 1976 $10.95–14.95 R 55, 70, 76, 80, 171 GRT SOUTHERN

34 Albany Hwy, Mount Barker, WA 6324 (098) 51 1704
fax (098) 41 6811
Open Thurs–Sun 10.30–4.30 **Production** 2000 cases
Winemaker Stephen Warne (Contract)
Principal Wines Ries, Tram Ries, Chard, Shir, Cab Franc.
Best Vintages W '82, '85, '87, '90 R '88, '89
Summary Irish-born medical practitioner Ken Lynch and his two children (including daughter Siobhan in charge of marketing) have quietly developed Chatsfield; competent contract winemaking at Goundrey Wines also helps.
Recommended Wines 1992 Chardonnay (outstanding wine with elegant melon and grapefruit aromas and subtle barrel ferment characters; wonderful mouthfeel and length, again with melon/grapefruit flavours, and again superbly handled oak; to 1997). 1992 Riesling (floral lime and passionfruit aromas and flavours; hints of botrytis add complexity; to 1996). 1991 Shiraz (high-toned cherry, spice and leaf aromas and flavours; will blossom when the finish softens; to 1998).

CHITTERING ESTATE B–CB Est 1982 $6.50–10 CD 39, 237, 324 PERTH HILLS

Chittering Valley Road, Chittering, WA 6084 (09) 571 8144
fax (09) 444 9056
Open Not **Production** 15 000 cases
Winemaker Francois Jacquard
Principal Wines Chard, Sem, Sauv Bl, Cab Mer, Pinot.
Summary One of the most interesting winery operations in Australia, with wealthy owners, extreme marketing skills and an intensely motivated winemaker producing wines of varying quality and style which are mainly exported, amongst other places, to Japan. The Chardonnay is full bodied and complex, international (rather than Australian) in style.

CLARENDON HILLS NR Est 1989 $16–21.50 R 21, 149 STHN VALES

Brookmans Road, Blewitt Springs, SA 5171 (08) 364 0227
fax (08) 364 1484
Open Not **Production** 1500 cases
Winemaker Roman Bratasiuk
Principal Wines Chard, Cab Sauv, Mer, Old Vines Grenache.
Summary Released with a fanfare of trumpets and much

excitement in 1991, with comparisons to '82 Ch Pichon-Lalande and '61 Ch Latour. Most of the wines have justified (as far as is possible) such extravagant comparisons, although one or two (such as the '91 Cabernet Sauvignon) have most certainly not. The future direction of Clarendon Hills was uncertain in 1993, following the dissolution of the founding partnership, but Roman Bratasiuk remains in charge.

Recommended Wines 1991 Shiraz (impenetrable purple colour with powerful, complex and concentrated liquorice and spice aromas and flavours; massive wine; to 2010). 1991 Merlot (smooth, clean bouquet with hints of leafy varietal character; excellent concentration and balance to the palate, with subtle red fruit flavours and sensitive use of oak; to 2005).

CLEVELAND NR Est 1985 $8.95–14.95 CD 55 MACEDON
Shannon's Road, Lancefield, Vic 3435 (054) 29 1449
fax (054) 29 1056
Open By appointment **Production** 2500 cases
Winemaker Keith Brien
Principal Wines Chard, Pinot, Cab Sauv and Sparkling Macedon under Cleveland label; Brien Family Selection Chard is second label.
Summary Cleveland made a promising debut with its 1989 vintage, and in particular with its sappy/strawberry Pinot Noir showing marked Burgundian character, even if the difficult vintage and the still relatively young vines meant a light bodied wine was inevitable. After a period of uncertainty, the 1992 wines fulfilled the promise of the initial releases.
Recommended Wines 1992 Cleveland Chardonnay (highly stylised, and quite stylish wine with pronounced oak and malolactic-type influences; should cellar well; to 1997). 1992 Cleveland Pinot Noir (brightly coloured, with oriental spices and dark plums intermingling on both bouquet and palate; of moderate weight, with balanced tannins; drink now).

CLIFF HOUSE NR Est 1983 $10.95–12.50 R SD TAMAR V
RSD 457, Kayena, Tas 7270 (003) 94 7454 fax (003) 94 7419
Open By appointment **Production** 2300 cases
Winemaker Julian Alcorso (Contract)
Principal Wines Chard, Ries, Pinot, Cab Sauv; 'Premium' is Cab/Pinot blend.
Summary Geoff and Cheryl Hewitt established four hectares of vineyard in the Tamar Valley area (a little distance away from the Tamar River) in 1983. The wines are made at Moorilla Estate and, as one would expect, are usually technically sound. The site, however, produces wines which are less robust than many of the Tamar Valley producers.
Recommended Wines 1992 Chardonnay (of light to medium weight with herbaceous/melon fruit; the mouthfeel and balance is good, and the wine may well develop nicely in bottle; to 1996). 1991 Cabernet Sauvignon (clean, fresh distinctly herbaceous aroma and flavour in the green olive/capsicum range; not unlike Chinon; to 1995).

CLONAKILLA CA–B Est 1971 $10–13 CD 64, 117 CANBERRA
Crisps Lane off Gundaroo Road, Murrumbateman, ACT 2582
(06) 251 1938
Open W'ends, hols 10–5 **Production** 500 cases
Winemaker Dr John Kirk

Principal Wines Sem Sauv Bl, Ries, Botrytis Sem, Cab Sauv, Cabernet, Shir, Muscat.

Best Vintages W '86, '87,' 90, '91, '92 R '86, '88, '90, '91, '92

Summary Distinguished scientist Dr John Kirk (among other things, the author of some interesting papers on the measurement of vineyard climate) presides over a tiny winery which has from time to time produced some excellent wines, although quality does vary somewhat with seasonal conditions.

Recommended Wines 1992 Shiraz (a return to top form after the thin '91, with dark fruits, spice and lots of weight and style; however, barrel sample). 1992 Riesling (fragrant, toasty aroma; crisp light bodied palate fleshed out with just a hint of sugar; well made; to 1995). 1992 Sauvignon Blanc (fresh, crisp, well made; not a great deal of varietal fruit, but helped by a touch of spicy oak).

CLOUD VALLEY NR Est 1991 $15 ML SD MORNINGTON P

15 Ocean View Avenue, Red Hill South, Vic 3937 (059) 89 2762
fax (059) 89 2700

Open Not **Production** 550 cases

Winemaker Tod Dexter (Contract)

Principal Wines Chard, Cab Sauv.

Summary Cloud Valley is a joint venture between Kathy and Bill Allen and Peter and Judy Maxwell. Each family has its own vineyard at Red Hill South, and the grapes are pooled and the wine made under contract at Stonier's Merricks. The Cabernet Sauvignon tends to be very leafy in Chinon style; the Chardonnay is light, fresh, crisp and citrus-tinged.

CLYDE PARK B–B Est 1980 $16–23 R 147, 251 GEELONG

Midland Hwy, Bannockburn, Vic 3331 (052) 81 1363
fax (052) 81 1349

Open Not **Production** 1200 cases

Winemaker Gary Farr

Principal Wines Chard, Pinot, Cab Sauv.

Best Vintages W '88, '89, '90, '91, '92 R '86, '88, '90, '91, '92

Summary Gary Farr's (of Bannockburn) own vineyard, producing small quantities of highly flavoured and distinctively styled wines, with Pinot a new addition to the line. The Chardonnay is consistently the best of the wines on offer.

COBAW RIDGE NR Est 1985 $14–15 CD SD MACEDON

Perc Boyer's Lane, East Pastoria via Kyneton, Vic 3444
(054) 235 227

Open W'ends 10–5, By appointment weekdays

Production 1000 cases

Winemaker Alan Cooper

Principal Wines Chard, Shir, Cab Sauv.

Summary Nelly and Alan Cooper have established Cobaw Ridge at an altitude of 610 metres in the hills above Kyneton. The site is replete with a self-constructed pole-framed mudbrick house and winery. Wine quality goes from strength to strength, and there is little doubt that the vineyard is exceptionally well-sited and managed.

Recommended Wines 1992 Chardonnay (excellent fruit intensity and length, with lovely grapefruit, fig and melon; to 1995).

1991 Shiraz (strong, cassis blackcurrant and mint fruit; great raw material which needed a touch more handling).

COFIELD WINES NR Est 1986 $8.50–15.50 CD SD NE VIC
Distillery Road, Wahgunyah, Vic 3687 (060) 33 3798
Open Mon–Sat 9–5, Sun 10–5 **Production** 2400 cases
Winemaker Max Cofield
Principal Wines Sem, Chenin, Chard, Cab Mer, Shir, Sparkl Burg, Pinot Chard Sparkl.
Summary District veteran Max Cofield, together with wife Karen, is developing a strong cellar door sales base by staging in-winery functions with guest chefs, and also providing a large barbeque and picnic area. The wine style is somewhat rustic.

COLDSTREAM HILLS NR Est 1985 $15–24 R 30, 147, 169, 170, 171, 173, 230 YARRA V
Lot 6, Maddens Lane, Coldstream, Vic 3770 (059) 64 9388
fax (059) 64 9389
Open Mon–Fri 12–2, w'ends 10–5 **Production** 21 000 cases
Winemakers James Halliday, Phillip Dowell
Principal Wines Varietal range Chard, Fumé, Pinot, Merlot, Cab Sauv, Cab Mer; Reserve range Chard, Pinot.
Best Vintages W '88, '90, '91, '92 R '88, '90, '91, '92
Summary The author's own winery, and therefore not rated; however, from five years limited show entries, Coldstream Hills has received 40 trophies, 82 gold, 77 silver and 94 bronze medals, a success rate of more than 80%.

COOINDA VALE NR Est 1985 $12.50 CD SD COAL RIVER
Bartonvale Road, Campania, Tas 7026 (002) 62 4227
Open By appointment **Production** 150 cases
Winemaker Andrew Hood (Contract)
Principal Wines Ries, Pinot.
Summary The tiny production means the wines are not widely known, even in southern Tasmania. However, the crisp, lifted 1992 Riesling and the concentrated, minty/essency 1992 Pinot Noir hold considerable promise, the latter emphasising the amount of ripeness and extract that can be obtained in the Campania/Coal River region.

COOLART VALLEY NR Est 1981 $11–15 CD SD
MORNINGTON P
Thomas Hill Road, Red Hill South, Vic 3937 (059) 89 2087
Open All w'ends Nov–Mar; first w'end month Apr–Oct
Production 450 cases
Winemaker Peter Cumming (Contract)
Principal Wines Sem, Chard, Ries, Cab Sauv, Cab Mer.
Summary Made an outstanding Cabernet Sauvignon in 1989, with unusual weight and depth for the year and perfect balance; a tangy, smoky 1990 Chardonnay rounded off an impressive debut. However, I have not tasted the '91 or '92 vintage wines in bottle.

• COOMBEND NR Est 1985 $14.50–16 ML SD EAST COAST, TAS
Coombend via Swansea, Tas 7190 (002) 57 8256
fax (002) 57 8484

Open By appointment **Production** 300 cases
Winemaker Freycinet (Contract)
Principal Wines Cab Sauv.
Summary John Fenn Smith has established 1.75 hectares of Cabernet Sauvignon (together with a little Cabernet Franc) on his 2600 hectare sheep station, choosing that part of his property which is immediately adjacent to Freycinet. All of the grapes are processed at Freycinet, with half being made and released under the Coombend label. The 1990 Cabernet Sauvignon, the first vintage, won the trophy for Best Tasmanian Wine in Older Vintage Classes at the 1992 Hobart Wine Show.
Recommended Wine 1991 Cabernet Sauvignon (very ripe and sweet, almost jammy aromas, with plummy/minty fruit and persistent tannins; a touch of sweet vanillin American oak adds to the attraction of the wine; to 2000).

COORINJA NR Est 1870 $8–10.50 CD SD PERTH HILLS
Toodyay Road, Toodyay, WA 6566 (096) 26 2280
Open Mon–Sat 8–5 **Production** 3200
Winemaker Michael Wood
Principal Wines Dry White, Claret, Herm, Burg, Port, Sherry, Muscat.
Summary An evocative and historic winery nestling in a small gully which seems to be in a time-warp, begging to be used as a set for a film. A recent revamp of the packaging accompanied a more than respectable 1990 Hermitage, with lots of dark chocolate and sweet berry flavour, finishing with soft tannins.

COPE WILLIAMS B–B Est 1977 $9.50–23 R SD MACEDON
Glenfern Road, Romsey, Vic 3434 (054) 29 5428 fax (054) 29 5655
Open 7 days 10–5 **Production** 6500 cases
Winemaker Michael Cope Williams
Principal Wines Chard, Cab Mer; d'Vine is second label, Ries, Chard and Cab Sauv; winery specialty sparkling wine, Macedon Brut and Rosé.
Summary One of the high country Macedon pioneers, specialising in sparkling wines that are full flavoured, but also producing excellent Chardonnay in the warmer vintages. A traditional 'English Green' type cricket ground is available for hire and booked out most days of the week from spring through till autumn.

CORIOLE BA–B Est 1969 $10.50–15.50 R 81, 148, 175, 193
STHN VALES
Chaffeys Road, McLaren Vale, SA 5171 (08) 323 8305
fax (08) 323 9136
Open Mon–Fri 9–5, w'ends 11–5 **Production** 12 000 cases
Winemaker Stephen Hall
Principal Wines Chard, Sem, Chenin, Sangiovese, Shir, Cab Shir, Cab Sauv; top-of-the-range red wines under Lloyd Reserve label.
Best Vintages W '84, '89, '90, '91 R '80, '84, '88, '90, 91
Summary Blessed with some great old vineyards, Coriole has been a consistent producer of rich, full flavoured red wines, often showing good use of oak. The white wines are less successful, with rather heavy-handed oak.
Recommended Wines 1990 Lloyd Reserve Shiraz (an immensely

rich, full bodied, firm wine with cabernet-like dark currant fruit and soft, lingering tannins; to 2010). 1991 Shiraz (full, rich, concentrated, with complex interplay between a hint of earthiness, dark chocolate fruit and a touch of American oak; to 2005). 1990 Cabernet Sauvignon (again, a very concentrated wine with dark chocolate aromas and full, ripe, fleshy fruit followed by substantial tannins; to 2005).

COSHAM WINES NR Est 1989 SD PERTH HILLS

Lot 44 Union Road, Carmel via Kalamunda, WA 6076
(09) 291 6514
Open Not **Production** 250 cases
Winemaker Anthony Sclanders
Principal Wines Chard, Pinot, Cab Mer.
Summary The newest of the Perth Hills ventures with a planned future production of 1000 cases, but no wines yet on the market.

COWRA ESTATE, THE CB–CB Est 1973 $10–18 R 47, 115 COWRA

Boorowa Road, Cowra, NSW 2794 (063) 42 1136 fax (02) 451 5670
Open Tues–Sat 11–5, Sun 12–5 **Production** 65 000 cases
Winemaker Simon Gilbert (Contract)
Principal Wines Ries, Gewurz, Sauv Bl, Directors Reserve Chard, Pinot, Cab Sauv.
Summary A major producer with a strong export base, the wines of which I have tasted many times, but which for a variety of reasons do not seem to realise the full potential of the Cowra region for full bodied white wines. It is not that they are bad wines; they are not, but they lack the style of the early Petaluma and the current Rothbury wines made from similar vintage sources.

CRABTREE OF WATERVALE CB–B Est 1979 $9–11 CD 20, 67, 184, 222 CLARE V

North Terrace, Watervale, SA 5452 (088) 43 0069
fax (088) 43 0144
Open 7 days 11–5 **Production** 2500 cases
Winemaker Robert Crabtree
Principal Wines Ries, Sem, Shir Cab, Cab Sauv, Muscat.
Best Vintages W '82, '86, '88, '90, '92 R '84, '86, '88, '90, '91
Summary The gently eccentric Robert Crabtree is one of the numerous great characters who inhabit the beautiful Clare Valley: the mixture of people, wine, history and beauty is a potent elixir, and you will not regret a visit to the winery, nor tasting the chewy, minty Shiraz Cabernet and full flavoured lime/toast Riesling.

CRAIG AVON B–B Est 1986 $19–23 R SD MORNINGTON P

Craig Avon Lane, Merricks North, Vic 3926 (059) 89 7465
Open Not **Production** 1000 cases
Winemaker Ken Lang
Principal Wines Chard, Cab Sauv, Pinot.
Summary The 1990 vintage produced pretty though typically light bodied wines for this new winery: the Chardonnay, with the attractive spicy oak which also made its appearance in a fresh Cabernet Sauvignon; the Pinot showed minty/spicy flavours which will appeal to some. However, the 1991 and 1992 vintages show far

r weight and extract, and promise a bright future for this producer.

Recommended Wines 1991 Cabernet Sauvignon (clean, potent fruit, obviously cool-grown yet ripe, with strong cassis flavours and great depth; to 2004). 1991 Chardonnay (crisp, clean, very cool-grown herbaceous/citrus style, with subtle oak and a long finish).

CRAIGIE KNOWE NR Est 1979 $19.45–25 R SD E COAST TAS

Craigie Knowe, Cranbrook, Tas 7190 (vineyard only); postal 173 Macquarie Street, Hobart, Tas (002) 23 5620
Open Not **Production** 350 cases
Winemaker Dr John Austwick
Principal Wines Cab Sauv.
Summary Makes a small quantity of full flavoured, robust Cabernet Sauvignon in a tiny winery as a weekend relief from a busy metropolitan dental practice.

CRAIGLEE A–A Est 1976 $13–15 CD 139 MACEDON

Sunbury Road, Sunbury, Vic 3429 (03) 744 1160 fax (03) 744 7905
Open By appointment **Production** 2500 cases
Winemaker Patrick Carmody
Principal Wines Chard, Shir, Cab Sauv, Pinot, Sparkl Burg.
Best Vintages W '85, '86, '87, '91, '92 R '85, '86, '88, '90, '91
Summary An historic winery with a proud nineteenth-century record; after a prolonged hiatus once again producing wine of the highest quality, most notably a vibrantly peppery Shiraz (reaching a great height in 1990), a smooth, deep flavoured Cabernet Sauvignon and a gold medal winning 1991 Chardonnay followed by an equally good 1992. The 1991 Shiraz is in very different style to the normal Craiglee wines, with concentrated, minty flavours and an unusually high degree of extract. It may need time to settle down.

CRAIGMOOR B–B Est 1858 $10–11 R 122 MUDGEE

Craigmoor Road, Mudgee, NSW 2850 (063) 72 2208
fax (063) 72 4464
Open Mon–Fri 9–4, w'ends 10–4 **Production** NFP
Winemaker Robert Paul
Principal Wines Sem Chard, Chard, Shir, Cab Sauv, Port.
Best Vintages W '84, '86, '90, '91, '93 R '82, '86, '90, '91, '93
Summary One of the oldest wineries in Australia to remain in continuous production, now subsumed into the Orlando/Wyndham group, with an inevitable loss of identity and individuality of wine-style, although the technical quality of the wines cannot be faulted.
Recommended Wines 1991 Chardonnay (soft, gentle, middle-of-the-road style with soft, gently peachy fruit; drink now).

CRANEFORD CB–B Est 1978 $10–15 CD 14, 126 ADELAIDE HILLS

Main Street, Springton, SA 5235 (085) 68 2220 fax (085) 68 2538
Open Wed–Mon 11–5 **Production** 2500 cases
Winemaker Colin Forbes
Principal Wines Ries, Chard, Shir, Cab Sauv.
Best Vintages W '81, '82, '88, '89 R '83, '88, '89, '90
Summary At times surprisingly mediocre Rhine Riesling, but some attractive red wines, most recently a vibrant, peppery spicy 1989

Shiraz following the very good minty 1988 Shiraz; Cab
Sauvignon, too, has been good.

CRANSWICK ESTATE C–CB Est 1976 $4.95–9.95 R 72, 227 MIA
Walla Avenue, Griffith, NSW 2680 (069) 62 4133
fax (069) 62 2888
Open Mon–Fri 10–4.30 **Production** 1 000 000 cases
Winemaker Andrew Schulz
Principal Wines Under Cranswick Estate label: Sem, Sem Chard,
Chard, Shir Cab, Shir Mer, Cab Sauv; under Barramundi label: Sem
Chard, Shir Mer, Dry White and Dry Red; under Redello label:
Classic Chablis and Shir Cab.
Summary Cranswick Estate has aggressively — and successfully —
focused on the export market, offering light bodied but technically
sound wines at highly competitive prices.

CRAWFORD RIVER CA–B Est 1982 $12–15 CD 48, 66, 70, 186 WESTERN VIC
Crawford via Condah, Vic 3303 (055) 78 2267 fax (055) 78 2267
Open 7 days 9–5 **Production** 3000 cases
Winemaker John Thomson
Principal Wines Ries, Beeren Ries, Sem Sauv Bl, Cab Sauv.
Best Vintages W '84, '86, '87, '88, '89 R '86, '88, '90, '91, '92
Summary Some exemplary Rieslings, Botrytis Rieslings and
Cabernet Sauvignons have been made by full-time grazier, part-time
winemaker John Thomson, who clearly has the winemaker's
equivalent of the gardener's green thumb.
Recommended Wines 1992 Beerenauslese Riesling (powerful
wine with plenty of concentration with lime juice and tropical fruit
flavours intermingling; very clean and well made; to 1995). 1992
Rhine Riesling (clean, crisp, well made wine with hints of
passionfruit and a refreshingly dry finish; to 1995).

CRUICKSHANK–CALLATOOTA ESTATE DC–C Est 1972 $8.30–12.50 CD SD UPPER HUNTER V
Wybong Road, Wybong, NSW 2333 (065) 47 8149
fax (065) 47 8144
Open Sum 9–6, Winter 9–5 **Production** 6200 cases
Winemaker Andrew Cruickshank
Principal Wines Rosé, Cab Sauv identified by cask and vat
numbers.
Summary Owned by Sydney management consultant John
Cruickshank and family. It typically produces fairly light bodied and
extremely regional (tarry) wines, but the 1991 vintage provided wines
with more weight and fruit than previously, the best for many years.

CULLEN WINES A–A Est 1971 $12.85–17.40 CD 20, 69, 115, 155, 171, 191, 204 MARGARET R
Caves Road, Willyabrup via Cowaramup, WA 6284 (097) 55 5277
fax (097) 55 5550
Open 7 days 10–4 **Production** 9000 cases
Winemaker Vanya Cullen
Principal Wines Sauv Bl, Chard, Sem (oaked), Classic Dry White,
Cab Mer, Pinot.

Best Vintages W '84, '86, '89, '90, '92 R '84, '86, '90, '91, '92

Summary One of the pioneers of Margaret River that has always produced long-lived wines of highly individual style. Winemaking has progressively passed from father Dr Kevin Cullen to wife Diana and now to daughter Vanya, one of the best-liked and most respected winemaking families in Australia.

Recommended Wines 1991 Cabernet Merlot (complex briary/berry, dark chocolate and cinnamon aroma with concentrated, ripe dark chocolate, plum and berry flavours, finishing with fine-grained tannins; to 2005). 1992 Semillon (fresh and lively with crisp fruit and spicy oak). 1992 Chardonnay (strong, complex textured wine with evident malolactic influence and weight; to 1996).

CURRENCY CREEK B–B Est 1969 $4.95–12.95 CD 48, 65, 98, 99, 123, 185 LANGHORNE CREEK
Winery Road, Currency Creek, SA 5214 (085) 55 4069
fax (085) 55 4100
Open 7 days 10–5 **Production** 8000 cases
Winemaker Phillip Tonkin
Principal Wines Chard, Sauv Bl, Ries, Seafood Dry White, Pinot, Gamay, Shir, Claret, Cab Sauv, Sparkl, fortifieds.
Best Vintages W '84, '86, '89, '90, '91 R '83, '84, '85, '87, '89, '90
Summary Constant name changes (Santa Rosa, Tonkins have also been tried) did not help the quest for identity or recognition in the marketplace, but the winery has nonetheless produced some outstanding wood-matured whites and pleasant soft reds selling at attractive prices.
Recommended Wines Methode Traditional Sparkling Brut (complex aroma showing full fruit and some autolysis; on the palate strong chardonnay fruit with some bite).

DALFARRAS B–B Est 1991 $9.95–12.95 R 42, 45, 163 GOULBURN V
PO Box 123, Nagambie, Vic 3608 (057) 94 2637
Open Not **Production** 8000 cases
Winemaker Alister Purbrick
Principal Wines Ries, Chard, Sem, Sauv Bl, Marsanne, Shir, Cab Sauv.
Summary The personal project of Alister Purbrick and artist wife Rosa Dalfarra, whose paintings adorn the labels of the wines. Alister, of course, is best known as winemaker at Chateau Tahbilk, the family winery and home, but this range of wines is intended to (in Alister's words) 'allow me to expand my winemaking horizons and mould wines in styles different to Chateau Tahbilk'.

DALRYMPLE NR Est 1987 $10–12 ML SD TAMAR V
Heemskerk/Lebrina Road, Pipers Brook, Tas 7254 (vineyard only); postal 116 Frankland Street, Launceston, Tas 7250 (003) 82 7222
fax (003) 31 3179
Open Sat–Sun 10–5 **Production** 900 cases
Winemaker Jean Baptiste Lecaillon (Contract for white wine), Nicholas Butler, Andrew Hood (Contract for red wine)
Principal Wines Chard, Pinot.
Summary A partnership between Jill Mitchell and her sister and

brother-in-law, Anne and Bertel Sundstrup, inspired by fath
Mitchell's establishment of the Tamarway Vineyard in the late
In 1991 Tamarway reverted to the Sundstrup and Mitchell
and it, too, will be producing wine in the future, probably under its
own label but sold ex the Dalrymple cellar door.

Recommended Wine 1991 Chardonnay (stylish, clean,
citrus/melon fruit with a hint of spicy oak; very well made; to 1996).

DALWHINNIE A–A Est 1976 $16–18 R 66, 120, 188, 319
PYRENEES
Taltarni Road, Moonambel, Vic 3478 (054) 67 2388
fax (054) 67 2237
Open 7 days 10–5 **Production** 3500 cases
Winemaker David Jones
Principal Wines Chard, Cab Sauv, Shir.
Best Vintages W '87, '88, '90, '91, '92 R '86, '88, '89, '90, '91,
'92
Summary Owned by distinguished architect Ewan Jones and
family, Dalwhinnie goes from strength to strength, making
outstanding wines right across the board. The wines all show
tremendous depth of fruit flavour, reflecting its relatively low-
yielding but very well maintained vineyards.
Recommended Wines 1991 Shiraz (extremely concentrated, with
hints of prune, blackcurrant and dark chocolate; massively
concentrated fruit and powdery tannins; to 2010). 1991 Cabernet
Sauvignon (similarly concentrated and deep, with sweet ripe berry
fruit aromas, briary/berry flavours and persistent tannins; to 2005).
1991 Chardonnay (complex and structured, built to last, with melon
fruit and subtle oak; to 1995).

DALYUP RIVER ESTATE NR Est 1987 $9 CD SD GRT
SOUTHERN
Murray's Road, Esperance, WA 6450 phone and fax (090) 76 5027
Open W'ends 10–4 **Production** 500 cases
Winemaker John Wade (Contract)
Principal Wines Ries, Chard, Shir.
Summary Light but fresh 1990 vintage white wines were a quiet
debut, but with contract-making by John Wade at Plantagenet the
future seems assured.

D'AQUINO'S NR Est 1952 $4.99–6.99 R SD ORANGE
129–133 Bathurst Road, Orange, NSW 2800 (063) 62 7381
Open 7 days 9.30–8 **Production** 3000 cases
Winemaker Rex D'Aquino
Principal Wines Table, fortified, Sparkl, flavoured wines.
Summary An interesting outpost of the industry: Rex D'Aquino
graduated from Roseworthy in 1981 and makes wines from grapes
purchased in various parts of Australia, as well as operating a bonded-
spirit store and bottling plant and a large retail shop offering wines
from most well-known Australian wineries.

D'ARENBERG BA–BA Est 1912 $6–15 CD 92, 98, 129, 181,
186, 207, 325 STHN VALES
Osborn Road, McLaren Vale, SA 5171 (08) 323 8206
fax (08) 323 8423

Open Mon–Fri 9–5, Sat/hols 10–5, Sun 12–4
Production 80 000 cases
Winemaker Chester Osborn
Principal Wines Chard, Ries, Sauv Chen Bl, Wh Burg, Wh Muscat, Shir Cab Sauv, Shir, Burg, Port.
Best Vintages W '86, '87, '88, '90, '92 **R** '88, '89, '90, '91, '92
Summary A rock of ages, yet showing some signs of moving with the times, flirting with avant-garde packaging while continuing to make soft, velvety McLaren Vale red wines which age with grace and the occasional startlingly good white wine. A sentimental favourite, I have to admit.
Recommended Wines 1989 Old Vines Shiraz (rich, sweetly ripe berry fruit and vanillin oak aroma, hint of gaminess, with the smooth patina which old vines give to the palate; lovely wine; to 2005). 1992 Noble Traminer Riesling (striking, spicy rich varietal aroma, merging into lychee, peach and apricot flavours, again with a touch of spice, on the palate; unusual but very impressive; drink now). 1990 Red Ochre Shiraz (spicy red cherry fruit, fresh and youthful; great value; drink now). 1989 Ironstone Pressings (clean, smooth, with hints of spice throughout; a fruity, rich blend of shiraz and grenache; to 1999).

DARLING ESTATE NR Est 1986 $9 CD 175 NE VIC
Whitfield/Myrtleford Road, Cheshunt, Vic 3678 phone and fax (057) 29 8396
Open By appointment **Production** 350 cases
Winemaker Guy Darling
Principal Wines Chenin, Pinot.
Summary A long-term grape grower in the King Valley, until 1991 a major supplier to Brown Bros, but with a parallel vineyard operation on the family tobacco farm.

DARLING PARK NR Est 1986 ML SD MORNINGTON P
Lot 1 Browne Lane, Red Hill, Vic 3937 (059) 89 2732 fax (059) 89 2254
Open W'ends 10–4 **Production** 300 cases
Winemaker Kevin McCarthy (Contract)
Principal Wines Chard, Cab Mer.
Summary With contract winemaking by Kevin McCarthy, wine quality should be assured once the vineyard becomes fully mature.

DARLINGTON ESTATE NR Est 1983 $9–15 CD 69, 312
PERTH HILLS
Lot 39 Nelson Road, Glen Forrest, WA 6071 (09) 299 6268 fax (09) 299 7107
Open Wed–Fri 12–5, w'ends & public hols 10–5
Production 2000 cases
Winemaker Balthazar van der Meer
Principal Wines Chard, Sem Sauv Bl, Chenin, Colomb, Shir, Cab Sauv, Port.
Summary In 1988 and 1989 Darlington showed just what the Perth Hills could achieve with Chardonnay, Semillon/Sauvignon Blanc and (in 1988) Cabernet Sauvignon — wines with great style, flavour and length. Subsequent vintages have disappointed except for a substantial, flavoursome 1989 Cabernet Sauvignon; no recent tastings.

DAVID TRAEGER WINES CB–CB Est 1988 $11.95–14.95 R
105, 174 GOULBURN V
399 High Street, Nagambie, Vic 3608 phone and fax (057) 94 2318
Open 7 days 10–5 **Production** 3000 cases
Winemaker David Traeger
Principal Wines Verd, Shir, Cab.
Summary David Traeger learnt much during his years as assistant
winemaker at Mitchelton, and produced a quite delectable 1991
Verdelho, with the aroma and flavour of a white peach and just a
touch of smoky oak. However, the 1992 Verdelho was not in the same
class.
Recommended Wine 1989 Cabernet (smooth, minty berry fruit,
although the wine has a slightly undermade character suggesting it
may have spent considerable time in tank; finishes clean).

DAWSON ESTATE CB–B Est 1980 $9–12 CD 27 HUNTER V
Londons Road, Lovedale, NSW 2325 (049) 90 2904
fax (049) 91 1886
Open 7 days 9–5 **Production** 4000 cases
Winemaker Ben Dawson
Principal Wines Chard, Tram Ries.
Best Vintages W '83, '86, '87, '89, '91
Summary A Chardonnay specialist producing wines of somewhat
variable quality, but at their best showing all of the buttery, peachy
richness one could hope for, and which repay cellaring.

DE BORTOLI CA–BA Est 1928 $4–30 CD 51–53, 67, 102, 216,
247 GRIFFITH
De Bortoli Road, Bilbul, NSW 2680 (069) 63 5253
fax (069) 63 5382
Open Mon–Sat 9–5.30 **Production** 3 million cases
Winemaker Darren de Bortoli
Principal Wines Botrytis Sem (now called Noble One), Chard,
Ries, Sauv Bl, Chab, Shir, Pinot, Cab Sauv, Mer principally under
Deen de Bortoli brand.
Best Vintages W '82, '84, '87, '90, '91 R '84, '87, '88, '90, '92
Summary Famous among the cognoscenti for its superb Botrytis
Semillon, which accounts for only a minute part of total production,
this winery was founded on low-priced varietal and generic wines that
neither aspired to nor achieved any particular distinction. Ever-
improving quality and financial and marketing acumen make de
Bortoli the fastest-growing large winery in Australia today.
Recommended Wines 1990 Noble One Botrytis Semillon (deep
yellow-gold colour; intense, complex, pungent bouquet; extremely
rich apricot and honey fruit flavours, with perfect balancing acidity;
tremendous length; to 1998). 1992 Dry Botrytis Semillon (bright,
glowing yellow-green colour; clean honeyed fruit with a hint of spicy
oak on the bouquet; some honey and fruit pastille flavours not unlike
viognier; very smooth; will build complexity with age; to 1998). 1992
Deen de Bortoli Chardonnay (fragrant passionfruit lime and
grapefruit aromas; very smooth, stylish wine on the palate with a nice
touch of barrel ferment oak and good length; a major surprise; drink
now). 1992 Premium Shiraz Cabernet (clean, sweet, red cherry fruit
with high-toned spicy American oak; to 1994).

DE BORTOLI BA–A Est 1971 $9.50–16 R 51–53, 67, 193 YARRA V
Pinnacle Lane, Dixons Creek, Vic 3775 (059) 65 2271
fax (059) 65 2442
Open Mon–Fri 9–5, w'ends 10–5.30 **Production** 100 000 cases
Winemakers Stephen Webber, David Slingsby-Smith
Principal Wines Chard, Ries, Shir, Pinot, Cab Sauv; second label
Windy Peak.
Best Vintages W '88, '90, '91, '92, '93 R '88, '90, '91, '92
Summary The former Chateau Yarrinya, now the quality arm of the
bustling de Bortoli group, run by Leanne de Bortoli and husband
Steven Webber, ex-Lindeman winemaker. Both the top label (de
Bortoli) and the second label (Windy Peak) offer wines of
consistently good quality and excellent value.
Recommended Wines 1992 Chardonnay (clean, soft, peachy fruit
with well balanced, subtle oak; plenty of flavour; very harmonious and
balanced, again with subtle oak interwoven with citrus/peach fruit).
1991 Cabernet Sauvignon (cool-grown, juicy cabernet with elegant
fresh red berry fruit, a hint of mint and a smooth, long finish; to 2000).
1992 Windy Peak Rhine Riesling (firm, reserved toasty aroma; classic
structure and flavour which will build with time in bottle; to 1997).

DELACOLLINE ESTATE B–B Est 1984 $10–15 ML SD PORT
LINCOLN
Whillas Road, Port Lincoln, SA 5606 (086) 82 5277
fax (086) 82 4455
Open Not **Production** 1000 cases
Winemaker Tim Knappstein (White), Neil Pike (Red) (Contract)
Principal Wines Ries, Fumé Bl, Cab Sauv.
Summary Joins Boston Bay as the second Port Lincoln producer;
the white wines are made under contract by Tim Knappstein and the
red wines by Neil Pike. The three hectare vineyard, run under the
direction of Tony Bassett, reflects the cool maritime influence, with
ocean currents that sweep up from the Antarctic.
Recommended Wines 1992 Rhine Riesling (fragrant, fine lime
and passionfruit aromas, delicate yet intense; fine, crisp and very long
on the palate; to 1997). 1991 Cabernet Sauvignon (spicy, leafy
tobacco-tinged aromas with considerable fragrance; fresh and fragrant
flavours, again with leafy notes, but neither bitter nor excessively
green; to 1995).

DELAMERE B–B Est 1983 $19 R SD PIPERS BROOK
Bridport Road, Pipers Brook, Tas 7254 (003) 82 7190
Open 7 days 10–5 **Production** 750 cases
Winemaker Richard H. Richardson
Principal Wines Chard, Pinot.
Best Vintages W '88, '89, '90, '91, '92 R '86, '87, '88, '90, '91
Summary Richie Richardson produces elegant, rather light bodied
wines which have a strong following. The Chardonnay has been most
successful, particularly in 1991, with a textured, complex, malolactic-
influenced wine with great creamy feel in the mouth. The Pinot Noir
always shows distinct varietal fruit, but very consistent tasting notes
show errant aromas deriving from old oak.
Recommended Wines 1991 Pinot Noir (has attractive, typically
soft and light, spicy/plummy fruit aroma and flavour, slightly blurred
by the oak; drink now).

DELATITE B–B Est 1982 $10–19 CD 55, 68, 120, 207, 224, 307
CENTRAL VIC
Stoneys Road, Mansfield, Vic 3722 (057) 75 2922
fax (057) 75 2911
Open Mon–Fri 10–6, w'ends 10–5 **Production** 9000 cases
Winemaker Rosalind Ritchie
Principal Wines Sauv Bl, Ries, Gewurz, Chard, Malb, Shir, Pinot, Sparkl.
Best Vintages W '82, '83, '86, '87, '91 R '82, '83, '86, '88, '90
Summary With its sweeping views across to the snow-clad alps, this is uncompromising cool-climate viticulture and the wines naturally reflect the climate. Light but intense Riesling and spicy Traminer flower with a year or two in bottle, and in years such as '88 and '90 the red wines achieve flavour and mouthfeel, albeit with a distinctive and all-pervasive mintiness.
Recommended Wine 1993 Sauvignon Blanc (fresh, gently herbaceous with good mouthfeel and even a touch of tropical fruit; drink now). 1992 Riesling (light, perfumed citrus and passionfruit aromas; a crisp, elegant palate; light but well balanced; to 1995).

DENNIS' DARINGA CB–B Est 1970 $14.40 R 21, 31, 48, 132, 134 STHN VALES
Kangarilla Road, McLaren Vale, SA 5171 (08) 323 8665
fax (08) 323 9121
Open 7 days 10–5 **Production** 4000 cases
Winemaker Peter Dennis
Principal Wines Sauv Bl, Chard, Cab Sauv, Shir, Cab Mer.
Summary Low profile winery which has made some excellent wines, notably the typically full-blown, buttery/peachy Chardonnay.

DEVIL'S LAIR NR Est 1981 $17.50–19.95 R 4, 54 MARGARET R
Rocky Road, Forest Grove via Margaret River, WA 6285
(09) 388 1717 fax (09) 381 5423; postal PO Box 212, Margaret River, WA 6285
Open via Captain Sterling Hotel, Nedlands, Sat 11–2
Production 10 000 cases
Winemaker Janice McDonald
Principal Wines Chard, Pinot, Cab Sauv.
Summary A relatively new but very substantial operation, with 40 hectares of vineyard and a 14 hectare lake stocked with trout and yabbies to service that vineyard and to beautify the landscape. The project of Philip Sexton, who started Redback Brewery, it is bound to play a major role in the development of Western Australia wine.
Recommended Wines 1991 Cabernet Sauvignon (a concentrated wine with sweet fruit aromas complexed by dark, briary characters and nice oak; similar ripe, dark cherry/berry fruit flavours and sweet vanillin oak on the palate; to 2003). 1992 Chardonnay (curious, scented, floraceous/lantana aromas lead on to a potent palate with similar vegetal/lime flavours; minimal oak; of uncertain cellaring future, but very interesting).

DIAMOND VALLEY BA–A Est 1976 $9–17 CD 20, 70, 81, 173, 187 YARRA V
Kinglake Road, St Andrews, Vic 3761 (03) 710 1484
fax (03) 710 1369

n Not Production 5000 cases
emaker David Lance
Principal Wines Ries, Chard, Pinot, Cabernet (Bordeaux blend).
Best Vintages W '84, '86, '89, '90, '92 **R** '86, '88, '90, '91, '92
Summary One of the Yarra Valley's finest producers of Pinot Noir, and an early pacesetter for the variety, making wines of tremendous style and crystal clear varietal character. They are not Cabernet Sauvignon look-alikes, but true Pinot Noir, fragrant and intense.
Recommended Wines 1991 Estate Pinot Noir (dark red purple in colour, with complex dark plum, chocolate and earth aromas; excellent flavour and structure, more intense and weighty than the celebrated 1990 vintage; to 1995). 1989 Semillon (scented, gently herbal, crisp fruit aromas with very direct, fresh and clean flavours; to 1997).

DOMAINE A NR Est 1973 $9–25 ML SD COAL R
Campania, Tas 7202 (002) 62 4174
Open By appointment **Production** 1000 cases
Winemaker Peter Althaus
Principal Wines Sauv Bl, Pinot, Cab Sauv, Cabernets.
Summary The striking new black label, dominated by the single, multicoloured 'A', signified the change of ownership from George Park to Swiss businessman Peter Althaus. The much expanded vineyard is of undoubted quality, a harbinger of the great potential of the Coal River region.

DOMAINE CHANDON A–A Est 1986 $22 R 156, 276 YARRA V
Greenpoint, Maroondah Highway, Coldstream, Vic 3770
(03) 739 1110 fax (03) 739 1095
Open 7 days 11–4.30 **Production** 60 000 cases
Winemakers Dr Tony Jordan, Wayne Donaldson
Principal Wines Meth Champ specialist, under various numbered Cuvee labels (eg 89.1) with occasional regional and varietal releases (eg Yarra Valley Blanc de Noirs 88.3). Green Point Vineyard is export label for sparkling wines and for tiny quantities of table wine sold only through cellar door.
Summary Wholly owned by Moet et Chandon and by far the most important wine facility in the Yarra Valley, superbly located with luxurious tasting facilities (a small tasting charge is levied). The wines are exemplary, thought by many to be the best produced by Moet et Chandon in any of its overseas subsidiary operations, a complex blend of French and Australian styles.
Recommended Wine Cuvee 90.1 (classically restrained, crisp bouquet with intense fruit yet not the least aromatic; on the palate fine, elegant and restrained, with soft, creamy chardonnay influence giving length and harmony, particularly to the back palate and finish).

• DONNELLY RIVER WINES NR Est 1986 SD GRT SOUTHERN
Lot 159 Vasse Highway, Pemberton, WA (097) 76 2052
fax (097) 76 2053
Open 7 days 9.30–4.30 **Production** 3500 cases
Winemaker Blair Mieklejohn, Kim Oldfield
Principal Wines Chard, Sem, Sauv Bl, Pinot, Cab Sauv.
Summary Donnelly River Wines draws upon 6 hectares of estate vineyards, planted in 1986 and which produced the first wines in

1990. The 1991 Chardonnay, a Sheraton Award winner, is the best credentialled wine of what is a substantial output by the standards of this still-emerging region.

DONOLGA C–B Est 1979 $5.75–7.80 CD SD STHN VALES
Main South Road, Aldinga, SA 5173 (085) 56 3179
Open 7 days 10–5 **Production** 8500 cases
Winemaker Nick Girolamo
Principal Wines Chard, Sauv Bl, Ries, Cab Sauv, Shir, Claret.
Best Vintages W '86, '89, '90, '91 R '80, '85, '86, '90
Summary Almost an anachronism in this day and age, selling entirely from cellar door to a local, largely ethnic clientele at prices that compete with the supermarket specials.

DONOVAN CB–B Est 1977 $10–14.50 R SD GRT WESTERN
Pomonal Road, Stawell, Vic 3380 (053) 58 2727
Open 7 days 10–4 **Production** 2000 cases
Winemaker Chris Peters
Principal Wines Ries, Dry Wh, Shir.
Best Vintages W '89, '90 R '82, '85, '87, '88
Summary Part-time winemaker and full-time school teacher Chris Peters quietly makes some attractively fragrant Riesling (an excellent crisp, toasty '91) and concentrated, powerful Shiraz for the Donovan family, most of which is sold cellar door and by mail order.

DOONKUNA ESTATE BA–BA Est 1973 $11–15 CD SD CANBERRA
Barton Highway, Murrumbateman, ACT 2582 (06) 227 5885
fax (06) 227 5085
Open By appointment **Production** 2000 cases
Winemaker Stephen Reed
Principal Wines Ries, Sauv Bl, Chard, Pinot, Shir, Cab Sauv.
Best Vintages W & R '85, '90, '91, '92
Summary With judicious help from consultants, Lady Janette Murray has continued the work of the late Sir Brian Murray, former Victorian Governor General, in making some of the best white wines in the Canberra district and forceful reds of somewhat lesser finesse, but turning for the better with minty-flavoured '90s.
Recommended Wines 1992 Sauvignon Blanc (an extremely well made wine with a fresh, crisp, gooseberry-accented bouquet; some tropical fruit flavours on the palate with very good mouthfeel; drink now). 1992 Chardonnay (fragrant, clean, grapefruit and melon aromas with a hint of oak spice; similar fresh grapefruit and melon flavours with quite pronounced clove/spice oak which should integrate with time; to 1996). 1992 Rhine Riesling (clean, lime and passionfruit aromas with a hint of herbaceousness; balanced by some residual sugar on the palate, makes for an easy commercial style; drink now).

DRAYTON'S CA–BA Est 1853 $6.90–25 R 78, 221 HUNTER V
Oakey Creek Road, Cessnock, NSW 2321 (049) 98 7513
fax (049) 98 7743
Open 7 days 9–5 **Production** 100 000 cases
Winemaker Trevor Drayton
Principal Wines Sem, Wh Burg, Ries, Chard, Verd, Sauv Bl, Herm, Cab Shir, Cab Mer; Oakey Creek is second label.

Best Vintages W '85, '86, '88, '90, '91 **R** '82, '85, '88, '89, '91

Summary A family owned and run stalwart of the Valley, producing honest, full flavoured wines which sometimes excel themselves and are invariably modestly priced.

Recommended Wines 1992 Verdelho (rich, tropical, fruit salad aroma and flavour, with honeyed sweetness on the palate, particularly interesting for the vintage). 1991 Hermitage Bin H8 (distinct pepper spice aromas, with slightly gamey overtones in the bouquet, leading on to a very spicy/peppery palate, most unusual for the district).

DROMANA ESTATE BA–BA Est 1982 $12–19 R 65, 66, 127
MORNINGTON P

Cnr Harrison's Road and Bittern-Dromana Road, Dromana, Vic 3936 (059) 87 3275 fax (059) 81 0714

Open 7 days Nov–April; May–Oct; w'ends 11–4, weekdays by appointment

Production 10 000 cases

Winemaker Garry Crittenden

Principal Wines Chard, Chenin, Sauv Bl, Rosé, Delicato, Nebbiolo, Pinot, Cab Mer; most under second label Schinus.

Best Vintages W '86, '88, '90, '91, '92 **R** '85, '88, '90, '91, '92

Summary The first of the Mornington Peninsula wineries to take a wholly commercial approach to winemaking and marketing. Intriguingly, having had great success in the United Kingdom, has withdrawn from there to concentrate its efforts in Australia, relying in part on a much enlarged and very attractive cellar door sales area.

Recommended Wines Dromana Estate 1990 Cabernet Merlot (as always, spotlessly clean, with dark berry and blackcurrant fruits and subtle oak, with plenty of weight and concentration; fine tannins; to 1997). 1992 Schinus Sauvignon Blanc (pungent, herbaceous and tobacco aromas, spotlessly clean; on the palate slightly more sweet fruit evident, but still in the crisp, direct herbaceous seafood style; drink now). 1991 Schinus Cabernet Sauvignon (quite luscious and ripe redcurrant and chocolate flavours, with soft tannins; easy style for early drinking).

• DULCINEA VINEYARD NR Est 1983 $8.30 CD SD
BALLARAT

RMB H974 Jubilee Road, Sulky, Ballarat, Vic 3352 (053) 34 6440

Open By appointment **Production** 800 cases

Winemaker Rod Stott, Paul Chambers

Principal Wines Chard, Sauv Bl, Pinot, Cab Sauv.

Summary Rod Stott is a part-time but passionate grape grower and winemaker who chose the name Dulcinea from *The Man of La Mancha* in which only a fool fights windmills. With winemaking help from Paul Chambers, he has produced a series of very interesting and often complex wines, all of which have had show success at one point or another in their career. The 1991 Chardonnay tasted from barrel was outstanding, but has developed some off characters in bottle that somewhat detract from the rich fruit.

DUNCAN ESTATE CB–B Est 1968 $9–12 CD 4 CLARE V
Spring Gully Road, Clare, SA 5453 (088) 43 4335

Open 7 days 10–4 **Production** 2000 cases

Winemaker Blair Duncan

Principal Wines Ries, Tram Ries, Sauv Bl, Shir, Mer, Cab Sauv.
Best Vintages W '84, '85, '89, '90, '91 R '88, '89, '90, '91, '92
Summary The Duncan family has been growing grapes in the Clare Valley since 1968, and first produced wines from its 7.4 hectares of vineyards in 1984, with son Blair Duncan (a Penfolds winemaker) directing proceedings. Over the years some attractive wines have been produced, with the Cabernet Merlot and Shiraz usually very good.
Recommended Wine 1991 Riesling (smooth, quite developed soft honey and lime flavours; hint of toastiness; now to 1995).

DYSON MASLIN BEACH NR Est 1984 $8.50–12.50 R 67
STHN VALES
Sherriff Road, Maslin Beach, SA 5170 (08) 386 1092
Open 7 days 10–5 **Production** 1600 cases
Winemaker Allan Dyson
Principal Wines Chard, Sauv Bl, Pinot, Cab Sauv, Sparkl.
Summary Owned by district veteran Allan Dyson. Typically for the district, Sauvignon Blanc has been one of the more consistent performers in the Maslin Beach portfolio, showing good varietal character and depth of flavour. No recent tastings.

EAGLE BAY ESTATE NR Est 1982 $12.50 CD SD MARGARET R
Eagle Bay Road, Eagle Bay, WA 6281 (097) 55 3346
Open 7 days 10–4 **Production** 880 cases
Winemaker F. G. Ley (Consultant Dorham Mann)
Principal Wines Sem, Sauv Bl, Shir.
Summary Limited tastings of initial releases have not impressed, but were insufficient to form a reasonable judgment. Consultant winemaker Dorham Mann has vast experience, and the area is, of course, one of the finest in Australia.

EAGLEHAWK ESTATE B–A Est 1856 $8.95 R 110, 282
CLARE V
Main North Road, Watervale, SA 5452 (088) 43 0003
fax (088) 43 0096
Open Mon–Fri 9–5, w'ends 12–4 **Production** 100 000 cases
Winemaker Stephen John
Principal Wines Ries, Fumé Bl, Sem, Shir Mer Cab.
Best Vintages W '80, '85, '87, '90, '92 R '80, '84, '86, '88, '90
Summary One of the three great legacies of the nineteenth century (Leasingham and Sevenhill being the others) with magnificent stone cellars. Since its acquisition by Wolf Blass (and its change of name from Quelltaler to Eaglehawk) the wines have been a model of consistency, predictability and economy.
Recommended Wines 1992 Rhine Riesling (high-toned, highly floral spicy/lime aromas and flavours in a thoroughly modern style). 1992 Chardonnay (fresh, crisp, almost sauvignon blanc-like cool fruit, with subtle oak; to 1994). 1990 Quelltaler Wood-aged Semillon (clean, relatively subtle oak, gradually building aromas; fine, well balanced palate with faintly herbaceous fruit and subtle oak; very good potential; to 1997).

ELAN VINEYARD NR Est 1980 $10 CD SD MORNINGTON P
17 Turners Road, Bittern, Vic 3918 (059) 83 1858
Open First w'end month 11–5 **Production** 100 cases

Winemaker Selma Lowther
Principal Wines Chard, Shir, Cab Mer.
Summary Selma Lowther, fresh from Charles Sturt University (as a mature age student) made an impressive debut with her spicy, fresh crisp 1990 Chardonnay. Production will increase rapidly from the tiny 1991 vintage; worth following.

ELDERTON B–B Est 1984 $8.95–26.50 R 175, 223 BAROSSA V
3 Tanunda Road, Nuriootpa, SA 5355 (008) 88 8500
fax (085) 62 2844
Open Mon–Fri 8.30–5, w'ends & public hols 11–4
Production 32 000 cases
Winemaker Neil Ashmead
Principal Wines Chab, Ries, Sparkl, Pinot, Shir Cab, Cab Mer, Herm.
Best Vintages W '80, '84, '86, '89, '92 R '82, '86, '87, '88, '90
Summary One of the more successful middle-sized wineries since its debut in 1984 (the substantial vineyards have been owned by the Ashmead family for much longer) driven by the tireless marketing zeal of Neil Ashmead, who is winemaker in name only.
Recommended Wines 1990 Shiraz Cabernet (light, fresh, crisp fruit aroma and similar fresh, red berry flavours, with soft tannins; drink now). 1987 Command Hermitage (pleasant, gently sweet fruit aromas and similar soft, mature fruit flavours backed by vanillin oak; drink now).

ELGEE PARK B–B Est 1972 $11–19 ML 72 MORNINGTON P
Wallaces Road, Merricks North, Vic 3926 (059) 89 7338
Open Not **Production** 1200 cases
Winemaker Tod Dexter (Contract)
Principal Wines Chard, Ries, Viog, Cab Mer.
Best Vintages W '82, '84, '88, '90, '92 R '82, '84, '88, '90,'92
Summary The pioneer of the Mornington Peninsula in its twentieth-century rebirth, owned by Baillieu Myer and family. The wines are now made at Stoniers Merricks, Elgee Park's own winery having been closed.
Recommended Wines 1990 Cabernet Sauvignon (attractive, clean, red berry fruit with subtle oak, fresh flavour and soft tannins; complete, stylish wine; to 1986). 1991 Chardonnay (strong smoky barrel ferment oak with crisp fruit and fairly pronounced acid; will benefit from bottle age; to 1997).

ELLENDALE ESTATE NR Est 1978 $8 CD SD SWAN V
Lot 109 Corona Way, Belhus, WA 6055 (09) 296 4581
Open By appointment **Production** NFP
Winemaker John Barrett Lennard
Principal Wines A range of varietal and generic table and fortified wines.
Summary Effectively in recess while it changes premises, with winemaking scheduled to restart in 1993. The accent has always been on no-frills wine of commensurately modest quality and price.

ELMSLIE WINES NR Est 1972 $15 ML SD TAMAR V
Upper McEwans Road, Legana, Tas 7277 (003) 30 1225
fax (003) 30 2161

Open By appointment **Production** 3000 cases
Winemaker Ralph Power
Principal Wines Cab Sauv, Pinot.
Summary A small, specialist red winemaker, from time to time blending pinot noir with cabernet. The fruit from the now fully mature vineyard has depth and character, but operational constraints mean that the style of the wine is often somewhat rustic.

ELSEWHERE BA–BA Est 1984 $12–15 CD SD HUON V
RSD 558, Glaziers Bay, Tas 7112 (002) 95 1509
Open Summer — Sun, or by appointment **Production** 3000 cases
Winemaker Andrew Hood (Contract)
Principal Wines Chard, Ries, Cab Sauv, Pinot.
Summary Eric and Lette Phillips' evocatively named Elsewhere Vineyard jostles for space with a commercial flower farm also run by the Phillips. It is a mark of the success of the wines that in 1993 some of the long established flower areas made way for additional chardonnay and riesling.
Recommended Wines 1991 Pinot Noir (strong, stylish bouquet with dark plum fruit and appropriately gamey overtones, leading on to a richly textured and flavoured palate with great mouthfeel; a cut above the 1990 Pinot Noir). 1990 Cabernet Sauvignon (dense red-purple in colour, with exceptionally ripe, dark currant and cassis aromas; wonderfully ripe blackcurrant and mulberry fruit, although the acid is ever so fractionally hard; a vintage role reversal, and much better than the more leafy 1991 Cabernet Sauvignon).

ELTHAM VINEYARDS NR Est 1990 $14.95–18.95 ML SD YARRA V
225 Shaws Roads, Arthurs Creek, Vic 3099 (03) 439 4688
fax (03) 439 5121
Open By appointment **Production** 850 cases
Winemaker George Apted, John Graves
Principal Wines Chard, Pinot, Cab Sauv.
Summary Drawing upon vineyards at Arthurs Creek and Eltham, John Graves (brother of David Graves of the illustrious Californian Pinot producer Saintsbury) produces tiny quantities of quite stylish Chardonnay and Pinot Noir, the former showing nice barrel ferment characters.

EPPALOCK RIDGE NR Est 1979 $13.50–16.50 CD SD BENDIGO
Metcalfe Pool Road, Redesdale, Vic 3444 (054) 25 3135
Open 7 days 10–6 **Production** 600 cases
Winemaker Rod Hourigan
Principal Wines Chard, Pinot, Shir, Cab Sauv.
Summary Full flavoured but rather tannic and astringent wines from 1989 and 1990 emanated from the former Romany Rye winery, which owns the original Flynn and Williams vineyard at Heathcote, and has long contracts with other local Bendigo region growers.

ERINACEA NR Est 1988 $14 CD SD MORNINGTON P
Devonport Drive, Rye, Vic 3941 (059) 88 6336
Open By appointment **Production** 350 cases
Winemaker Ron Glyn Jones

...al Wines Chard, Cab Sauv, Cab Franc.

...ry Medical practitioner Dr Ron Jones added a winemaking ... viticulture degree to his qualifications in 1988, and as well as making tiny quantities of wine acts as a consultant to others in the region. The 1990 Chardonnay was an uncertain start, appearing high in volatile acidity.

ETTAMOGAH NR Est 1978 $4.50–10.50 CD SD STHN NSW

Tabletop Road, Tabletop via Albury, NSW 2640 (060) 26 2366
Open Mon–Sat 9–5, Sun 9–4 **Production** 3500 cases
Winemaker Brian Wilson
Principal Wines Champ, Chard, Sem, Ries, Mos, Spat Lex, Cab Sauv, fortifieds.
Summary Formerly called Coopers Tabletop, now under the care of former Griffith-based winemaker Brian Wilson, who brings with him a wealth of experience and who is concentrating on fortified wines.

EVANS FAMILY A–A Est 1979 $15–17.50 R 125 HUNTER V

Palmers Lane, Pokolbin, NSW 2321 (049) 98 7333
Open By invitation **Production** 2900 cases
Winemaker Rothbury (Contract)
Principal Wines Chard, Sparkl, Gamay, Pinot.
Best Vintages W '82, '84, '86, '87, '88, '91 R '91
Summary Sold chiefly through the extended Evans family and friends — who are invited to regular no-charge lunches with Len and Trish Evans, who (in Len's words) 'are aiming to create a gentle wine-house feeling'. Given the great quality of the unctuous, buttery Chardonnay, the value rating should be AAA.
Recommended Wine 1991 Chardonnay (mainstream Hunter style with honeyed, buttery, fleshy fruit; already weighty and viscous in the mouth; I would prefer to drink it sooner rather than later).

EVANS & TATE A–A Est 1972 $13.85–27.95 R 48, 62, 112,

120, 163, 165, 238 SWAN V & MARGARET R
Metricup Road, Willyabrup, WA 6284 (09) 296 4666 Gnangara Estate or (097) 55 6244 Redbrook Estate fax (09) 296 1148
Open Mon–Fri 10.30–4.30, w'ends 11–4.30 Gnangara or 7 days 10.30–4.30 Redbrook
Production 20 000 cases
Winemakers Brian Fletcher, Krister Jonsson
Principal Wines Classic Dry White, Sauv Bl, Sem, Chard, Verd, Shir, Herm, Cab Sauv, Mer.
Best Vintages W '88, '89, '90, '91, '92 R '86, '88, '90, '91, '92
Summary Single-handedly changed perceptions of the Swan Valley red wines in the '70s before opening its highly successful Margaret River operation which goes from strength to strength. The arrival of the immensely talented and experience Brian Fletcher as winemaker should guarantee the continuation of its success.
Recommended Wines 1992 Margaret River Semillon (deliciously fresh and fragrant wine with tropical/passionfruit overtones to the bouquet; fragrant, faintly spicy palate with harmony and length). 1991 Margaret River Cabernet Sauvignon (a wholly exceptional wine, with superb toasty oak, masses of dark berry and cassis fruit; outstanding structure and tannin balance; to 2015). 1990 Margaret River Merlot (strong spicy oak intermingling with fragrant, sweet berry fruit;

wonderfully silky texture; to 2000). 1992 Two Vineyards Chardonnay (fresh, crisp, slightly herbaceous fruit with a lively palate and a delicate but long finish; to 1996). 1992 Gnangara Shiraz Cabernet (strong marzipan oak is dominant, but there is sweet berry fruit and the wine is clean; some will like the oak, others will find it over the top; to 1998).

FAIRFIELD NR Est 1959 $6.50–12.50 CD SD NE VIC

Murray Valley Highway, Browns Plains via Rutherglen, Vic 3685 (060) 32 9381

Open Mon–Sat 10–5, some Sun 12–5 **Production** NFP

Winemaker Stephen Morris

Principal Wines Wh Herm, Mos, Rosé, Shir, Cab Sauv, Durif, fortifieds.

Summary Specialist in red and fortified wines made with nineteenth-century wine equipment housed in the grounds of the historic Fairfield Mansion built by G. F. Morris. A tourist must.

FELSBERG NR Est 1983 SD GRANITE BELT

Townsends Road, Glen Aplin, Qld 4381 (07) 300 1946

Open Thur–Mon 9.30–4.30 **Production** 1500 cases

Winemaker Otto Haag

Principal Wines Chard, Ries, Mer, Cab Mer, Shir.

Summary After a prolonged gestation, opened for business in late 1991; a full range of the 1991 vintage wines tasted early in their life showed a variety of winemaking problems that needed to be addressed before the wines were bottled. No more recent tastings.

FERGUSSON'S CB–B Est 1968 $8.50–17.50 CD SD YARRA V

Wills Road, Yarra Glen, Vic 3775 (059) 65 2237 fax (059) 65 2405

Open 7 days 11–5 **Production** 5000 cases

Winemaker Christopher Keyes

Principal Wines Meth Champ, Ries, Chard, LH Lexia, Sauv Bl, Shir, Cab Sauv, Cab Mer, some from the Yarra Valley, some from elsewhere.

Best Vintages W '86, '88, '90, '91, '92 **R** '82, '83, '86, '87, '90, '91

Summary The combined restaurant-winery complex is one of the most frequently visited spots in the Yarra Valley, catering both for the general tourist and the wine lover. Both Yarra Valley and non Yarra Valley sourced wines are available for sale; the Yarra Valley wines can be extremely attractive.

Recommended Wines 1990 Benjamin Cabernet Sauvignon (clean, aromatic bouquet with cedary, scented lemony oak; elegant wine on the palate with modulated dark berry fruit flavours and fine tannins; to 2000). 1992 Chardonnay (fresh, tangy melon and grapefruit aromas and flavours, with considerable length to the finish; to 1997). 1991 Shiraz (dense, concentrated fruit in the dark cherry/blackcurrant spectrum, with soft tannins; an echo of unusual oak character slightly distracts; to 1998).

FERMOY ESTATE NR Est 1985 $13.50–14.90 CD SD

MARGARET R

Metricup Road, Willyabrup, WA 6284 (097) 55 6285

fax (097) 55 6251

Open 7 days 11–4.30 **Production** 6500 cases

Winemaker Michael Kelly
Principal Wines Sem, Sauv Bl, Pinot, Cab Sauv.
Summary Owned by Western Mining Corporation executive John Anderson, with a number of vintages now under its belt. After a great start, wine style has gone down a particular path, which emphasises structure and downplays fruit aroma and flavour, an approach that appeals to some but not to others.

FISHBURN & O'KEEFE NR Est 1991 $13.50–15 CD SD DERWENT, TAS

c/o Meadowbank Vineyard, Glenora, Tas 7140 (002) 86 1238
fax (002) 86 1168
Open 7 days Richmond Wine Centre, 27 Bridge St, Richmond
Production 1500 cases
Winemaker Greg O'Keefe
Principal Wines Ries, Chard, Pinot, Cab Sauv, Sparkl.
Summary Wine consultant and contract winemaker Greg O'Keefe, formerly winemaker at Normans, has joined forces with Hutchins schoolteacher Mike Fishburn to produce wines made from grapes purchased from various growers across Tasmania, but with an estate vineyard in the course of establishment.
Recommended Wines 1991 Brut (a very correct sparkling wine with some appropriate yeasty characters in the bouquet, followed by a crisp and clean palate with well balanced acidity and dosage).

FLOWERDALE NR Est 1976 $13–16 CD SD CENTRAL VIC

Yea Road, Flowerdale, Vic 3717 (03) 606 4612
Open Sat/Sun 10–5 **Production** 500 cases
Winemaker Ros Ritchie (Contract)
Principal Wines Chard, Chenin, Tram Ries, Pinot.
Summary It seems that in all except the warmest years the climate at Yea is just too cool to allow the grapes to gain the level of flavour and weight we expect from classic varieties.

FLYNN & WILLIAMS NR Est 1979 $14 ML SD MACEDON

Flynns Lane, Kyneton, Vic 3444 (054) 22 2228
Open Not **Production** 600 cases
Winemakers L. Williams, J. Flynn
Principal Wines Cab Sauv.
Best Vintages R '81, '82, '88, '91
Summary Produces a sought-after, single wine made from 100% Cabernet Sauvignon grown at Kyneton, a sub-district of Macedon able to produce wonderful red wines in warmer vintages, exemplified by the '88 and '91 vintages.

FRANKLAND ESTATE BA–BA Est 1988 $11.73–12.65 CD 178 GRT SOUTHERN

RMB 705, Frankland, WA 6396 (098) 55 1555 fax (098) 55 1583
Open By appointment 10–4 **Production** 12 000 cases
Winemaker Jane Gilham
Principal Wines Ries, Chard, Sauv Bl, Cab Sauv/Franc/Mer.
Summary A rapidly growing Frankland River operation, situated on a large sheep property owned by Barrie Smith and Judy Cullam. The 14 hectare vineyard has been established progressively since 1988, and a winery built on the site for the 1993 vintage (prior to which

time the wines were made at Alkoomi).

Recommended Wines 1992 Rhine Riesling (intense, s~~
bouquet, with similar attractive lime-flavoured fruit on th~~
well balanced; to 1998). 1992 Sauvignon Blanc (bright green~~
colour with light citrus passionfruit and gooseberry aroma~~, ~~
light on the palate, but will build in the short term; to 1995).

FRASER NR Est 1987 $10–12 CD SD HUNTER V
Lot 5 Wilderness Road, Rothbury, NSW 2321 (049) 30 7594
fax (049) 33 1100
Open 7 days 10–5 **Production** 1900 cases
Winemaker Peter Fraser
Principal Wines Chard, Dry White, Shir, Malbec.
Best Vintages W '87, '90, '91, '92, '93 R '87, '89, '90, '91
Summary The first wines released were excellent, but subsequent
vintages as have been tasted are rather disappointing, with erratic
oak handling a problem. No recent tastings, however.

FREYCINET A–A Est 1980 $14–23 R 21, 48, 149, 233 EAST
COASTAL TAS
Tasman Highway via Bicheno, Tas 7215 (002) 57 8384
fax (002) 57 8454
Open 7 days 9–5.30 **Production** 4000 cases
Winemaker Geoff Bull
Principal Wines Ries, Chard, Pinot, Cab Sauv, Cab Franc.
Summary The four hectare Freycinet vineyards are beautifully
situated on the sloping hillsides of a small valley. The soils are Podsol
and decaying granite with a friable clay subsoil, and the combination
of aspect, slope, soil and heat summation produce red grapes of
unusual depth of colour and ripe flavours. The white grapes, too, are
of high quality, but clearly the East Coast around Bicheno is
peculiarly suited to pinot noir, and Freycinet has produced the best
Pinot Noirs so far from Tasmania.
Recommended Wines 1991 Pinot Noir (rich, plummy/spicy
bouquet, redolent with fruit, and a wonderfully velvety palate,
crammed with similar spicy/plummy fruit; outstanding Pinot Noir in a
ripe, lush style; to 1996). 1992 Pinot Noir (spicy/peppery/plummy
fruit with some tannins; shows great promise; much in the style of the
1991; cask sample). 1992 Chardonnay (complex, honeyed/nutty/
buttery aroma and flavour, with rich mouthfeel; in Freycinet style,
much richer than most Tasmanian Chardonnays; early developing).
1991 Cabernet Sauvignon (powerful cassis and dark berry fruit; fully
ripe style, finishing with fine tannins; only a whisper of herbaceous
characters).

GALAFREY B–B Est 1977 $8.50–14 CD 43, 63 GRT SOUTHERN
145 Lower Sterling Terrace, Albany, WA 6330 (098) 41 6533
fax (098) 51 2022
Open Mon–Sat 10–5 **Production** 4000 cases
Winemaker Ian Tyrer
Principal Wines Chard, Ries, Muller, Pinot, Shir, Cab Sauv.
Best Vintages W '83, '87, '90, '91, '92 R '85, '88, '90, '91
Summary Despite his unconventional winery (in a 100-year-old
converted woolstore) and his idiosyncratic sense of humour, Ian
Tyrer is a serious winemaker ever trying to improve quality within

the constraints of a modest budget. His 1990 and 1991 white wines are proof of that success.

Recommended Wines 1991 Rhine Riesling (very high quality wine with fine, cool-grown lime juice aromas, tinged with just a delicate touch of herbaceousness; well balanced, long palate in which the fruit is not forced; trophy winner 1993 Sydney International Wine Competition; to 1997). 1990 Shiraz (strong, dense fruit with some spice underlying the berry characters; fractionally gamey which might upset the technical palate; to 1998).

GALAH WINES B–A Est 1986 $9 ML SD ADELAIDE HILLS

Box 231, Ashton, SA 5137 phone and fax (08) 390 1243
Open Not **Production** 1000 cases
Winemaker Stephen George
Principal Wines Shir, Cab Mer, Cabernets.
Best Vintages R '86, '88, '89, '90
Summary A unique operation run by Stephen George, consultant winemaker at Wendouree and winemaker at Ashton Hills; it has a one-off licence allowing mail-list sales only, and the wines are purchased in bulk or selected as cleanskins from other makers or made by Stephen George from vineyard sources across South Australia. Some astonishing bargains appear on each list.
Recommended Wines 1991 Clare Valley Shiraz (ripe, liquorice and mint aromas, with strong minty fruit and persistent tannins on the palate; to 2000). 1991 Shiraz Cabernet (solid but as yet slightly subdued bouquet; sweeter, riper palate with blackcurrant fruit; to 1997).

GARDEN GULLY B–B Est 1987 $8.30–14.90 CD SD GRT WESTERN

Garden Gully, Great Western, Vic 3377 (053) 56 2400
fax (053) 56 2400
Open Mon–Fri 10.30–5.30, w'ends 10–6 **Production** 2500 cases
Winemaker Brian Fletcher
Principal Wines Chard, Ries, Shir, Meth Champ, Sparkl Burg.
Best Vintages W '88, '89, '90, '91 R '88, '89, '90, '91
Summary Given the skills and local knowledge of the syndicate which owns Garden Gully, it is not surprising the wines are consistently good across the entire range: an attractive stone cellar door sales area is an additional reason to stop and pay a visit.
Recommended Wines 1991 Chardonnay (exceptionally complex, stylish bouquet in a Burgundian mould with grapefruit/melon and well integrated and balanced oak; the palate is also very complex, with oak slightly more dominant than on the bouquet but still having intense fruit; to 1997). 1991 Sparkling Burgundy (richly fruity, with liquorice, sweet blackcurrant and spice flavours, but happily lower dosage and hence less sweet on the finish than most Sparkling Burgundies).

GATEWAY ESTATE NR Est 1989 SD HUNTER V

Cnr Broke & Branxton Roads, Pokolbin, NSW 2321 (049) 98 7844
Open 7 days 10.30–4 **Production** 3000 cases
Winemaker Colin Peterson
Principal Wines Chard, Sem, Wh Burg.
Summary A new, principally cellar door operation; the wines are made by Colin Peterson at Wollundry, but quality is unknown.

GEHRIG BROS C–CB Est 1858 $6–15 CD 72 NE VIC
Cnr Murray Valley Highway & Howlong Road, Barnawartha,
3688 (060) 26 7296
Open Mon–Sat 9–5, Sun 10–5 **Production** 5000 cases
Winemaker Brian Gehrig
Principal Wines Chenin, Ries. Sauternes, Pinot, Shir, Cab Sauv,
fortifieds.
Best Vintages W '84, '86, '88, '90, '92 R '83, '86, '88, '90, '92
Summary An extremely antiquated winery — even by the
standards of north eastern Victoria — which is being slowly
modernised; the fortified wines are still a great deal better than the
table wines.

GEMBROOK HILL NR Est 1983 $18–21 R SD YARRA V
Launching Place Road, Gembrook, Vic (059) 68 1622
Open Not **Production** 2000
Winemaker Dr Ian Marks
Principal Wines Sauv Bl, Chard, Pinot.
Summary The six hectare Gembrook Hill Vineyard is situated on
rich, red volcanic soils two kilometres north of Gembrook in the
coolest part of the Yarra Valley. The vines are not irrigated, with
consequent natural vigour control. Pinot Noir will join the range of
wines produced in late 1993.
Recommended Wines 1992 Sauvignon Blanc (ultra herbal style,
crisp and bracing, very much reflecting the cool climate; great with
seafood; drink now).

GEOFF MERRILL B–B Est 1980 $16–19.50 R 147, 169, 171,
209, 289 STHN VALES
Cnr Pimpala & Byards Roads, Reynella, SA 5161 (08) 381 6877
fax (08) 322 2244
Open Mon–Fri 9–5 Sun 12–5 **Production** 6000 cases
Winemaker Geoff Merrill
Principal Wines Sem Chard, Cab Sauv.
Best Vintages W '82, '84, '86, '87, '88 R '80, '82, '85, '88, '90
Summary The premium label of the three wines made by Merrill
(Mount Hurtle — see separate entry — and Cockatoo Ridge being
the other two); always given bottle age, the wines reflect the desire of
this otherwise exuberant winemaker for elegance and subtlety,
although one wonders whether the choice of oak type is not a little
outmoded.
Recommended Wines 1988 Geoff Merrill Semillon Chardonnay
(soft bottle-developed traditional Australian White Burgundy style,
with full-blown, honeyed/buttery fruit; drink now). 1990 Cabernet
Sauvignon Franc Merlot (in typical Merrill style, relying on elegance
rather than fruit power, with cedary, dusty notes; drink now).

GIACONDA BA–B Est 1985 $20–25 ML 12, 49, 147 CENTRAL
VIC
Cnr Wangaratta & McClay Roads, Beechworth, Vic 3747 phone and
fax (057) 27 0246
Open By appointment **Production** 1000 cases
Winemaker Rick Kinzbrunner
Principal Wines Chard, Cab Mer, Cab Franc, Pinot.
Best Vintages W '86, '89, '90, '91, '92 R '85, '86, '88, '90, '91

Summary Wines that have a super-cult status and which, given the tiny production, are extremely difficult to find. All have a cosmopolitan style befitting Rick Kinzbrunner's international winemaking experience.

Recommended Wines 1992 Pinot Noir (complex, stylish, plummy/tobacco bouquet; tremendous power and distinction to a fully ripe palate balanced by stalk tannins; the best Giaconda Pinot yet; to 1997). 1992 Chardonnay (very much reflects the winemaking techniques used, needing time for the chalky edges to the fruit to settle down; has the structure and weight to do so; to 1998). 1991 Cabernet (light, faintly stemmy bouquet, but excels on the palate with good structure and plenty of character; to 1999).

GILBERTS NR Est 1980 SD GRT SOUTHERN
RMB 438 Albany Hwy, Kendenup via Mt Barker, WA 6323
(098) 51 4028
Open 7 days 9–5 while wine available **Production** 300 cases
Winemaker John Wade (Contract)
Principal Wines Ries, Chard.
Summary The now mature vineyard, coupled with contract winemaking by John Wade at Plantagenet, has produced small quantities of high quality Rhine Riesling and Chardonnay; the tiny production sells out quickly each year, both wines showing strong varietal character allied with the backbone that one comes to expect from the region.

GLENARA NR Est 1971 $10.90–18.90 CD SD ADELAIDE HILLS
126 Range Road, North Upper Hermitage, SA 5131 phone and fax (08) 380 5056
Open 7 days 10–5 **Production** 5500 cases
Winemaker Trevor Jones
Principal Wines Ries, Chard, Rosé, Shir, Cab Sauv, Ries Beerenauslese.
Summary Glenara has been owned by the Verrall family since 1924; the first vines were planted in 1971, the first wine was made in 1975, and the winery was built as recently as 1988. Between 1983 and 1988 the wines produced by Glenara were made under contract at Kellermeister.

GLENAYR NR Est 1975 $12–16 ML SD COAL R
Back Tea Tree Road, Richmond, Tas 7025 (vineyard only); postal PO Box 38, Richmond, Tas 7025 (002) 622 2388 fax (002) 44 7234
Open Not **Production** 200 cases
Winemaker Chris Harrington (at Domaine A)
Principal Wines Ries, Pinot, Cab Sauv.
Summary Produces the rich, full bodied reds for which the Coal River region of Tasmania seems destined to become known, the solid, plummy and rich 1991 Pinot adding to some previously impressive Cabernets.

GLENBOTHY NR Est 1987 $9.50–12.50 ML SD NORTH TAS
RSD 282 Glenwood Road, Rilbia, TAS 7258 (003) 43 0773
Open By appointment **Production** 350 cases
Winemaker Greg O'Keefe (Contract)
Principal Wines Ries, Pinot, Cab Sauv.

Summary A light but exceptionally stylish sappy/cherry-flavoured 1991 Pinot Noir won a trophy at the 1992 Tasmanian Regional Wine Show. Unfortunately, the 1992 vintage grown at this isolated vineyard on the North Esk River, south of Launceston, was destroyed by frost.

Recommended Wine 1991 Cabernet Sauvignon (clean, fresh with a hint of mint in the aroma, with similar fresh leafy/minty brightly flavoured fruit on the palate; light bodied, early drinking style).

GLENFINLASS NR Est 1971 $7–12 CD SD WELLINGTON

Elysian Farm, Parkes Road, Wellington, NSW 2820 (068) 45 2011 or (068) 45 2221

Open Sat 9–5 or by appointment **Production** 500 cases

Winemaker Brian G. Holmes

Principal Wines Sauv Bl, Shir, Cab Sauv.

Summary The weekend and holiday hobby of Wellington solicitor Brian Holmes, who has wisely decided to leave it at that. I have not tasted the wines for many years, but the last wines I did taste were competently made.

GLENGARRY VINEYARD NR Est 1981 $14.50 R SD TAMAR V

Loop Road, Glengarry, Exeter, Tas 7275 (003) 96 1340 fax (003) 34 2273

Open Not **Production** 600 cases

Winemaker Heemskerk (Contract)

Principal Wines Pinot, Cab Sauv.

Summary Glengarry has passed through several owners in recent years, and is now owned by Mike Beamish; the output from the three hectares of Pinot Noir and one hectare of Cabernet Sauvignon in bearing is currently processed at Heemskerk. The vineyards are being extended with new plantings of Chardonnay, and the future focus will be on Pinot Noir and Chardonnay.

• GLOUCESTER RIDGE VINEYARD NR Est 1985 $12–17 CD SD GRT SOUTHERN

Burma Road, Pemberton, WA 6260 (097) 76 1035 fax (097) 61 1390

Open 7 days 10–4 **Production** 3000 cases

Winemaker Virginia Willcock (Contract)

Principal Wines Chard, Res Chard, Ries, Sauv Bl, Pinot, Cab Franc, Cab Sauv, Mer, Port.

Summary Gloucester Ridge was one of the early vineyards to be established in the emerging Pemberton region, and is the only vineyard located within the Pemberton town boundary, en route to the Gloucester Tree. For the time being, the wines are made under contract at Redgate.

GNADENFREI ESTATE NR Est 1979 SD BAROSSA V

Seppeltsfield Road, Marananga via Tanunda, SA 5353 (085) 62 2522

Open 7 days 10–5.30 **Production** 9000 cases

Winemaker Malcolm Seppelt

Principal Wines Ries, Gewurz, Fronti, Shir, Cab Sauv, Pinot Herm, Port, Sparkl.

Summary A small and somewhat reclusive cellar door operation, which increasingly relies on wines made at other wineries.

●**GOLDEN GRAPE ESTATE** NR Est 1985 $11.95–22.95 CD
SD HUNTER V
Oakey Creek Road, Pokolbin, NSW 2321 (049) 98 7588
fax (049) 98 7730
Open 7 days 10–5 **Production** NFP
Winemaker Michael Sansen
Principal Wines Sem, Chard, Alsacienne, Shir, Cab Herm, Port,
Sparkl.
Summary German-owned and unashamedly directed at the tourist,
with a restaurant, barbeque and picnic areas, wine museum and
separate tasting room for bus tours. Golden Grape Estate is established
on the site of the old Barrie Drayton Happy Valley Winery. The
substantial range of wines are of diverse origins and style.

GOLVINDA NR Est 1971 SD GIPPSLAND
RMB 4635 Lindenow Road, Lindenow South via Bairnsdale, Vic 3865
(051) 57 1480
Open 7 days 9–6 **Production** NFP
Winemaker Robert Guy
Principal Wines Ries, Chenin, Chard, Cab Sauv.
Summary Robert Guy pioneered the Gippsland area, and produced
some attractive wines in the late '70s but the spark faded thereafter;
by no means all of the wines now sold are of Gippsland origin.

GOONA WARRA BA–BA Est 1863 $14–15 CD 178
MACEDON
Sunbury Road, Sunbury, Vic 3429 (03) 744 7211 fax (03) 744 7648
Open W'ends 10–6 **Production** 2000 cases
Winemaker John Barnier
Principal Wines Chard, Sem, Pinot, Cab Franc.
Best Vintages W '86, '88, '90, '91, '92 R '86, '88, '90, '91, '92
Summary An historic stone winery, established under this name by
a nineteenth-century Victorian Premier, which also houses an
excellent restaurant and tasting complex. It is only 30 minutes drive
from Melbourne (or 10 minutes north of Tullamarine Airport).
Recommended Wines 1991 Chardonnay (potent grapefruit
aromas with attractive smoky oak; extremely smooth palate with
strong grapefruit flavours and perfectly integrated oak; to 1997). 1991
Semillon (very clean and fragrant, with a most appealing blend of
herbaceous and riper, tropical fruit aromas; similarly attractive, fleshy,
multi-flavoured palate with soft, spicy oak; to 1995). 1991 Cabernet
Franc (bright red-purple in colour, with fresh redcurrant bouquet and
soft oak; beautifully handled oak is again a feature of the palate with
most attractive flavour, weight and feel; no tobacco characters at all;
lovely now but will hold to 1996). 1991 Semillon (fresh, crisp and
vibrant with a touch of sophisticated barrel-ferment oak; citrus-tinged
palate again showing some clever oak handling, and fairly
pronounced acidity; should develop well; to 1997).

GOUNDREY BA–A Est 1978 $11.95–18.95 R 67, 178, 303 GRT
SOUTHERN
Muir Highway, Mount Barker, WA 6324 (098) 51 1777
fax (098) 51 1997
Open Mon–Sat 10–4.30, Sun 11–4.30 **Production** 30 000 cases
Winemaker Stephen Warne

Principal Wines Under the premium Windy Hill label Ries, Chard, Cab Sauv; under slightly lower priced Langton label Chenin, Mount Barker Classic White, Shir, Mount Barker Classic Red, Cab Mer.

Best Vintages W '82, '89, '90, '91, '92 R '81, '85, '87, '88, '91

Summary Now the largest winery in the region, with the long-term potential to become larger again, although the recession in Australia severely pruned its ambitions. Has settled down to be a reliable producer of well priced wines, at times rising above their station.

Recommended Wines 1992 Windy Hill Chardonnay (very rich, concentrated honey, peach and grapefruit aromas, with a high flavoured, honeyed peach, apricot and grapefruit palate, suggesting a degree of botrytis infection in the grapes but which ends up making a most interesting wine; drink now). 1992 Langton Sauvignon Blanc Semillon (soft, sweet, gooseberry bouquet with plenty of mouthfeel and richness; fruit rather than oak driven, lemony but not tough; drink now). 1989 Windy Hill Cabernet Sauvignon (concentrated, briary, dark fruit and subtle oak, with good structure and weight; to 2002).

GRAND CRU ESTATE B–B Est 1981 $12.50–22.00 R 68, 127, 167, 207 ADELAIDE HILLS
Ross Dewell's Road, Springton, SA 5235 (085) 68 2378
fax (085) 68 2799
Open 7 days 10–5 **Production** 4000 cases
Winemaker K. J. Seppelt
Principal Wines Ries, Chard, Cab Sauv, Herm, Sparkl.
Best Vintages W '85, '86, '88, '90 R '86, '87, '88, '90
Summary Karl Seppelt successfully orchestrates his contract winemakers (Petaluma makes the white and sparkling wines) but, despite his prior position as Seppelt marketing director, has been less successful in obtaining the recognition (and the distribution) these often good wines deserve.
Recommended Wines 1990 Chardonnay Methode Champenoise (clean, direct, stylish, with powerful fruit and low dosage; much more complexity and spine than most Blanc de Blancs).

GRANITE CELLARS NR Est 1991 $7–12.50 CD SD GRANITE BELT
Lot 9 New England Highway, Glen Aplin, Qld 4381 (076) 83 4324
fax (076) 83 4335
Open Thurs–Mon 9–5 **Production** 1000 cases
Winemaker Robert Gray
Principal Wines Sem, Shir, Cab Sauv.
Summary A new venture of Rumbalara partner Bob Gray, with the first wines released end 1991; also incorporates a BYO restaurant. The few wines tasted to date are hard to recommend.

GRANT BURGE B–B Est 1988 $8.30–15.60 CD 32, 80, 181, 250 BAROSSA V
Jacobs Creek, Tanunda, SA 5352 (085) 63 3700 fax (085) 63 2807
Open 7 days 10–5 **Production** 70 000 cases
Winemaker Grant Burge
Principal Wines Chard, Ries, Sauv Bl, Sem, Fronti, Mer, Cab Sauv, Shir; Meshach is premium old-vine Shiraz; Oakland is non vintage red and white label.

Summary As one might expect, this former Krondorf wunder-kid makes consistently good, full flavoured and smooth wines chosen from the pick of the crop of his extensive vineyard holdings; the immaculately restored/rebuilt stone cellar door sales buildings are another attraction.

Recommended Wines 1990 Shiraz (rich and concentrated, with very sophisticated and successful American oak handling; to 1997). 1992 Frontignac (extremely flowery, intensely fruity, moderately sweet; well balanced acidity and finish; they do not come much better; drink now). 1990 Cabernet Sauvignon (smooth, clean, well balanced with smooth, ripe, dark berry fruit and soft tannins; now to 1996).

•**GRANTON VINEYARD** NR Est 1991 SD TAMAR V
Rowbottoms Road, Granton, Tas phone and fax (002) 63 7457
Open Not **Production** 1300 cases
Winemaker Steve Lubiana
Principal Wines Chard, Pinot, Sparkl.
Summary Steve Lubiana has moved from one extreme to the other, having run Lubiana Wines at Moorook in the South Australian Riverlands for many years before moving to the Tamar Valley region of Tasmania to set up a substantial winery which will act as both contract maker and maker for its own label wines. It has 1.3 hectares of estate Pinot Noir and Chardonnay planted and will rely on purchased grapes for much of its intake.

•**GREEN VALLEY VINEYARD** NR Est 1980 $10.95–13.95
SD MARGARET R
Sebbes Road, Forest Grove via Margaret River, WA 6286
(09) 384 3131
Open Sat & public hols 10–6, Sun 10–4 **Production** 1500 cases
Winemaker Contract
Principal Wines Ries, Chard, Muller Thurgau, Cab Sauv.
Summary Owners Ed and Eleanore Green commenced the development of Green Valley Vineyard in 1980, producing tiny quantities of the first white wine in 1987 and the first red wine in 1990. The 1991 Cabernet Sauvignon won a bronze medal at the 1992 Perth Show, competing in the open classes.

GREVILLEA ESTATE NR Est 1980 $8.50–12.80 CD SD SOUTH
COAST
Buckajo Road, Bega, NSW 2550 (064) 92 3006
Open 7 days 9–5 **Production** 4600 cases
Winemaker Nicola Collins
Principal Wines Chard, Gewurz, Tram Ries, Cab Sauv, Pinot.
Summary A tourist-oriented winery that successfully sells all of its surprisingly large production through cellar door and to local restaurants.

GROSSET BA–A Est 1981 $11.95–16.95 R 21, 31, 48, 108, 128,
149, 162, 204 CLARE V
King Street, Auburn, SA 5451 (088) 49 2175 fax (088) 49 2292
Open Wed–Sun 10–5 **Production** 5000 cases
Winemaker Jeffrey Grosset
Principal Wines Ries (Watervale and Polish Hill), Noble Ries, Sem Sauv Bl, Chard, Gaia (Cab Mer blend).

Best Vintages W '82, '86, '87, '90, '92 **R** '82, '86, '90, '91, '92

Summary Jeffrey Grosset served part of his apprenticeship at the vast Lindeman Karadoc winery, moving from the largest to one of the smallest when he established Grosset Wines in its old stone winery. He now crafts the wines with the utmost care from grapes grown to the most exacting standards; all need a certain amount of time in bottle to fill out and gain complexity.

Recommended Wines 1990 Gaia (outstanding wine with superb vibrant cassis and dark cherry fruit augmented by charred, spicy oak; to 2000+). 1992 Polish Hill Riesling (elegant, crisp, faintly toasty wine with very good length and acidity; to 1997). 1992 Semillon Sauvignon Blanc (elegant herbaceous fruit with cool grown characters and tingling acidity; to 1995). 1992 Noble Riesling (intense apricot and lime juice botrytis influence; moderately sweet palate with balancing acidity; to 1995).

HAINAULT VINEYARD C–CB Est 1980 $11–15 R SD PERTH HILLS

Walnut Road, Bickley, WA 6076 (09) 293 8339 fax (09) 293 8339

Open Thurs–Sun 10–5 **Production** 2200 cases

Winemaker Peter Fimmel

Principal Wines Gewurz, Sem, Chard, Cab Mer, Pinot.

Best Vintages W '84, '85, '87, '89, '92 **R** '85, '87, '88, '91, '92

Summary Peter Fimmel has been the guiding force in the Perth Hills, and his commitment to wine is absolute. I simply wish I could be more enthusiastic about his wines or believe the Perth Hills is the right area for Pinot Noir, Fimmel's particular love.

HALCYON DAZE B–B Est 1982 $12–18 CD SD YARRA V

Lot 15 Uplands Road, Lilydale, Vic 3140 phone and fax (03) 726 7111

Open By appointment **Production** 750 cases

Winemaker Richard Rackley

Principal Wines Ries, Chard, Pinot, Cabernet.

Summary One of the lower-profile wineries with small, pre-dominantly estate grown production and no external consultancy advice. Rhine Riesling ages with grace, as does the Cabernet Sauvignon. Both the recommended wines were available for sale mid 1993.

Recommended Wines 1988 Rhine Riesling (most attractive soft bottle-developed wine with clean but full lime fruit and plenty of weight; ready but will hold to 1996). 1988 Cabernet Sauvignon (dense aromas with plenty of fruit and life, fleshy, rich and meaty on the palate, with balanced tannins; to 1998).

HANGING ROCK CA–B Est 1982 $7–28 CD 140 MACEDON

The Jim Jim, Jim Road, Newham, Vic 3442 (054) 27 0542 fax (054) 27 0310

Open 7 days 10–5 **Production** 10 000 cases

Winemakers John Ellis

Principal Wines 'Macedon' Sparkl; 'Jim Jim' Sauv Bl; 'Victoria' Chard, Cab Mer, Pinot; 'Heathcote' Shir; 'Picnic' Red and White.

Best Vintages W '88, '90, '91, '92 **R** '87, '88, '90, '92

Summary The Macedon area has proved very marginal in spots, and the Hanging Rock vineyards, with their lovely vista towards the Rock, are no exception. John Ellis has thus elected to source additional grapes from various parts of Victoria, in order to produce an interesting and diverse style of wines. The low-priced Picnic White and Picnic Red, with the striking label, have been particularly successful.

Recommended Wines 1990 Heathcote Shiraz (hugely concentrated and luscious fruit with massive, essency American oak and strong tannins; an extreme style which has won 9 gold medals; to 2010). 1992 Jim Jim Sauvignon Blanc (ultra cool climate, direct, crisp, cleansing herbal/tobacco aroma and flavour; strictly seafood; drink now). 1990 Victoria Pinot Noir (distinct carbonic maceration characters, giving gamey/tobacco aromas, and also contributing much to the palate, which is a little on the stalky side; nonetheless, interesting wine; drink now).

● **HANNS CREEK ESTATE** NR Est 1987 $10–16 CD SD MORNINGTON P
Kentucky Road, Merricks North, Vic 3926 (059) 89 7266
fax (059) 89 7500
Open W'ends 11–5 **Production** 900 cases
Winemaker St Huberts (Contract)
Principal Wines Chard, Pinot, Cab Sauv; Harlequin is second label.
Summary Denise and Tony Aubrey-Slocock have established a three hectare vineyard on the slopes of Merricks North. The 1991 vintage wines were an uncertain start, but it is early days yet.

HAPP'S CB–B Est 1978 $6.30–14.98 CD 11 MARGARET R
Commonage Road, Dunsborough, WA 6281 (097) 55 3300
fax (097) 55 3846
Open 7 days 10–5 **Production** 7000 cases
Winemaker Erl Happ
Principal Wines Chard, Verd, Shir, Mer, Cab Mer, Margaret River Red, Port.
Best Vintages W '88, '89, '90, '91 R '84, '86, '88, '91
Summary Former schoolteacher turned potter and winemaker Erland Happ brings a highly intelligent mind to bear on all his endeavours, suffering fools not at all. A very good Chardonnay made its debut in 1990, but Merlot (and Cabernet Merlot) remains the winery specialty, although I personally have problems with the style.
Recommended Wines 1992 Chardonnay (a complex wine showing cool-grown fruit, malolactic fermentation influences and a harmonious palate; fruit a little light at this stage, but should grow in bottle; to 1996).

HARCOURT VALLEY NR Est 1976 $9.50–12.50 CD SD BENDIGO
118 km post, Calder Highway, Harcourt, Vic 3453 (054) 74 2223
Open 7 days 9–6 **Production** 2000 cases
Winemaker John Livingstone
Principal Wines Chard, Ries, Shir, Cab Sauv.
Best Vintages W '89, '90, '91, '92 R '84, '87, '89, '90, '92
Summary Traditional producer of rich, full bodied red wines typical of the district, but sporadic (and largely outdated) tastings since ownership changed preclude evaluation.

HARDY A–A Est 1853 $6–22 R 22–26, 181, 320 STHN VAL
Reynella Road, Reynella, SA 5161 (08) 381 2266 fax (08) 381
Open 7 days 10–4.30
Production 10 000 tonnes (650 000 case equivalent)
Winemakers David O'Leary, Tom Newton
Principal Wines A large range of brands, moving upwards from
the Bird series, next the Siegersdorf series, next the Hardy Collection
and finally super premium Eileen Hardy; all major varieties and
generic styles covered.
Best Vintages W '81, '87, '90, '91, '92 R '80, '81, '87, '89, '90
Summary 1992 marked the end of a family dynasty as Thomas
Hardy became part of the publicly listed BRL Hardy Limited group,
it being no secret that it was Berri Renmano (hence the BRL in the
corporate name) which was the groom and Hardy the reluctant bride.
The merged group is extremely powerful in terms of volume, edging
the Orlando Wyndham group out of second place in the hierarchy.
Hardy's problems came not from Australia but from its overseas
investments, particularly Ricasoli in Italy, and the Hardy wines and
brands will continue in much the same vein as before.
Recommended Wines 1992 Siegersdorf Chardonnay (plenty of
rich, peachy, buttery fruit with almost tropical overtones, and a nice
touch of commercially induced oak; drink now). 1991 Collection
Chardonnay (complex, rich textured wine with strong oak and some
barrel ferment influence; does have fruit; drink now). 1992 Nottage
Hill Rhine Riesling (soft, clean floral lime aroma and flavour, with a
subliminal hint of sweetness; to 1995). 1990 Collection Cabernet
Sauvignon (clean wine of moderate weight, with hints of mint, a
touch of herbaceousness and nicely judged French and American oak
influence; to 1997).

• **HARTZVIEW WINE CENTRE** NR Est 1988 SD HUON V
RSD 1034 Gardners Bay, Tas 7112 (002) 95 1623
Open 7 days summer, Wed–Sun autumn, w'ends winter 10–5
Production NFP
Winemaker Andrew Hood (Contract)
Principal Wines Chard, Pinot.
Summary Robert Patterson is a graduate of the applied science
(viticulture) course at Charles Sturt University and Anthea Patterson is
a graduate of the wine marketing course at Adelaide University
(Roseworthy campus). They thus bring the full range of skills to
Hartzview Vineyard and Wine Centre which, as well as ultimately
selling Hartzview wines produced from the three hectare vineyard
established in 1988, also offers wines from other small Tasmanian
wineries including Panorama, Milnathort, Wellington, Pig and Whistle
(fruit wines), Wattley Creek, Lake Barrington Estate and Tolosa.

HAY RIVER NR Est 1974 $18 R 171 GRT SOUTHERN
Denmark Road, Mt Barker, WA 6324
Open Not **Production** 1000 cases
Winemaker Goundrey Wines
Principal Wines Cab Sauv.
Summary Used to produce high quality Cabernet Sauvignon, deep
in colour and with ever-present cassis/mint aroma and flavour, but the
'88 and '89 vintages have not impressed. Sold almost entirely in
Western Australia through retail outlets only.

● **HAY SHED HILL** NR Est 1987 $10–$15 CD SD MARGARET R
RSM 398 Harmans Mill Road, Willyabrup, WA 6280 (097) 55 6234
fax (09) 383 1064
Open W'ends & hols 10–5 **Production** 2600 cases
Winemaker John Smith
Principal Wines Sauv Bl, Sem, Pitchfork Pink (Rosé), Cab Sauv
(light, unwooded), Cab Sauv (Conventional).
Summary The former Sussex Vale vineyard has been resuscitated
and vastly improved by the Morrison family; a six-year business plan
devised by marketing director Elizabeth Morrison has resulted in the
first wines being made in 1990 by John Smith at another winery, and
each intervening vintage up to 1993 likewise. In that year a
substantial (120 tonne capacity), functional and aesthetically
excellent winery was constructed adjacent to the old hay shed from
which the winery takes its name. Designed by architect Chris
Willcox, it is an outstanding piece of architecture.
Recommended Wines 1990 Cabernet Sauvignon (bright red
purple colour with perfectly ripened fruit and equally well judged
fruit and oak balance; firm but not aggressive tannins; to 2000+). 1992
Semillon (extremely complex and rich for a young wine tasted ex
barrel; strong toasty oak; if the balance is kept, could be outstanding).

HAYWARD'S NR Est 1975 $6.50–9 CD SD GOULBURN V
Lot 18A Hall Lane, Seymour, Vic 3660 (057) 92 3050
Open Mon–Sat 9–6, Sun 10–6 **Production** Over 500 cases
Winemaker Sid Hayward
Principal Wines Ries, Shir, Cab Sauv, Cab Shir.
Summary Hayward's of Whiteheads Creek (to give it its full name)
produces massive, raw, tannic red wines that defy conventional
evaluation and demand both tolerance and patience.

HEATHCOTE B–B Est 1982 $8–13.50 R 2 BENDIGO
183–185 High Street, Heathcote, Vic 3523 (054) 33 2595
fax (054) 33 3081
Open 7 days 10–6 **Production** Varies; grapes sold in some vintages
Winemaker Nigel Sneyd
Principal Wines Chard, Chenin, Gewurz, Pinot, Cab Sauv, Cab
Shir.
Summary Good producer of white wines, most notably a spicy
Gewurztraminer and tangy barrel-fermented Chardonnay; the red
wines are flavoursome, though not quite in the same league. Has had
a very low profile in Australia in recent times, but scored a huge
success in a French wine competition with its 1990 Chardonnay. The
arrival of winemaker Nigel Sneyd could well herald a major revival in
the fortunes (and wine quality) of Heathcote.

HEEMSKERK BA–B Est 1967 $13.95–29.95 R 65, 66, 102, 126,
265 PIPERS BROOK
Pipers Brook, Tas 7254 (003) 30 1900 fax (003) 30 2092
Open Nov–Apr 10–5 **Production** 12 000 cases
Winemaker Jean Baptiste Lecaillon
Principal Wines Ries, Botrytis Ries, Chard, Pinot, Cab Sauv,
Sparkl (Jansz).
Best Vintages W '82, '84, '88, '91, '92 R '82, '84, '86, '90, '91
Summary After years of relatively disappointing performance, has

well and truly turned the corner, no doubt due to the influence of Jean Baptiste Lecaillon.

Recommended Wines 1991 Pinot Noir (while of only light to medium weight, has excellent varietal character and style; plums, strawberries and a hint of sappiness are interwoven with subtle oak; long finish; a worthy successor to the very good 1990 wine; to 1995). 1992 Riesling (scented, toasty, crisp and clean bouquet; hints of lime and passionfruit on the palate will build with further age; the wine has good mouthfeel and balance; to 1996). 1991 Chardonnay (clean, scented citrus fruit aromas; crisp, clean and tight, with complex structure, reserved style, but with a very good finish; to 1998). 1990 Jansz Cuvee (crisp, high acid style with quite particular dry, nutty flavours; powerful yet elegant; the limitation if any lies in the high acidity).

HEGGIES BA–B Est 1971 $12–18.50 R 140–144, 326 ADELAIDE HILLS
Cnr Heggies Range & Tanunda Creek Roads, Adelaide Hills, SA (Vineyard only) (085) 64 2423
Open Not **Production** 17 000 cases
Winemaker Simon Adams
Principal Wines Ries, Botrytis Ries, Chard, Cabernets.
Best Vintages W '86, '87, '90, '91 R '86, '87, '88, '90, '92
Summary Heggies was the second of the high altitude (570 metres) vineyards established by S Smith & Sons (Yalumba), with plantings on the 120 hectare former grazing property commencing in 1973. The red wines are typically rather lean, but the white wines are never less than good, and not infrequently outstanding.
Recommended Wines 1992 Botrytis Riesling (bright green-yellow with fresh, fragrant lime juice aromas; very pure lime juice Riesling flavours, with perfectly balanced acidity to go with the intense sweetness; now to 1996). 1990 Chardonnay (has developed superbly in bottle with complex, sweet honeyed fruit on the bouquet and intense, cool-grown citrus and peach flavours on the palate with a long finish, now to 1996).

HELM'S CB–B Est 1974 $10–16 CD 3, 64 CANBERRA
Butt's Road, Murrumbateman, ACT 2582 (06) 227 5536
fax (06) 227 5953
Open Thurs–Mon 10–5 **Production** 2000 cases
Winemaker Ken Helm
Principal Wines Ries, Chard, Premium Dry White, Cab Sauv, Cab Mer.
Summary One of the more commercially oriented and energetic of the Canberra district wineries. White wine quality has always been somewhat unpredictable, the red wines (particularly the Cabernet Merlot) being far more dependable.
Recommended Wines 1992 Rhine Riesling (potent, clean, full passionfruit/lime aroma and flavour; well made, highly commercial style with just a hint of sweetness; to 1994). 1991 Cabernet Merlot (strong cassis berry fruit with a hint of mint; needs time to settle down; to 1998).

HENKE NR Est 1974 $10–14 ML SD GOULBURN V
Lot 30A Henke Lane, Yarck, Vic 3719 (057) 97 6277
Open By appointment **Production** 250 cases

ker Tim & Caroline Miller

l Wines Shir, Shir Cab.

ry Produces tiny quantities of deep coloured, full flavoured, d wines known only to a chosen few; in 1993 reds from the 1988 vintage were still available at cellar door.

HENLEY PARK NR Est 1935 $7.50–16.50 CD SD SWAN V
Swan Street, West Swan, WA 6055 (09) 296 4328
fax (09) 296 1313
Open Mon–Sat 9–6, Sun 10–6 **Production** 3500 cases
Winemaker Vincent Desplat
Principal Wines Chenin, Chard, Verd Chard, Fronti, Mousse, Cab Sauv, fortifieds.
Best Vintages W '88, '90, '91 R '80, '84, '87, '88
Summary Henley Park is owned by a Danish businessman (since 1987), has a French winemaker, and nestles in the heartland of the Yugoslavian wineries of the Swan Valley, indeed a tribute to multiculturalism. I have not tasted any of the wines recently.

HENSCHKE A–A Est 1868 $11–35 R 102, 119, 147, 169, 170, 264 ADELAIDE HILLS
Moculta Road, Keyneton, SA 5353 (085) 64 8223
fax (085) 64 8294
Open Mon–Fri 9–4.30, Sat 9–12 **Production** 35 000 cases
Winemaker Stephen Henschke
Principal Wines Chard, Chenin, Gewurz, Ries, Sauv Bl, Sem, Cab Sauv, Hill of Grace, Mount Edelstone and Cyril Henschke are the great red wine labels; Lenswood (Adelaide Hills) the new addition.
Best Vintages W '82, '85, '87, '89, '90 R '82, '84, '86, '88, '90
Summary Unchallenged as one of the top half dozen wineries in Australia, and has gone from strength to strength over the past 13 years or so under the guidance of Stephen and Prue Henschke. The red wines fully capitalise on the very old, low yielding, high quality vines and are superbly made with sensitive but positive use of new small oak; the same skills are evident in the white wine making.
Recommended Wines 1992 Semillon (lovely wine with complex fruit flavours, peachy and almost Chardonnay-like with excellent oak integration; to 1998). 1992 Lenswood Giles Pinot Noir (stylish, aromatic plum and spice aroma, very tangy, complex Burgundian palate with spice and sappiness; drink now). 1990 Mount Edelstone (strong dark fruit, plum and liquorice aroma; structured, rich palate with dark red fruits, a hint of gaminess and soft tannins; to 2010). 1990 Hill of Grace (wonderfully smooth yet deep; powerful, classic velvet fist in iron glove; hints of berry, earth and dark chocolate; to 2020). Also strongly recommended: 1990 Cyril Henschke Cabernet Sauvignon, 1991 Lenswood Croft Chardonnay, 1990 Lenswood Abbotts Prayer Merlot Cabernet.

HERCYNIA NR Est 1979 $7–14 CD SD HILLTOPS
Prunevale Road, Kingsvale, NSW 2587 (063) 84 4243
fax (063) 84 4292
Open W'ends 9–5 **Production** 300 cases
Winemaker Keith John Doldissen (Consultant)
Principal Wines Ries, Chard, Sauv Bl, Pinot, Port, Muscat.
Best Vintages W '85, '86, '88, '89, '91 R '85, '88, '89, '91

Summary The Doldissen family commenced the development of their eight hectare vineyard in 1979, producing the first wines in 1985. Much of the production is sold to other makers, notably in the Canberra district.

HERITAGE BA–A Est 1984 $10–12.30 R CD 146, 226
BAROSSA V
Seppeltsfield Road, Marananga via Tanunda, SA 5352
(085) 62 2880
Open 7 days 11–5 **Production** 4500 cases
Winemaker Stephen Hoff
Principal Wines Ries, Chard, Shir, Cab Franc.
Best Vintages W '86, '87, '88, '90, '91 R '86, '88, '90, '91
Summary A little-known winery which deserves a far wider audience, for Stephen Hoff is apt to produce some startlingly good wines. At various times the Chardonnay, Rhine Riesling (from Old Clare Valley vines) and Shiraz have all excelled.
Recommended Wines 1991 Rhine Riesling (classic, toast and lime flavours, intense yet not heavy; early developing style but of great quality).

HERITAGE FARM NR Est 1987 $3.50–8.50 CD SD MURRAY R
RMB 1005 Murray Valley Highway, Cobram, Vic 3655
(058) 72 2376
Open 7 days 10–5 **Production** 1600 cases
Winemaker Kevin Tyrrell
Principal Wines Ries, Chard, generic whites and reds, fortifieds.
Summary A relatively recent arrival on the scene; I have not tasted any of the wines.

• HERITAGE WINES OF STANTHORPE NR Est 1992
$9.50–12.50 ML SD GRANITE BELT
New England Highway, Cottonvale, Qld 4375 (076) 85 2197
Open 7 days 8–7 **Production** 2000 cases
Winemaker Stan Aliprandi (Contract)
Principal Wines Sem, Sauv Bl, Chard, Muscat, Shir, Cab Sauv.
Summary Owners Bryce and Paddi Kassulke buy grapes from other Granite Belt vineyards, notably Winewood and Bungawarra, and use the services of industry veteran Stan Aliprandi, the highly controversial former part-owner of San Bernadino in Griffith. The operation is tourist oriented, with extensive barbeque and picnic areas, with the initial wines offered able to be purchased in bulk or cleanskins from other makers.

• HERONS RISE VINEYARD NR Est 1984 $12.50–20 CD SD
STHN TAS
Saddle Road, Kettering, Tas 7155 (002) 67 4339
Open 7 days 11–5 **Production** 120 cases
Winemaker Bruce Gilham (Contract)
Principal Wines Ries, Muller Thurgau, Pinot
Summary Sue and Gerry White run a small stone country guest house in the D'Entrecasteaux Channel area, and basically sell the wines from the surrounding one hectare of vineyard to those staying at the guest house. The postal address for bookings is PO Box 271, Kettering.

HICKINBOTHAM NR Est 1981 $14.95–23.75 R 188, 296
MORNINGTON P
Cnr Wallaces Road & Nepean Highway, Dromana, Vic 3936
(059) 81 0355 fax (059) 81 0355
Open Sun 11–5 **Production** 3000 cases
Winemaker Andrew Hickinbotham
Principal Wines Chard, Sauv Bl, Cabernets from various regions.
Best Vintages W '82, '88, '89, '90, '92 R '83, '86, '89, '90, '91
Summary After a peripatetic period and a hiatus in winemaking, Hickinbotham has established a permanent vineyard and winery base at Dromana. It continues to make small parcels of wine from grapes purchased from various parts of Victoria, but is increasingly concentrating on Mornington Peninsula grapes. Wine quality and style have been variable, but the completion of the new on-site winery may well see a turn for the better.

HIGHBANK NR Est 1988 $14 CD SD COONAWARRA
Coonawarra, SA 5263 (087) 37 2020
Open W'ends 9–5; or by appointment **Production** 700 cases
Winemaker Dennis Vice
Principal Wines Chard, Cab blend.
Summary Mount Gambier lecturer in viticulture Dennis Vice makes a tiny quantity of smooth, melon-accented Chardonnay of good quality which is sold through local restaurants and cellar door.

HIGH WYCOMBE NR Est 1975 $7–14 CD SD BAROSSA V
Bethany Road, Bethany via Tanunda, SA 5352 (085) 63 2776
Open 7 days 9–4.30 **Production** 1000 cases
Winemaker Colin Davis
Principal Wines Ries, Fronti, Mos, Shir, Cab Sauv, Muscat, Port.
Summary Colin and Angela Davis run what they describe as the smallest winery in the Valley and a holiday cottage complex, selling all of their wine on-site.

HILL SMITH ESTATE BA–A Est 1982 $13.20–13.80 R
140–144, 192, 206, 326 ADELAIDE HILLS
c/o Yalumba Winery, Angaston, SA 5353 (085) 64 2423
fax (085) 64 2549
Open Not **Production** 10 000 cases
Winemaker Andrew Murphy
Principal Wines Chard, Sauv Bl, Shir, Cab Sauv.
Best Vintages W '87, '88, '90, '91, '92 R '87, '88, '90, '91, '92
Summary Drawing upon two discrete and distinct vineyards, the home vineyard at an altitude of 380 metres planted to Shiraz and Cabernet Sauvignon, and a hills vineyard at an altitude of 550 metres planted principally to Chardonnay, Sauvignon Blanc and Semillon, the Hill Smith Estate brand was originally created for the export market. Its success in those markets, in particular the value for quality ratio, has led to both domestic and international distribution.
Recommended Wines 1990 Cabernet Shiraz (complex, cedary aroma with great depth of flavour; dark fruit and dark chocolate characters with well balanced oak; smooth but robust texture; to 1999). 1990 Chardonnay (rich, unctuous, tropical fruit aromas, suggesting some botrytis influence; similar rich almost tropical fruit).

•HILLSTOWE WINES BA–BA Est 1980 $10–22 R 34, 55, 185, 188 STHN VALES
Sand Road, McLaren Vale, SA 5171 (08) 323 8645
fax (08) 323 8903
Open Not **Production** 9000 cases
Winemaker Martin Shaw (Contract)
Principal Wines Vineyard and varietally identified Chard, Sauv Bl, Pinot and Cab Mer from McLaren Vale, Adelaide Hills (Udy's Mill) and Yarra Valley.
Summary Long-term viticulturists David Paxton and Chris Laurie have entered into winemaking with great flair but relatively little publicity. High quality fruit and the skills of contract winemaker Martin Shaw have proved a potent combination.
Recommended Wines 1991 McLaren Vale Chardonnay (tremendously intense grapefruit and melon fruit flavours with stylish barrel ferment oak in the background; sophisticated and elegant; to 1996). 1992 Udy's Mill Chardonnay (fragrant, tangy melon and grapefruit flavours with subtle, spicy oak and good acidity; long finish; to 1997). 1992 McLaren Vale Sauvignon Blanc (potent herbal/grassy/tobacco aromas and flavours; crisp seafood style aping that of Marlborough).

HJT B–B Est 1979 $9.90–16.50 CD SD NE VIC
Keenan Road, Glenrowan, Vic 3675 (057) 66 2252
Open Fri/Sat/hols 10–5 **Production** 1000 cases
Winemaker Harry Tinson
Principal Wines Ries, Chard, Chenin, LP Chenin, Pinot, Cab Sauv, Mer, Cab Pinot, Port.
Best Vintages W '84, '85, '87, '90, '91 R '85, '86, '87, '88, '90
Summary Harry Tinson, ex-Bailey's winemaker and revered for his Muscats and Tokays, produced a legendary Chardonnay in 1984 and (to a degree) deservedly lives off the reputation of that wine; it and subsequent Chardonnays have been the pick of the crop.

HOLLICK B–BA Est 1983 $10.50–19.50 R 29, 34, 84, 185, 204, 304 COONAWARRA
Racecourse Road, Coonawarra, SA 5263 (087) 37 2318
fax (087) 37 2952
Open 7 days 9–5 **Production** 17 000 cases
Winemakers Pat Tocaciu, Ian Hollick
Principal Wines Chard, Ries, Meth Champ, Pinot, Shir, Cab Sauv, Cab Mer, Shir; Ravenswood is deluxe label.
Best Vintages W '86, '88, '89, '90, '91 R '84, '85, '88, '90, '91
Summary Hollick has, if it were possible, added to the reputation of Coonawarra since it released its first wines in the mid '80s. Winner of many trophies (including the most famous of all, the Jimmy Watson), its wines are invariably well crafted and competitively priced.
Recommended Wines 1992 Chardonnay (clean, smooth, easy style, well balanced with subtle melon and fig fruit, needing a little time to build complexity; to 1995). 1990 Cabernet Merlot (solid, smooth berry fruit with subtle oak, and a mix of redcurrant and dark chocolate flavours; to 1997). 1990 Ravenswood Cabernet Sauvignon (very powerful wine which is, however, largely driven by the mix of French and American oak used in its production; to 2000).

... OAK B–B Est 1983 $15–18.50 R 11, 181, 258 TAMAR V
...6 Rowella, West Tamar, Tas 7270 (003) 94 7577
...03) 94 7350
Open 7 days 12–5 **Production** 1800 cases
Winemaker Nick Butler
Principal Wines Pinot, Cab'Sauv.
Summary The Butler family produce tremendously rich and strongly flavoured red wines from the vineyard, situated on the banks of the Tamar River, that takes its name from the grove of oak trees planted around the turn of the century and originally intended for the making of tennis racquets. Together with Marion's Vineyard, it suggests that this section of the Tamar Valley may even be too warm for Pinot Noir; certainly it is best suited to Cabernet Sauvignon and Chardonnay.
Recommended Wines 1990 Cabernet Sauvignon (scented, fresh, elegant fruit with quite pronounced sweet vanillin American oak; fine-grained tannins; to 2000). 1991 Cabernet Sauvignon (solid, rich and deep fruit with strong American oak influence; masses of depth and structure; to 2005).

HOPPERS HILL NR Est 1990 $10–12 CD SD CENTRAL TABLELANDS
Googodery Road, Cumnock, NSW 2867 (063) 67 7270
Open W'ends 11–5 **Production** NFP
Winemaker Robert Gilmore
Principal Wines Chard, Sauv Bl, Dry White, Cab Franc Mer, Cab Sauv.
Summary The Gilmores planted their vineyard in 1980 using organic growing methods and using no preservatives or filtration in the winery, which was established in 1990. Not surprisingly, the wines cannot be judged or assessed against normal standards, but may have appeal in a niche market.

HORSESHOE VALLEY NR Est 1986 $14–16 R 69 UPPER HUNTER V
Horseshoe Road, Horseshoe Valley via Denman, NSW 2328
(065) 47 3528
Open By appointment **Production** NFP
Winemaker John Hordern
Principal Wines Sem, Sem Chard, Chard.
Summary Seems to have fallen by the wayside after a wonderful start in 1987.

HOUGHTON A–A Est 1836 $7.99–12.99 R 22–26, 85, 203 SWAN V
Dale Road, Middle Swan, WA 6055 (09) 274 5100
fax (09) 274 5372
Open Mon–Sat 10–5 **Production** 300 000 cases
Winemaker Peter Dawson
Principal Wines Wh Burg, Chab, Sem, Verd, Ries, Rosé, Cab Sauv, Shir Malb under four ranges: Show Reserve, Gold Reserve, Houghtons Standard and Wildflower Ridge.
Best Vintages W '82, '83, '87, '89, '93 R '82, '83, '90, '92, '93
Summary The A–A rating may seem extreme, but is very deliberate and is in no small measure justified by Houghton White Burgundy, one of Australia's largest selling white wines, almost entirely

consumed within days of purchase but which is superlative with seven or so years bottle age. To borrow a phrase of the late Jack Mann, 'There are no bad wines here'.

Recommended Wines 1992 White Burgundy (quite fragrant, with citrus and passionfruit nuances early in its life; fruit rather than oak driven; is guaranteed to blossom with age; to 2000). 1991 Semillon (complex, tangy and stylish; an intense fruit-driven wine that will develop further in bottle; to 1997). 1990 Wildflower Ridge Shiraz (ripe curranty/berry full blown rich with sophisticated spicy oak; great at the price; to 1996). 1991 Gold Reserve Verdelho (strong tropical/ honeysuckle fruit with pronounced varietal flavour and well balanced acidity; drink now). 1989 Gold Reserve Cabernet Sauvignon (fresh and smooth with red berry fruit, a touch of charred oak and a crisp, cleansing finish; to 1998).

HOWARD PARK A–B Est 1986 $12.50–29.95 R 12, 46, 59, 183 GRT SOUTHERN
Lot 11, Little River Road, Denmark, WA 6333 (098) 48 1261
fax (098) 48 2064
Open Not **Production** 3000 cases
Winemaker John Wade
Principal Wines Ries, Cab Mer under Howard Park label; Madfish Bay Premium Dry White and Dry Red is second label.
Best Vintages W '86, '88, '90, '91, '92 **R** '86, '88, '90, '91, '92
Summary Just two wines, made with infinite care by the diminutive but vastly experienced and skilful John Wade, and which vie with each other for longevity: the classic, lightly citrus/lime accented Riesling needs at least five years, the almost startlingly aromatic, cassis-flavoured and spice-tinged Cabernet Sauvignon a decade or more.
Recommended Wine 1992 Madfish Bay Dry White (brilliant light green colour with grapefruit and passionfruit aromas and flavours which continue to build in the glass; very good mouthfeel and acid balance; to 1995).

HUGO WINES CB–B Est 1982 $9.50–14.50 R 115, 163, 258 STHN VALES
Elliott Road, McLaren Flat, SA 5171 (08) 383 0098
fax (08) 383 0446
Open 7 days 10.30–5 **Production** 5000 cases
Winemaker John Hugo
Principal Wines Ries, Chard, Cab Sauv, Shir, Port, Muscat.
Best Vintages W '84, '86, '87, '90, '92 **R** '83, '86, '87, '88, '90
Summary A winery that came from relative obscurity to prominence with some lovely ripe, sweet '88 reds which, while strongly American oak influenced, were quite outstanding. Subsequent vintages have not been up to the same high standard, largely due to less skilled use of oak.
Recommended Wines Tawny Port (clean, showing some aged rancio characters with appropriate cleansing finish, and overall good style).

HUNGERFORD HILL CB–B Est 1967 $8.50–17 CD 124, 195 HUNTER V
Cnr McDonalds and Broke Roads, Pokolbin, NSW 2321
(049) 98 7666 fax (049) 98 7682

Open Mon–Fri 9–4.00, w'ends 10–4.30 **Production** 18 000 cases
Winemaker Jay Tulloch

Principal Wines Sem, Sem Sauv Bl, Chard, Pinot, Shir, Cab Mer, under standard and Show Reserve labels.

Summary The Hungerford Hill Winery has been sold to McGuigan Brothers Ltd but the brand continues in the Penfold Group ownership, where it quietly fades away.

Best Vintages W '83, '84, '86, '87, '92 R '83, '84, '86, '87, '89, '92

Recommended Wine 1992 Chardonnay (sophisticated oak handling helps a wine that does not have great fruit weight, but does have some style and length; infinitely better than the Semillon of the same vintage).

HUNTER ESTATE C–B Est 1972 $7.40–10.70 R 122, 204
HUNTER V
Hermitage Road, Pokolbin, NSW 2321 (049) 98 7521
Open 7 days 9–5 **Production** 20 000 cases
Winemaker Neil McGuigan

Principal Wines Chard, Fumé, Sem, Sem Verd, Tram Ries, Wh Burg, Pinot, Shir, Cab Sauv.

Best Vintages W '83, '87, '89, '91 R '85, '87, '89, '91

Summary A minor offshoot of the Wyndham empire, producing a somewhat mixed bag of wines but always showing strong fruit and no regional astringency.

HUNTINGTON ESTATE B–BA Est 1969 $6.50–9.50 CD 42, 43
MUDGEE
Cassilis Road, Mudgee, NSW 2850 (063) 73 3825
fax (063) 73 3730
Open Mon–Sat 9–5, Sun 11–3 **Production** 20 000 cases
Winemakers Bob & Susan Roberts

Principal Wines Sem, Chard, Pinot Rosé, Cab Sauv, Cab Mer, Shir, Pinot.

Best Vintages W '82, '84, '86, '89, '91 R '81, '84, '86, '89, '91, '92

Summary Bob Roberts is one of the nicest men in an industry that seems to attract nice people, but that does not necessarily flow through to wine quality. Happily, in the case of Huntington Estate it does: Bob makes textured, complex red wines that age with extreme grace.

Recommended Wines 1983 Cabernet Sauvignon (wonderfully soft, aged, earthy/tobacco aromas with sweet fruit and a touch of American oak on the palate; fully mature but holding). 1992 Semillon Chardonnay (fresh melon/peach fruit aromas, soft and clean on the palate; to 1995). 1990 Shiraz (clean cherry fruit, bouquet with no tarry, regional characters; relatively light palate with clean fresh fruit and soft tannins; to 1997).

HUNTLEIGH C–CB Est 1975 $9–11 CD SD BENDIGO
Tunnecliffes Lane, Heathcote, Vic 3523 (054) 33 2795
Open W'ends & public hols 10–5.30 **Production** 300 cases
Winemaker Leigh Hunt

Principal Wines Tram Ries, Cab Sauv, Shir.

Summary A retirement hobby with robust, rather astringent red wines that need time in bottle to lose some of the rough edges, typified by the 1989 Leckies Vineyard She-Oak Hill Shiraz.

HUNT'S FOXHAVEN ESTATE NR Est 1978 $7–11 CD SD
MARGARET R
Canal Rocks Road, Yallingup, WA 6282 (097) 55 2232
fax (09) 291 6052
Open School hols 11–5 or by appointment **Production** 500 cases
Winemaker David Hunt
Principal Wines Ries, Sem Sauv Bl, Cab Sauv.
Summary Has only just commenced commercial operations, and is still tiny. The only wines tasted suggest David Hunt is still learning the trade.

IDYLL VINEYARD CB–B Est 1966 $9.65–14.30 R 72, 269
GEELONG
265 Ballan Road, Moorabool, Vic 3221 (052) 76 1280
fax (052) 76 1537
Open Tues–Sun 10–5 & public hols Mon **Production** NFP
Winemaker Dr Daryl Sefton
Principal Wines Idyll Blush, Gewurz, Chard, Bone Idyll (light, unoaked Shir), oak-aged Shir, Cab Shir, Cab Sauv; Sefton Estate is second label.
Best Vintages W '84, '86, '90, '91, '92 R '80, '82, '86, '89, '90
Summary A stalwart of the region, producing wines in an individual style (pungent, assertive Traminer, long-vatted reds) that are almost as well known and appreciated overseas as they are in Australia
Recommended Wine 1992 Shiraz (a radical departure in style, early-bottled with clean, rich and sweet red berry fruit and soft vanillin oak; to 1997).

INGOLDBY BA–A Est 1973 $10–16.50 CD 12, 67, 95, 181, 275
STHN VALES
Ingoldby Road, McLaren Flat, SA 5171 (08) 383 0005
fax (08) 383 9467
Open Mon–Fri 9–5, w'ends 11–5 **Production** 16 000 cases
Winemaker W. Clappis
Principal Wines Chard, Sauv Bl, Ries, French Colomb, Cab Shir.
Best Vintages W '80, '82, '86, '88, '90 R '85, '86, '87, '88, '90
Summary Bill Clappis is a larger-than-life character who does not allow his irreverence to overshadow the serious business of successfully marketing wines that are consistently very good, with Chardonnay, Sauvignon Blanc and Cabernet Sauvignon at the forefront.
Recommended Wines 1990 Cabernet Sauvignon (solid, archetypal Southern Vales cabernet with sweet dark cherry and dark chocolate fruit, pronounced vanillin American oak and soft persistent tannins; to 2000). 1992 French Colombard (fresh, lively, tingling wine with very neatly balanced acidity and a hint of residual sugar; drink now).

INNISFAIL VINEYARDS NR Est 1980 $10.50–16.50 R 72
GEELONG
Cross Street, Batesford, Vic 3221 (052) 761 258 fax (052) 23 2720
Open Sun 10–5 or by appointment **Production** 2000 cases
Winemaker Ron Griffiths

Principal Wines Ries, Chard, Cab Sauv.

Summary This four hectare vineyard released its first wines in 1988, made in a small but modern winery on-site with a chewy, complex Chardonnay from both 1989 and 1990 attesting to the quality of the vineyards. Neither '91 nor '92 vintages tasted.

IRONBARK RIDGE VINEYARD NR Est 1984 $14 ML SD IPSWICH

Middle Road Mail Service 825, Purga, Qld 4306 (07) 28 1440
fax (07) 391 1908
Open By appointment **Production** 450 cases
Winemaker Peter Scudamore-Smith MW
Principal Wines Chard.

Summary Ipswich is situated on the coastal side of the Great Dividing Range, and the high summer humidity and rainfall will inevitably provide challenges for viticulture here. Style is still to settle down under the guidance of Peter Scudamore-Smith, for whom Ironbark Ridge is very much a part-time interest.

Recommended Wine 1992 Chardonnay (light, clean, fresh, citrus melon fruit, curiously lacking ripeness and tending hard early in its life; may develop in bottle).

IRON POT BAY B–B Est 1988 $13.50–14 ML SD TAMAR V

West Bay Road, Rowella, Tas 7270 (003) 94 7320
fax (003) 94 7346
Open By appointment **Production** 1000 cases
Winemaker Andrew Hood (Contract)
Principal Wines Chard, Sauv Bl Sem.

Summary Rod and Kyra Cuthbert have established an immaculate two hectare vineyard, utilising an open lyre trellis system and a high density (5000 vines per hectare) planting. It takes its name from a bay on the nearby Tamar River and is strongly maritime influenced.

Recommended Wines 1992 Unwooded Chardonnay (clean, aromatic, peach-accented fruit of light to medium weight; well balanced acid and good mouthfeel; to 1995). 1992 Sauvignon Blanc Semillon (clean, bright, crisp and fresh; in cool, discrete style, but could do with a little more flesh; drink now).

JACKSON'S HILL NR Est 1984 $12–18 CD SD HUNTER V

Mount View Road, Mount View, NSW 2321 (049) 90 1273
Open W'ends 9–5 or by appointment **Production** 800 cases
Winemaker Mike Winborne
Principal Wines Sem, LH Sem, Cab Franc, Cab Sauv Cab Franc, fortified Cab Franc.

Summary A new arrival on the spectacularly scenic Mount View Road making tiny quantities of wine sold exclusively through the cellar door.

Recommended Wine 1991 Cabernet Franc (fresh, elegant wine with lemony oak, tending to show regional rather than varietal character but nicely balanced; to 1995).

JADRAN NR Est 1967 $6–12 CD SD SWAN V

Reservoir Road, Orange Grove, WA 6109 (09) 459 1110
Open Mon–Sat 10–8, Sun 11–5 **Production** NFP
Winemaker Steve Radojkovich
Principal Wines Ries, Herm, generic white and red table, Sparkl, fortifieds.

Summary A quite substantial operation which basically se[rves] local clientele, occasionally producing wines of quite surp[rising] quality from a variety of fruit sources. The 1990 Shiraz sh[ows] attractive scented cherry fruit with a touch of spice.

JAMES HASELGROVE C–C Est 1981 $7.90–22.50 CD SD
STHN VALES & COONAWARRA
Main Penola-Naracoorte Road, Coonawarra, SA 5263
(08) 323 8706 and Foggo Road, McLaren Vale, SA 5171
(08) 323 8706 fax (08) 323 8049
Open Mon–Fri 9–5, w'ends 10–5 **Production** 17 000 cases
Winemaker Nick Haselgrove
Principal Wines Meth Champ, Chab, Chard, Ries, Gewurz, Cab Shir, Shir, Cab Sauv, Port; variously from Coonawarra and Southern Vales fruit.
Best Vintages W '82, '84, '90, '91, '92 R '82, '84, '90, '91, '92
Summary Now owned by Australian Premium Wines Pty Limited, which has provided the funds necessary for the purchase of new winemaking equipment and new oak. James Haselgrove is no longer involved with the company, but 26-year-old Nick Haselgrove continues as winemaker. The 1990 and 1991 vintage wines are mediocre, but presumably 1992 and 1993 will see a turnaround in the fortunes of the brand.

JANE BROOK ESTATE CB–CB Est 1972 $10.50–14.50 CD SD
SWAN V
Toodyay Road, Middle Swan, WA 6056 (09) 274 1432
fax (09) 274 1211
Open Mon–Sat 10–5, Sun 12–5 **Production** 11 000 cases
Winemaker David Atkinson, Candy Jonsson
Principal Wines Chenin, Chard, Sauv Bl, Ries, Fronti, Cab Mer, Cab Sauv, fortifieds.
Best Vintages W '83, '84, '88, '91, '92 R '81, '84, '88, '90, '91
Summary An attractive winery that serves alfresco lunches every day and produces a range of wines from both Swan Valley and Mount Barker fruit that never offend but which seldom scale the heights.
Recommended Wines 1992 Mount Barker Rhine Riesling (pungent and intense, with strong lime and passionfruit aromas and flavours; to 1996).

JASPER HILL A–BA Est 1975 $13.50–23 R 12, 21, 149, 225
BENDIGO
Drummonds Lane, Heathcote, Vic 3523 (054) 33 2528
fax (054) 33 3143
Open W'ends 10–6 **Production** 3000 cases
Winemaker Ron Laughton
Principal Wines Georgia's Paddock Ries, Shir, Emily's Paddock Shir, Cab Franc.
Best Vintages W '86, '90, '91, '92, '93 R '86, '88, '90, '91, '92
Summary Much admired survivor of the 1987 bushfires which make red wines full of character and flavour, typically needing a decade or more in bottle to start showing their best; 1990 produced two outstanding red wines in this mould. The Riesling is often ignored, but can be every bit as good.
Recommended Wines 1991 Georgia's Paddock Shiraz (big, rich,

ripe but not overripe wine with massively dense aroma and flavour, and mouthfilling persistent tannins; to 2010). 1991 Emily's Paddock Shiraz Cabernet Franc (dense, sweet, concentrated fruit aromas, with rich berry flavours, mint and tannins; to 2010).

JASPER VALLEY NR Est 1976 $4.20–12 CD SD SOUTH COAST
RMB 880 Croziers Road, Berry, NSW 2535 (044) 64 1596
Open 7 days 9.30–5.30 **Production** 1100 cases
Winemaker Contract
Principal Wines Wh Burg, Ries, Tram Ries, Mos, Summer Red, Cab Sauv and Ports; also non-alcoholic fruit wines.
Summary A strongly tourist-oriented winery with most of its wine purchased as cleanskins from other makers. Features two acres of lawns, barbeque facilities and sweeping views.

JEIR CREEK CB–B Est 1984 $9–14 CD 96, 152 CANBERRA
Gooda Creek Road, Murrumbateman, ACT 2582 (06) 227 5999
fax (06) 227 5900
Open Fri–Sun and public hols 10–5 **Production** 2000 cases
Winemaker Rob Howell
Principal Wines Ries, Sauv Bl, Chard, Pinot, Shir, Cab Mer, Botrytis Sem.
Summary Rob Howell came to part-time winemaking through a love of drinking fine wine, and is intent on improving both the quality and consistency of his wines.
Recommended Wines 1992 Sauvignon Blanc (pleasant, crisp, clean and direct style which is well balanced though not intense; drink now).

JENKE VINEYARDS NR Est 1989 $7.50–12 CD 71 BAROSSA V
Barossa Valley Way, Rowland Flat, SA 5352 (085) 24 4154
fax (085) 24 4154
Open 7 days 10–4.30 **Production** 2350 cases
Winemaker Kym Jenke
Principal Wines Ries, Sem, Chard, Shir, Cab Sauv.
Summary The Jenkes have been vignerons in the Barossa since 1854, and have over 25 hectares of vineyards; a small part of the production is now made and marketed through a charming restored stone cottage cellar door.

JIM BARRY CA–BA Est 1974 $5–40 CD 30, 35, 64, 102, 119, 306 CLARE V
Main North Road, Clare, SA 5453 (088) 42 2261
fax (088) 42 3752
Open Mon–Fri 9–5, w'ends 9–4 **Production** 55 000 cases
Winemaker Mark Barry
Principal Wines Ries, Chablis, Sauv Bl, Chard (unwooded), Cab Mer, Cab Sauv. The Armagh is a Grange pretender.
Best Vintages W '84, '86, '89, '91 R '80, '84, '88, '90, '91
Summary This is a family-run winery that seems to have surmounted marketing problems of a few years ago; it produces a range of wines in substantial quantities which can offer very good value for money.
Recommended Wines 1990 The Armagh Shiraz (impenetrable colour, hugely concentrated aroma and massively rich, almost thick

flavour and structure; not for everyone and certainly not for the faint hearted; to 2030). 1992 Sauvignon Blanc (strong tobacco/herbal aromas with direct, intense fruit flavours; surprising wine for the region; drink now). 1990 Cabernet Sauvignon (clean, fresh and bright with simple sweet fruit; to 1995).

JINGALLA CB–B Est 1979 $9–15.50 CD 71, 125, 155 GRT SOUTHERN

RMB 114 Bolganup Dam Road, Porongurup, WA 6324 phone and fax (098) 53 1023

Open 7 days 10.30–5 **Production** 1250 cases
Winemaker Goundrey Wines (Contract)
Principal Wines Ries, Sem, LH Sem, Verd, Rouge, Shir, Cab Sauv.
Best Vintages W '84, '86, '89, '90, '91 R '86, '87, '88, '89
Summary Jingalla has provided some attractive wines over the past three or four years, although fruit flavour and intensity tends to be a little on the light side, and a limited oak budget sometimes leaves its mark. Verdelho is a winery specialty, with attractive fleshy/peachy fruit flavours.

JOHN GEHRIG C–B Est 1976 $6.50–19.90 CD 3, 184 NE VIC

On Oxley to Milawa Road, Oxley, Vic 3678 phone and fax (057) 27 3395

Open 7 days 9–5 **Production** 5000 cases
Winemaker John Gehrig
Principal Wines Ries, Chenin, Chard, Sparkl, Verd, Pinot, Cab Mer, fortifieds.
Best Vintages W '80, '87, '88, '90, '92 R '82, '88, '90, '91, '92
Summary Honest, if seldom exciting, wines; the occasional Chardonnay, Pinot Noir and Cabernet Merlot have, however, risen above their station.

JONES NR Est 1864 SD NE VIC

Chiltern Road, Rutherglen, Vic 3685 (060) 32 9496

Open Mon–Sat 9–5, w'ends and hols 10–5 **Production** NFP
Winemaker Les Jones
Principal Wines Chab, Ries, Wh Burg, Light Red, Dry Red, Ports and other fortifieds.
Summary An ultra-reclusive and ultra-traditional winery (despite the garish labels) making no-frills wines. Les Jones even regards details of his current wines and prices as 'my business only'.

JUD'S HILL B–B Est 1977 $8.99–16.95 R 2, 33, 115 CLARE V

Farrell Flat Road, Clare, SA 5343 (vineyard only)
Open Not **Production** NFP
Winemaker Brian Barry
Principal Wines Ries, Chab, Cab Sauv, Cab Mer; Gleesons Ridge is newly introduced second label.
Summary Brian Barry is an industry veteran with a wealth of winemaking and show judging experience. His is nonetheless in reality a vineyard-only operation, with a substantial part of the output sold as grapes to other wineries, and the wines made under contract at various wineries albeit under Brian Barry's supervision. As one would expect, the quality is reliably good.
Recommended Wines 1992 Rhine Riesling (exceptionally scented,

fragrant and spicy, with high flavoured, spicy, passionfruit characters on the palate, all suggesting the use of some enzymes in the making; highly commercial style with masses of flavour). 1990 Cabernet Sauvignon (mint, cassis and fresh earth aromas intermingle; smooth palate with mint and red berry flavours, finishing with soft tannins; to 1996).

KAESLER FARM NR Est 1990 $7.50–13.70 CD SD BAROSSA V
Barossa Valley Way, Nuriootpa, SA 5355 (085) 62 2711
fax (085) 62 2788
Open 7 days 10–5 **Production** 3000 cases
Winemaker Roger Harbord (Contract)
Principal Wines Prestige Sem, Rhine Ries, Old Vine Shir, Cab Sauv, fortifieds.
Summary Toby and Treena Hueppauff purchased Kaesler Farm, with its 12 hectares of vines, in 1985, and since 1990 have had the wines made under contract by Roger Harbord at Basedows.
Recommended Wines 1992 Prestige Semillon (while scented, lemony oak dominates the bouquet and palate, the fruit is there, with plenty of weight on the mid to back palate; short-term development to 1995). 1991 Old Vines Shiraz (attractive red cherry fruit of light to medium weight, showing that old vines do not necessarily produce heavy, extractive wines; the oak is slightly raw, but will settle down with age; to 1998).

KAISER STUHL C–B Est 1931 $4.30–11.80 R 124, 195
BAROSSA V
Tanunda Road, Nuriootpa, SA 5355 (085) 62 0389
fax (085) 62 1669
Open 7 days 8.30–5
Production 1.3 million cases
Winemaker Steve Chapman
Principal Wines Black Forest, generic whites under Bin Nos (Bin 44, 55, 66, 77); Claret Bin 33; Red Ribbon Shir as premium release; Sparkl (Summer Wine); also extensive cask and flagon range.
Best Vintages W '82, '84, '86, '90, '92 R '82, '84, '86, '90, '92
Summary Yet another brand that seems to be struggling to retain its identity within the Penfold Wine Group. Green Ribbon Riesling, alas, is no more, while the 1988 and 1989 Red Ribbon Shiraz lack the fruit of bygone years and are driven by what can only be described as pedestrian oak.

KARA KARA NR Est 1977 $10–12 CD SD PYRENEES
Sunraysia Highway via St Arnaud, Vic 3478 (054) 96 3294
Open 7 days 10–6 **Production** 1300 cases
Winemaker Steve Zsigmond
Principal Wines Fumé Bl, Chard Sem, Sauv Bl, Cab Sauv.
Summary Hungarian-born Steve Zsigmond comes from a long line of vignerons, and sees Kara Kara as the eventual retirement occupation for himself and wife Marlene. The first step has been the decision to have their production contract made by Mitchelton (previously the grapes were sold) with predictably consistent results over the first few years.
Recommended Wine 1992 Sauvignon Blanc (full, developed, forward style with appreciable oak, plenty of weight and flesh, though not varietal — more semillon-like; drink now).

KARINA CA–B Est 1984 $10–12.50 CD 68 MORNINGTON P
Harrisons Road, Dromana, Vic 3936 phone and fax (059) 81 0137
Open W'ends 11–5 **Production** 1500 cases
Winemaker Graeme Pinney
Principal Wines Ries, Sauv Bl, Chard, Mer, Cab Sauv.
Best Vintages W '88, '89, '91, '92 **R** '89, '90, '91
Summary The white wines are characteristically light bodied and
elegant, the red wines much richer, led by the 1990 and 1991
Cabernet Sauvignons (with a little Merlot blended in) which have
abundant, very ripe berry fruit with cassis/blackcurrant overtones.

KARRELEA ESTATE B–B Est 1982 $8–14 CD SD GRT
SOUTHERN
Duck Road, Mount Barker, WA 6324 (098) 51 1838
Open Fri–Sun/hols 10–5 **Production** 200 cases
Winemaker John Wade
Principal Wines Ries, Sauv Bl, Pinot, Cab Sauv Franc Mer,
Pinot.
Best Vintages W '87, '89, '90 **R** '87, '88
Summary A consistent producer of excellent lime/passionfruit
Rieslings which have won gold medals; the elegant
Cabernet/Franc/Merlot blend can also be good, proving that the
strictly organic grape-growing methods used are not a whimsical folly.

KARRIVALE B–B Est 1979 $11–11.50 CD 55, 155 GRT
SOUTHERN
Woodlands, Porongurup, WA 6324 (098) 53 1009
fax (098) 53 1129
Open Wed–Sun 10–5 **Production** 350 cases
Winemaker John Wade
Principal Wines Ries
Best Vintages W '89, '90, '91, '92
Summary A tiny Riesling specialist in the wilds of the Porongurups
forced to change its name from Narang because Lindemans felt it could
be confused with its Nyrang Hermitage brand; truly a strange world.
Recommended Wines 1992 Rhine Riesling (firm, intense, tightly
structured wine with good length and bright, lively flavours; to 1997).
1991 Special Rhine Riesling (rich, soft, rounded, fleshy lime and
honey fruit; to 1994). 1991 Rhine Riesling (pleasant wine with hints
of lime juice; still fresh and with attractive mouthfeel; to 1996).

KARRIVIEW NR Est 1986 $11.50–$17.50 CD 155 GRT
SOUTHERN
Scotsdale Road, Denmark, WA 6333 (098) 40 9381
Open Summer: Fri–Sun 10–5, winter: w'ends 10–5
Production 530 cases
Winemaker John Wade (Contract)
Principal Wines Ries, LP Ries, Chard, Pinot.
Summary One of the newest arrivals which announced its presence
in no uncertain fashion by winning two trophies at the 1990 Mount
Barker Show for its stylish, elegant, oaky 1990 Chardonnay.
Recommended Wine 1992 Pinot Noir (relatively light, but strongly
styled gamey/stalky Burgundian overtones; gold medal winner 1992
Mount Barker Show; drink now).

KATNOOK ESTATE BA–B Est 1979 $12.60–22.25 CD 148, 268 COONAWARRA

Off main Penola-Naracoorte Road, Coonawarra, SA 5263
(087) 37 2394 fax (087) 37 2397

Open Mon–Fri 8–4.30, w'ends & public hols 10–4

Production 25 000 cases (including Riddoch label)

Winemaker Wayne Stehbens

Principal Wines Under Katnook label Ries, Sauv Bl, Chard, Mer, Pinot, Cab Sauv, Sparkl; under second label Riddoch Chard, Sauv Bl, Cab Shir, Shir.

Best Vintages W & R '86, '88, '90, '91

Summary The prestige label of the vast Coonawarra Machinery Company empire, with access to the very best grapes from large vineyard holdings and also to some high level consultancy advice. The Katnook wines are made in very limited quantities, the volume coming through the Riddoch label.

Recommended Wines 1992 Katnook Estate Sauvignon Blanc (smooth, clean, balanced fruit showing good ripeness with passionfruit and gooseberry aromas and flavours; deserves its many gold medals; drink now). 1991 Riddoch Chardonnay (clean, rich, buttery aromas with soft oak; smooth, medium weight palate with harmonious fruit and oak; drink now). 1989 Riddoch Cabernet Shiraz (solid, sweet, fresh fruit of medium weight and a hint of leafiness; not complex but still fresh, and showing well for a difficult vintage; may have been bottled late; to 1995).

KAY BROS AMERY DB–CB Est 1890 $4–15.50 CD 27 STHN VALES

Kay Road, McLaren Vale, SA 5171 (08) 323 8211 fax (08) 323 9199

Open Mon–Fri 9–5, w'ends 12–5 **Production** 6500 cases

Winemaker Colin Kay

Principal Wines Sauv Bl, LH Fronti, Cab Sauv, Shir, Pinot, fortifieds.

Best Vintages R '86, '89, '90, '91, '92

Summary A traditional winery with a rich history and some priceless old vines; while the white wines are not recommended, the red wines and fortified wines can be very good. Of particular interest is Block 6 Shiraz, made from 100-year-old vines.

Recommended Wines 1990 Block 6 Shiraz (dense, impenetrable colour with deep, concentrated briary aromas and similarly concentrated dark berry and bitter chocolate flavours, with soft, lingering tannins; to 2010). 1989 Block 6 Shiraz (clean, strong, sweet vanillin coconut oak and fleshy red berry fruit; highly seductive, commercial wine; to 2005).

KELLERMEISTER CB–B Est 1970 $7–25 CD SD BAROSSA V

Barossa Valley Highway, Lyndoch, SA 5351 (085) 24 4303
fax (085) 24 4880

Open 7 days 9–6 **Production** 5000 cases

Winemaker Trevor Jones

Principal Wines Chard, Sauv Bl, Ries, Gewurz, Sem Wh Burg, Shir, Cab Sauv, Sparkl, fortifieds.

Best Vintages W '82, '86, '88, '90, '91 R '80, '84, '86, '90, '92

Summary Specialises in older vintage wines made in traditional fashion, an extraordinary array of which are on offer at enticing prices, including Rhine Rieslings back to 1984, red wines back to 1982 and Vintage Ports back to 1978.

KELLYBROOK CA–CB Est 1970 $8–17.50 CD 20, 95 YARRA V
Fulford Road, Wonga Park, Vic 3115 (03) 722 1304
fax (03) 722 2092
Open Mon–Sat 9–6, Sun 11–6 **Production** 3500 cases
Winemaker Darren Kelly, Peter Draper
Principal Wines Meth Champ, Apple Brandy, Sparkling Cider, Old Gold Cider, Chard, Ries, Gewurz, Mos, Colomb, Pinot, Shir, Cab Sauv.
Summary A cider and apple brandy maker turned winemaker; notwithstanding that apples are much more difficult to work with than grapes, the ciders and apple brandy (formerly called Calvados) remain highlights and are strongly recommended. Peter Draper's arrival should see a marked improvement in table wine from 1993.

• KEVIN SOBELS WINES NR Est 1992 SD HUNTER V
Cnr Broke & Halls Roads, Pokolbin, NSW 2321 phone and fax (049) 98 7766
Open 7 days 10–5 **Production** 3000 cases
Winemaker Kevin Sobels
Principal Wines Chard, Sem, Tram, Pinot.
Summary Veteran winemaker Kevin Sobels has found yet another home, using 10.5 hectares of vineyards to produce wines sold through cellar door and mail order, with very limited retail representation. The cellar door offers light meals, picnic and barbeque facilities.

KILLAWARRA CB–B Est 1975 $6.30–11.50 R 124, 197 BAROSSA V
Tanunda Road, Nuriootpa, SA 5355 (085) 62 0389
fax (085) 62 1669
Open See Penfolds **Production** NFP
Winemaker John Duval
Principal Wines Brut, Premier Brut, Brut Reserve.
Summary Purely a brand name of the Penfolds group, but capable of coming up with one or two surprisingly good wines from time to time, particularly the sparkling wines, the best of which are not infrequently declassified sparkling wines from the very best of the Seaview/Seppelt range.
Recommended Wines 1989 Reserve Brut (powerful, complex, rich wine with lots of flavour and yeast autolysis development, tending fractionally sweet on the finish, but great at the price). 1990 Premier Brut (another very complex wine with echoes of French Champagne, particularly in the slightly aldehydic overtones).

KILLERBY VINEYARDS BA–B Est 1973 $10–15.50 R 50, 108, 175, 186 MARGARET R
Minninup Road off Lakes Road, Gelorup, WA 6230 (097) 95 7222
fax (097) 95 7835
Open 7 days 10–5 **Production** 10 000 cases
Winemaker Matt Aldridge
Principal Wines Chard, Sem, April White and April Red, Cab Sauv, Pinot, Shir, Port.
Best Vintages W '88, '89, '91, '92 R '85, '87, '89, '91

Summary The Killerby family are long-term residents of the south-west; Anna Killerby, herself a Roseworthy graduate, is the fourth generation and is married to Matt Aldridge, formerly of Rosemount and now chief winemaker at Killerby. The 16 hectares of vines were established by Anna's father, the late Dr Barry Killerby, in 1973 and are now fully mature.

Recommended Wines 1992 Chardonnay (fine melon/fig fruit with subtle yet complex barrel ferment characters; well structured wine; to 1995). 1992 Semillon (potent, spicy American oak is fairly dominant, but there is length to the fruit and the wine is clean; to 1996).

KINGS CREEK BA–B Est 1981 $17 CD 55 MORNINGTON P
237 Myers Road, Bittern, Vic 3918 (059) 82 1715
Open Sun 11–5 **Production** 800 cases
Winemakers Kathleen Quealy, Kevin McCarthy
Principal Wines Chard, Pinot, Cab Sauv.
Summary Has followed its trophy winning 1990 Pinot Noir with an even better wine in 1991, marvellously stylish and Burgundian; the 1991 Chardonnay is also excellent.

KINGSLEY B–B Est 1984 $10–12 CD 72 WESTERN VIC
50 Bancroft Street, Portland, Vic 3305 (055) 23 1864
Open 7 days 1–4 **Production** 2000 cases
Winemaker Seppelt (Contract)
Principal Wines Ries, Botrytis Ries, Cab Sauv.
Summary Situated in the very cool Drumborg region of south-western Victoria. While intensely flavoured Rhine Rieslings are a highlight, Cabernet Sauvignon will prove difficult to fully ripen in most years and often shows excessively herbal characteristics.
Recommended Wines 1992 Botrytis Riesling (intense lime and apricot botrytis aroma and flavour, with pleasantly soft acidity; to 1995).

KNIGHT'S GRANITE HILLS CB–B Est 1979 $9–16 R 92 MACEDON
Lancefield-Mia Mia Road, Baynton RSD 391, Kyneton, Vic 3444 (054) 23 7264 fax (054) 23 7288
Open Mon–Sat 10–6, Sun 12–6 **Production** 4000 cases
Winemaker Lew Knight
Principal Wines Ries, Chard, Shir, Cab Sauv.
Best Vintages R '81, '82, '88, '91, '92
Summary Introduced Australia to the spicy/peppery style of Shiraz almost a decade ago; at their best these wines are superb, as was the '91 Shiraz tasted ex-cask, but they are sometimes adversely affected by late bottling. No recent tastings from bottle.

KNIGHT'S VINES NR Est 1986 $8.50–10.50 CD 72, 92 MUDGEE
Henry Lawson Drive, Mudgee, NSW 2850 (063) 73 3954 fax (063) 72 2399
Open Mon–Fri 10–4, w'ends 9–5 **Production** NFP
Winemaker Peter Knights
Principal Wines Sem, Chablis, Wh Burg, Claret and fortifieds.
Summary A very small winery concentrating chiefly on generic table and fortified wines, which has recently changed hands (and name — it was formerly Caloola).

• KNOWLAND ESTATE WINES NR Est 1990 $not fixed SD
MUDGEE
Mt Vincent Road, Running Stream, NSW 2850 (063) 58 8420
fax (063) 58 8423
Open By appointment **Production** 80 cases
Winemaker Peter Knowland
Principal Wines Shir, Pinot.
Summary The former Mount Vincent Winery which sells much of
its grape production from the 3.5 hectares of vineyards to other
makers, but which proposes to increase production under its own
label from the 1993 vintage.

KOMINOS CB–B Est 1976 $8–11 CD SD GRANITE BELT
New England Highway, Severnlea, Qld 4352 (076) 83 4311
Open 7 days 9–4.30 **Production** NFP
Winemaker Tony Comino
Principal Wines Chenin, Sem, Chard, Light Red, Shir, Cab Sauv.
Summary Tony Comino is a dedicated viticulturist and winemaker;
in late 1991 wines to impress were a peachy/melon 1990 Chardonnay,
a lively herbal/berry 1990 Cabernet Sauvignon and a promising
concentrated 1991 Shiraz. No more recent tastings.

• KOPPAMURRA WINES NR Est 1973 $4.50–7.50 ML SD
COONAWARRA
Joanna via Naracoorte, SA 5271 (08) 271 4127 fax (08) 271 0726
Open Not **Production** 1000 cases
Winemaker John Greenshields
Principal Wines Botrytis Ries, Cab Mer, Naracoorte Ranges Dry
Red.
Summary Koppamurra has been revived after a period of relative
inactivity. The seven hectare vineyards that owner John Greenshields
commenced to plant way back in 1973 have continued in production,
but most of the grapes have been and continue to be sold to other
makers. The vineyards, incidentally, are established on a patch of terra
rossa soil which is well north of the main viticultural area, halfway
between Coonawarra itself and Naracoorte. The wines are made at
other facilities under John Greenshields' supervision and, as the Late
Harvest Riesling attests, can be excellent.
Recommended Wine 1992 Late Harvest Botrytis Riesling (very
clean, lime aromas of moderate intensity; on the palate, firm, clean,
fully sweet Riesling fruit, with the lusciousness balanced by crisp
acidity; to 1996).

KROEMER ESTATE NR Est 1986 $9.50–15.50 CD SD
BAROSSA V
Tanunda, SA 5352 (085) 63 3375 fax (085) 63 3758
Open Mon–Fri 10–4.30, w'ends 10–5
Production 2000 cases
Winemaker Roger Harbord (Contract)
Principal Wines Sylv, Ries, Sparkl, Shir, Cab Sauv.
Summary Opened its doors on 30 June 1990 specialising — of all
unlikely grapes — with Sylvaner; the '86 vintage (first) has matured
surprisingly well, but subsequent attempts have been less
convincing. On the other side of the ledger, an elegant, toasty 1990
Rhine Riesling showed Roger Harbord's skill.

KRONDORF B–B Est 1978 $6.15–15 R 110, 197, 210
BAROSSA V
Krondorf Road, Tanunda, SA 5352 (085) 63 1245
fax (085) 62 3055
Open 7 days 9–5 **Production** 120 000
Winemaker Nick Walker
Principal Wines Ries, Chab, Sem, Chard, Fronti, Herm, Shir Cab, Cab Sauv.
Best Vintages W '86, '87, '90, '92 R '80, '81, '86, '88, '92
Summary Yet another winery that found itself as part of a larger group in 1991, this time under the aegis of Mildara. The brands seem reasonably strong, and little overt change has eventuated.
Recommended Wines 1992 Barossa Valley Riesling (clean and rich with flowery, generous, lime-accented fruit, with good length, weight and acidity; to 1996). 1992 Show Reserve Chardonnay (very sophisticated barrel ferment oak handling, with fair intensity to fruit and pleasing acidity; its bloodlines suggest it will develop quickly; to 1995). 1991 Shiraz Cabernet (rich, full, ripe fruit with some briary notes and soft, fleshy, accessible structure; to 1996).

KYEEMA ESTATE NR Est 1986 $9–12 ML SD CANBERRA
PO Box 282, Belconnen, ACT 2616 (06) 254 7557 (AH)
Open Not **Production** 400 cases
Winemaker Andrew McEwin
Principal Wines Sem, Chard, Shir, Cab Sauv.
Summary By the time of publication, Andrew McEwin expects to have his winery fully functioning at Murrumbateman after several years of making bits and pieces of wine here, there and everywhere. If the winery has a specialty it is undoubtedly its Semillon, the '90, '91 and '92 vintages of which were all good wines, the latter winning a gold medal at the Yass Show in 1993.

LAANECOORIE B–B Est 1982 $16.95 R SD PYRENEES
Bendigo Road, Betley, Vic 3472 (vineyard only); postal RMB 1330, Dunolly, Vic 3472
Open Not **Production** 1500 cases
Winemaker John Ellis (Contract)
Principal Wines A single Bordeaux-blend dry red of Cab Franc, Cab Sauv and Merlot in roughly equal proportions.
Summary John McQuilten's four hectare vineyard produces grapes of consistently high quality, and competent contract winemaking by John Ellis at Hanging Rock has done the rest.
Recommended Wine 1990 Laanecoorie (ripe, lush, berry fruit with overtones of mint and a touch of gaminess; soft tannins; to 1998).

LADBROKE GROVE NR Est 1982 $6–11 CD 67
COONAWARRA
Coonawarra Road, Penola, SA 5277 (087) 37 2997
Open 7 days 9–4 **Production** 1200 cases
Winemaker Ken Ward
Principal Wines Ries, LP Ries, Shir.
Summary Leads a somewhat shadowy existence outside the mainstream of Coonawarra wineries; wine quality has been variable, but it does have two hectares of hand-pruned shiraz planted by John Redman in the 1960s upon which to draw.

LAKE BREEZE NR Est 1987 $7.40–13.90 CD SD LANG
CREEK
Step Road, Langhorne Creek, SA 5255 (085) 37 3017
fax (085) 37 3267
Open 7 days 10–5 **Production** 800 cases
Winemaker Greg Follett
Principal Wines Chard, White Fronti, Cab Sauv, Cab Mer Shir,
the last labelled Bernoota, Tawny Port.
Summary The Follett family have been farmers at Langhorne
Creek since 1880, grape growers since the 1930s. Since 1987 a small
proportion of their grapes has been made into wine, and a cellar door
sales facility was opened in early 1991. The '90, '91 and '92 vintage
wines show a strong oak influence (the White Frontignac excepted)
with the Chardonnay exhibiting pungent smoky bacony oak, the red
wines strong American oak to go with rich fruit.

LAKE GEORGE CB–B Est 1971 $10–12.60 R SD CANBERRA
Federal Highway, Collector, NSW 2581 (048) 48 0039
Open Not **Production** 300 cases
Winemaker Dr Edgar F. Riek
Principal Wines Chard, Pinot, Cab Sauv, Mer.
Best Vintages W '86, '88, '90, '91, '92 R '84, '86, '88, '91, '92
Summary Dr Edgar Rick is an inquisitive, iconoclastic winemaker
who is not content with his role as Godfather and founder of the
Canberra district, forever experimenting and innovating. His fortified
wines, vintaged in North East Victoria but matured at Lake George,
are very good.

LAKE'S FOLLY A–A Est 1963 $18 CD 50, 264 HUNTER V
Broke Road, Pokolbin, NSW 2321 (049) 98 7507 fax (049) 98 7322
Open Mon–Sat 10–4 **Production** 4000 cases
Winemaker Stephen Lake
Principal Wines Chard, Cab Sauv.
Best Vintages W '81, '83, '86, '91, '92 R '81, '85, '89, '90, '91
Summary The first of the weekend wineries to produce wines for
commercial sale, Lake's Folly has been long revered for its Cabernet
Sauvignon and thereafter its Chardonnay. Very properly, terroir and
climate produce a distinct regional influence and thereby a distinctive
wine style. Some find this attractive, others are less tolerant of the
style.
Recommended Wines 1992 Chardonnay (stylish wine with clean
melon fruit, good intensity and length; good development potential;
to 1997). 1991 Cabernet Sauvignon (firm, cherry-accented fruit with
just a touch of astringency merging into blackcurrant flavours on the
palate; soft, lingering tannins; to 2005).

• LALLAGULLY VINEYARD NR Est 1988 $15 R SD NTH TAS
Brooks Road, Lalla, Tas 7250 (003) 31 2325
Open By appointment
Production 200 cases
Winemaker Andrew Hood (Contract)
Principal Wines Chard, Pinot.
Summary Owners Rod and Kim Ascui have established one hectare
each of Pinot Noir, Chardonnay and Sauvignon Blanc, producing the
first tiny crop in 1992.

LAMONT B–A Est 1978 $5.50–11 CD SD SWAN V
Bisdee Road, Millendon, WA 6056 (09) 296 4485
Open Wed–Sun 10–5 **Production** 4000 cases
Winemaker Corin Lamont
Principal Wines Wh Burg, Chard, Sweet Wh, Cab Rosé, Cab,
Mer, fortifieds.
Best Vintages W '81, '85, '89, '90 R '81, '83, '85, '89
Summary Corin Lamont is the daughter of the late Jack Mann, and
makes her wines in the image of those her father used to make,
resplendent in their generosity. Lamont also boasts a superb restaurant.

LANCEFIELD NR Est 1983 $9.80–18.80 CD 72, 285 MACEDON
Woodend Road, Lancefield, Vic 3435 (054) 29 1217
fax (054) 29 1041
Open W'ends 12–6 **Production** 2000 cases
Winemaker John Ellis (Contract)
Principal Wines Gewurz, Colomb, Chard, Cab Mer, Mer Cab
Franc, Sparkl; Pattersons is the second label for wines from other
parts of Victoria
Best Vintages W '86, '88, '89, '91, '92 R '86, '90, '91
Summary Offers a mixture of wines sourced variously from
Macedon and other regions relying in part upon the restaurant and
live entertainment to draw custom. The wines are light but well
enough made.

LA PROVENCE NR Est 1956 $17–21 CD SD TAMAR V
407 Lalla Road, Lalla, Tas 7267 (003) 95 1290
Open 7 days 10–5 **Production** 480 cases
Winemaker Jean-Baptiste Lecaillon (Contract)
Principal Wines Chard, Ries, Sem, Pinot.
Summary La Provence incorporates the pioneer vineyard of
Frenchman Jean Miguet, now owned by Stuart and Kay Bryce who
purchased it in 1980 and who have expanded the original 1.3 hectare
vineyard to a little over three hectares as well as grafting over unsuitable
Grenache and Cabernet (left from the original plantings) to Chardonnay
and Pinot Noir.

LARK HILL B–B Est 1978 $9–15 CD 134, 175 CANBERRA
RMB 281 Gundaroo Road, Bungendore, NSW 2621 (06) 238 1393
Open Thurs–Mon & public hols 10–5 **Production** 2500 cases
Winemakers Dr David & Sue Carpenter
Principal Wines Ries, Ausl Ries, Chard, Pinot, Cab Mer.
Best Vintages W '86, '88, '90, '91, '92 R '87, '88, '90, '91, '92
Summary For long the most consistent all-round winemaker in the
district, which has returned to form after an uncharacteristic wobble.
Recommended Wines 1992 Chardonnay (complex barrel
fermentation, spicy oak with firm, clean fruit and good mouthfeel; to
1995). 1992 Cabernet Sauvignon (fairly leafy, cool climate style of
light to medium weight; to 1996).

• **LATARA WINES** NR Est 1979 $9.50–11 CD SD HUNTER V
Cnr McDonalds & Deaseys Roads, Pokolbin, NSW 2320
(049) 98 7320
Open Sat 9–5, Sun 9–4 **Production** 250 cases
Winemaker Ian Riggs (Contract)

Principal Wines Sem, Cab Sauv, Shir.

Summary The bulk of the grapes produced on the five hectare Latara vineyard, which was planted in 1979, are sold to Brokenwood. A small quantity is vinified for Latara and sold under its label. As one would expect, the wines are very competently made and are of show medal standard.

LAURISTON CB–B Est 1985 $11.60–19.95 R 22–26, 321 ADELAIDE PLAINS

Heaslip Road, Angle Vale, SA 5117 (08) 284 7000
fax (085) 83 2224

Open Mon–Fri 9–5, Sat 11–5, Sun 1–5 **Production** 10 000 cases
Winemaker Colin Glaetzer

Principal Wines Meth Champ, Chard, Ries, Cab Sauv Shir, Port, Muscat.

Summary The Lauriston wines are purchased either from other members of the Berri Renmano group or from external sources across southern Australia; the wine styles vary accordingly.

Recommended Wines Show Tawny Port (some earthy spirit characters aid complexity; the wine is very well structured and balanced, with a pleasantly dry finish). Show Muscat (a surprisingly rich and concentrated wine, with similar earthy spirit characters which are attractive; well made, meritorious wine). 1991 Chardonnay (deep gold-yellow in colour with masses of buttery/butterscotch fruit; by now most probably past its best, but at the time a good example of the extreme peaches and cream style).

LAWSON HILL NR Est 1985 $8.50–13 CD SD MUDGEE

Henry Lawson Drive, Eurunderee, Mudgee, NSW 2850
(063) 73 3953

Open Thurs, Fri, Mon 9.30–4, w'ends 9.30–5
Production 2000 cases
Winemaker Various Contract and José Grace

Principal Wines Sem Chard, Tram Ries, Verd, Cab Mer, Pinot, Port.

Summary Former music director and arranger (for musical acts in Sydney clubs) José Grace and wife June run a strongly tourist-oriented operation situated next door to the Henry Lawson Memorial, offering a kaleidoscopic array of wines produced from 8 hectares of vineyard and made under contract.

LEASINGHAM CB–BA Est 1893 $5.95–9.95 R 22–26, 203, 302 CLARE V

7 Dominic Street, Clare, SA 5453 (088) 42 2555 fax (088) 42 3293
Open Mon–Fri 8.30–5.30, w'ends 10–4 **Production** 95 000 cases
Winemaker Roger Rowe

Principal Wines Hutt Creek Chab, Ries, Claret and Domaine Chard, Ries, Sem, Shir, Cab Malb.

Best Vintages W '84, '86, '87, '90, '92 R '80, '82, '89, '90, '92

Summary A model of marketing discipline and clarity, unusual in this day and age; both the Hutt Creek and Domaine ranges are no less commendable for their consistency of quality and value for money, however little this may be recognised by the public.

Recommended Wines 1991 Domaine Chardonnay (while showing a fair degree of sophisticated oak input does have tangy fruit and plenty of overall flavour; drink now). 1990 Domaine Shiraz (strong, sweet berry fruit on a lusciously full palate; quite subtle oak).

LECONFIELD BA–BA Est 1974 $6–15 R 12, 16, 55, 63, 115, 127, 274 COONAWARRA

Main Penola-Naracoorte Road, Coonawarra, SA 5263
(087) 37 2326 fax (087) 37 2285

Open 7 days 9–5 **Production** 38 000 cases (including contract)

Winemaker Ralph Fowler

Principal Wines Ries, Chard, Shir, Cab Sauv.

Best Vintages W '83, '86, '90, '91 R 82, '88, '90, '91

Summary Under the sure hand of Ralph Fowler, Leconfield is now restored to its former glory — indeed, with the exception of some curiously inconsistent tasting notes for the 1992 Chardonnay, the quality right across the range is better than it ever has been.

Recommended Wines 1992 Rhine Riesling (crisp, clean and fresh with very pure, classic varietal aroma and flavour showing no hint of enzyme assistance, the length of flavour is assisted by just a hint of sweetness; to 1996). 1991 Cabernet Sauvignon (full, ripe and concentrated fruit with abundant red berry flavours, a hint of spice and deftly handled oak; to 2005).

LEEUWIN ESTATE BA–B Est 1974 $12.40–40 R 65, 69, 127, 245 MARGARET R

Gnarawary Road, Margaret River, WA 6285 (097) 57 6253
fax (097) 57 6364

Open 7 days 10–4.30 **Production** 30 000 cases

Winemaker Bob Cartwright

Principal Wines Ries, Sauv Bl, Chard, Cab Sauv, Pinot; premium range Art Series, second label Prelude.

Best Vintages W '81, '82, '86, '87, '91 R '82, '87, '88, '89, '91

Summary The Horgan family retains both a shareholding and managerial role in Leeuwin Estate, and the restructured company has (happily) continued the long-term marketing and promotional strategy set in easier times. All in all, remains one of the benchmark wineries in Australia.

Recommended Wines 1987 Chardonnay (a quite beautiful wine, reminiscent of the '82, with extremely intense citric/grapefruit flavours, well integrated oak and a long, lingering finish; to 1998). 1988 Chardonnay (much richer, with far sweeter fruit and strong barrel ferment oak; has more flavour but is less elegant than the '87; to 1995). 1987 Cabernet Sauvignon (a controversial style, with powerful, intense herbaceous fruit; has length; the green bean characters will worry some). 1991 Rhine Riesling (almost Germanic floral aromas with crisp, clean and lively fruit on the palate; to 1997).

LEFROY BROOK NR Est 1986 $21.95 R SD GRT SOUTHERN

Glauder Road, Pemberton, WA 6260 (09) 386 8385

Open Not **Production** 300 cases

Winemaker Peter Fimmel

Principal Wines Chard, Pinot.

Summary One of the first Pemberton producers to come on-stream; the '89 and '90 vintages showed problems in the winery, perhaps due to the very small quantities, and give no real indication of the potential of the region.

LELAND ESTATE NR Est 1986 $11.75 ML 115 ADELAIDE HILLS
PO Lenswood, SA 5240 (08) 389 6928
Open Not **Production** 500 cases
Winemaker Rob Cootes
Principal Wines Sauv Bl, Pinot.
Summary Former Yalumba senior winemaker Rob Cootes, with a
Master of Science Degree, deliberately opted out of mainstream life
when he established Leland Estate, living in a split-level, one-
roomed house built from timber salvaged from trees killed in the Ash
Wednesday bush fires. The 1991 Sauvignon Blanc is as piercingly
rich in gooseberry varietal flavour as any from the exciting Lenswood
district in the Adelaide Hills.

LENTON BRAE ESTATE NR Est 1983 $11–18 CD SD
MARGARET R
Willyabrup Valley, Margaret River, WA 6285 (097) 55 6255
Open 7 days 10–6 **Production** 4000 cases
Winemaker Dorham Mann (Consultant)
Principal Wines Chard, Sauv Bl, Cab Sauv.
Summary Former architect and town planner Bruce Tomlinson has
built a strikingly beautiful winery, but will not stand for criticism of
his wines. For the record, the 1992 Chardonnay is the best of the
current releases.

LEO BURING BA–BA Est 1931 $7.50–11.80 R 124, 195
BAROSSA V
c/o Seppelt, Seppeltsfield via Tanunda, SA 5352 (085) 63 2184
fax (085) 63 2804
Open Mon–Fri 8.30–5, Sat 10.30–4.30, Sun 11–4 **Production** NFP
Winemakers Rob Ruediger, John Vickery (Consultant)
Principal Wines A range of varietally and regionally identified
wines coming from Barossa and surrounds (predominantly
Coonawarra and Padthaway), with emphasis on Ries, Chard and Cab
Sauv. Deluxe wines are Reserve Bin Rieslings.
Best Vintages W '84, '88, '90, '91, '92 R '84, '86, '87, '88, '90
Summary Yet another member of the Penfolds Wine Group that is
but a shadow of its former self in terms of sales, but which still has
some marvellous aged Rieslings in its repertoire and one or two very
interesting red wines.
Recommended Wines 1990 Rhine Riesling Bin DWT 13 (firm,
discrete, classic style, relatively unevolved, and in transition from
primary to secondary flavours; be patient and you will be rewarded; to
2005). 1990 Cabernet Sauvignon Bin DR 505 (a very big, ripe and
generous wine with lots of fruit but even more oak; a slightly lighter
touch would have produced an absolutely outstanding wine; to 2005).

LESNIK FAMILY NR Est 1986 SD HUNTER V
Branxton Road, Pokolbin, NSW 2321 (049) 98 7755
fax (049) 98 7750
Open 7 days 9–5 **Production** 3500 cases
Winemaker Josef Lesnik
Principal Wines Sem, Ries, Chard, Tram Ries, LP Sem, Shir, Cab
Sauv, fortifieds.
Summary A no-holds-barred tourist-oriented cellar door operation
offering wines from estate grown grapes; quality has been variable but

g, stylish 1991 barrel-fermented Chardonnay justifiably
Small Producers Class at the 1992 Royal Sydney Wine
quent show success at the Hunter Valley Wine Show
performance was not a fluke.

LILLYDALE VINEYARDS NR Est 1976 $9–17 R 68 208 YARRA V

Lot 10 Davross Court, Seville, Vic 3139 (059) 64 2016

Open 7 days 10–5 **Production** 9000 cases

Winemaker Alex White

Principal Wines Ries, Sauv Bl, Gewurz, Chard, Pinot, Cab Sauv; second label is Yarra Range.

Best Vintages W '82, '84, '86, '90 **R** '85, '86, '90, '91

Summary One of the larger wineries in the Valley and one of the old hands. The wines are deliberately made in a reserved style; Alex White is not one who believes in spending a great deal of money on new oak, preferring that the grapes (and the wine) should do the talking, helped by bottle development. Recent tastings in wine shows have not impressed.

LILLYPILLY ESTATE CB–B Est 1982 $6.55–10.90 CD 175, 207 MIA

Lillypilly Road, Leeton, NSW 2705 (069) 53 4069 fax (069) 53 4980

Open Mon–Sat 10–5.30, Sun by appointment **Production** 9000 cases

Winemaker Robert Fiumara

Principal Wines Ries, Chard, Tram Ries, Botrytis Noble Ries, Noble Muscat, Cab Sauv, Herm, Port.

Best Vintages W '82, '84, '85, '89 **R** '84, '85, '89

Summary The best wines by far are the botrytised white wines, with the Noble Muscat of Alexandria unique to the winery; these wines have both style and intensity of flavour and can age well.

Recommended Wines 1990 Noble Muscat of Alexandria (intense, grapy muscat aromas with almost mead-like overtones to the bouquet, with strongly botrytis influenced flavour; intense acidity to balance the sweetness, and a long finish).

LINDEMANS A–A Est 1908 $9.80–19.50 124, 195, 287 COONAWARRA & PADTHAWAY

Main Penola-Naracoorte Road, Coonawarra, SA 5263

(087) 36 3205 fax (087) 36 3250

Open 7 days 10–4 **Production** NFP

Winemakers Phillip John, Greg Clayfield

Principal Wines Under the Lindeman label, Padthaway Ries, Chard, Sauv Bl, Pinot; Limestone Ridge Shir Cab, Pyrus and St George Cab Sauv; under the Rouge Homme label Chard, Pinot, Cab Shir and Cab Sauv.

Best Vintages W & R '82, '86, '88, '90, '91

Summary Clearly the strongest brand other than Penfolds in the SABH-owned Penfolds Wine Group, with some great vineyards and a great history. The run of good vintages from 1990 add further interest and strength, as does the upgrading of the packaging and the quality of the Rouge Homme red wines (see separate entry).

Recommended Wines 1991 Padthaway Chardonnay (complex, oaky/nutty/buttery textured wine in the full and rich end of the spectrum; on track record should cellar well, but I am not sure). 1985

Nursery Riesling (a classic release from the past, remarkably youthful, crisp and fresh with spicy lime fruit; should hold to 2000). 1990 Commemorative Coonawarra Cabernet Sauvignon (very strong, concentrated sweet vanilla and red berry fruit, almost creamy in texture, with vanillin oak very apparent; to 2010).

LINDEMANS BA–BA Est 1870 $11.70–65 R 124, 195, 287 HUNTER V

McDonalds Road, Pokolbin, NSW 2321 (049) 98 7501
fax (049) 98 7682
Open 7 days 9–5 **Production** 60 000 cases
Winemaker Phillip John
Principal Wines Standard wines under annually changing Bin Nos of Sem, Chab, Wh Burg, Sem Chard, Chard, Red Burg, Herm; deluxe releases under Reserve Bin label and occasional older classic release label.
Best Vintages W '68, '70, '79, '87, '91 R '65, '83, '86, '87, '91
Summary Only time will tell where Lindemans Hunter Valley wines are eventually positioned in the SABH empire; certainly, the vineyards which produced the great wines of the '50s and '60s are gone forever, but the red wines in particular have shown a renaissance in recent years.
Recommended Wines 1983 Red Burgundy Reserve Bin 6600 (released in magnum in 1993; wonderfully powerful wine with dark plum and liquorice aroma and flavour, with persistent but well balanced tannins; to 2010 and beyond). 1992 Chardonnay Bin 8081 (pleasant citrus/melon fruit with quite pronounced oak which will integrate with time; to 1995). 1992 Chablis Bin 8075 (made not from the traditional semillon — in Hunter Valley terms — but from chardonnay, which was particularly successful for Lindemans in 1992; smooth, gently peachy fruit and just a faint hint of spicy oak)

LINDEMANS KARADOC CA–BA Est 1963 $4.60–7.60 R 124, 195, 287 MURRAY R

Nangiloc Road, Karadoc via Mildura, Vic 3500 (050) 24 0303
fax (050) 24 0324
Open Mon–Sat 10–4.30 **Production** 3.5 million cases
Winemaker Phillip John (Chief)
Principal Wines Under Lindeman label Bin 65 Chardonnay leads the way; also Bin 50 Burgundy; under both Lindeman and Leo Buring Premier Selection label Chab, Chard, Rh Ries, Sauv Bl, Sem Chard, Cab Shir, Cab Sauv; also winery-linked Matthew Lang range Chab, Ries, Tram Ries, Wh Burg, Claret.
Best Vintages W '85, '87, '90, '91, '92 R '80, '81, '84, '85, '90
Summary Now the production centre for all of the Lindeman and Leo Buring wines, with the exception of special lines made in the Coonawarra and Hunter wineries. The biggest and most modern single facility in Australia allowing all important economies of scale, and the major processing centre for the beverage wine sector (casks, flagons and low-priced bottles) of the SABH empire. Its achievement in making four million bottles of Bin 65 Chardonnay a year is extraordinary given the quality and consistency of the wines.

LIRRALIRRA ESTATE CB–CB Est 1981 $8–15 SD YARRA V

Paynes Road, Lilydale, Vic 3140 (03) 735 0224

Open W'ends & hols 10–6 **Production** 350 cases
Winemaker Alan Smith, David Lloyd (Consultant)
Principal Wines Sem, Sauv Bl, Pinot, Cabernets.
Summary Off the beaten track and one of the lesser-known Yarra Valley wineries; owner Alan Smith originally intended to make a Sauternes-style wine from Semillon, Sauvignon Blanc and Muscadelle, but has found the conditions do not favour the development of botrytis and is hence producing dry red and white wines.

LITTLE RIVER NR Est 1934 $8–11 CD 150 SWAN V
Cnr West Swan Road & Forest Roads, West Swan, WA 6055
(09) 296 4462 fax (09) 296 1022
Open 7 days 10–5.30 **Production** 6500 cases
Winemaker Stephen Murfit
Principal Wines Chen, Chard, Saut, Verd, Cab Sauv, Shir, fortifieds.
Summary Following several quick changes of ownership (and of consultant winemakers) the former Glenalwyn has gone through a period of change, but is nonetheless aggressively marketing its wines ex cellar door offering, amongst other things, the only 'Spatlese Sauterne' I have ever heard of.

LITTLE'S CB–CB Est 1983 $11–15 CD SD HUNTER V
Lot 3 Palmers Lane, Pokolbin, NSW 2321 (049) 98 7626
fax (049) 98 7867
Open 7 days 10–4.30 **Production** 6000 cases
Winemaker Ian Little
Principal Wines Sem, Chard, Sem Chard, Gewurz, Pinot Herm, Shir, Cab Sauv, Port.
Best Vintages W '85, '86, '87, '88, '91 R '85, '86, '87, '88, '91
Summary A successful cellar door operation with friendly service and friendly wines: aromatic, fresh and sometimes slightly sweet white wines and light, inoffensive red wines. The Vintage Port can be excellent, and the Semillon and Semillon Chardonnay greatly benefit from a few years in bottle.

LOCHVIE NR Est 1985 $9.50 CD 296 YARRA V
28 Lavender Park Road, Eltham, Vic 3095 (03) 439 9444
fax (03) 439 3694
Open Sun 9–6, or by appointment **Production** 400 cases
Winemaker John Lewis
Principal Wine Cab Mer.
Summary A minute back-room winery; the 1992 wine won a bronze medal at the 1992 Lilydale Wine Show.

LONG GULLY ESTATE CB–CB Est 1982 $11.20–20 CD SD 296 YARRA V
Long Gully Road, Healesville, Vic 3777 (03) 807 4246
fax (03) 807 2213
Open W'ends 12–5 **Production** 25 000 cases
Winemaker Peter Florance
Principal Wines Chard, Sauv Bl, Sem, Ries, Mer, Pinot, Cab Sauv, Shir.
Best Vintages W '86, '87, '88, '90, '91 R '87, '88, '89, '90, '91
Summary An aggressively expanding producer having success in

both domestic and export markets with Chardonnay, Pinot Noir and Cabernet Sauvignon, which from time to time have enjoyed considerable show success. Quality can, however, be variable.

LONGLEAT C–B Est 1984 $7.95–15 CD 29, 184 GOULBURN V
Old Weir Road, Murchison, Vic 3610 (058) 26 2294
fax (058) 26 2510
Open Mon–Sat 9–5, Sun 10–5 **Production** 2500 cases
Winemaker Mark Schulz, Alister Purbrick (Consultant)
Principal Wines Ries, Sauv Bl, Chard, Spat, Cab Sauv, Shir, fortifieds, Sparkl.
Summary Very strongly flavoured and structured wines (made at Chateau Tahbilk) have a great deal of personality but not a great deal of finesse; the oaky but high flavoured '90 Chardonnay had success in various forums.

LOVEGROVE OF COTTLES BRIDGE B–B Est 1988 $10–22
CD SD YARRA V
1420 Heidelberg-Kinglake Road, Cottlesbridge, Vic 3099
(03) 718 1569 fax (03) 718 1028
Open W'ends & hols 11.30–6.00 **Production** 1000 cases approx
Winemaker Various contract
Principal Wines Chard, Pinot, Cab Mer; Dunmoochin is second label.
Summary A recently opened cellar door gives visitors to the pretty and distinctively different Diamond Valley sub-region a chance to taste some very well made wines.
Recommended Wines 1992 Chardonnay (clean, melon/fig fruit in typical restrained Yarra Valley style, and subtle oak; needs time in bottle and will repay cellaring; to 1998). 1991 Pinot Noir (complex stemmy/briary/sappy aromas with similar flavours on the palate but with a core of quite sweet fruit; good varietal character; to 1995).

LOWE FAMILY NR Est 1987 $11.40 R 68 MUDGEE
Ashbourne Vineyard, Tinja Lane, Mudgee, NSW 2850
(063) 72 1762
Open Not **Production** 1000 cases
Winemaker David Lowe
Principal Wines Chard.
Summary The family vineyard of former Rothbury winemaker David Lowe, making typically rich, full bodied Chardonnay, albeit in tiny quantities. I have not tasted recent vintages.

• LYRE BIRD HILL WINES NR Est 1986 $10–15 CD SD
SOUTH GIPPSLAND
Inverloch Road, Koonwarra, Vic 3594 phone and fax (056) 64 3204
Open W'ends & hols 11–5 **Production** 500 cases
Winemaker Owen Schmidt
Principal Wines Ries, Chard, Pinot, Shir.
Summary Owen and Robyn Schmidt have established a two hectare vineyard, half planted to Pinot Noir and the rest to tiny quantities of Riesling, Chardonnay, Cabernet Sauvignon, Traminer and Shiraz. Until the plantings come into full bearing, small quantities of additional fruit are purchased from other south Gippsland growers. A 1991 Shiraz showed promising spice, red cherry and mint fruit flavours.

McALISTER VINEYARDS B–B Est 1975 $17 CD 1͞7͞͞ 281
GIPPSLAND
Golden Beach Road, Longford, Vic 3851 phone and
fax (051) 49 7229
Open By appointment **Production** 600 cases
Winemaker Peter Edwards
Principal Wines A single wine, The McAlister, a blend of Cab
Sauv, Cab Franc Mer.
Summary The McAlister Vineyards are situated on the most
easterly finger of the Strzelecki Hills, and the climate is strongly
maritime influenced both by sea breezes and by the Gippsland lake
system. The plantings of 70% Cabernet Sauvignon and Cabernet
Franc and 30% Merlot were established with a Bordeaux-style wine
in mind, and owner/winemaker Peter Edwards has succeeded in his
aim.
Recommended Wine 1991 The McAlister (firm, lean, sinewy,
but with concentrated fruit and dark berry fruit background; to 2003).

McGUIGAN BROTHERS NR Est 1992 $7.95–11.95 R 82, 83,
314 HUNTER V
PO Box 31, Branxton, NSW 2335 (049) 98 7400 fax (049) 98 7401
Open 7 days 10–5 **Production** 120 000 cases
Winemaker Neil McGuigan
Principal Wines Bin 7000 Chard, First Harvest Sem Chard, Bin
6000 Verd, Black Shir, Bin 4000 Cab Sauv; more limited releases of
Shareholder Reserve wines.
Summary After successfully raising funds through a public share
issue in 1991, McGuigan Wines Limited released its first wines in
April 1992 without having by then built or acquired a winery. That
acquisition followed at the end of 1992, when McGuigan Brothers
purchased the Hungerford Hill Winery (although not the brand). The
style of the wines is unashamedly commercial and in no way aimed at
the connoisseur; the marketing genius of Brian McGuigan (supported
by wife Fay) is presently being focused on the United States.

McIVOR CREEK C–CB Est 1973 $7.85–12.95 CD 2 BENDIGO
Costerfield Road, Heathcote, Vic 3523 (054) 33 3000
fax (054) 33 2609
Open 7 days 10–5.30 **Production** 4000 cases
Winemaker Peter Turley
Principal Wines Ries, Sem, Sauv Bl, Shir, Cab Sauv, fortifieds.
Best Vintages W '86, '87, '89 R '87, '88, '89
Summary The beautifully situated McIvor Creek winery is well
worth a visit, and does offer wines in diverse styles of which the red
wines are the most regional. No recent tastings.

McMANUS NR Est 1972 $4–8 SD MIA
Rogers Road, Yenda, NSW 2681 (069) 68 1064
Open 7 days 9–5 **Production** 700 cases
Winemaker Dr David McManus
Principal Wines Chard, Dry White, Cab Sauv, Malb, Mer, Shir,
Pinot Malb Shir.
Summary An extremely idiosyncratic winery run by Griffith GP Dr
David McManus, his sister and other family members. Natural
winemaking methods lead to considerable variation in quality, but
the prices are from another era.

McWILLIAMS HANWOOD CB–A Est 1877 $5.80–15.40 R
90, 107, 205, 210, 319 MIA
Winery Road, Hanwood, NSW 2680 (069) 62 1333
fax (069) 62 1941
Open Mon–Sat 9–5.30, Sun 10–4 **Production** 1.4 million cases
Winemaker Jim Brayne

Principal Wines Under Inheritance label Chablis, Ries, Tram Ries, Wh Burg, Shir, Cab; under Hanwood label Ries, Chard, Cab Sauv; also limited volume premium regional releases from Coonawarra, Hilltops, Eden Valley etc.

Summary The best wines to emanate from the Hanwood winery are in fact those made from other regions, notably Hilltops in New South Wales, Coonawarra and Eden Valley; it is a strategy that has been successful and is likely to gain momentum.

Recommended Wines 1991 Barwang Cabernet Sauvignon (rich, ripe, mouthfilling cassis berry fruit with beautifully handled oak; exceptionally high quality wine). 1989 Semillon Sauternes (deep gold, with complex, strongly botrytis-influenced apricot and cumquat aromas and flavours; good length and balancing acidity; drink now). Bin MC11 Liqueur Muscat (dark green brown in colour; very concentrated and rich, showing obvious barrel age; plum pudding aromas and flavours; great length).

McWILLIAMS MT PLEASANT BA–BA Est 1880
$5.25–15.85 R 90, 107 HUNTER V
Marrowbone Road, Pokolbin, NSW 2321 (049) 98 7505
fax (049) 98 7761
Open Mon–Fr 9–4, w'ends 10–4 **Production** 80 000 cases
Winemaker Phillip Ryan

Principal Wines An ever-expanding series of wines now appear under various incarnations of the Mount Pleasant label; one needs a doctorate in wine label interpretation to fathom whether these are simply Mount Pleasant brands or whether they are indeed Hunter Valley sourced. Price is the best guide.

Best Vintages W '82, '86, '87, '90, '91 R '83, '86, '87, '91

Summary McWilliams Elizabeth (a pure Hunter wine) is now the only mature Hunter Semillon generally commercially available, and is an undervalued and underpriced treasure with a consistently superb show record. Under the skilled hand of Phillip Ryan, the small-run premium Mount Pleasant wines are also flourishing and worth the identification effort; Chardonnay, in particular, has enjoyed outstanding show success in recent years, but the small-volume Rosehill, OP & OH and similar Hermitage releases can also be excellent.

Recommended Wines 1987 Elizabeth Semillon (relatively forward and developed compared to the usual Elizabeth style, showing some honey and toast characters more akin to the classic Lindeman Hunter style; typically bone dry finish; now to 2000). 1986 Elizabeth Semillon (complex citrussy/smoky/honeyed aromas; clean, long, faintly herbaceous palate showing excellent varietal fruit with good acidity; now to 2005). 1991 Mountain Range Chardonnay (full yellow colour with soft, rich buttery/nutty aromas and flavours and a particularly rich, viscous finish; drink now). 1989 Homestead Chardonnay (big, rich, full blown buttery, toasty wine showing both regional character and bottle development; drink now).

• **MACEDON RIDGE NR** Est 1985 $35 ML 140 MACEDON
'Brook Farm', McDonalds Lane, Hesket, Vic 3442 (054) 27 0524
Open Not **Production** 500 cases
Winemaker John Ellis (Contract)
Principal Wines Sauv Bl, Pinot, Sparkl.
Summary Macedon Ridge is the venture of well known radio and
television personality Derryn Hinch. The immaculate vineyard was
established in 1985, producing its first commercial crop in 1991. The
1992 production was all directed to sparkling wine, due for release at
the end of 1993 at a suitably awe-inspiring price.

MADDENS LANE WINERY NR Est 1989 $15 ML SD YARRA V
Maddens Lane, Gruyere via Coldstream, Vic 3770 (059) 64 9279
Open By appointment **Production** 150 cases
Winemaker Various Contract
Principal Wines Sauv Bl Sem, Chard.
Summary A small and intermittent producer, selling its grapes in
some years and in others having the wine vinified. It is the former
Prigorjie Winery, now owned by Geoffrey Norris.

MADEW B–B Est 1984 $15 CD 18 CANBERRA
Furlong Road, Queanbeyan, ACT 2620 (06) 299 2303
Open W'ends & pub hols 11–5 **Production** 700 cases
Winemaker Greg Tilbrook
Principal Wines Ries, Chard, Cab Mer.
Summary There was a revolution in wine quality with the 1990
vintage; earlier vintages were very ordinary indeed, and in fact no wines
were released from '88 or '89. The appointment of Oenotec as
consultants did the trick; a superb '90 Chardonnay, with sophisticated
oak and full of peach and passionfruit, followed by a beautifully handled
crisp, toasty 1991 Rhine Riesling, show the potential of the winery.

MAGLIERI CA–B Est 1972 $2.50–13 CD 67, 78, 120 STHN VALES
Douglas Gully Road, McLaren Flat, SA 5171 (08) 383 0177
fax (08) 383 0136
Open Mon–Sat 9–4, Sun 12–4 **Production** 1800 tonnes
Winemaker John Loxton
Principal Wines Prolific Italian-accented range of generic and
varietal table wines; Spumante, fortified and flavoured wines; also
Ries, Sem Chard, Shir Cab Sauv.
Summary Maglieri has always described itself as the 'House of
Lambrusco', and just to prove the point produces a white Lambrusco
that might surprise the Italians but which adds another dimension to
the conventional red Lambrusco. Its wooded white wines tend to be
heavy handed and a little oily, the red wines at times rustic but
invariably generously proportioned and full of character.
Recommended Wines 1991 Cabernet Sauvignon (dense, ripe,
clean, sweet berry and chocolate bouquet; big chewy palate with dark
chocolate and blackcurrant fruit; 1997-2005). 1990 Shiraz (soft, ripe
and full in quintessential Southern Vales style; sweet plum and dark
chocolate fruit, round and mouthfilling; to 1998).

MAIN RIDGE ESTATE B–B Est 1975 $9–15 CD SD
MORNINGTON P
Lot 48 William Road, Red Hill, Vic 3937 (059) 89 2686

Open 7 days 12–5 **Production** 1000 cases
Winemaker Nat White
Principal Wines Chard, Pinot, Pinot Meunier, Cab Sauv.
Best Vintages W '86, '88, '90, '91, '92 R '86, '88, '90, '91, '92
Summary Nat White gives meticulous attention to every aspect of his viticulture and winemaking, doing annual battle with one of the coolest sites on the Peninsula. Only in the most favourable growing seasons (such as 1992) do the wines gain the richness and weight the market expects. The 1992 wines are highly recommended.

MAIR'S COALVILLE VINEYARD B–B Est 1985 $15 R SD
GIPPSLAND
Moe South Road, Moe South, Vic 3825 (051) 27 4229
fax (051) 27 2148
Open By appointment **Production** 250 cases
Winemaker Dr Stewart Mair
Principal Wines A single red wine, predominantly Cab Sauv with a little Cab Franc, Malbec and Mer labelled Coalville Red.
Best Vintages R '83, '84, '85, '87, '91
Summary Dr Stewart Mair has fashioned a remarkably consistent wine from his small vineyard, on the lean side perhaps, but with the elegance that comes from very cool-grown fruit.
Recommended Wines 1990 Coalville Red (cool-grown, firm red berry fruit with a touch of astringency and subtle oak; to 1997).

MALCOLM CREEK NR Est 1982 $14 R 133 ADELAIDE HILLS
Bonython Road, Kersbrook, SA 5231 (08) 389 3235
Open W'ends & hols 10–4 **Production** 400 cases
Winemaker Reg Tolley
Principal Wines Chard, Cab Sauv.
Summary The tiny hobby vineyard of Tolley's chief Reg Tolley, the vinous equivalent of a bus conductor's holiday; the wines are smooth, clean and somewhat simple, but are released with significant bottle age.

MANNING PARK NR Est 1979 $9.50–12.50 CD SD STHN VALES
Cnr Olivers & Chalkhill Roads, McLaren Vale, SA 5171
(08) 323 8209
Open 7 days 9–5 **Production** NFP
Winemaker Allan McLean
Principal Wines Ries, Fumé, Wh Burg, Saut, Herm, Cab Sauv, Port, Muscat.
Summary A low-key cellar door operation that places special emphasis on old (and expensive) tawny ports.

MARIENBERG CB–B Est 1966 $10.85–14 R 82 STHN VALES
c/o Hill International Wines (02) 630 5429 fax (02) 583 2729
Open Not **Production** 20 000 cases
Winemaker Various Contract
Principal Wines Chab, Chard, Ries, Sem Chard, Shir, Cab Sauv.
Summary The Marienberg brand was purchased by the Hill group of companies in late 1991 following the retirement of Ursula Pridham. Releases under the new regime have been honest, full flavoured wines.

MARION'S VINEYARD NR Est 1980 $15–18 CD SD TAMAR V
Foreshore Drive, Deviot, Tas 7275 (003) 94 7434 fax (003) 94 7434
Open 7 days 10–5 **Production** 1800 cases
Winemaker Mark Semmens
Principal Wines Chard, Muller, Pinot, Cab Sauv.
Best Vintages W '84, '86, '88, '90, '92 R '84, '86, '88, '90, '92
Summary Produces the exceptionally strong flavoured and strongly structured reds for which the Tamar Valley is noted, and which are quite unlike most other Tasmanian wines.
Recommended Wines 1990 Chardonnay (smooth fig and melon fruit with harmonious oak balance and integration; aging well in bottle; to 1996). 1988 Cabernet Sauvignon (primary fruit aromas and flavours softening into cedary characters, but with blackcurrant fruit still lingering and fine, supple tannins on a long finish; to 1999).

MARKEITA CELLARS NR Est 1974 SD CENT WEST NSW
Mitchell Highway, Neurea, NSW 2820 (068) 46 7277
Open 7 days 8.30–6 **Production** 1600 cases
Winemaker Keith Reinhard
Principal Wines Fronti, Shir, Cab Sauv, numerous Ports.
Summary Full-bodied red wines and fortifieds, some purchased elsewhere, are dispensed in containers of all shapes and sizes to both locals and passing tourists.

MARKWOOD ESTATE NR Est 1971 $10–18 CD SD NE VIC
Morris Lane, Markwood, Vic 3678 (057) 27 0361
Open 7 days 9–5 **Production** 900 cases
Winemaker Rick Morris
Principal Wines Chard, Cab Sauv, Shir, Muscat, Tokay, Port.
Summary A member of the famous Morris family, Rick Morris shuns publicity and relies virtually exclusively on cellar door sales for what is a small output.

MARRON CREEK NR Est 1988 $12.50 ML SD GRT SOUTHERN
Frankland-Rocky Gully Road, Frankland, WA 6396 (098) 55 2278
Open Not **Production** 400 cases
Winemaker Kim Hart
Principal Wines Chard, Cab Sauv.
Summary Marron Creek is the weekend and out-of-hours occupation for Alkoomi winemaker Kim Hart and her husband. The fleshy, red berry 1989 Cabernet Sauvignon, with its sophisticated American oak, is an outstanding wine, the 1990 Chardonnay somewhat idiosyncratic but good.

MARSH ESTATE B–B Est 1971 $11–$14 CD SD HUNTER V
Deasey Road, Pokolbin, NSW 2321 (049) 98 7587
fax (049) 98 7884
Open Mon–Fri 10–4.30, w'ends 10–5 **Production** 4000 cases
Winemaker Peter Marsh
Principal Wines Chard, Sem, Tram Ries, Champ, Saut, Herm, Cab Sauv, Port.
Best Vintages W '83, '86, '87, '89, '91 R '83, '86, '87, '89, '91
Summary Through sheer consistency, value-for-money and unrelenting hard work, the Marsh family (who purchased the former Quentin Estate in 1978) has built up a sufficiently loyal cellar door

and mail-list clientele to allow all of the considerable production to be sold ex-winery. Wine style is always direct, with oak playing a minimal role and prolonged cellaring paying handsome dividends.

MASSONI BA–B Est 1984 $22 R 72 MORNINGTON
Mornington-Flinders Road, Red Hill, Vic 3937 (059) 89 2060
fax (059) 89 2348
Open By appointment **Production** 1750 cases
Winemaker Contract
Principal Wines Chard, Pinot, Cab Sauv, Sparkl.
Summary Highly regarded former Melbourne restaurateur Leon Massoni has formed a joint venture with Yellowglen founder Ian Home, which will lead to a significant increase in the output of the Massoni wines as well as the release of a sparkling wine under the 'Home' brand. One of the stated objectives is also to increase the complexity of the Chardonnay — a wine that in many vintages has been impressively complex in any event.
Recommended Wines 1991 Chardonnay (full flavoured wine with peach and citrus flavours and pronounced toasty barrel ferment oak; to 1995). 1991 Pinot Noir (quite firm, with appreciable charred oak; fairly tight, sappy style with great structure for ageing; to 1996).

MAXWELL CB–B Est 1979 $6–14 CD 176 STHN VALES
26 Kangarilla Road, McLaren Vale, SA 5171 (08) 323 8200
fax (08) 323 8900
Open 7 days 10–5 **Production** 4000 cases
Winemaker Mark Maxwell
Principal Wines Chard, Sem, Sauv Bl, Shir, Cab Mer, Cab Sauv, Port, Mead.
Summary Full flavoured, rather traditional wines (and excellent mead) are the order of the day, although Mark Maxwell is forever experimenting, dropping some styles and introducing others.
Recommended Wine 1992 Semillon (pungent, crisp, grassy, unoaked style; the 12.4% alcohol gives the wine weight and feel on the palate, though it remains trenchantly grassy; drink now).

MEADOWBANK CB–B Est 1974 $14–15 CD 14, 48, 103, 258 DERWENT
Glenora, Derwent Valley, Tas 7410 (002) 86 1269
fax (002) 86 1133
Open 7 days 11–5 **Production** 2000 cases
Winemaker Greg O'Keefe
Principal Wines Chard, Ries, Pinot, Cab Sauv, Shir.
Summary The Ellis family have been grape growers for many years, originally selling to Hickinbotham Winemakers but now producing their own wines, with former Normans' winemaker Greg O'Keefe in charge.
Recommended Wine 1992 Riesling (clean, crisp, herbaceous fruit with well balanced acidity; well made wine; to 1996).

MERRICKS ESTATE B–B Est 1978 $19.95 R 68 MORNINGTON P
Thompsons Lane, Merricks, Vic 3916 (03) 612 7285 fax (03) 629 4035
Open First w'end month 12–5 **Production** 2000 cases
Winemaker Alex White

Principal Wines Chard, Shir, Cab Sauv.

Summary Melbourne solicitor George Kefford, together with wife Jacquie, runs Merricks Estate as a weekend and holiday enterprise as a relief from professional practice. Right from the outset it has produced very distinctive, spicy, cool climate Shiraz which has accumulated an impressive array of show trophies and gold medals.

Recommended Wine 1991 Chardonnay (attractive, clean melon and peach fruit with minimal oak impact; good mouthfeel and balance; to 1995).

• MERRIVALE WINES NR Est 1993 $ CD SD STHN VALES
Olivers Road, McLaren Vale, SA 5171 (08) 323 9196
Open Fri–Sun & pub hols 11–5, Mon 1–3 **Production** NFP
Winemaker Brian Light
Summary Brian Light, long-term (and continuing) winemaker at Normans, with wife Kay, has purchased the Merrivale winery and revived the operation after a lapse of some years. With Brian Light's unquestioned skills as a winemaker and his family's access to high quality Adelaide Hills fruit Merrivale should be a label to follow.

MIDDLETON WINERY NR Est 1979 $7.50–10 CD 80 STHN VALES
Flagstaff Hill Road, Middleton, SA 5213 (085) 55 4136
fax (085) 55 4108
Open Fri–Sun 10–5 **Production** 5000 cases
Winemaker Nigel Catt
Principal Wines Ries, Sauv Bl, Sem Sauv Bl, Cab, Herm.
Summary Nigel Catt has demonstrated his winemaking skills at Andrew Garrett and elsewhere, so wine quality should be good; despite its decade of production, I have never seen or tasted its wines.

MILDARA BA–A Est 1955 $8–24 R 110, 210 COONAWARRA
Main Penola-Naracoorte Road, Coonawarra, SA 5263
(087) 36 3339
Open 7 days 9–5 **Production** 150 000 cases
Winemaker Gavin Hogg
Principal Wines Jamieson's Run red is a volume brand leader, Jamieson's Run Chardonnay is a later addition. Alexanders is top of the range Bordeaux blend; also varietal Herm and Cab Sauv.
Best Vintages R '81, '82, '86, '88, '90
Summary In a space of four vintages Jamieson's Run red was established as one of Australia's mid-price brand leaders, contributing handsomely to group profit and picking up a Jimmy Watson Trophy along the way, attesting to the outstanding winemaking skills behind it. The other wines are fully representative of region and price.
Recommended Wines 1990 Jamiesons Run (fragrant and sophisticated, with spicy American oak woven into bright, fresh fruit and appropriately light tannins; excellent value; drink now). 1992 Jamieson's Run Chardonnay (fresh, clean gentle peach and melon fruit; subtle oak; harmonious, light to medium bodied wine; by far the best Chardonnay under the Jamiesons label to date). 1988 Alexanders (cedary cigar box aroma and flavours with dark, briary berry fruit on the palate; some Coonawarra 'greens'; to 1996).

MILDARA CB–BA Est 1888 $7.40 R 110, 210 MURRAY R
Wentworth Road, Merbein, Vic 3505 (050) 25 2303
fax (050) 25 3300
Open 7 days 9–5 **Production** 1 million cases
Winemaker Alan Harris
Principal Wines Church Hill Chard, Fumé Bl, Cab Mer; also
makes fine Sherries (Chestnut Teal, George and Supreme) and
superb Pot Still Brandy.
Summary A somewhat antiquated Merbein facility remains the
overall group production centre following its acquisition of Wolf
Blass, although all of its premium wines are sourced from and made at
Coonawarra. The Church Hill range is dependable, the Sherries
good.

MILLINUP ESTATE NR Est 1989 $11–14.50 CD SD GRT
SOUTHERN
RMB 1280 Porongurup Road, Porongurup, WA 6324 (098) 53 1105
Open Mon–Fri 10–4 **Production** 220 cases
Winemaker John Wade (Contract)
Principal Wines Ries, Cab Mer.
Summary The Millinup Estate vineyard was planted in 1978, when
it was called Point Creek. Owners Peter and Lesley Thorn purchased
it in 1989, renaming it and having the limited production vinified by
John Wade at Plantagenet.

MILNATHORT NR Est 1983 $9–10 ML SD STHN TAS
Channel Highway, Birchs Bay, Tas 7162 (vineyard only); postal
PO Box 4, Woodbridge, Tas 7162 (002) 67 4750 fax (002) 67 4601
Open Not **Production** 80 cases
Winemaker Andrew Hood (Contract)
Principal Wines Ries, Cab Sauv.
Summary Although production is minuscule, quality has been
consistently high over the 1990 and 1991 vintages. The Riesling is
well made, but the interesting wine from this far southern vineyard is
Cabernet Sauvignon: clearly, the vineyard enjoys favourable ripening
conditions.
Recommended Wines 1991 Cabernet Sauvignon (complex and
stylish, soft, plummy bouquet with similar fruit flavours on the palate
together with a touch of spice; does fall away ever so slightly on the
finish; to 1997).

MINTARO WINES CB–B Est 1986 $9–12 CD SD CLARE V
Leasingham Road, Mintaro, SA 5415 (088) 43 9046
Open 7 days 9–5 **Production** 2000 cases
Winemaker James Pearson
Principal Wines Ries, Cab Sauv.
Summary Has produced some very good Rhine Riesling over the
years, developing well in bottle. The Cabernet Sauvignon, by
contrast, has tended to dullness and/or bitterness.

MINTON GROVE C–C Est 1970 $8–9.95 R 43, 232 ADELAIDE
PLAINS
Heaslip Road, Angle Vale, SA 5117 (08) 284 7700
fax (08) 284 7711
Open Not **Production** 14 000 cases

Winemaker Lindsay Stanley
Principal Wines Chard, Sem Chenin, Sauv Bl Colomb, Shir, Cab Sauv.
Summary Minton Grove is now the principal domestic label of Anglesey Estate; the Angelsey Estate label is used in Victoria and in export markets, but the moderately priced wines are in fact the same under either label.

MINYA, THE NR Est 1974 $8–12.50 SD GEELONG
Minya Lane, Connewarre, Vic 3227 (052) 64 1397
Open Hols & w'ends, or by appointment
Production 1600 cases
Winemaker Susan Marwood
Principal Wines Gewurz, Grenache, Cab Sauv, Mer, Shir.
Summary Geoff Dans first planted vines in 1974 on his family's dairy farm, followed by further plantings in 1982 and 1988. I have not tasted any of the wines.

MIRAMAR B–B Est 1977 $7–15 CD SD MUDGEE
Henry Lawson Drive, Mudgee, NSW 2850 (063) 73 3874
fax (063) 73 3854
Open 7 days 9–5 **Production** 7000 cases
Winemaker Ian MacRae
Principal Wines Sem, Sem Chard, Chard, Sauv Bl, Ries, Tram Ries, Rosé, Pinot, Shir, Cab Sauv, Port.
Best Vintages W '82, '84, '86, '87, '91 R '82, '84, '85, '86, '91
Summary Has achieved fame for highly concentrated, tangy, complex Chardonnay which ages superbly; the '81 was a gold medal and trophy winner in 1990, and the '88 is headed down the same track. Overall, the white wines are better than the reds, but the latter do benefit from cellaring.

MIRANDA CA–A Est 1939 $2.50–$25 CD 35, 111, 180, 205, 254 MIA
57 Jondaryan Avenue, Griffith, NSW 2680 (069) 62 4033
fax (069) 62 6944
Open 7 days 9–5 **Production** Over 1 000 000 cases
Winemaker Shayne Cunningham
Principal Wines Under premium Wyangan label Chard, Sem, Ries, Sauv Bl, Cab Mer, Sauterne, Herm; numerous other table and fortified wines under Miranda and Mirrool Creek labels.
Summary In recent years, Miranda has produced some startlingly good wines, no doubt due to its purchases of Clare and Barossa Valley grapes, followed by its acquisition of the Barossa Rovalley winery. Some of the Chardonnays in particular have scored very highly in shows, but it is not always easy to tell which wine ends up under which label; seemingly, both Mirrool Creek and Wyangan ranges have done extremely well.
Recommended Wines 1992 Wyangan Estate Chardonnay (stylish, elegant wine with tight fruit and particularly impressive length of flavour; to 1994). 1990 Wyangan Estate Botrytis Semillon (extremely rich bouquet with strong apricot and dried peach aromas and flavour, balanced by cleansing acidity; to 1994). Mirrool Creek Vat 91 Cabernet Shiraz (attractive, clean and fresh spicy berry flavours, soft tannins; drink now while it retains its freshness).

MISTY VALLEY WINES NR Est 1986 $12–15 ML SD YARRA V
Lot 1 Greenwood Lane, Steel's Creek, Vic 3775 (059) 625 083
fax (03) 853 5929
Open Not **Production** 400 cases
Winemaker John Ellis (Contract)
Principal Wines Gewurz, Chard, Pinot.
Summary Both the Gewurztraminer and the Chardonnay from 1990
left no doubt about the potential of this small but beautiful vineyard;
the wines are principally sold through the mailing list, the address
being PO Box 240, Healesville, Vic 3777.

MITCHELL CELLARS B–B Est 1975 $10–14 CD 30, 80, 139,
150, 204, 271 CLARE V
Hughes Park Road, Sevenhill via Clare, SA 5453 (088) 43 4258
fax (088) 43 4340
Open 7 days 10–4 **Production** 12 000 cases
Winemaker Andrew Mitchell, Neil Pike
Principal Wines Ries, Sem (wood aged), Shir, Cab Sauv.
Best Vintages W '80, '82, '84, '90, '92 R '80, '82, '84, '86, '88,
'90
Summary A Clare Valley stalwart, producing typically long-lived
Rieslings and Cabernet Sauvignons in mainstream regional style.
Recommended Wines 1992 Semillon (clean, firm tangy/lemony
fruit with subtle oak; has excellent mouthfeel and length; great
development potential; to 2000). 1991 Cabernet Sauvignon
(unusually full, ripe and fleshy, with masses of body and quite
pronounced tannins; to 2005).

MITCHELTON CA–BA Est 1974 $4.95–22.95 CD 65, 120, 191,
209, 213, 217 GOULBURN
Mitchelltown via Nagambie, Vic 3608 (057) 94 2710
fax (057) 94 2615
Open Mon–Sat 9–5, Sun & hols 10–5
Production 1500 tonnes (95 000 case equivalent)
Winemaker Don Lewis
Principal Wines Ries, Sauv Bl, Marsanne, Chard, Cab Sauv, Shir,
Pinot, Sparkl; Print Label for each vintage's top red wine; Classic
Release for cellar-aged releases of back vintage.
Best Vintages W '80, '81, '86, '90, '91 R '82, '86, '87, '90, '91
Summary Since the Schelmerdine family acquired a substantial
interest in Mitchelton in 1991, thereby entering into partnership with
the Valmorbida family, the fortunes of Mitchelton have been on the
ascendant. New chief executive Chris Ainstee brings international
experience to the job, and nowadays 70% of production is exported.
Recommended Wines 1992 Riesling (fine, fragrant passionfruit
lime and other citrus aromas and flavour; very well balanced; on track
record will age well; to 1997). 1992 Sauvignon Blanc (a surprise
package, offering fragrant, gooseberry fruit with passionfruit
overtones; quite sweet, although this appears to be fruit rather than
residual sugar sweetness; drink now). 1991 Reserve Cabernet
Sauvignon (dense colour; full, concentrated, dark-fruited bouquet;
rich, concentrated, dark berry fruit flavour with persistent tannins,
high quality; 1997-2005). 1990 Reserve Marsanne (in typical style,
driven by its strong spicy/nutmeg oak, but there is fruit there; drink
now). 1991 Preece Cabernet Sauvignon (an unusual wine, with

marked cedary/cigar box overtones to dark berry fruit with delicately astringent tannins; to 1996).

MONBULK DC–C Est 1984 $8.50–12.90 CD SD YARRA V
Macclesfield Road, Monbulk, Vic 3793 (03) 756 6965
Open W'ends 12–5 **Production** 1000 cases
Winemaker Paul Jabornik
Principal Wines Chard, Ries, Pinot, Cab Sauv, Shir; also kiwifruit wines.
Summary Originally concentrated on kiwifruit wines, but now extending to table wines; the very cool Monbulk sub-region should be capable of producing wines of distinctive style, but the table wines are (unfortunately) not of the same standard as the kiwifruit wines.

MONICHINO CB–B Est 1962 $7–21 CD 175 NTH GOULBURN R
Berrys Road, Katunga, Vic 3640 (058) 64 6452 fax (058) 64 6538
Open 7 days 9–5 **Production** 11 000 cases
Winemaker Carlo Monichino
Principal Wines Chard, Fumé, Cab Sauv, Cab Shir, Cab Franc, Cab Mal, Shir, fortifieds.
Summary An altogether surprising winery that quietly makes very clean, fresh white wines in which the fruit character has been carefully preserved.

MONTARA CB–B Est 1970 $7–14.50 CD 50, 72, 120 GRT WESTERN
Chalambar Road, Ararat, Vic 3377 (053) 52 3868
fax (053) 52 4968
Open Mon–Sat 9.30–5, Sun 12–4 **Production** 8000 cases
Winemaker Mike McRae
Principal Wines Chard, Ries, Ondenc, Chasselas, Pinot, Shir, Cab Sauv, Port.
Best Vintages W '85, '86, '88, '90, '91 R '84, '86, '88, '90, '91
Summary Reliable maker of full flavoured, soft and generous wines which anomalously produces Pinot Noir of, at times, exceptional style and varietal character. The '89 was another success, although increasing competition from southern Victoria with this variety may prove difficult to overcome in the future.

MONTROSE B–A Est 1974 $6.95–9.95 R 122, 227 MUDGEE
Henry Lawson Drive, Mudgee, NSW 2850 (063) 73 3853
fax (063) 73 3795
Open Mon–Fri 9–4, w'ends 10–4 **Production** 50 000 cases
Winemaker Robert Paul
Principal Wines Chard, Chab, Wh Burg, Sem, Poet's Corner Dry White, Saut, Shir, Poet's Corner Dry Red, Cab Sauv.
Best Vintages W '84, '86, '89, '90, '91 R '82, '86, '89, '90, '91, '93
Summary A small piece of the Orlando/Wyndham empire, acting partly as a grape and bulk wine source for that empire and partly as a quality producer in its own right, making typically full flavoured whites and deep coloured reds.
Recommended Wines 1992 Poet's Corner Dry White (rich, sweet, gently tropical fruit aromas with some passionfruit and tangy citrus flavours, finishing with good acidity). 1992 Poet's Corner Dry

Red (attractive, fresh red berry fruits, with a hint of spice; of light to medium weight and soft tannins; early drinking style).

MOONDAH BROOK ESTATE BA–BA Est 1968 $10.10–18 R 22–26, 85, 321 SWAN V
Gingin (vineyard only), WA 6503
Open Not **Production** 90 000 cases
Winemaker Paul Lapsley
Principal Wines Chard, Chenin, Verdelho, Cab Sauv.
Summary Part of the Houghton Wine Group which has its own special character as it principally draws its fruit from the Gingin vineyard, 70 km north of the Swan Valley. Recently it has excelled even its own reputation for reliability with some quite lovely wines.
Recommended Wines 1992 Chenin Blanc (floral, intense fruit with tropical, passionfruit and fruit salad flavours, lively and fresh; as good a Chenin Blanc as you will find; drink now). 1991 Cabernet Sauvignon (fine, clean, red berry fruit in elegant, lighter style; soft tannins; to 1995). 1992 Chardonnay (tangy and stylish bouquet, with a subliminal hint of toasty oak; not especially weighty or complex palate, but the sort of wine to encourage the second glass; now to 1995). 1992 Verdelho (fresh, very protected fruit with hints of passionfruit; crisp acidity on the finish; drink now).

MOOREBANK ESTATE NR Est 1987 $13.50–16.50 CD 12 HUNTER V
Palmers Lane, Pokolbin, NSW 2321 (049) 98 7610
Open Wed–Sun 10–4 **Production** 1300 cases
Winemaker Iain Riggs (Contract)
Principal Wines Chard, Sem, Gewurz, Merlot.
Best Vintages W '87, '88, '89, '91
Summary A newly opened winery with contract winemaking by Iain Riggs of Brokenwood.
Recommended Wine 1992 Chardonnay (big, broad, warm style with honeyed/peachy fruit; drink now).

MOORILLA ESTATE B–B Est 1958 $13.50–19.50 CD 2, 149, 181 DERWENT
655 Main Road, Berriedale, Tas 7011 (002) 49 2949
fax (002) 49 4093
Open 7 days 10–6 **Production** 12 000 cases
Winemaker Julian Alcorso
Principal Wines Ries, Chard, Gewurz, Cab Sauv, Pinot.
Best Vintages W '81, '87, '89, '91, '92 R '81, '84, '90, '91, '92
Summary While Julian Alcorso remains as winemaker, majority ownership of Moorilla has passed out of the family. The good news, as it were, of the change of ownership has been the injection of substantial additional equity that, amongst other things, has allowed the purchase of the St Matthias Vineyard which will henceforth supply grapes to Moorilla.
Recommended Wines 1992 Chardonnay (sophisticated wine with attractive fresh melon and fig fruit; deftly handled touch of spicy oak and typically fine acidity; to 1997). 1992 Rhine Riesling (crisp, herbaceous style with a touch of residual sugar to balance the fractionally green fruit; very well made). 1992 Gewurztraminer (clean and fresh; although light in body, does have beautifully articulated

lychee and spice varietal character). 1990 Cabernet Sauvignon (clean, fresh, direct red berry and cassis fruit and quite firm tannins; an impressive wine; to 1998).

MOOROODUC ESTATE A–BA Est 1983 $20.95 R 68, 181
MORNINGTON P
Derril Road, Moorooduc, Vic 3936 (03) 696 4130 (03) 696 2841
Open First w'end each month 12–5 **Production** 1600 cases
Winemaker Dr Richard McIntyre
Principal Wines Chard, Pinot, Cab Sauv.
Best Vintages W and R '86, '88, '90, '91, '92
Summary Dr Richard McIntyre, originally with consultant Nat White, produces one of the richest, most complex Chardonnays in the region, with grapefruit/peach fruit set against sumptuous spicy oak; the '88, '89 and '90 Chardonnays were of the highest quality. The 1990 Cabernet Sauvignon, too, was an excellent wine for the year, but was surpassed as a young wine by the great 1991 Cabernet Sauvignon with its lush, perfectly ripened cassis-accented fruit.
Recommended Wines 1992 Chardonnay (tremendously rich, full, toasty honeyed wine, with the texture increased by partial malolactic fermentation; early developing). 1992 Pinot Noir (very deep colour, with strong, quite minty fruit; fractionally hard on the finish).

MORNINGSIDE NR Est 1980 $10–12.50 ML SD STHN TAS
Middle Tea Tree Road, Tea Tree, Tas 7017 (002) 68 1748
Open Not **Production** 120 cases
Winemaker Peter Bosworth
Principal Wines Ries, Pinot, Cab Sauv.
Summary The name Morningside was given to the old property on which the vineyard stands because it gets the morning sun first. The property on the other side of the valley was known as 'Eveningside' and, consistently with the observation of the early settlers, the Morningside grapes achieve full maturity with good colour and varietal flavour. Production is, as yet, tiny but will increase as the 1.5 hectare vineyard matures.

MORNINGTON VINEYARDS B–B Est 1988 $16 R 175
MORNINGTON P
Moorooduc Road, Mornington, Vic 3931 phone and
fax (059) 74 2097
Open Not **Production** 800 cases
Winemaker Tod Dexter (Contract)
Principal Wines Chard, Pinot.
Summary As with so many Mornington Peninsula vineyards, a high degree of viticultural expertise, care and attention coupled with skilled contract winemaking has paid dividends. If there is to be a criticism, it is in the lack of concentration of flavour, something that will come as the vineyards mature.

MORRIS A–A Est 1859 $4.80–32 CD 122, 236 NE VIC
Mia Mia Road, Rutherglen, Vic 3685 (060) 26 7303
fax (060) 26 7445
Open Mon–Sat 9–5, Sun 10–5 **Production** 32 000 cases
Winemaker David Morris
Principal Wines Sem, Botrytis Sem, Chard, Sauv Bl, Ries, Cab

Sauv, Shir, Durif, Muscat, Tokay, Port, Sherry.

Summary One of the greatest of the fortified winemakers, some would say the greatest. If you wish to test that view, try the Old Premium Muscat and Old Premium Tokay which, at $32 a bottle (cellar door), are absolute bargains given their age and quality. The table wines are dependable, the white wines all being made by owner Orlando. The Durif is a winery specialty of awesome power and longevity.

Recommended Wines Old Premium Liqueur Muscat (deep, green-tinged colour with intensely concentrated, raisined aroma and plum pudding flavours, intensely sweet on the mid palate but finishes relatively dry). Old Premium Tokay (mahogany and olive green colour with rich, concentrated cold tea and butterscotch aroma and flavour; slightly more elegant in style than the Muscat, and preferred by many winemakers for that precise reason).

MOSS BROTHERS CB–B Est 1985 $13–18 CD 125

MARGARET R
Caves Road, Willyabrup, WA 6280 (097) 55 6270
fax (097) 55 6298

Open 7 days 10–5.30 **Production** 4500 cases

Winemakers Jane & David Moss

Principal Wines Chard, Sem, Sauv Bl, Cabs, Moses Rock White and Red.

Summary After a somewhat uncertain start with the early vintages, has improved markedly in terms of both consistency and quality. The improbable blend of cabernet and pinot noir works despite itself.

Recommended Wines 1992 Cabernet Pinot Noir (of light to medium weight with very fresh red berry fruit and just a hint of leafiness; subtle oak and smooth overall texture; to 1995). 1991 Cabernet Merlot (bright colour, clean, cool-grown cabernet fruit aroma and flavour; fresh, firm palate, though slightly short on the finish).

MOSS WOOD A–BA Est 1969 $18–26 R 20, 65, 126, 155, 171, 193, 288 MARGARET R

Metricup Road, Willyabrup via Cowaramup, WA 6284
(097) 55 6266 fax (097) 55 6303

Open By appointment **Production** 4500 cases

Winemaker Keith Mugford

Principal Wines Sem (wood mat), Sem, Chard, Cab Sauv, Pinot.

Best Vintages W '83, '85, '87, '88, '90 R '83, '85, '87, '90, '91

Summary Widely regarded as one of the best wineries in the region, capable of producing glorious Semillon (the best outside the Hunter Valley) in both oaked and unoaked forms, unctuous Chardonnay and elegant, gently herbaceous, superfine Cabernet Sauvignon which lives for many years.

Recommended Wines 1992 Chardonnay (stylish wine with spicy oak and melon and citrus fruit; good acidity and length; now to 1998). 1992 Wood Matured Semillon (well integrated and subtle smoky-spice oak complements perfectly balanced, faintly herbaceous fruit; 1996-2005). 1991 Cabernet Sauvignon (complex amalgam of aromas, with briary dark fruits, good depth and extract on the palate, with dark berry fruit, subtle oak and strong tannins; to 2005). 1992 Semillon (hints of honey underlain by some grassy/herbal fruit; should develop well; to 2000).

MOUNT ALEXANDER D–CD Est 1984 $10–14 CD SD
BENDIGO
Calder Highway, North Harcourt, Vic 3453 (054) 74 2262
fax (054) 74 2553
Open 7 days 10–5.30 **Production** 6000 cases
Winemaker Keith Walkden
Principal Wines A wide range of various table wines, sparkl,
fortifieds, meads and liqueurs.
Summary A substantial operation with 12 hectares of vineyards
planted to all the right varieties. Wine quality, unhappily, leaves
much to be desired.

MOUNT ANAKIE C–C Est 1968 $10–18 R SD GEELONG
Staughton Vale Road, Anakie, Vic 3221 (052) 84 1452
fax (052) 84 1405
Open Tues–Sun 11–6 **Production** 8000 cases
Winemaker Otto Zambelli
Principal Wines Ries, Chard, Sem, Dolcetto, Cab, Cab Franc,
Shir, Tawny Port.
Summary Also known as Zambelli Estate, and has produced some
excellent wines (under its various ownerships and winemakers), all
distinguished by their depth and intensity of flavour. The most
recently tasted wines were decidedly unconvincing, a pity given the
infectious enthusiasm of owner Otto Zambelli.

MOUNT AVOCA B–B Est 1978 $9.50–14.60 CD 140–144, 270
PYRENEES
Moates Lane, Avoca, Vic 3467 (054) 65 3282 fax (054) 65 3544
Open Mon–Fri 9–5, w'ends 10–5 **Production** 11 000 cases
Winemakers John Barry, Rodney Morrish
Principal Wines Sauv Bl, Chard, Sem, Cab Sauv, Shir.
Best Vintages W '87, '88, '90, '91, '92 R '87, '88, '90, '91, '92
Summary A substantial winery that has for long been one of the
stalwarts of the Pyrenees region.
Recommended Wines 1991 Chardonnay (tangy, with some
volatile lift and a touch of charry oak on the bouquet, and bite and
flavour to the palate; to 1996). 1990 Shiraz (of light to medium weight
with clean, bright, fresh berry fruit; something of a departure in style
for Mount Avoca). 1989 Cabernet Sauvignon (concentrated,
gamey/earthy, ripe, dark berry fruit and pronounced tannins; to 1998).

MOUNT CHALAMBAR B–B Est 1978 $10–13 R CD 48, 55
GRT WESTERN
Tatyoon Road, Ararat, Vic 3377 (053) 54 3207
Open See Mt Langi Ghiran **Production** 1000 cases
Winemaker Trevor Mast
Principal Wines Ries, Chard, Sparkl.
Summary Sparkling wine making has, it seems, gone into recess,
leaving the focus of attention on full flavoured, lime-accented Rhine
Riesling and barrel-fermented Chardonnay.

MOUNT DUNEED C–C Est 1970 $15–17 CD 72 GEELONG
Feehan's Road, Mount Duneed, Vic 3216 (052) 64 1281
Open Sat 9–5, Sun 12–5 **Production** 1000 cases

Winemaker Ken Campbell
Principal Wines Sem Sauv Bl, Ries, Botrytis Sem, Cab Malb, Cab Sauv.
Summary Rather idiosyncratic wines are the order of the day, some of which can develop surprisingly well in bottle; the Botrytis Noble Rot Semillon has, from time to time, been of very high quality.

MOUNT HELEN CB–CB Est 1978 $14.50–19.50 R 42, 127, 166, 171, 181, 278 CENTRAL GOULBURN

Strathbogie Ranges (vineyard only), Vic 3666 (054) 821 911
Open See Tisdall **Production** 6500 cases
Winemaker Toni Stockhausen
Principal Wines Chard, Ries, Sauv Bl, LH Gewurz, Cab Mer, Pinot, Sparkl.
Best Vintages W '84, '86, '87, '90, '92 R '84, '86, '87, '88, '90
Summary Mount Helen has always promised a great deal, and occasionally delivers it. For reasons I do not profess to understand wine quality is not always what it should be, with some extreme winemaker interpretations appearing on the one hand and vineyard problems on the other. Mount Helen, incidentally, is a separate vineyard and brand owned by Tisdall, and — since mid 1993 — indirectly by Mildara Blass.
Recommended Wines 1992 Sauvignon Blanc (light, crisp, faintly herbal seafood style which really needs a touch more fruit sweetness but is well enough made). 1990 Cabernet Merlot (clean but light fresh berry bouquet; rather more weight on the palate, with similar fresh red berry fruit and faintly dusty tannins; has four gold medals to its credit; to 1998).

MOUNT HORROCKS CB–CB Est 1982 $10–14 CD 16, 105, 115, 118, 133 CLARE V

Mintaro Road, Leasingham, SA 5452 (088) 43 0005
fax (088) 43 0150
Open 7 days 10–5 **Production** 3500 cases
Winemaker Jeffrey Grosset (Contract — previous)
Principal Wines Ries, Sem, Wood Aged Sem, Chard, Cab Mer, Cordon Cut Riesling.
Best Vintages W '82, '85, '86, '89, '91 R '82, '85, '87, '90, '91
Summary Mount Horrocks was sold by its founders, the Ackland brothers, in mid 1993; at the time of going to press, the future direction of the winery was uncertain.
Recommended Wines 1992 Cordon Cut Riesling (lime, peach and passionfruit aroma and flavour with good balancing acidity; not complex but well balanced; to 1995). 1991 Cabernet Merlot (fresh fruit aromas with hints of earth and caramel-tinged oak; smooth, fresh red berry and mint flavours with good acidity; needing time to develop when first released; to 1997).

MOUNT HURTLE BA–BA Est 1897 $9–12 CD 147, 169, 209, 289 STHN VALES

Cnr Pimpala & Byards Roads, Reynella, SA 5161 (08) 381 6877 fax (08) 322 2244
Open Mon–Fri 9–5, Sun 12–5 **Production** 21 000 cases (total group production)
Winemaker Geoff Merrill

Principal Wines Sem Sauv Bl, Cab Sauv.
Best Vintages W '86, '87, '89, '90, '91 **R** '84, '85, '86, '88, '90, '91

Summary Once seen, the stridently flamboyant label of Mount Hurtle is not easily forgotten, which is no doubt precisely what Geoff Merrill intended. The style of the wine in the bottle is altogether more restrained and elegant, with the accent on freshness and varietal clarity. The name is that of the beautiful century-old stone winery at which all the Merrill brands are made.

Recommended Wines 1992 Sauvignon Blanc (fresh, clearly articulated varietal Sauvignon with gently crisp fruit; direct un-oaked seafood style; drink now). 1991 Chardonnay (of medium weight, with clean, soft melon and peach fruit, and gentle oak; pleasant easy-drinking style). 1992 Grenache (vivid bright red with fresh red cherry fruit, and a nice touch of sappiness to give a cleansing cut to the finish; drink now).

MOUNT IDA B–B Est 1978 $16.50 R 42, 127, 166, 171, 181 BENDIGO

Northern Highway, Heathcote, Vic 3523 (054) 82 1911
Open At Tisdall **Production** 1500 cases
Winemaker Toni Stockhausen
Principal Wines Shir.
Best Vintages '82, '85, '90, '91

Summary Established by the famous artist Leonard French and Dr James Munro, but purchased by Tisdall after the 1987 bushfires. Up to the time of the fires wonderfully smooth, rich red wines with almost voluptuous sweet, minty fruit were the hallmark. After a brief period during which the name was used as a simple brand (with various wines released) has returned to a single estate-grown wine.

Recommended Wines 1990 Shiraz (brightly coloured wine with fine, sweet cherry fruit; the oak is a little raw and needs to integrate; five gold medals to its credit; to 2000).

MOUNT LANGI GHIRAN A–A Est 1969 $9.50–16.50 R 48, 65, 66, 101, 127, 150, 323 GRT WESTERN

Warrak Road, Buangor, Vic 3375 (053) 54 3207 fax (053) 54 3277
Open Mon–Fri 9–5, w'ends 12–5 **Production** 24 000 cases
Winemaker Trevor Mast
Principal Wines Chard, Ries, Cab Sauv, Shir, Circa (a regional blend), Red and White is second label.
Best Vintages W '84, '85, '87, '91, '92 **R** '86, '88, '89, '91, '92

Summary A maker of outstanding cool climate peppery Shiraz, crammed with flavour and vinosity, and very good Cabernet Sauvignon. The Shiraz points the way for cool climate examples of the variety, for weight, texture and fruit richness all accompany the vibrant pepper-spice aroma and flavour.

Recommended Wines 1991 Langi Shiraz (textbook richness and varietal character with ripe plum/prune fruit aromas, rich, textured palate with plum pudding spice characters and fine tannins; to 2005). 1990 Langi Cabernet Sauvignon (dark chocolate, dark berry and mint aromas and flavours; the tannins need time to soften; to 2003).

MOUNT MAGNUS NR Est 1933 $4.95–9.50 CD SD GRANITE BELT

Donnellys Castle Road, Pozieres, Qld 4352 (076) 85 3313

Open 7 days 9–5 **Production** NFP
Winemaker Andrew Braithweight
Principal Wines Sem Chard, Ries, Gewurz Tram, LP Sem, Cab Sauv.
Summary This is one of the oldest vineyards in the district, which has had a chequered history that has included numerous changes of ownership and winemakers. I have not tasted the wines for several years.

MOUNT MARTHA VINEYARD NR Est 1986 $11–14.50 ML SD MORNINGTON P
Range Road, Mount Martha, Vic 3934 (059) 74 2700
fax (059) 74 4007
Open Not **Production** 750 cases
Winemaker Kevin McCarthy (Contract)
Principal Wines Chard, Sauv Bl, Cab Sauv.
Summary The two hectare Mount Martha Vineyard is owned by the Matson and Scalley families, overlooking Port Phillip Bay on undulating loam. Competent contract winemaking should ensure the quality of the wines.

MOUNT MARY A–A Est 1971 $20–24 ML 21, 149 YARRA V
Coldstream West Road, Lilydale, Vic 3140 (03) 739 1761
Open Not **Production** NFP
Winemaker Dr John Middleton
Principal Wines Chard, Sauv Bl Sem Muscat, Pinot, Cabernets (Bordeaux blend).
Summary Superbly refined, elegant and intense Cabernets, and usually outstanding and long lived Pinot Noirs fully justify Mount Mary's exalted reputation; the white Bordeaux blend of Semillon, Muscadelle and Sauvignon Blanc is good, though not quite in the same class.

MOUNT PRIOR NR Est 1860 $6.50–16.90 CD 121 NE VIC
Cnr River Road & Popes Lane, Rutherglen, Vic 3685 (060) 26 5591
fax (060) 26 7456
Open 7 days 10–5 **Production** 9000 cases
Winemaker Garry Wall
Principal Wines Chard, Carignan, LP Ries, Chenin, Wh Burg, Durif, Herm, Cab Sauv, Shir, Sparkl, fortifieds.
Summary Re-established in 1989 after a disastrous foray into exports to the United States; the experience of Garry Wall should ensure quality.

MOUNT VIEW ESTATE C–CB Est 1971 $12–14 CD SD HUNTER V
Mount View Road, Mount View, NSW 2325 (049) 90 3307
fax (049) 91 1289
Open 7 days 9–5 **Production** 1200 cases
Winemaker Harry Tulloch
Principal Wines Chard, Verd, Shir, Pinot, Cab Sauv, fortifieds.
Best Vintages W '86, '87, '88, '91, '92 R '81, '83, '86, '87, '91
Summary Some new oak would help the table wines immeasurably; the range of fortified wines is rather better.

MOUNT VINCENT DB–C Est 1980 $12–15 CD SD MUDGEE
Common Road, Mudgee, NSW 2850 (063) 72 3184
Open Mon–Sat 10–5, Sun 10–4 **Production** 2000 cases
Winemaker Jane Nevell
Principal Wines Ries, Cab Sauv, Liqueur Muscat, Meads, Mead Ale.
Summary The table wines are made without preservatives, and simply show how difficult it is to make wine this way. The meads are very good, also the mead ale.

• MOUNT WILLIAM WINERY NR Est 1987 $12 CD 100 MACEDON
Mt William Road, Tantaraboo, Vic 3764 (054) 29 1595
fax (054) 29 1998
Open 7 days 10–6 **Production** 200 cases
Winemakers Murray Cousins, Michael Cope-Williams
Principal Wines Sem, Pinot, Sparkl Burg.
Summary Adrienne and Murray Cousins established four hectares of vineyards between 1987 and 1992, planted to Pinot Noir, Cabernet Franc, Semillon and Chardonnay. The Cabernet Franc is to be used as part of a base wine for Sparkling Burgundy, while the Chardonnay is not expected to come into bearing for several years. The wines are made under contract (Cope Williams), and are sold through a stone tasting room cellar door facility which was completed in 1992.

MOUNTADAM BA–B Est 1970 $15–30 R 65, 66, 102, 120, 131, 258 ADELAIDE HILLS
High Eden Road, High Eden Ridge, SA 5235 (08) 362 8804
fax (08) 362 8942
Open 7 days 11–4 **Production** 30 000 cases
Winemaker Adam Wynn
Principal Wines Three ranges: Mountadam, David Wynn and quasi-organic Eden Ridge.
Best Vintages W '81, '84, '87, '89, '90 R '81, '84, '88, '90, '91
Summary One of the leading small wineries, founded by David Wynn and run by winemaker son Adam Wynn, which initially offered only the Mountadam range at relatively high prices. The subsequent development of the three ranges of wines has been very successful, judged both by the winemaking and wine marketing viewpoint.
Recommended Wines 1991 Mountadam Chardonnay (complex, weighty, concentrated wine with strong buttery malolactic influence, and real authority to the finish; to 1999). 1991 David Wynn Shiraz (a wine with absolutely exemplary shiraz varietal character, concentrated and rich, with some pepper and spice, but essentially driven by dark, liquorice-accented fruit; to 2000). 1991 David Wynn Cabernet Sauvignon (clean, solid dark berry fruit with hints of chocolate and blackcurrant; has depth, and finishes with soft tannins; to 2000). 1991 Eden Ridge Shiraz (extraordinary, almost essency redcurrant/cassis/dark cherry aromas and very high-toned dark cherry flavours; to 1996).

MOUNTAIN CREEK NR Est 1973 $12.50 ML SD PYRENEES
Mountain Creek Road, Moonambel, Vic 3478
Open W'ends by appointment **Production** 1600 cases
Winemaker Taltarni (Contract)

Principal Wines Sauv Bl, Cab Sauv.

Summary Brian Cherry acquired the Mountain Creek Vineyard in 1975 and has slowly extended it. The first wine was made in 1987, all or part of the grapes before and in some years since then sold to other Pyrenees wineries. The wine is made under contract, and shows all of the substance and weight for which the district is renowned. The 1990 Sauvignon Blanc and '88 Cabernet Sauvignon were both commendable wines.

MOUNTILFORD NR Est 1981 $8–9.50 CD SD MUDGEE

Vincent Road, Ilford, NSW 2850 (063) 58 8544

Open 7 days 10–4 **Production** 3000 cases

Winemaker Don Cumming

Principal Wines Chard, Tram, Ries, Pinot, Shir Cab, Port.

Summary Surprisingly large cellar door operation which has grown significantly over the past few years. I have not, however, had the opportunity of tasting the wines.

MOUNTVIEW WINES NR Est 1991 $8–12 CD SD GRANITE BELT

Mount Sterling Road, Glen Aplin, Qld 4381 (076) 83 4316

Open W'ends & hols 9–5 **Production** 700 cases

Winemaker David Price

Principal Wines Chablis, Chard, Light Red, Cab Mer, Shir.

Summary David and Linda Price are refugees from the Sydney rat race operating a small, neat, red cedar farm-style winery. Both the 1990 and 1991 Shiraz were clean, well made wines with good varietal fruit and a pleasant touch of sweet American oak.

MUDGEE WINES NR Est 1963 $7.50–9 CD SD MUDGEE

Henry Lawson Drive, Mudgee, NSW 2850 (063) 72 2258

Open Mon–Sat 10–5, Sun 12–5 **Production** 1000 cases

Winemaker Jennifer Meek

Principal Wines Chard, Gewurz, Crouchen, Ries, Rosé, Shir, Pinot, Cab Sauv.

Summary All of the wines are naturally fermented with wild yeasts and made without the addition of any chemicals or substances including sulphur dioxide, a very demanding route particularly with white wines. For some consumers, any shortcoming in quality will be quite acceptable.

MURRAY ROBSON B–B Est 1974 $13.50–19 CD SD HUNTER V

Halls Road, Pokolbin, NSW 2321 (049) 98 7539 fax (049) 98 7746

Open 7 days 9–5 **Production** 12 800 cases

Winemaker Murray Robson

Principal Wines A range of evocative labels including Murray Robson, Pepper Tree Vineyard, Frost Hollow, Mulberry Row, Ploughmans and Sundial of blended wines and traditional varietals including Chard, Sem, LH Sem, Pinot, Herm, Cab Sauv and Muscat.

Best Vintages W '82, '87, '89, '91, '92 R '83, '87, '89, '90, '91

Summary With partner James Fairfax providing all of the necessary capital, the fortunes of Murray Robson are decidedly on the ascendent. Production is increasing apace, the winery has doubled in size, while the historic convent guest house and the restaurant (run by Robert Molines) constitute a most impressive complex that is understandably very well patronised.

Recommended Wines 1991 Murray Robson Cabernet Sauvignon (firm, complex, powerful, dusty Cabernet with appropriately impressive tannins and tremendous potential; to 2005). 1992 Traminer (excellent varietal aroma and flavour, with delicate spicy lychee fruit; the residual sugar is quite evident but legitimate in the style).

MURRINDINDI CB–B Est 1979 $16.95 CD SD STHN VIC
Cummins Lane, Murrindindi, Vic 3717 (057) 97 8217

Open Not **Production** 2000 cases

Winemaker Alan and Hugh Cuthbertson

Principal Wines Chard, Cab.

Summary Not quite in the Yarra Valley nor in Macedon but (like Flowerdale) in a climate so cool it is marginal for table winemaking and perhaps better suited to sparkling wine. The warmest years have produced some elegant Chardonnays and Cabernet Merlots.

Recommended Wine 1992 Chardonnay (light melon/citrus fruit in slightly green Chablis style; well made).

• MURRUMBATEMAN WINERY NR Est 1972 SD Canberra
Barton Highway, Murrumbateman, NSW 2582 (06) 227 5584

Open 7 days 10–5 **Production** 1100 cases

Winemaker Duncan Leslie

Principal Wines Ries, Sauv Bl, Chard, Shir, Cab Sauv.

Summary Revived after a change of ownership, the Murrumbateman Winery draws upon 2.3 hectares of vineyards and also incorporates an a la carte restaurant and function room together with picnic and barbeque areas.

• NEPEAN WINES NR Est 1987 $13.50–15 ML SD
MORNINGTON P
'Moonah', Truemans Road, Rosebud, Vic 3939 (069) 28 4638
fax (069) 28 4606

Open Not **Production** 550 cases

Winemaker Various Contract

Principal Wines Chard, Pinot.

Summary Nepean Wines is a joint venture between the Leslie and Matear families; the main vineyards are situated on limestone-based soils behind Rye on the southern Mornington Peninsula in one of the coolest vineyard sites. The 1991 vintage wines were very light and crisp, precisely in the style desired by the proprietors.

NICHOLSON RIVER A–BA Est 1978 $9–19 CD SD 225
GIPPSLAND
Liddells Road, Nicholson, Vic 3882 (051) 56 8241 fax (051) 56 8433

Open 7 days 10–5 preferably by appointment

Production 1500 cases

Winemaker Ken Eckersley

Principal Wines Sem, Chard, Ries, Pinot, Cabernets; second label is Montview.

Best Vintages W '86, '87, '88, '91, '92

Summary The fierce commitment to quality in the face of the temperamental Gippsland climate and frustratingly small production has been handsomely repaid by some stupendous Chardonnays.

Recommended Wine 1991 Chardonnay (golden yellow colour with massively rich and complex aroma and flavour, honeyed butterscotch and toasty oak; already there).

NIOKA RIDGE DB–C Est 1979 $6.80–12 CD SD HILLTOPS
Barwang Road, Young, NSW 2594 (063) 82 2903
Open 7 days 9–6 **Production** 2200 cases
Winemaker Phil Price
Principal Wines Chard, Ries, Cab Shir, Cab Malb, fortifieds.
Summary A winery that struggles hard to overcome the difficulties of isolation, not always succeeding.

NOON'S NR Est 1976 $10.50–13 CD SD STHN VALES
Rifle Range Road, McLaren Vale, SA 5171 (08) 270 4253
fax (08) 323 8290
Open 7 days 10–5 **Production** 2500 cases
Winemaker David Noon
Principal Wines Rosé, Cab Sauv, Burg, Dry Red, Shir, Shir Cab, Port.
Summary Massive wines made in wholly idiosyncratic style.

NORMANS BA–BA Est 1851 $4–50 CD 42–45, 63, 197, 247 STHN VALES
Grants Gully Road, Clarendon, SA 5157 (08) 383 6138
fax (08) 383 6089
Open Mon–Sat 10–5, Sun 11–5 **Production** 120 000 cases
Winemaker Brian Light
Principal Wines Ries, Chard, Fumé, Chenin, Chablis, Pinot, Herm, Cab Sauv, fortifieds, under the Chandlers Hill, White Label and top-of-the-range Chais Clarendon labels.
Best Vintages W '82, '85, '90, '91, '92 R '82, '84, '86, '88, '90
Summary Consistent producers of wines which, within their price categories, have considerable appeal. Always smooth and well crafted, they can reach great heights under the Chais Clarendon label and equally great value under the Chandlers Hill label.
Recommended Wines 1990 Chais Clarendon Cabernet Sauvignon (harmonious, balanced yet powerful wine with concentrated fruit and smoothly integrated oak; to 2007). 1990 Chais Clarendon Shiraz (extremely youthful dark cherry, berry and currant fruit flavours, needing time in bottle to soften and become more complex). 1992 Chandlers Hill Fumé Blanc (crisp, bracing, direct, herbaceous fruit with just a touch of compensating residual sugar; drink now). 1992 White Label Chardonnay (pleasant melon and peach fruit; very smooth on the mouth with subtle oak; subliminal touch of sweetness; drink now).

NOTLEY GORGE NR Est 1983 $10–14.50 ML SD TAMAR V
Loop Road, Glengarry, Tas 7275 (vineyard only) (003) 96 1166
fax (003) 96 1200
Open By appointment **Production** 1800 cases
Winemaker Doug Bowen, Andrew Hood (Consultant)
Principal Wines Sauv Bl, Chard, Pinot, Cab Sauv, Cab Mer (light red).
Summary Marine engineer Doug Bowen (no relation to the Doug Bowen of Coonawarra) spreads his favours around, having his Sauvignon Blanc processed at Domaine A, Chardonnay at Rochecombe

and Pinot Noir crushed at Notley Gorge, pressed at Holm Oak and then returned to Notley Gorge for maturation in the former apple orchard cool store, a building which just happened to be on the property and which precipitated him into wine production.

Recommended Wines 1991 Chardonnay (extremely stylish, complex wine showing outstanding barrel ferment oak influence together with textured citrus and melon fruit; to 1998). 1992 Sauvignon Blanc (crisp, clean, direct herbaceous/asparagus style, but with good mouthfeel and acid balance; drink now).

OAKRIDGE ESTATE BA–B Est 1982 $10–26 CD 125, 186 YARRA V

Aitken Road, Seville, Vic 3139 (059) 64 3379 fax (059) 64 2061

Open W'ends & hols 10–5 **Production** 2000 cases

Winemaker Michael Zitzlaff

Principal Wines Cab Sauv under Quercus and Reserve labels.

Best Vintages R '82, '84, '86, '90, '91

Summary Has provided some of the greatest Yarra Valley Cabernets; the vintage rating reflects some young vine influence between 1986 and 1990. Shortly prior to the 1993 vintage, Oakridge was offered for sale or lease, so its future is not entirely certain. If the Zitzlaff family retains ownership and control, the focus will be on the outstanding Reserve Cabernet Sauvignon.

Recommended Wines 1990 Reserve Cabernet Sauvignon (beautifully articulated and weighted blackcurrant cabernet fruit showing perfect ripening and very good tannins; fruit rather than oak driven; to 2010).

OAKVALE CB–B Est 1893 $10–18.50 CD 33, 260 HUNTER V

Broke Road, Pokolbin, NSW 2321 (049) 98 7520 fax (049) 98 7747

Open 7 days 9–5 **Production** 5000 cases

Winemaker Barry Shields

Principal Wines Sem, Sem Chard, Chard, Fronti, Muscat, Shir, fortifieds.

Best Vintages W '88, '89, '91 R '88, '89, '90, '91

Summary Former Sydney solicitor Barry Shields seems content with the change in his lifestyle as he presides over the historic Oakvale Winery, which he purchased from the Elliott family over a decade ago. The emphasis is on Semillon, Chardonnay and a blend of the two in both oaked and unoaked versions, most of which are offered with three to five years bottle age.

Recommended Wines 1988 Peachtree Semillon (as so often with aged Hunter Semillons gives the impression of some oak, when in fact none has been used in this wine; soft, honeyed fruit in a fairly light mould, with crisp acid finish; now mature). 1991 Chardonnay (clean, smooth harmonious honey and peach flavours, with soft acidity; early maturing). 1989 Peppercorn Shiraz (starting to develop sweet, earthy regional notes in the bouquet, with soft chewy and faintly spicy sweet fruit on the palate; now to 1998).

OLD BARN NR Est 1990 $5–10 CD SD BAROSSA V

Langmeil Road, Tanunda, SA 5352 (085) 63 0111

Open Mon–Fri 9–5, w'ends & hols 11–4 **Production** 3000 cases

Winemaker Various contract

Principal Wines Ries, Dry White, Light Dry Red, Quaffing Red,

Cab Shir, Cab Mal, fortifieds.

Summary Owned by a partnership of Barry and Elizabeth Chinner and Janet Hatch, with an honorary establishment date of 1861, being the date of construction of the old stone barn from which the wines are exclusively sold. The wines themselves are either made elsewhere or purchased from other makers for the Old Barn label.

OLD CAVES WINERY NR Est 1979 $7.50–13.50 CD SD
GRANITE BELT
New England Highway, Stanthorpe, Qld 4380 (076) 81 1494
fax (076) 81 2722
Open 7 days 9–5 **Production** 2500 cases
Winemaker David Zanatta
Principal Wines Chard, Shir, Cab Sauv and a range of generic wines in both bottle and flagon, including fortifieds.
Summary A range of wines tasted from the 1990 and 1991 vintages showed significant winemaking problems, but over the years Old Caves has produced some pleasant wines.

OLIVE FARM CB–B Est 1829 $8.80–12 CD SD SWAN V
77 Great Eastern Highway, South Guildford, WA 6055
(09) 277 2989 fax (09) 279 4372
Open Mon–Fri 10–5, Sat 9–3 **Production** 9500 cases
Winemaker Ian Yurisich
Principal Wines Verd, Chenin, Chab, Sem, Chard, Gewurz, Cab Shir, Herm, Cab Sauv, Cab Shir Mer, Sherry, Port, Sparkl.
Summary The oldest winery in Australia in use today, and arguably the least communicative. The ultra-low profile tends to disguise the fact that wine quality is by and large good.

OLIVERHILL NR Est 1973 $3.50–11 CD SD STHN VALES
Seaview Road, McLaren Vale, SA 5171 (08) 323 8922
Open 7 days 10–5 **Production** 1300 cases
Winemaker Vincenzo Berlingieri
Principal Wines Great Outdoors white and red, Chard, Shir Cab, Port and Muscat.
Summary Vincenzo Berlingieri's towering presence once extended to Sydney promotional trips; these days he is content to run Oliverhill without fanfare and, with his wife Kiawngo, run a unique Italian-Chinese restaurant. Open 7 days for lunch and dinner by appointment.

ORLANDO A–A Est 1847 $6–29 R 122, 211, 236 BAROSSA V
Sturt Highway, Rowland Flat, SA 5350 (085) 24 4500
fax (085) 21 3100
Open Mon–Fri 9.30–5, w'ends 10–4 **Production** NFP
Winemaker Phil Laffer
Principal Wines A plethora of brands (in ascending order) including Coolabah casks and flagons, Jacobs Creek, RF, Gramps (the last three covering all styles), St Hugo Cab Sauv, St Hilary Chard, St Helga Ries, Flaxmans Gewurz, Lawsons Shir, Steingarten Ries and Jacaranda Ridge Cab Sauv. All of the major grape varieties are represented.
Best Vintages W '82, '85, '86, '90, '92 R '82, '86, '88, '90, '91
Summary As befits a group of this size, Jacobs Creek is an

enormously successful international brand that has done particularly well in the United Kingdom and is doubtless the financial jewel in the Orlando crown.

Recommended Wines 1992 RF Chardonnay (stylish wine with distinct cool, citrus fruit aromas and subtle oak; to 1995). 1992 Gramps Chardonnay (very stylish wine with excellent fruit length and intensity; flavours of peach, melon and fig with nicely handled oak; to 1997). 1992 RF Sauvignon Blanc (surprisingly crisp and punchy wine with pronounced herbal/tobacco fruit and a clean, crisp dry finish; drink now). 1989 St Hugo Cabernet Sauvignon (strongly American oak driven with soft, easily accessible fruit; arguably yesterday's style, but some would disagree; drink now).

PADTHAWAY ESTATE, THE NR Est 1980 $16–20 R 86–90
PADTHAWAY
Keith-Naracoorte Road, Padthaway, SA 5271 (087) 65 5039
fax (087) 65 5097
Open 7 days 10–5 **Production** 6000 cases
Winemaker Nigel Catt, Pam Dunsford (Consultant)
Principal Wines Chard, Sparkl, Pinot.
Summary The only functioning winery in Padthaway, set in the superb grounds of the estate in a large and gracious old stone woolshed; the homestead is in the Relais et Chateaux mould, offering luxurious accommodation and fine food. The combined experience of new winemaker Nigel Catt (who also serves at Middleton Estate) and consultant Pam Dunsford could well see a significant improvement in wine style.
Recommended Wines 1992 Chardonnay (of light to medium weight, discrete and understated, but has real style and nicely balanced melon fruit and oak; to 1996).

PALMARA NR Est 1984 $12 CD SD COAL R
Main Road, Richmond, Tas 7025 (002) 622 462; postal PO Box 75, Rosny Park, Tas 7018
Open Summer 10–6, winter 10–4 **Production** 150 cases
Winemakers Allan Bird, Andrew Hood
Principal Wines Chard, Richmond Ries, Pinot, Cab Sauv.
Summary Allan Bird has the Palmara wines made for him by Andrew Hood, all in tiny quantities. The Pinot Noir has performed consistently well since 1990.
Recommended Wine 1992 Pinot Noir (solid wine with plummy/spicy fruit and good texture in the mouth; to 1995).

PANKHURST WINES NR Est 1986 $12 ML SD CANBERRA
Old Woodgrove, Woodgrove Road, Hall, NSW 2618 (06) 230 2592
fax (06) 273 1936
Open Not **Production** 2000 cases
Winemaker Dr Roger Harris (Contract)
Principal Wines Chard Sem, Chard Sauv Bl, Pinot, Cab Mer.
Summary Agricultural scientist and consultant Allan Pankhurst and wife Christine (with a degree in pharmaceutical science) have established a three hectare, split canopy vineyard. The strongly flavoured, chewy 1990 Cabernet Merlot, redolent with sweet berry fruit, augurs well for the future, as does contract winemaking in the skilled hands of Dr Roger Harris.

PANORAMA CB–CB Est 1974 $10–13 ML 48 HUON V
193 Waterworks Road, Dynnyrne, Tas 7005 (002) 23 1948
Open 7 days 10–5 **Production** 500 cases
Winemaker Steve Ferencz
Principal Wines Chard, Sauv Bl, Pinot, Cab Sauv.
Summary The quality of the underlying fruit, particularly with the red wines, is not in doubt: these have great colour and startling richness of flavour in years such as 1990 and 1991. The full potential has sometimes been held back by problems with indifferent oak, but not so in the case of the superb 1990 Cabernet Sauvignon.
Recommended Wine 1992 Sauvignon Blanc (pronounced oak on both bouquet and palate, showing barrel ferment characters and nutty/spicy flavours; the oak itself is of good quality but does threaten the fruit in terms of balance).

PARINGA ESTATE BA–A Est 1985 $15–18 CD 72
MORNINGTON P
44 Paringa Road, Red Hill South, Vic 3937 (059) 89 2669
Open W'ends & hols 11–5 **Production** 1200 cases
Winemaker Lindsay McCall
Principal Wines Chard, Cab Sauv, Pinot, Shir.
Summary Rising star of the Mornington Peninsula scene, originally making an impact with its vibrantly spicy Shiraz, but now adding an outstanding Pinot and a very good Chardonnay to the portfolio.
Recommended Wines 1992 Pinot Noir (intense, powerful and stylish wine with red cherry, plum and spice fruit, cut by an appropriate touch of sappiness; to 1995). 1991 Shiraz (spotlessly clean, vibrant spicy red berry fruit of light to medium weight; to 1997). 1992 Chardonnay (full, sweet, ripe peachy fruit, typical of the vintage in Mornington; succulent and mouthfilling).

PARKER WINES NR Est 1968 $10.40–28 R 68 HUNTER V
McDonalds Road, Pokolbin, NSW 2321 (049) 98 7585
fax (049) 98 7732
Open 7 days 9.30–4.30 **Production** 26 000 cases
Winemaker David Lowe
Principal Wines Sem, Chard, Pinot, Shir.
Summary Established as Tamburlaine, this seemingly ill-starred winery became Tamalee, then Sobels and now Parker — named after its new owner Stan Parker. With ex-Rothbury chief winemaker David Lowe in charge it is reasonable to hope — and indeed expect — that the fortunes of what is now Parker Wines will take a turn for the better. Certainly, production is increasing in leaps and bounds.

PARKER COONAWARRA ESTATE BA–B Est 1975
$16.99–29.95 R 55, 93, 101, 188, 241 COONAWARRA
Penola Road, Coonawarra, SA 5263 (02) 357 3376
fax (02) 358 1517
Open Not **Production** 2000 cases
Winemaker Ralph Fowler (Contract)
Principal Wines Cab Sauv under two labels, Parker Estate and Parker Estate Terra Rosa First Growth.
Summary Parker Coonawarra Estate is a joint venture between the Parker, Fowler and Balnaves families: John Parker, former chairman of Hungerford Hill; Doug Balnaves, long-term viticulturist in

Coonawarra; and Ralph Fowler, winemaker at Leconfield and contract maker for Parker Coonawarra Estate. The partnership grows 400 tonnes of fruit a year, and selects the best 30 tonnes for the Parker label. All of the wines released to date have shown very opulent fruit and no less opulent oak, and are at the richest end of the spectrum of Australian wine style.

Recommended Wines 1990 Terra Rossa First Growth Cabernet Sauvignon (impenetrable, youthful purple-red colour, with concentrated fruit aromas and flavours, but even more pronounced oak; needs time to come into balance; to 2010). 1991 Terra Rossa First Growth Cabernet Sauvignon (deep colour, with luscious, sweet, scented and ripe cassis, blackcurrant, mint and vanilla aroma and flavour; a huge wine in every respect; to 2010).

PARKLANE WINES NR Est 1986 $8–12 CD SD CANBERRA
Brooklands Road, via Hall, ACT 2618 phone and fax (06) 230 2263
Open W'ends 11–5 **Production** 2500 cases
Winemaker Alwyn Lane
Principal Wines Ries, Fumé Bl, Chard, Pinot, Cabernets.
Summary Alwyn and Margaret Lane run the 8 hectare vineyard and winery as a full-time occupation, making only estate grown wines, and with plans to increase production to 4500 cases by 1996. In the meantime, the Lanes have lost no time in stirring local viticultural politics.

PASSING CLOUDS B–B Est 1974 $12.50–18 CD 12, 115, 173, 175, 266 BENDIGO
Kurting Road, Kingower, Vic 3517 (054) 38 8257
Open 7 days 10–5 **Production** 1800 cases
Winemaker Graeme Leith
Principal Wines Shir Cab, Shir, Angel Blend, Pinot.
Best Vintages R '82, '84, '86, '90, '91
Summary Graeme Leith is one of the great personalities of the industry, with a superb sense of humour, and makes lovely regional reds with cassis, berry and mint fruit. His new innovation, 1991 Angel Blend, is a typical piece of labelling whimsy; it is in fact a Cabernet Sauvignon, Cabernet Franc and Merlot blend.
Recommended Wine 1992 Shiraz (very clean, sweet, ripe red cherry bouquet with exuberant, youthful and juicy cassis berry flavours; a striking, early-bottled style).

PATRITTI DC–B Est 1926 $2.50–6.50 CD SD ADELAIDE PLAINS
13–23 Clacton Road, Dover Gardens, SA 5048 (08) 296 8261
fax (08) 296 5088
Open Mon–Sat 9–6 **Production** 65 000 cases
Winemakers G. & J. Patritti
Principal Wines A kaleidoscopic array of table, sparkling, fortified and flavoured wines (and spirits) offered in bottle and flagon.
Summary One of the old-style winemaker-cum-merchant offering wines and spirits at old-style prices.

PATTERSONS B–B Est 1982 $11–18 ML SD GRT SOUTHERN
28 Montem Street, Mount Barker, WA 6324 (098) 51 2063
Open By appointment **Production** 1000 cases
Winemaker John Wade (Contract)

Principal Wines Chard, Shir, Pinot.

Best Vintages R & W '88, '90, '91, '92

Summary Schoolteachers Sue and Arthur Patterson have grown Chardonnay and grazed cattle as a weekend relaxation for a decade; a vertical tasting of their Chardonnay (made by various contract makers) since 1986 showed the worth of relaxation — the wines had real style and flavour. The 1992 debut of the '90 Shiraz, with crisp, fragrant pepper spice, was no less impressive.

PAUL CONTI CB–B Est 1968 $6–14 CD 55, 68, 109 SW COASTAL

529 Wanneroo Road, Wanneroo, WA 6065 (09) 409 9160
fax (09) 309 1634

Open Mon–Sat 9.30–5.30 **Production** 8000 cases

Winemaker Paul Conti

Principal Wines Chard, Chenin, Fronti, Herm, Cab Sauv, Red and White Port.

Best Vintages W '82, '86, '89, '90, '92 R '82, '87, '85, '87, '89, '90

Summary A low-key operation that consistently makes clean, smooth dry white wines, intensely fruity and slightly sweet Frontignac and fresh cherry/berry flavoured Hermitage.

Recommended Wines 1992 Late Picked Frontignac (fragrant spicy/grapy bouquet; beautifully handled wine, with intense grape flavour and very good acid/sugar balance; drink now).

PAULETTS B–B Est 1983 $9.50–12 CD 68, 127, 130, 178 CLARE V
Polish Hill Road, Polish Hill River, SA 5453 (088) 43 4328
fax (088) 43 4202

Open 7 days 10–5 **Production** 5000 cases

Winemaker Neil Paulett

Principal Wines Sauv Bl, Ries, LH Ries, Chard, Shir, Cab Mer, Sparkl.

Best Vintages W '84, '86, '87, '90, '91 R '85, '87, '89, '90, '91

Summary The recent completion of the winery and cellar door sales facility marks the end of a development project that began back in 1982 when Neil and Alison Paulett purchased a 47 hectare property with a small patch of old vines and a house in a grove of trees (which were almost immediately burnt by the 1983 bushfires). The beautifully situated winery is one of the features of the scenic Polish Hill River region.

Recommended Wines 1992 Rhine Riesling (ample lime and toast fruit with good weight; pleasantly dry finish; to 1996). 1991 Shiraz (concentrated bouquet with briary notes; fresh cherry, prune and red plum flavours; fruit rather than oak driven; to 1999). 1990 Cabernet Merlot (clean, dusty cabernet aromas and flavours; Bordeaux-like in its slightly leafy overtone; some sweet oak; to 1997).

PAUL OSICKA B–BA Est 1955 $11–14 CD 72 GOULBURN V
Graytown, Vic 3608 (057) 94 9235

Open Mon–Sat 10–5, Sun 12–5 **Production** NFP

Winemaker Paul Osicka

Principal Wines Chard, Ries, Cab Sauv, Herm, Port.

Best Vintages W '89, '90, '91, '92 R '86, '87, '90, '91, '92

Summary Produces red wines that are never less than good, and are sometimes outstanding; for example the '89 Shiraz was wonderfully rich, minty and spicy.

PEEL ESTATE NR Est 1974 $11.50–16 R 109, 188, 286 SW COASTAL
Fletcher Road, Baldivis, WA 6210 (09) 524 1221 fax (09) 524 1625
Open 7 days 10–5 **Production** 5000 cases
Winemaker Will Nairn
Principal Wines Chard, Chenin (wood mat), Verd, Shir, Cab Sauv, Zinfandel, Port.
Summary Will Nairn has concentrated on wood-matured Chenin Blanc and light but elegant reds, with some success; recent oak handling has not been convincing, but the underlying wine quality is good. Insufficient recent tastings to justify a rating.

PENDARVES ESTATE NR Est 1986 $13–16 ML 68 HUNTER V
Lot 10 Old North Road, Belford, NSW 2335 (065) 74 7222 or
(02) 913 1088
Open W'ends 11–5 **Production** 3200 cases
Winemaker Mark Davidson, Greg Silkman (Contract)
Principal Wines Chard, Verd, Sem Sauv Bl, Pinot Chambourcin, Shir, Cab Mer Mal.
Summary The perpetual motion general practitioner and founder of the Australian Medical Friends of Wine, Dr Philip Norrie, is a born communicator and marketer, as well as a wine historian of note. He also happens to be a passionate advocate of the virtues of Verdelho, inspired in part by the high regard held for that variety by vignerons around the turn of the century.

PENFOLDS A–A Est 1844 $6–90 R 124, 195, 287 BAROSSA V
Tanunda Road, Nuriootpa, SA 5355 (085) 62 0389
fax (085) 62 2494
Open Mon–Fri 9–5, Sat 10–5, Sun 1–5 **Production** 745 000 cases
Winemaker John Duval
Principal Wines As with the other majors the emphasis is on brands, allied with long-established Bin number products. Bin 28 Kalimna, 128 Coonawarra Claret, 389 Cab Shir, 707 Cab Sauv; newly introduced Bin 407 Cab Sauv; brands include Minchinbury Sparkl, Koonunga Hill Claret, Magill Estate, Clare Estate, St Henri Claret and Grange Herm. Has fairly recently moved into Chard and Sem Chard.
Best Vintages R '55, '62, '66, '71, '76, '82, '83, '86, '88, '90
Summary Makes what has often been described as Australia's only first growth claret — Grange Hermitage — a wine that can age with exceptional grace for over 30 years. Strongly flavoured, complex, oak-influenced wines have always been its forte; Bin 707 Cabernet Sauvignon has comprehensively replaced St Henri Claret as the second wine in the line-up, while Koonunga Hill is regarded as one of the best budget-priced reds available throughout the year. Minchinbury sparkling wine is a brand leader in its category.
Recommended Wines 1990 Bin 407 Cabernet Sauvignon (clean, full, sweetly ripe blackcurrant fruit with well balanced oak; the wine has excellent structure, weight and length; to 2010). 1990 Bin 28 Shiraz (extremely rich, sweet, concentrated chewy wine with plum pudding fruit aromas, hints of chocolate on the palate and abundant,

soft tannins; best in the line for many years; to 2010). 1990 Bin 128 Coonawarra Shiraz (again, one of the best in the series for many years, albeit in very different style to the Bin 28, with pronounced cedary fruit, hints of spice and liquorice). 1987 Grange Hermitage (dense purple-red in colour with exceptional dark berry and dark chocolate aromas, pronounced oak and very solid tannins; another great wine in the line, but not drinkable for 20 years; to 2025). 1991 Koonunga Hill (an extraordinary wine at its price, with full, rich, chewy, dark berry and dark chocolate flavours; soft persistent tannins; to 2005). 1992 Semillon Chardonnay (sophisticated spicy oak and fresh fruit bouquet; full, rich, smooth, mouthfilling white burgundy style; clever winemaking; drink now).

PENINSULA ESTATE NR Est 1985 $12–20 R SD
MORNINGTON P
Red Hill Road, Red Hill, Vic 3937 (059) 89 2866
Open W'ends 11–5 **Production** 3000 cases
Winemaker Daniel Greene
Principal Wines Chard, Pinot, Cab; Point Nepean is second label.
Summary A relative newcomer, but one of the larger operations on the Mornington Peninsula, now with former Elgee Park winemaker Daniel Greene in charge of winemaking. The 1992 Point Nepean Chardonnay is clean and fresh with a nice touch of spicy oak, even if a little on the light side.

PENLEY ESTATE BA–BA Est 1988 $12–22 R 69, 126, 226, 264, 310 COONAWARRA
McLeans Road, Coonawarra, SA 5263 (08) 366 4106
fax (08) 231 0589
Open W'ends & hols 10–4 **Production** 7000 cases
Winemaker Kym Tolley
Principal Wines Chard, Shir Cab, Shir, Cab Sauv, Methode Champ.
Summary An ultra-ambitious and potentially high-profile winery, sparing no expense in its quest for quality and having success right from the outset; production will ultimately be estate grown, the early wines having been made from purchased grapes.
Recommended Wines 1991 Chardonnay (extremely elegant but complex wine with some barrel ferment characters, strong citrus/melon fruit and the structure to develop nicely in bottle; to 1995). 1990 Cabernet Sauvignon (extremely generous, rich and full blown style with sweet vanillin American oak, bitter chocolate and dark red berry fruit; soft tannins; to 2005). 1990 Shiraz Cabernet (smooth but classy wine with some secondary cedar and berry aromas; red berry fruit and a hint of chocolate on a smooth and well balanced palate; to 1997).

PENOWARRA NR Est 1978 SD COONAWARRA
Main Penola-Naracoorte Road, Penola, SA 5277 (087) 37 2458
Open Most Sat/Sun 9–5 **Production** 500 cases
Winemaker Ken Ward
Principal Wines Ries, Shir, Cab Sauv, Wh Port.
Summary A low-profile cellar door operation making no frills wine: those last tasted were adequate but not exciting.

PENWORTHAM WINE CELLARS NR Est 1985
$7.50–14.50 CD 145 CLARE V
Government Road, Penwortham, SA (088) 43 4345
Open W'ends & public hols 10–5 **Production** 2000 cases
Winemaker Richard Hughes
Principal Wines Ries, Muscat Fronti, Burg, Cab Sauv, Port.
Summary A Clare Valley new arrival; I have not tasted the wines.

PEPPERS CREEK NR Est 1986 $15 CD SD HUNTER V
Broke Road, Pokolbin, NSW 2321 phone and
fax (049) 98 7532
Open Wed–Sun 10–5 **Production** 800 cases
Winemaker Peter Ireland
Principal Wines Sem, Chard, Shir, Mer.
Summary A combined winery and antique shop. The red wines
previously tasted were clean and full flavoured.

PETALUMA A–A Est 1976 $14–28 R 147, 169, 171, 190, 202, 251 ADELAIDE HILLS
Spring Gully Road, Piccadilly, SA 5151 (08) 339 4122
fax (08) 339 5253
Open 7 days 10.30–5.30 (at Bridgewater Mill) **Production** 40 000
cases
Winemaker Brian Croser
Principal Wines Ries, Chard, Coonawarra (a Cabernet blend), ,
Merlot, Croser (sparkling), Sharefarmers (a Cabernet blend from a
vineyard adjacent to Coonawarra).
Best Vintages W '80, '87, '90, '91 R '87, '88, '90, '91
Summary After joining the lists of the Australian Associated Stock
Exchanges in early 1993, raising significant additional capital,
acquiring Tim Knappstein Wines and with other acquisitions planned,
Petaluma is poised to take another leap forward. It is already widely
regarded as one of Australia's finest producers of table and sparkling
wines, with a reputation which it skillfully projects and protects.
Recommended Wines 1992 Rhine Riesling (in typical Petaluma
mould, reserved, bone dry, crisp, gently toasty, crying out for bottle
age; to 2000). 1991 Croser (intriguing blend of citrus and bready Pinot
Noir influences; firm, crisp, citrus-tinged palate, with good structure
and length). 1991 Chardonnay (fine and long in the mouth, citrus and
melon fruit, a touch of barrel ferment influence, subtle malolactic
fermentation input; good structure; to 1998). 1991 Merlot (voluptuous
mix of red berry fruits, superbly handled French oak, with fine
tannins and structure; to 2000). 1990 Coonawarra (complex spicy oak
with sweet red berry fruit; a much more opulent and extroverted style
than the white wines from the Petaluma stable; to 2003).

PETER LEHMANN CB–BA Est 1980 $9.95–18.50 R 86–90, 289 BAROSSA V
Samuel Road off Para Road, Tanunda, SA 5352 (085) 63 2500
fax (085) 63 3402
Open Mon–Fri 9.30–5, w'ends 10.30–4.30 **Production** NFP
Winemaker Peter Lehmann
Principal Wines Chard, Ries, Sem (wood matured), Noble Sem,
Cab Sauv, Clancy's Gold Preference; Cellar Collection Ries, Chard;
Stonewall Shir Cab blend.

Best Vintages W '82, '84, '87, '91, '92 R '80, '84, '88, '90, '91

Summary The stalwart of the Barossa Valley, which he knows better and loves more than anyone else. The substantial production reflects grower loyalty and very competent winemaking: these constantly good, sometimes superb wines always give you extra value for money. In mid 1993 a very successful public share issue was completed, guaranteeing the future of the winery.

Recommended Wines 1990 Cellar Collection Cabernet Malbec (clean, fragrant and sweet; minty, redcurrant fruit and very sophisticated handling of spicy, high-toned oak; altogether utterly seductive; to 2000). 1991 Cellar Collection Chardonnay (a cunningly made wine with full, sweet oak and unusually deftly handled American oak). 1991 Shiraz (clean, bright, fresh, high flavoured wine with lots of red cherry fruit and spicy, toasty American oak; now to 1998). 1990 Cabernet Sauvignon (clean, pleasant, easy, soft, commercial style, with slightly cosmetic oak but well enough handled; to 1998).

PETERSONS CB–CB Est 1971 $12–17 CD 40 HUNTER V
Mount View Road, Mount View, NSW 2325 (049) 90 1704
fax (049) 91 1344
Open Mon–Sat 9–5, Sun 10–5 **Production** 10 500 cases
Winemaker Gary Reed
Principal Wines Sem, Sauternes, Chard, Pinot, Shir, Cab Sauv.
Summary Petersons may have slipped from the high pedestal on which it once sat but retains its marketplace image. The 1991 Shiraz is made in what might loosely be called 'a contemporary style', seemingly using high-toned American bluegrass-type oak; some will accept, indeed enjoy, this level of oak; others will not.

PEWSEY VALE B–BA Est 1961 $11–14 R 140–144, 326
ADELAIDE HILLS
Browne's Road, Pewsey Vale, Adelaide Hills, SA (vineyard only)
Open Not (see Yalumba) **Production** 27 000 cases
Winemaker Alan Hoey
Principal Wines Ries, Botrytis Ries, Sauv Bl, Cab Sauv.
Best Vintages W '84, '86, '90, '91, '92 R '86, '87, '90, '91, '92
Summary Pewsey Vale was a famous vineyard established in 1847 by Joseph Gilbert, and it was appropriate that when S. Smith & Son (Yalumba) began the renaissance of the high Adelaide Hills plantings in 1961, they should do so by purchasing Pewsey Vale. Right from the outset, the decision to seek cooler growing conditions through altitude was proved correct, with a long line of extremely distinguished Rhine Rieslings the result.

Recommended Wine 1992 Rhine Riesling (crisp, clean and toasty, with length and style; now to 1997).

PFEIFFER CB–B Est 1880 $7.90–16.20 CD SD 300 NE VIC
Distillery Road, Wahgunyah, Vic 3687 (060) 33 3158
fax (060) 33 3158
Open Mon–Sat 9–5, Sun 11–4
Production 10 000 cases
Winemaker Christopher Pfeiffer
Principal Wines Chard, Ries, Spat Fronti, Gamay, Pinot, Shir Cab, Cab, fortifieds.
Summary Ex-Lindeman fortified winemaker Chris Pfeiffer

occupies one of the historic wineries that abound in the north-east, and which is worth a visit on this score alone. The fortified wines are good, and the table wines have improved considerably over recent vintages.

•PIANO GULLY WINES NR Est 1987 $12–15 CD SD GRT SOUTHERN
Piano Gully Road, Manjimup, WA 6258 (097) 723 5583
Open W'ends & public hols 10–5 **Production** 450 cases
Winemaker Blair Meiklejohn
Principal Wines Chard, Pinot, Cab Sauv, Concerto.
Summary Piano Gully takes its name from a turn-of-the-century attempt by a local landowner to import a piano from England which, having safely made its way to the nearest railway station, was then being carried to its final destination by bullock dray; it fell from the dray and was irreparably damaged. The four hectare vineyard was established in 1987 on rich Karri loam, 10 kilometres south of Manjimup, with the first wine made from the 1991 vintage.

•PIBBIN WINERY NR Est 1985 $12 ML 74 ADELAIDE HILLS
Sandow Road, Verdun, SA 5245 (08) 388 7375 fax (08) 388 7685
Open Not **Production** 900 cases
Winemaker Roger Salkeld
Principal Wines Pinot; Sparkl Pinot and Sparkl Burg planned.
Summary The 2.5 hectare Pibbin Vineyard, near Verdun, is managed on organic principles; owners Roger and Lindy Salkeld explain the name 'Pibbin' is a corruption of a negro spiritual word for Heaven, adding that while the wines may not have achieved that lofty status yet, the vineyard has. And indeed, the 1991 Pinot Noir was pretty much a starting effort.

PICCADILLY FIELDS NR Est 1989 $14.90–19.45 SD
ADELAIDE HILLS
Udy's Road, Piccadilly, SA 5151 (08) 272 2239
Open Not **Production** 1000 cases
Winemaker Sam Virgara
Principal Wines Chard, Mer Cab Franc.
Summary A tiny winery which takes its name from that part of the Adelaide Hills made famous by Petaluma. The 1991 Merlot Cabernet Franc tasted from cask had massive flavour and tannins; if it was tamed before bottling, it could add a new dimension to the wines of the region.

PIERRO A–B Est 1980 $16–30 R 65, 155, 288 MARGARET R
Caves Road, Willyabrup via Cowaramup, WA 6285 (097) 55 6220
fax (097) 55 6308
Open 7 days 10–5 **Production** 4000 cases
Winemaker Michael Peterkin
Principal Wines Chard, Sem Sauv Bl, Pinot.
Best Vintages W '86, '87, '89, '90, '92 R '87, '91, '92
Summary Dr Michael Peterkin is another of the legion of Margaret River medical practitioners who, for good measure, married into the Cullen family. Pierro is renowned for its stylish white wines, which often exhibit tremendous complexity, although Michael Peterkin is nervous about any reference to or comparison with French Burgundies (or their making).

Recommended Wines 1992 Semillon Sauvignon Blanc (firm, crisp, tightly structured herbaceous fruit which has very good length and mouthfeel; drink now). 1991 Chardonnay (potent wine with melon, grapefruit and peach flavours and pronounced oak influence; to 1997).

PIESSE BROOK NR Est 1974 $10–12 CD SD PERTH HILLS
226 Aldersyde Road, Bickley, WA 6076 (09) 293 3309
Open Sat 1–5, Sun 10–5 **Production** 500 cases
Winemaker Brian Murphy
Principal Wines Chard, Cabernova, Cab Shir, Shir, Cab Mer, Cabernet.
Summary Surprisingly good red wines made in tiny quantities. The first Chardonnay was made in 1993.

PIETER VAN GENT NR Est 1979 LR CD $6.80–14 CD SD MUDGEE
Black Springs Road, Mudgee, NSW 2850 (063) 73 3807
Open Mon–Sat 9–5, Sun 11–4 **Production** 4500 cases
Winemaker Pieter van Gent
Principal Wines Chard, Fronti, Muller, Sticky, Cab Sauv, Cab Mer, Pipeclay Port and other fortifieds.
Summary Many years ago Pieter van Gent worked for Lindemans, before joining Craigmoor but moving to his own winery in 1979 where he has forged a strong reputation and following for his fortified wines in particular, although the range extends far wider. The wines are seldom seen outside cellar door.

PIKES B–B Est 1985 $9–13 CD 147, 169, 171, 258 CLARE V
Polish Hill River Road, Sevenhill, SA 5453 (088) 43 4249
fax (088) 43 4353
Open W'ends & public hols 10–4 **Production** 10 000 cases
Winemaker Neil Pike
Principal Wines Ries, Sauv Bl, Chard, Shir, Cab Sauv.
Best Vintages W '85, '86, '90, '91, '92 R '85, '86, '87, '90, '91
Summary Owned by the relatively young Pike brothers, one of whom (Andrew) is a senior viticulturist with Penfolds, the other (Neil) winemaker at Mitchells, where the wines are in fact made. Strongly flavoured and structured wines are increasingly the order of the day, which will appeal to those who look for total impact rather than finesse or subtlety.
Recommended Wines 1992 Rhine Riesling (crisp, clean, zesty fruit; will cellar well; to 1997). 1990 Cabernet Sauvignon (strong, potent, dense wine, perhaps a little extractive; to 2005).

PIPERS BROOK BA–B Est 1974 $9.90–20.30 R 48, 86–89, 191, 204, 291 PIPERS BROOK
Bridport Road, Pipers Brook, Tas 7254 (003) 82 7197
fax (003) 82 7226
Open W'ends Nov 10–4 **Production** 25 000 cases
Winemaker Andrew Pirie
Principal Wines Chard, Ries, Gewurz, Pinot, Opimian (Mer Cab) under Pipers Brook label; Summit Chardonnay is deluxe release; Tasmanian Wine Co is second label producing Sem, Chard, Pinot, Cab Sauv.

Best Vintages W '82, '84, '85, '91, '92 R '82, '86, '88, '90, '92

Summary Dr Andrew Pirie founded the Pipers Brook region; an immensely knowledgeable and skilled viticulturist and winemaker, he heads a progressive and ever-growing company, producing some of the most beautifully packaged of all Australian wines.

Recommended Wines 1992 Rhine Riesling (lime and passionfruit flavours with a distinct cool climate herbaceous edge; ever so slightly broad and phenolic). 1991 Chardonnay (firmly constructed with secondary stony characters in semi-Chablis style; has considerable length; should age extremely well; to 1999).

PIRRAMIMMA C–C Est 1892 $8–15.40 R 29, 101, 178 STHN VALES

Johnston Road, McLaren Vale, SA 5171 (08) 323 8205
fax (08) 323 9224

Open Mon–Fri 9–5, Sat 10–5, Sun/hols 12–4

Production 40 000 cases

Winemaker Geoff Johnston

Principal Wines Chard, Sauv Bl, Sem, Chab, Ries, Cab Sauv, Cab Mer, Shir, Port

Summary In the latter part of the 1980s much of the time and attention (and cash resources) of the Johnston family (owners of Pirramimma) were devoted to establishing 80 hectares of new plantings of Chardonnay, Pinot Noir and Cabernet Sauvignon. That phase of development having been completed, the Johnstons intend to turn their attention once again to the production of the wines of the quality which made Pirramimma so well known in the 1970s and early '80s.

PLANTAGENET A–A Est 1968 $7.50–25 CD 65, 128, 133, 139, 165, 182, 302 GRT SOUTHERN

Albany Highway, Mount Barker, WA 6324 (098) 51 1150
fax (098) 51 1839

Open Mon–Fri 9–5, w'ends 10–4 **Production** 12 000 cases

Winemaker John Wade

Principal Wines Chard, Ries, Chenin, Sauv Bl, Fronti, Fleur, Pinot, Shir, Cab.

Best Vintages W '82, '83, '86, '91, '92 R '80, '82, '85, '86, '90

Summary The senior winery in the Mount Barker region which has hit an absolute purple patch over the past year or so, making superb wines across the full spectrum of variety and style.

Recommended Wines 1992 Omrah Vineyard Chardonnay (outstanding example of un-oaked Chardonnay, with intense grapefruit and melon aromas and flavours, and tremendous length to the palate; the absence of oak is in no way a limiting factor; to 1997). 1992 Chardonnay (stylish, elegant and intense wine with excellent cool climate grapefruit/melon fruit and subtle barrel ferment influence; to 1998). 1990 Shiraz (complex gamey, spicy peppery wine, fleshy and round in the mouth; again that touch of gaminess which is in no way a fault; has vinosity; to 1996). 1989 Cabernet Sauvignon (complex, sweet fruit and charred spicy oak bouquet, with lovely red berry fruit, sophisticated spicy oak flavours; supple, silky and harmonious; to 2000).

PLATT'S C–C Est 1983 $9–12 CD SD MUDGEE

Mudgee Road, Gulgong, NSW 2852 (063) 74 1700

Open 7 days 9–5 **Production** 4000 cases
Winemaker Barry Platt
Principal Wines Chard, Sem, Gewurz, Cab Sauv.
Summary Inconsistent and often rather unhappy use of oak
prevents many of the wines realising their potential.

PLUNKETTS WHITEGATE BA–A Est 1980 $8.95–11.95 CD
175 CENTRAL GOULBURN
Whitegate, Upton Road, Avenell, Vic 3664 (057) 96 2275
fax (057) 96 2118
Open 7 days 10–5 **Production** 4000 cases
Winemaker Sean Plunkett
Principal Wines The top-of-the-range wines are released under the
Strathbogie Range label (Cab Mer and Chard), the 'standard' wines
under the Blackwood Ridge brand of Ries, Sauv Bl, Sem, Cab Mer.
Summary The Plunketts family first planted grapes way back in
1968, establishing 3 acres with 25 experimental varieties. Commercial
plantings commenced in 1980, with 40 hectares now under vine.
While holding a vigneron's licence since 1985, Plunketts did not
commence serious marketing of the wines until 1992.
Recommended Wines 1990 Strathbogie Ranges Chardonnay
(extremely attractive melon and grapefruit flavours with a touch of
spicy French oak; long, intense and stylish; to 1996). 1992 Blackwood
Ridge Chardonnay (fresh and crisp, with good fruit intensity; not
especially complex, but should grow nicely in the bottle; to 1998).
1991 Strathbogie Ranges Chardonnay (attractive barrel ferment
characters with citrus and melon fruit, complexed by apparent
malolactic fermentation; tight, ageworthy structure; to 1999).

POKOLBIN ESTATE NR Est 1980 $13–17 CD SD HUNTER V
McDonalds Road, Pokolbin, NSW 2321 (049) 98 7524
fax (049) 98 7765
Open 7 days 10–6 **Production** 1125 cases
Winemaker Trevor Drayton
Principal Wines Wh Burg, Chard, Tram Ries, Sem, Shir, Cab
Sauv.
Summary An unusual outlet, offering its own-label wines made
under contract by Trevor Drayton, together with the wines of Lakes
Folly, Peacock Hill and Pothana, and with cheap varietal 'cleanskins'.
Wine quality under the Pokolbin Estate label is very modest.

• POOLE'S ROCK VINEYARD NR Est 1988 $16 R ML
124a, 273 HUNTER V
Lot 41 Wollombi Road, Broke, NSW 2330 (02) 247 5358
fax (02) 251 3302
Open Not **Production** 1500 cases
Winemaker Iain Riggs (Contract)
Principal Wines Chard
Summary Sydney merchant banker David Clarke has had a long
involvement with the wine industry, ranging from his chairmanship of
the Royal Sydney Wine Show Committee through to an earlier
partnership with Sydney retailer Andrew Simon in Wollombi Brook, to
chairmanship of McGuigan Brothers Limited. The 5 hectare Poole's
Rock vineyard, planted purely to Chardonnay, is his own personal
venture, producing very a full flavoured wine in 1991.

● **POPLAR BEND** NR Est 1988 $11.50–12 ML SD
MORNINGTON P
RMB 8655 Main Creek Road, Main Ridge, Vic 3928 (059) 89 6046
Open By appointment **Production** 240 cases
Winemaker Keith Dunstan
Principal Wines Pinot, Pinot Chloe, Cab, Sparkl Pinot.
Summary The quasi retirement venture of Melbourne journalist,
author and raconteur Keith Dunstan and wife Marie. The label of
Pinot Chloe depicts Chloe in all her glory, and would be calculated to
send the worthy inhabitants of the Bureau of Alcohol, Tobacco and
Firearms (of the United States) into a state of cataleptic shock.

PORT PHILLIP ESTATE NR Est 1987 $11.95–14.95 CD SD
MORNINGTON P
261 Red Hill Road, Red Hill, Vic 3937 (059) 89 2708
fax (059) 89 2891
Open W'ends 12–5 **Production** 2500 cases
Winemaker Alex White (Contract)
Principal Wines Chard, Pinot, Cab Mer, Shir.
Summary The vineyard of leading Melbourne Queen's Counsel
Jeffrey Sher, which released its first wine from the 1991 vintage. The
wines augur well for the future.
Recommended Wines 1991 Cabernet Merlot (strong, scented
amalgam of leaf, red berry and tobacco; sweet berry fruit, some leafy
notes, a touch of charred oak and soft tannins coalesce on the palate;
to 1996). 1991 Pinot Noir (sophisticated spicy nutmeg oak tends to
slightly overpower the fruit, but there is quite good varietal character;
drink now).

● **PORTREE VINEYARD** BA–BA Est 1983 $7.50–16.50 ML SD
MACEDON
Powells Track via Mt William Road, Lancefield, Vic 3455
(054) 29 1422
Open By appointment **Production** 800 cases
Winemaker Various Contract
Principal Wines Chard, Rosé, Cab Franc Merlot.
Summary Owner Ken Murchison selected his four hectare Macedon
vineyard after studying viticulture at Charles Sturt University and
being strongly influence by Dr Andrew Pirie's doctoral thesis. The
current release wines are clear evidence of very skilled viticulture in a
cool region.
Recommended Wines 1992 Chardonnay (complex and rich, with
totally surprising weight and style given the climate; well handled
oak; to 1997). 1991 Cabernet Franc Merlot (spotlessly clean and fresh
redcurrant and cherry in an attractive light bodied style; drink now).
1992 Rosé (a very well made wine with grassy Cabernet Franc fruit
and a touch of sweetness which come together, rather than clashing
as one might think; drink now).

POTHANA NR Est 1983 $9–12 ML SD HUNTER V
Carramar, Belford, NSW 2335 (065) 74 7164
Open By appointment through Pokolbin Estate
Production 2000 cases
Winemaker David Hook
Principal Wines Chard, Sem, Pinot.

Summary Principally sold through Pokolbin Estate and by mailing list; the '91 Chardonnay is a soft, buttery/toasty wine in mainstream Hunter Valley style.

PRIMO ESTATE A–A Est 1979 $6.50–22 CD 116, 280
ADELAIDE PLAINS
Old Port Wakefield Road, Virginia, SA 5120 (08) 380 9442
fax (08) 380 9696
Open Mon–Fri 9–5, Sat/hols 10–4.30, closed 1 Jan to 31 May each year
Production 12 000 cases
Winemakers Joseph Grilli, Peter Godden
Principal Wines Colomb, Chard, Botrytis Ries, Shir, Cab Sauv, Joseph Cab Mer, Joseph Cab Sauv (double pruned); Joseph Cab Moda Amarone.
Best Vintages W '82, '84, '87, '90, '92 R '81, '85, '86, '90, '91
Summary Roseworthy dux Joe Grilli has risen way above the constraints of the hot Adelaide Plains to produce an innovative and always excellent range of wines.
Recommended Wines 1991 Joseph Cabernet Sauvignon (employs the 'double-pruned' technique; concentrated, sweet berry fruit with dusty tannins and outstanding structure; to 2000). 1991 Joseph Cabernet Merlot (briary, dark chocolate fruit flavours with exceptional depth; again fine and dusty tannins with finesse and strength to the structure; to 2000). 1992 Colombard (a wholly remarkable wine with a brilliantly crisp and clean bouquet touched with herbal/gooseberry aromas, and an intense, long palate). 1991 Chardonnay (sophisticated, fragrant, oak-influenced bouquet; hightoned, slightly aggressive oak on the palate but with good depth of Chardonnay fruit; drink now).

PRINCE ALBERT B–B Est 1975 $12 ML 33 GEELONG
100 Lemins Road, Waurn Ponds, Vic 3221 phone and
fax (052) 41 8091
Open By appointment **Production** 300 cases
Winemaker Bruce Hyett
Principal Wines Pinot.
Best Vintages R '82, '85, '90, '91, '92
Summary Australia's true Pinot Noir specialist (it has only ever made the one wine) which also made much of the early running with the variety: the wines always show good varietal character, although some are a fraction simple.

QUEEN ADELAIDE CB–B Est 1858 $7 R 124 BAROSSA V
181 Flinders Street, Adelaide, SA 5000 (08) 236 3400
fax (08) 224 0964
Open Not **Production** NFP
Winemaker Penfolds Group winemakers
Principal Wines Chab, Chard, Ries, Sauv Bl, Spat Lexia, Wh Burg, Pinot, Claret, Sparkl.
Summary The famous brand established by Woodley Wines, and some years ago subsumed into the Seppelt and now Penfolds Wine Group. It is a pure brand, without any particular home, either in terms of winemaking or fruit sources, but ironically quality has increased since its acquisition by Seppelt. It was the first maker to offer unwooded (and slightly sweet) Chardonnay on to the Australian market.

READS NR Est 1972 $7.50–13 CD SD NE VIC
Evans Lane, Oxley, Vic 3678 (057) 27 3386 fax (057) 27 3559
Open Mon–Sat 9–5, Sun 10–6 **Production** 1900 cases
Winemaker Kenneth Read
Principal Wines Ries, Chard, Sauv Bl, Crouchen, Cab Shir, Cab
Sauv, Port.
Summary Limited tastings have not impressed, but there may be a
jewel lurking somewhere, such as the medal-winning 1990 Sauvignon
Blanc.

REDBANK B–B Est 1973 $7.50–54 CD 177, 208 PYRENEES
Sunraysia Highway, Redbank, Vic 3467 (054) 67 7255
fax (054) 67 7248
Open Mon–Sat 9–5, Sun 10–5 **Production** 5100 cases
Winemaker Neil Robb
Principal Wines Chard, Sally's Paddock, Cab Sauv, Shir, Herm,
Port; Long Paddock is second label.
Best Vintages R '81, '82, '86, '88, '91
Summary Neil Robb makes very concentrated wines, full of
character; the levels of volatile acidity can sometimes be intrusive,
but are probably of more concern to technical tasters than to the
general public.
Recommended Wine 1991 Sally's Paddock (rich and concentrated
with redcurrant and mint fruit, and well tuned tannins running
through the palate; subtle oak; to 2005).

REDGATE CB–CB Est 1977 $7–18 CD 27, 54, 112, 113, 114,
279 MARGARET R
Boodjidup Road, Margaret River, WA 6285 (097) 57 6208
fax (097) 57 6308
Open 7 days 10–5 **Production** 12 500 cases
Winemakers Paul Ullinger, Virginia Willock
Principal Wines Chenin, Sauv Bl Sem, Sem, Spat Ries, Pinot,
Cab Shir, Cab Sauv, Wh Port; some varieties offered under Reserve
label.
Best Vintages W '83, '85, '87, '91, '92 R '82, '84, '85, '88, '91
Summary Twenty hectares of vineyard provide the base for one of
the larger wineries of the Margaret River region which probably has a
lower profile than it deserves. The wines are solid, but a degree of
astringency seems to run through many of them. I am not too
convinced about the merits of the Reserve range.
Recommended Wines 1992 Chardonnay (clean and fresh aroma
with hints of tropical, peachy fruit and subtle oak; light, fresh Chablis
style on the palate; drink now). 1992 Botrytis Riesling (surprisingly
rich, weighty and intense, with pronounced botrytis-induced apricot
characters; to 1995).

• **RED HILL ESTATE** NR Est 1989 $13.95–19.95 CD SD
MORNINGTON P
53 Red Hill Shoreham Road, Red Hill South, Vic 3937 (059) 89 8660
Open W'ends & public hols 12–5 **Production** 2500 cases
Winemaker Jenny Bright
Principal Wines Chard, Pinot, Cab Sauv, Sparkl.
Summary Sir Peter Derham and family completed the construction

of an on-site winery in time for the 1993 vintage, ending a period in which the wines were made at various wineries under contract arrangements. The 8 hectare vineyard is one of the larger plantings on the Mornington Peninsula, and the newly opened tasting room has a superb view across the vineyard to Westernport Bay and Phillip Island.

Recommended Wines 1992 Chardonnay (light, crisp and faintly herbal fruit, but well made, and has the length of flavour to promise development in bottle; to 1995). 1992 Pinot Noir (pronounced carbonic maceration making characters, but there is plummy varietal fruit; drink now). 1991 Brut (firm, biscuity Pinot Noir-influenced wine which has been well made, even if it is a little youthful).

REDMAN CB–CB Est 1966 $7.90–14.90 R 22–26 COONAWARRA
Main Penola-Naracoorte Road, Coonawarra, SA 5253
(087) 36 3331 fax (087) 36 3013
Open Mon–Sat 9–5, w'ends 10–4 **Production** 20 000 cases
Winemaker Bruce Redman
Principal Wines Claret, Cab Sauv.
Best Vintages R '84, '86, '88, '90, '92
Summary The Redman wines are not bad, but they should be among the best of Coonawarra — which they are not. A lack of interest (or investment) in new oak is one problem, off-taints and lack of fruit intensity another. The 1990 Cabernet Sauvignon shows what the vineyard and winery can achieve.
Recommended Wine 1990 Cabernet Sauvignon (stylish, smooth, red berry fruit with good concentration, soft tannins and a nice touch of oak; comprehensively the best wine for many years).

RENMANO B–BA Est 1914 $7.95 R 22–26, 212, 256
RIVERLANDS
Sturt Highway, Renmark, SA 5341 (085) 86 6771 fax (085) 86 5939
Open Mon–Sat 9–5 **Production** 1.6 million cases
Winemakers Reg Wilkinson, David Nelson, John Griffiths
Principal Wines Chairmans Selection Chard, Sauv Bl, Ries, Tram Ries, Cab Sauv, Herm, Port.
Best Vintages W '84, '85, '88, '91, '92 R '84, '85, '88, '90, '92
Summary The unctuous, buttery Chardonnay (foremost) and Cabernet Sauvignon lead the Chairmans Selection range, which is remarkable both for its consistency of style and for its value for money. Whether the style of the wines will continue to gain the same acceptance in the future as it has in the past remains to be seen; certainly, it is made for immediate consumption and does not repay cellaring.
Recommended Wines 1992 Chairmans Selection Chardonnay Bin 104 (sweet, vanillin/coconut American oak style which hangs together well enough and is well balanced for immediate drinking). 1992 Chairmans Selection Rhine Riesling Bin 604 (attractive lifted spicy wine with good length and quite surprising depth and style).

REYNOLDS YARRAMAN B–B Est 1967 $14–16 CD 56, 65, 102 UPPER HUNTER V
Yarraman Road, Wybong, Muswellbrook, NSW 2333
(065) 47 8127 fax (065) 47 8013
Open Mon–Sat 10–4, Sun 11–4 **Production** 5000 cases

Winemaker Jon Reynolds
Principal Wines Chard, Sem, Cab Sauv, Cab Mer.
Summary Formerly Horderns Wybong Estate, now owned by talented ex-Houghton and Wyndham winemaker Jon Reynolds' and wife Jane. The red wines released to date have been full of flavour and character, the white wines a little disappointing given Reynolds' track record.

RIBBON VALE ESTATE CB–CB Est 1977 $12.75–15.25 R 130, 177 MARGARET R
Lot 5 Caves Road, Willyabrup via Cowaramup, WA 6284
(097) 55 6272
Open W'ends 10–5 **Production** 3000 cases
Winemaker Mike Davies
Principal Wines Sem, Sauv Bl, Sem Sauv Bl, Cab Mer, Cab Sauv, Merlot.
Best Vintages W '85, '88, '91, '92, '93 R '85, '87, '88, '90, '91
Summary When in form, makes crisp, herbaceous Semillon and Sauvignon Blanc (and blends), ideal seafood wines, and austere, very firm Cabernets all in mainstream regional style.
Recommended Wines 1992 Sauvignon Blanc (in riper mould with fair fruit weight and nice gooseberry flavours; drink now). 1991 Merlot Cabernet (massive weight, concentration and extract, with pronounced tannins and powerful fruit; a typical Margaret River style; 1998-2005).

RICHARD HAMILTON B–B Est 1972 $7–14 CD 115, 130, 185, 274 STHN VALES
Willunga Vineyards, Main South Road, Willunga, SA 5172
(085) 56 2288 fax (085) 56 2868
Open Mon–Sat 10–5, Sun 11–5 **Production** NFP
Winemaker Ralph Fowler
Principal Wines Chard, Sem Sauv Bl, Cab Sauv, Shir, Pinot, Port, Sparkl.
Best Vintages W '86, '88, '90, '91, '92 R '84, '86, '90, '91, '92
Summary With the arrival of Ralph Fowler as winemaker and Brian Miller as marketing manager the quality, consistency and profile of Richard Hamilton wines are on the rise.
Recommended Wines 1991 Hut Block Cabernet Sauvignon (very concentrated, ripe, blackcurrant fruit with strong tannins; juicy, concentrated style made from 45-year-old Cabernet vines). 1991 Old Vines Shiraz (ultra peppery, spicy style, made from 100-year-old vines; retains pepper/spice characters notwithstanding its 13% alcohol; to 1998).

RICHMOND GROVE C–B Est 1977 $6.95–9.95 R 122 HUNTER V
Hermitage Road, Pokolbin, NSW 2321 (049) 98 7792
fax (049) 98 7783
Open Mon–Fri 9.30–5, w'ends 10–4 **Production** NFP
Winemaker Steve Clarkson
Principal Wines Chab, Chard, Dry White, Tram Ries, Wh Burg, Herm, Mer, Cab Sauv; Cowra Vineyard range of Verd and Chard is a new addition.
Summary With 422 hectares of vineyard, including the state-of-the-

art 242 hectare Cowra Vineyard established over a 12 month period at a cost of $6 million, Richmond Grove is a major producer both on its own account and for the other members of the Orlando Wyndham Group. The wines are reliable, if unashamedly commercial in style.

RIDGE WINES, THE DC–C Est 1984 $9.20–12.50 CD SD
COONAWARRA

Naracoorte Road, Coonawarra, SA 5263 (087) 36 5071
Open 7 days 9–5 **Production** 2000 cases
Winemaker Sid Kidman
Principal Wines Ries, Cab Sauv, Shir.
Best Vintages W '84, '87, '88, '89 R '84, '86, '87, '88
Summary Quite simply, the quality should be better given the area and Sid Kidman's viticultural expertise.

•RIVENDELL NR Est 1987 SD MARGARET R

Lot 328 Wildwood Road, Yallingup, WA 6282 (097) 55 2090
fax (097) 55 2295
Open 7 days 10–5 **Production** 750 cases
Winemaker Mike & Jan Davies
Principal Wines Sem Sauv Bl, LH Sem, Shir Cab.
Summary With 13.5 hectares of vineyards coming into bearing, production for Rivendell will increase significantly over the coming years. The cellar door sales facility is in a garden setting complete with restaurant. An unusual sideline is the sale of 50 types of preserves, jams and chutneys.

RIVERINA WINES CA-B Est 1971 $3–6.20 CD 42–45, 176, 292 MIA

Farm 1, 305 Hillston Road, Tharbogang, NSW 2680 (069) 62 4122
fax (069) 62 4628
Open Mon–Sat 9–6, Sun 10–3 **Production** 1.6 million cases
Winemaker John Casella
Principal Wines Fifteen varieties are processed, the overwhelming proportion of which is sold in bulk; bottled wine releases under the Riverina and Ballingal Estate labels.
Summary One of the large producers of the region chiefly selling wine in bulk to other producers, but the Ballingal Estate label is one to watch, particularly from the '91 vintage: the wines have won a number of show medals.
Recommended Wine 1991 Ballingal Estate Premium Selection Chardonnay (surprisingly elegant wine, with fragrant passionfruit and grapefruit aromas and flavours; fine structure and considerable length; to 1996).

ROBERT HAMILTON CB–B Est 1942 $5–10 CD 33, 80, 176
ADELAIDE HILLS

Springton Wine Estate, Hamilton's Road, Springton, SA 5235
(085) 68 2264
Open 7 days 10–4 **Production** 12 000 cases
Winemaker Robert Hamilton
Principal Wines Ries, Chard, Sem, Chab, Wh Burg, Shir, Cab Sauv, fortifieds.
Summary A traditional range of wines sold at traditional prices; the reds are usually the best, and occasionally very good.

ROBINSONS FAMILY NR Est 1969 $9–18 CD 134 GRANITE BELT
Curtins Road, Ballandean, Qld 4382 (076) 32 8615
fax (076) 39 2718
Open 7 days 10–5 **Production** 4000 cases
Winemakers Rod MacPherson, Philippa Hambledon
Principal Wines Chard, Lyra White, Cab Mal, Cab Sauv, Shir, Shir Cab, Sparkl.
Best Vintages One of the most fascinating vineyards, wandering in pieces through undulating bush and scrub, producing wines of at times ferocious power and intensity that have not been quite tamed in the winery. Changes in the winemaking team and a deliberate strategy of reducing extract should see better balanced and more reliable wines in the future.

ROBINVALE NR Est 1976 $3.50–7.90 CD SD MURRAY R
Sea Lake Road, Robinvale, Vic 3549 (050) 26 3955
fax (050) 26 1123
Open Mon–Sat 10–6, Sun 1–6 **Production** 10 000 cases
Winemaker Bill Caracatsanoudis
Principal Wines Chard, Chenin, Wh Burg, Marsanne, Saut, Merl, Shir, Cab Sauv, fortifieds.
Summary Producers of a fascinating range from bio-dynamic grape juice, non-alcoholic wines, flavoured, fortified, Greek and standard table wines. Indeed, it is the only winery fully accredited with the Bio-Dynamic Agricultural Association of Australia. The wines will appeal chiefly to those for whom such matters are important.

ROCHECOMBE B–B Est 1985 $11.50–17.50 CD 48, 72, 92 PIPERS BROOK
Baxter's Road, Pipers River, Tas 7252 (003) 82 7122
fax (003) 82 7240
Open 7 days 9–5 **Production** NFP
Winemakers Brigitte & Bernard Rochaix
Principal Wines Chenin, Ries, Sauv Bl, Chard, Pinot, Cab Sauv Franc.
Summary A Swiss/Australian joint venture with considerable ambition; 13 hectares of (by Australian standards) immaculate, close-planted vineyard, with a further 20 hectares due to be planted by 1995 and a high-tech winery to boot.
Recommended Wines 1992 Chardonnay (restrained bouquet with faint melon/grapefruit aromas; a creamy, malolactic fermentation-induced texture to the palate, but does retain freshness and crispness; overall in European rather than Australian style). 1991 Sauvignon Blanc (pronounced tobacco/herbal bouquet, quite rich and concentrated; the wine has full texture and mouthfeel, round almost fleshy, and showing strong varietal character; to 1995). 1990 Cabernet Franc (attractive, clean, crisp, tangy, herbaceous Bordeaux style that perhaps won't appeal to traditional palates but which I enjoy; low oak; to 1997).

ROCHFORD CB–CB Est 1987 $9–18.50 ML 175 MACEDON
Romsey Park, Rochford, Vic 3442 (054) 29 1428 fax (054) 29 1066
Open Not **Production** 1200 cases
Winemaker Bruce Dowding
Principal Wines Ries, Rosé, Cab Sauv, Pinot.

Summary Construction engineer-cum-restaurateur-cum-grape grower and winemaker Bruce Dowding (and partner Sheila Hawkins) hit the headlines with their '90 and '91 Pinot Noirs, proving the suitability of the variety to the Macedon region. The Cabernet Sauvignon, however, has fairly consistently lacked ripe fruit.

ROCKFORD B–B Est 1984 $7.90–15.90 CD SD 220 BAROSSA V
Krondorf Road, Tanunda, SA 5352 (085) 63 2720
fax (085) 63 3787
Open 7 days 11–5 **Production** 12 000 cases
Winemaker Robert O'Callaghan
Principal Wines Eden Valley Ries, Botrytis Ries, Basket Press Shir, Black Shir, Port, Sparkl.
Best Vintages W '86, '88, '90, '91, '92 R '85, '87, '90, '91, '92
Summary The wines are sold through Adelaide retailers only (and cellar door) and are unknown to most eastern states wine drinkers, which is a great pity for these are some of the most individual, spectacularly flavoured wines made in the Barossa today, with an emphasis on old low-yielding dry land vineyards.
Recommended Wine 1989 Basket Press Shiraz (soft, relatively light aromas, but with more weight and extract on the palate, showing dark berry fruit, a hint of chocolate and soft tannins; to 1998).

ROMAVILLA CB–CB Est 1863 $5–24 CD SD WEST QLD
Northern Road, Roma, Qld 4455 phone and fax (074) 22 1822
Open Mon–Fri 8–5, Sat 9–4 **Production** 2000 cases
Winemaker David Wall
Principal Wines Fourteen varietal and generic table wines and 13 fortified wine styles including Madeira and Tawny Port are on sale at the winery.
Summary An amazing historic relic, seemingly untouched since its nineteenth-century heyday, producing eminently forgettable table wines but still providing some extraordinary fortifieds, including a truly stylish Madeira made from Riesling and Syrian (the latter variety originating in Persia).

• **ROSABROOK ESTATE** NR Est 1980 $6–10.80 CD SD MARGARET R
Rosa Brook Road, Margaret River, WA 6285
Open 7 days 11–5 **Production** 2000 cases
Winemaker Eric Hayle-Mills (supervising contract making elsewhere up to 1993)
Principal Wines Sem, Ries, Chard, Cab Mer, Cab Sauv.
Summary The 7 hectare Rosabrook Estate vineyards have been established progressively since 1980, with no less than 9 varieties planted. The cellar door facility is housed in what was Margaret River's first commercial abattoir, built in the early 1930s, with a winery under construction mid 1993. The grapefruity 1993 Chardonnay and the cherry and spice 1993 Shiraz tasted from cask showed great promise.

ROSEMOUNT ESTATE BA–A Est 1969 $9.50–36 R 120, 135–138, 198, 211, 299 UPPER HUNTER V
Rosemount Road, Denman, NSW 2328 (065) 47 2467
fax (065) 47 2742

Open Mon–Sat 10–4, Sun 12–4 **Production** over 500 000 cases
Winemaker Philip Shaw
Principal Wines Tram Ries, Chab, Wh Burg, Sem, Ries, Chard, Fumé, Shir, Cab Shir, Cab Sauv, Pinot, Sparkl. Roxburgh is top of many labels including Giants Creek, Whites Creek, Kirri Billi, Show Reserve and Diamond Label.
Best Vintages W '80, '84, '87, '90, '92 R '80, '82, '84, '88, '90
Summary Roxburgh Chardonnay is arguably Australia's most famous and is certainly a flagbearer for this large and successful winery, which has been one of the export leaders, setting an exemplary path of consistency and value for money wherever it sells.
Recommended Wines 1992 Fumé Blanc (complex but soft, gently herbaceous fruit with a touch of cinnamon; soft, clean finish; drink now). 1992 Giants Creek Chardonnay (big, rich, buttery wine with pronounced oak influence throughout; early developing; drink now). 1991 Roxburgh Chardonnay (extraordinary, scented butter menthol aromas; massive weight and flavour on the palate, consistent with its 14% alcohol). 1990 Show Reserve Cabernet Sauvignon (classic cedary, leafy, Cabernet aroma, Bordeaux-like; complex cedary/leafy/berry fruit with firm tannins; to 2000). 1991 Diamond Label Shiraz (solid, ripe and full flavoured with cherry/berry fruit and a soft finish; to 1995).

ROSENBERG CELLARS CB–BA Est 1985 $8–10 CD SD

CLARE V
Main North Road, Watervale, SA 5452 (088) 43 0131
Open W'ends 10–5 **Production** NFP
Winemaker Terry Blanden
Principal Wines Chenin, Cottage White, Sparkl, Rosé, Shir.
Summary The wines, basically white and usually with residual sugar, are made under contract at Eaglehawk and Sevenhill; not surprisingly, quality is good, particularly at the price.

ROSEWHITE VINEYARDS NR Est 1983 $8–11 CD SD NE

VIC
Happy Valley Road, Happy Valley via Myrtleford, Vic 3737
(057) 52 1077
Open Fri–Mon, Wed 10–5 **Production** 500 cases
Winemaker Joan Mullett
Principal Wines Chard, Traminer, Pinot, Shir, Cab Sauv.
Summary After a career with the Victorian Department of Agriculture, agricultural scientists Ron and Joan Mullett began the establishment of Rosewhite in 1983, and have since established a little over two hectares of vineyards at an altitude of 300 metres. A 1989 Pinot Noir indicated the area had real potential for this variety, but I have not tasted subsequent vintages.

ROSSETTO CB–B Est 1930 $2.95–22 R 48 MIA

Farm 576, Beelbangera, NSW 2686 (069) 63 5214
fax (069) 63 5542
Open Mon–Sat 8.30–5.30 **Production** 7 million litres
Winemaker Ralph Graham
Principal Wines Mt Bingar generic and varietal casks; a kaleidoscopic range of flavoured and fortified wine; premium table wines under Rossetto label.

Summary A winery with an interesting mix of products, with 50% of total sales coming from the Mount Bingar range of 4 litre casks, 40% being provided by fortified wines, cocktail wines and 12 000 cases of Rossetto premium table wines. The latter can offer very good value.

Recommended Wine 1992 Mount Bingar Semillon (strong tropical peach and passionfruit aromas and flavours, seemingly botrytis influenced, with American oak flavours; drink now).

ROTHBURY ESTATE BA–A Est 1968 $12.95–18.95 R 48, 86–90, 251 HUNTER V
Broke Road, Pokolbin, NSW 2321 (049) 98 7555 fax (049) 98 7553
Open 7 days 9.30–4.30 **Production** 250 000 cases
Winemakers Peter Hall (Chief), Keith Hall (Red)
Principal Wines Chard, Sem, Sauv Bl, Ries, Pinot, Herm, Shir Cab, under a range of labels and brands.
Best Vintages W '84, '86, '89, '91, '93 R '83, '87, '89, '91, '93
Summary Increasingly concentrating its efforts on Chardonnay at the top end and a range of merchant labels (including Scribbly Bark) and Denman Estate at the value end of the market. Obstinately, I continue to buy and cellar its Semillon, but do admire its voluptuous, barrel fermented Reserve Chardonnays from both Cowra and the Hunter Valley, and no less the spectacular, fruity/oaky Shiraz.
Recommended Wines 1992 Barrel Fermented Chardonnay (wonderfully complex, aromatic bouquet with citrus fruit and obvious barrel ferment characters; long, balanced and harmonious palate, with oak evident but not overly aggressive; outstanding wine; to 1994). 1991 Shiraz (exceptionally ripe, rich and sweet berry and chocolate fruit with some American oak evident; abundant soft tannins; to 2005). 1991 Reserve Shiraz (intense berry fruit with strong, spicy vanillin oak; hugely concentrated; strong tannin; to 2010). 1992 Cowra Chardonnay (clean, well balanced and flavoured no-frills Chardonnay with slight tropical overtones to peach/melon fruit; good acidity; to 1995).

ROTHERHYTHE NR Est 1969 $18 R SD TAMAR V
Hendersons Lane, Gravelly Beach, Exeter, Tas 7251 (003) 34 0188
Open 7 days 10–4 at Delamere **Production** 1300 cases
Winemaker Dr Steven Hyde
Principal Wines Chard, Pinot, Cab Mer.
Summary The softly spoken Dr Steven Hyde is one of the nice guys of the wine industry, and I simply wish I could be more enthusiastic about the wines. Sulphide-derived astringency has been a consistent problem, but the 1992 Chardonnay and 1991 Cabernet Sauvignon are certainly pointing in the right direction and suggest better things are in store.

ROUGE HOMME B–B Est 1954 $8–9 R 124, 195, 287
COONAWARRA
Main Penola-Naracoorte Road, Coonawarra, SA 5263
(087) 36 3205 fax (087) 36 3250
Open Mon–Sat 10–4 **Production** 35 000 cases
Winemaker Paul Gordon
Principal Wines Chard, Pinot, Cab Shir, Cab Sauv.
Best Vintages W & R '86, '88, '90, '91
Summary Rouge Homme might be described as the warrior brand

for the Lindeman Wine Group, with a limited number of carefully styled and priced wines which all sell for under $10.

Recommended Wines 1990 Shiraz Cabernet (the revamped and relabelled Claret, emanating from the great '90 vintage; strong, briary/berry fruit, moderately pronounced American oak, and soft tannins; to 2005). 1991 Chardonnay (fairly oaky style but very smooth and stylish, with citrus and peach flavours; those who like oak might well rate it as outstanding; to 1996).

ROVALLEY ESTATE BA–A Est 1919 $2.95–6.90 CD 91, 97, 111, 151 BAROSSA V
Sturt Highway, Rowland Flat, SA 5352 (085) 24 4537 fax (085) 24 4066
Open Mon–Fri 9–4.30, w'ends 11–4.30 **Production** 30 000 cases
Winemakers Shayne Cunningham, Mos Kaesler
Principal Wines Premium table wines under Barossa Rovalley Ridge label; a full range of fortifieds and sparkling wines.
Summary Since its acquisition by Miranda Wines, the quality of the top end of the Rovalley Estate wines has been transformed, with some astonishingly good wines made in 1992.
Recommended Wines 1992 Show Reserve Chardonnay (superb handling of oak in a complex and stylish wine with deep fruit and strong barrel ferment characters; drink now). 1992 Rhine Riesling (highly floral, spicy bouquet; attractive, long flavoured palate with very good fruit intensity).

• RUKER WINES NR Est 1991 $10 CD SD CANBERRA
Barton Highway, Dickson, ACT 2602 (06) 230 2310
Open W'ends & public hols 10–5 **Production** 500 cases
Winemaker Richard Ruker
Principal Wines Ries, Gewurz.
Summary Barbara and Richard Ruker, with the assistance of eldest daughter Niki, planted two hectares of riesling and traminer in 1984. The cellar door cum winery is a farm shed, subsequently converted to an office and then to its present function; it is finished with heavy wooden beams salvaged from a railway bridge near Tarago and clad with the remains of an old slab hut, while the tables are made from huge red and yellow box trees cut down when the vineyard was planted. The first wines were made in 1991, and I have not tasted them.

RUMBALARA NR Est 1974 $5.50–12 CD SD GRANITE BELT
Fletcher Road, Fletcher, Qld 4381 (076) 84 1206 fax (076) 83 4324
Open 7 days 9–5 **Production** 3000 cases
Winemaker Bob Gray
Principal Wines Ries, Sem, Shir, Pinot, Cab Sauv, fortifieds, Cider.
Best Vintages W '84, '86, '90, '91, '92 R '86, '87, '88, '92
Summary Over the years has produced some of the Granite Belt's finest, honeyed Semillon and silky, red berry Cabernet Sauvignon, but quality does vary and has recently disappointed, though the peachy '91 Semillon shows some character.

RYECROFT CB–B Est 1888 $7.45–11.50 R 14, 48, 80, 301 STHN VALES
Ingoldby Road, McLaren Flat, SA 5171 (08) 383 0001
Open Mon–Sat 10–5, Sun 12–4 **Production** NFP

Winemaker Not known at time of publication

Principal Wines Tradition Cab Shir and Mer; Contemporary Chard; Flame Tree Red and White, Flame Tree varietals Chard, Sauv Bl, Shir, Cab Shir Mer.

Summary Following its acquisition by Rosemount Estate in late 1991 wine quality has become very much more consistent, even if unashamedly commercial.

Recommended Wines 1992 Flame Tree Sauvignon Blanc (cool, intense herbal grassy style with crisp acidity). 1991 Tradition Cabernet Shiraz Merlot (ripe, almost essency dark plum and chocolate fruit, with soft tannins; smooth and mouthfilling).

RYMILL RIDDOCH RUN BA–B Est 1973 $14–24 R 82, 101, 102, 139 COONAWARRA

Old Penola Estate, Penola, SA 5277 (087) 36 5001
fax (087) 36 5040

Open Not **Production** 18 000 cases

Winemaker John Innes

Principal Wines Chard, Sauv Bl, Shir, Cab Sauv.

Summary The Rymills are descendants of John Riddoch, and have long owned some of the finest Coonawarra soil upon which they have grown grapes since 1973. Peter Rymill has made a small amount of Cabernet Sauvignon since 1987, and has now plunged headlong into commercial production, with winemaker John Innes presiding over the striking winery portrayed on the label.

Recommended Wines 1991 Shiraz (masses of sweet cassis and dark cherry fruit woven through with soft tannins; a wholly seductive wine; to 2002). 1992 Sauvignon Blanc (full, rich, ripe fruit, with fleshy gooseberry flavours; just a fraction sweet for some tastes).

SADDLERS CREEK B–B Est 1989 $11.50–15 CD SD HUNTER V

Marrowbone Road, Pokolbin, NSW 2321 (049) 91 1770
fax (049) 91 1778

Open 7 days 9–5 **Production** 5000 cases

Winemaker Craig Brown-Thomas

Principal Wines Vosges Chard, Tram Ries, Sem Chard, Sem Sauv Bl, Fumé Bl, Herm, Cab Mer, Bluegrass Cab Sauv.

Summary An impressive newcomer to the district producing consistently full flavoured and rich wines, with the 1990 red wines showing lovely fresh, sweet fruit and the 1991 whites having the softness and concentration one expects from this vintage.

SALISBURY ESTATE B–A Est 1977 $7–11 R 81, 101, 112, 113, 139, 323 MURRAY R

Nangiloc Road, Nangiloc, Vic 3494 (050) 24 6800
fax (050) 24 6605

Open Mon–Sat 10–4.30

Production 11 million litres; 50 000 case labelled production

Winemaker David Martin

Principal Wines A multiplicity of labels, but all very carefully targeted; Australian retail is limited to Salisbury Estate varietals and Salisbury Estate Reserve; Milburn Park is exclusively for restaurants; Castle Crossing for chain stores and wine clubs; Tennyson Vineyards for Australian mail orders and export; Barrier Reef and Acacia Ridge for export.

Summary Salisbury Estate is the tip of the iceberg of the Alambie Wine Company, which typically processes around 4 million litres of wine a year, selling all but a fraction of the very best in bulk to other wineries. Not surprisingly, the quality of these modestly priced wines has been of medal winning standard.

Recommended Wines 1992 Salisbury Estate Chardonnay (clean, smooth and honeyed, with surprising fruit weight and development; drink now). 1992 Salisbury Estate Show Reserve Chardonnay (complex rich and weighty, although the fruit is not much different to the standard wine; drink now). 1992 Salisbury Estate Chardonnay Semillon (unexpectedly stylish and elegant, with strong charred oak influence and a clean finish; impressive making; drink now). 1992 Salisbury Estate Sauvignon Blanc Semillon (very cleverly made with fresh fruit and spicy American oak; drink now).

SALTRAM CA–BA Est 1859 $7.50–35 R 146 BAROSSA V
Angaston Road, Angaston, SA 5353 (085) 64 2200
fax (085) 64 2876
Open Mon–Fri 9–5, w'ends 10–5 **Production** 190 000 cases
Winemaker Nigel Dolan
Principal Wines A full range of varietal wines under the Estate, Classic, Mamre Brook Private Reserve and Pinnacle labels; Mr Pickwick Port is the top Tawny Port.
Best Vintages W '82, '86, '88, '90 R '84, '86, '88, '90
Summary I have more than once (and perhaps somewhat rudely) suggested that international spirit and wine giant Seagram has entirely forgotten about this furthest outpost of its empire. Certainly, Saltram has seldom, if ever, flexed its muscles during its decade of Seagram ownership, and most people would agree has not realised its potential, even though it can and does produce some excellent wines.
Recommended Wines 1992 Classic Sauvignon Blanc (rich, generous, gooseberry fruit with attractive balance of flavours, including herbal nuances, with a wholly acceptable hint of sweetness; drink now). 1988 Pinnacles Selection Cabernet Sauvignon (attractive, clean, red berry/redcurrant fruit with harmonious oak; while a powerful wine is very well balanced with soft tannins; to 2000). 1990 Classic Semillon (soft, bottle-developed style with some honeyed fruit followed by a light crisp finish; drink now).

SAMPHIRE NR Est 1982 $7 CD SD ADELAIDE HILLS
Watts Gully Road, Kersbrook, SA 5231 (08) 389 3183
Open 7 days 9–5 by appointment **Production** 90 cases
Winemaker Tom Miller
Principal Wines Riesling (from the 0.4 hectare vineyard).
Summary Next after Scarp Valley, the smallest winery in Australia offering wine for sale; pottery also helps. Tom Miller has one of the more interesting and diverse CVs, with an early interest in matters alcoholic leading to the premature but happy death of a laboratory rat at Adelaide University and his enforced switch from biochemistry to mechanical engineering.

SANDALFORD CB–C Est 1840 $9.30–27.16 R 86–90, 139, 244
SWAN V & MARGARET R
West Swan Road, Caversham, WA 6055 (09) 274 5922
fax (09) 274 2154

Open Mon–Sat 10–5, Sun 11–5 **Production** 43 000 cases
Winemaker Bill Crappsley
Principal Wines Caversham Range (Dry White, Chenin Verd, Cab), Premium range Margaret River (Ries, LH Ries, Verd, Shir, Cab); fortifieds including Sandalera.
Summary A consistent under-performer over recent years that will hopefully take on a new lease of life with the arrival of Bill Crappsley as chief winemaker. The vineyard resources are good, and there is no reason why there should not be a sharp increase in wine quality.
Recommended Wines Sandalera (mahogany greenish rim; raisined, complex obvious rancio with chocolate and caramel flavours, classic Swan Valley fortified).

SAND HILLS NR Est 1920 $5.60–9 CD SD CENTRAL WEST NSW

Sandhills Road, Forbes, NSW 2871 (068) 52 1437
Open Mon, Thurs–Sat 9–5, Sun 12–5 **Production** 400 cases
Winemaker John Saleh
Principal Wines Chab, Dry Wh, Mos, Spat Ries, Rosé, Burg, Cab Shir, fortifieds.
Summary Long owned by Jacques Genet, and now by the Saleh family, who know much about the appreciation of fine wine but are still learning how to make it.

SANDSTONE B–B Est 1988 $17–18 R 46, 68, 127, 313 MARGARET R

Lot 5 Caves Road, Willyabrup via Cowaramup, WA 6284
(097) 55 6271 fax (097) 55 6292
Open Not **Production** 1000 cases
Winemaker Mike Davies
Principal Wines Sem, Cab.
Summary The family operation of consultant winemakers Mike and Jan Davies, who also operate very successful mobile bottling plants. The wines are made at Ribbon Vale, where the Davies work as consultants and contract winemakers for others.
Recommended Wines 1992 Semillon (typically rich, full blown Sandstone style, distinct from most Margaret River wines; full, almost heavy in texture, with pronounced American oak influence; drink now). 1990 Cabernet Sauvignon (strong but clean wine with dark berry fruit, sweet vanillin oak and moderately strong tannins; 1995-2000).

SCARBOROUGH A–B Est 1987 $18.50–20 CD SD HUNTER V

Gillards Road, Pokolbin, NSW 2321 (049) 98 7563
fax (049) 98 7786
Open 7 days 9–5 **Production** 5000 cases
Winemaker Ian Scarborough
Principal Wines Chard, Pinot.
Best Vintages W '87, '88, '89, '90, '91
Summary Ian Scarborough put his white winemaking skills beyond doubt during his years as a consultant, and his exceptionally complex and stylish Chardonnay is no disappointment. Marketing and promotion, however, remain at a low level.
Recommended Wines 1989 Chardonnay (deep yellow in colour, with very full, developed toast and butterscotch bouquet;

153

exceedingly rich, buttery, unctuous palate; in extreme style, but does it very well; drink now). 1988 Chardonnay (yellow orange colour, with complex, sweet cumquat/mandarin-tinged bouquet, suggestive of some botrytis; very sweet, ripe, peachy fruit flavours; once again, in the full frontal style of the maker; drink now).

SCARPANTONI ESTATES NR Est 1979 $8–14 CD 3, 42, 67, 74, 167, 290 STHN VALES

Scarpantoni Drive, McLaren Flat, SA 5171 (08) 383 0186
fax (08) 383 0490

Open 7 days 10–5 **Production** 10 000 cases

Winemakers Michael & Filippo Scarpantoni

Principal Wines Ries, Chard, Botrytis Ries, Cab Sauv, Cab Mer.

Summary A large number of wines tasted in various shows have consistently disappointed all the judges, myself included, but every now and then Scarpantoni comes up with a top wine.

SCARP VALLEY NR Est 1978 $15 ML SD PERTH HILLS

6 Robertson Road, Gooseberry Hill, WA 6076 (09) 454 5748

Open Not **Production** 27 cases

Winemaker Peter Fimmel (Contract)

Principal Wines Hermitage.

Summary Owner Robert Duncan presides over what has to be the smallest producer in Australia, with one quarter acre of shiraz producing a single cask of wine each year if the birds do not get the grapes first. Recently introduced netting should help alleviate that problem. The 1990 vintage, tasted in March '93, was a pleasant wine, light and clean with gently minty fruit, and can be found in local Perth Hills restaurants and liquor stores.

SCHMIDTS TARCHALICE C–C Est 1984 $7–20 CD SD BAROSSA V

Research Road, Vine Vale via Tanunda, SA 5352 (085) 63 3005
fax (085) 63 3616

Open Mon–Sat 10–5, Sun 12–5 **Production** 1000 cases

Winemaker Christopher Schmidt

Principal Wines Ries, Chard, Sem, Gewurz, Pinot, Cab Sauv, Port.

Summary Vanillin oak-flavoured Semillon and Chardonnay are among the better wines, but develop very quickly.

SCOTCHMANS HILL BA–A Est 1982 $16–16.50 R 21, 149, 262 GEELONG

Scotchman's Road, Drysdale, Vic 3222 (052) 51 3176
fax (052) 53 1743

Open 7 days 10.30–4.30 **Production** 10 000 cases

Winemaker Robin Brock

Principal Wines Chard, Ries, Pinot, Cabernet.

Summary In fact situated on the Bellarine Peninsula, south-east of Geelong, with a very well equipped winery and first-class vineyards. Has consistently made one of the outstanding value-for-money Pinot Noirs over the past three years, and is strongly recommended.

Recommended Wines 1991 Pinot Noir (both bouquet and palate show strong making influence, with complex carbonic maceration characters intermingling with rich plummy fruit; the wine is round and soft in the mouth as befits Pinot Noir; to 1995).

SEAVIEW CA–A Est 1850 $6.60–20 R 124, 197, 287 STHN VALES
Chaffeys Road, McLaren Vale, SA 5171 (08) 323 8250
fax (08) 323 9308
Open Mon–Fri 9–4, Sat 11–5, Sun 11–4 **Production** 500 000 cases
Winemaker Ed Carr
Principal Wines Chab, Ries, Tram Ries, Wh Burg, Chard, Cab Shir, Cab Sauv, Sparkl under Seaview and Edmond Mazure labels.
Best Vintages W '85, '87, '90, '91 R '86, '88, '90, '91
Summary A maker of sturdy, reliable white wines, red wines that are frequently absurdly underpriced and perhaps suffer in consequence and, of course, of some of the country's best known sparkling wines, which have gone from strength to strength over recent years.
Recommended Wines 1990 Pinot Chardonnay Brut (wonderfully harmonious, smooth elegant wine with the chardonnay influence obvious but not too much so; long in the mouth and perfectly balanced; richly deserves the cascade of gold medals and trophies that have descended on it). 1989 Edmond Mazure Brut (complex, smoky, yeasty autolysis characters with richness, weight and length to the palate; well balanced acidity; outstanding sparkling wine). 1992 Rhine Riesling (firm, dry, toasty style with crispness and length, perhaps fractionally hard but should develop well; to 1996). 1990 Cabernet Sauvignon (rich and textured with abundant American oak, some dark fruit and chocolate flavours and well balanced tannins; outstanding value at the price; to 2000).

SELDOM SEEN NR Est 1987 $8–12 CD SD MUDGEE
Craigmoor Road, Mudgee, NSW 2850 (063) 72 4482
Open 7 days 9.30–5 **Production** 4000 cases
Winemaker Barry J. Platt
Principal Wines Sem, Chard, Tram Ries, Cab Shir.
Summary A major grape grower that reserves a proportion of its crop for making and release under its own label. Quality has been inconsistent.

SEPPELT A–A Est 1850 $4–2000 R 124, 195, 287 BAROSSA V
Seppeltsfield via Tanunda, SA 5352 (085) 62 8028
fax (085) 62 8333
Open Mon–Fri 8.30–5, Sat 10.30–4.30, Sun 11–4 **Production** NFP
Winemakers Ian McKenzie, James Godfrey
Principal Wines Seppelt has had the habit of spawning brands with gay abandon; the most humble is Glen Osmond Claret, followed by the Queen Adelaide range, Moyston and Chalambar, the Gold Label range, the Black Label range and the Premium range, including what one suspects to be transients such as Harpers Range, Corella Ridge, Ironbark and so forth. Regional-based wines include Dorrien, Drumborg and Partalunga.
Best Vintages W '82, '85, '86, '90, '91 R '82, '86, '88, '90, '91
Summary A multi-million dollar expansion and renovation program has seen the historic Seppeltsfield winery become the production centre for the Seppelt wines, adding another dimension to what was already the most historic and beautiful major winery in Australia. Seppeltsfield has always been the centre for fortified wine production, including the annual release of century-old Para Liqueur

Ports with a price of around $2000 a bottle. Many magnificent tawny and liqueur ports and sherries (all Australia's finest) are available at far more normal prices. Likewise, there are high quality table wines such as Dorrien Cabernet Sauvignon, and the numerous premium wines incorporating Padthaway material.

Recommended Wines 1992 Rhymney Sauvignon Blanc (an exhilarating blend of Padthaway and Tumbarumba grapes providing a crisp, intensely flavoured wine with exceptional gooseberry and herbal varietal fruit, properly uninfluenced by oak; drink now). 1991 Corella Ridge Chardonnay (rich, complex, scented oak and intense melon/fig/citrus fruit flavours; exemplary wine in its class; to 1995). 1990 Harpers Range Cabernet (elegant cedary/leafy wine of light to medium body, in Chinon (Loire Valley) style and unusual in the Australian marketplace; to 1997). 1977 Para Liqueur Tawny Port (extremely complex wine with strong wood-aged, rancio characters and also a certain amount of background oak flavour; fine, gently biscuity drying finish). 1992 Gold Label Rhine Riesling (lime, passionfruit and herbaceous flavours intermingle in a wine with plenty of style and a long finish; to 1996).

SEPPELT GREAT WESTERN A–A Est 1866 $7–25 R 124, 287 GRT WESTERN

Moyston Road, Great Western, Vic 3377 (053) 56 2202
fax (053) 56 2300

Open Mon–Sat 9–5, Sun 12–4 **Production** NFP

Winemaker Ian McKenzie (chief)

Principal Wines Meth Champ comprising (from the bottom up) Brut Reserve, Imperial Reserve, Rosé Brut, Fleur de Lys, Vintage Brut and Salinger; also various varietal and regional sparkling wines of high quality; also premium regional Chard, Ries, Herm; finally various brands including much-diminished Chalambar and Moyston.

Summary Australia's foremost producer of sparkling wine, always immaculate in its given price range but also producing excellent Great Western-sourced table wines, especially long-lived Hermitage.

Recommended Wines 1989 Jean Trouette (excellent mousse, with bright, fresh and clean citrus aromas; on the palate there are more bready Pinot flavours evident, which add to complexity and length). 1989 Salinger (bright yellow-green colour with good mousse; a firm, crisp, citrus-toned wine that is crisp to the point of hardness, but does have great length). 1989 Fleur de Lys (good colour and mousse, with pleasant lemony Blanc de Blanc flavours and well balanced sweetness on the finish). Non Vintage Brut Reserve (excellent wine at its price, and very much in the mainstream Seppelt style with clean, lemony, Chardonnay fruit driving the wine and a crisp, clean finish).

SERENELLA ESTATE C–C Est 1981 $9.50–13.50 CD 21, 149 UPPER HUNTER V

Mudgee Road, Baerami via Denman, NSW 2333 (065) 47 5168
fax (065) 47 5164

Open Mon–Sat 10–4, Sun 11–4 **Production** 6000 cases

Winemaker Letitia Ceccini

Principal Wines Chard, Sem, Wh Burg, Cab Sauv, Herm, Shir.

Summary With 32 hectares of vineyards, Serenella is part grape grower and part winemaker, and in turn part of the broader based Serenella Pastoral Company. The winery also undertakes contract winemaking for others. Wine quality is modest; by and large, the white wines are better than the red.

SETTLEMENT WINE COMPANY NR Est 1976 $10–15 ML SD STHN VALES

c/o Torresan Wine Estates, Martins Road, McLaren Vale, SA 5171
(08) 386 3644

Open Not **Production** 500 cases

Winemaker Dr David Mitchell

Principal Wines Cab Sauv, Port.

Summary A shadow of its former self but still selling (for example) Dr David's Plasma Port, packaged in a genuine glass drip bottle.

SETTLERS CREEK NR Est 1971 $9.95–12.95 CD SD MUDGEE

c/o Augustine, George Campbell Drive, Mudgee, NSW 2850
(063) 72 3880

Open 7 days 10–4 **Production** 2500 cases

Winemaker Jon Reynolds (Contract)

Principal Wines Chard, Pinot.

Summary Has had a somewhat unsettled existence, but with Jon Reynolds now making the wine under contract good things can be expected.

SEVENHILL CELLARS B–BA Est 1851 $5–14 CD 43, 72, 126, 173, 176 CLARE V

College Road, Sevenhill via Clare, SA 5453 (088) 43 4222
fax (088) 43 4382

Open Mon–Fri 8.30–4.30, Sat & hols 9–4 **Production** 6000 cases

Winemakers Brother John May, John Monten

Principal Wines Wh Burg, Ries, Cab Sauv, Cab Sauv Malb, Mer Cab Franc, Shir, other red blends; Port.

Best Vintages W '87, '88, '89, '90, '92 R '80, '86, '89, '90, '92

Summary One of the historical treasures of Australia; the oft-photographed stone wine cellars are the oldest in the Clare Valley, and winemaking is still carried out under the direction of the Jesuitical Manresea Society and, in particular, Brother John May.

Recommended Wines 1992 Rhine Riesling (fragrant, toasty/fruity classic Clare Riesling, with fresh citrus-tinged fruit; a touch of sweetness does not detract; to 1997). 1991 Shiraz Touriga Grenache (clean, spicy, sweet fruit of light to medium weight; a blend of expediency, perhaps, but very attractive early drinking style). 1991 Shiraz (clean and fresh, with red berry fruit and considerable sweet vanillin American oak; to 1996).

SEVILLE ESTATE A–A Est 1972 $10–17.50 ML SD YARRA V

Linwood Road, Seville, Vic 3139 (059) 64 4556 fax (059) 64 3585

Open Not **Production** 1500 cases

Winemaker Dr Peter McMahon

Principal Wines Chard, Ries, Beeren, Shir, Pinot, Cab Sauv.

Best Vintages W '82, '86, '88, '90 R '86, '88, '90, '91

Summary To be perfectly honest, there is an element of inconsistency in the quality of the Seville wines which the A–A rating does not indicate; on the other hand, the great majority are beyond criticism. The heavily botrytised Riesling, released usually as a Beerenauslese but sometimes Trockenbeerenauslese, is a tour-de-force made in minuscule quantities but of the highest possible quality.

Recommended Wines 1990 Shiraz (gloriously fresh and vibrant peppery/spicy red cherry fruit with plenty of richness in the mouth and perfectly balanced soft tannins; to 2005). 1990 Cabernet Sauvignon (a very elegant wine with complex dark berry mint and leaf bouquet and flavour; soft tannins, but good acidity; to 2005).

SHANTELL B–B Est 1981 $11–16 CD 175 YARRA V
Melba Highway, Dixons Creek, Vic 3775 (059) 65 2264
fax (059) 65 2331
Open W'ends & hols 10–5 **Production** 1400 cases
Winemakers Shan & Turid Shanmugam
Principal Wines Sem, Chard, Pinot, Cab Sauv.
Best Vintages W '88, '89, '90, '91, '92 R '88, '89, '90, '91, '92
Summary The substantial and now fully mature Shantell vineyards provide the winery with a high quality fruit source; part is sold to other Yarra Valley makers, the remainder vinified at Shantell.
Recommended Wines 1990 Cabernet Sauvignon (solid, deep and ripe with concentrated cassis berry fruit, a touch of mint and strong tannins; to 2005). 1992 Semillon (crisp, herbaceous and tangy; no oak influence; good acidity; to 1994).

SHAW AND SMITH A–A Est 1990 $15–21 R 48, 65, 66, 109, 116, 127, 165, 323 STHN VALES
Flaxman Valley Road, Adelaide, SA 5152 (08) 370 9911
fax (08) 370 9339
Open Not **Production** 8000 cases
Winemaker Martin Shaw
Principal Wines Chard, Sauv Bl.
Summary The partnership of Michael Hill Smith, Australia's first Master of Wine, and Martin Shaw, premier 'Flying Winemaker', has predictably produced faultless wines.
Recommended Wines 1991 Chardonnay (elegant, cool-grown melon fruit, with a hint of barrel ferment; stylish and developing slowly; to 1996). 1992 Sauvignon Blanc (crisp, clean, direct herbaceous style with crisp acidity; drink now).

SHOTTESBROOKE CB–CB Est 1984 $13–17 R 42, 48, 80, 126, 127, 178, 226 STHN VALES
Ryecroft Vineyard, Ingoldby Road, McLaren Flat, SA 5171
(08) 383 0001 fax (08) 383 0456
Open Mon–Fri 9–5, w'ends 12–5 **Production** 4000 cases
Winemaker Nick Holmes
Principal Wines Sauv Bl, Chard, Cab Mer Malbec, Mer.
Summary The label of Ryecroft winemaker Nick Holmes, made from grapes grown on his vineyard at Myponga, at their best showing clear berry fruit, subtle oak and a touch of elegance. Recent releases have been disappointing.

SILOS, THE NR Est 1985 $8.50–14 CD SD SOUTH COAST
Princes Highway, Jaspers Brush, NSW 2535 (044) 48 6082
Open 7 days 10–5 **Production** 1400 cases
Winemaker Alan Bamfield
Principal Wines Chard, Sem, Sauv Bl, Shir, Mal, Port.

Summary Aimed purely at the tourist trade; wine quality has left much to be desired, but a delightful, light, pepper-spice 1990 Shiraz redressed the balance.

SIMON HACKETT NR Est 1981 $11–13.20 R SD 227 STHN VALES

Off McMurtrie, McLaren Vale, SA 5171 (08) 331 7348
Open Not **Production** 8500 cases
Winemaker Simon Hackett
Principal Wines Sem, Chard, Cab Sauv.

Summary Simon Hackett makes his wines at various wineries before maturing and packaging them at his own maturation establishment. Wine quality has varied somewhat over the years, but hit a high spot with the '91s and in particular the tangy, lively and zesty '91 Semillon.

SIMONS NR Est 1978 $8–10 CD SD CANBERRA

Badgery Road, Burra Creek, Queanbeyan, NSW 2620
(06) 236 3216
Open W'ends 9–5 **Production** 100 cases
Winemaker Lloyd Simons
Principal Wines Chard, Tram Ries, Mer.

Summary The tiny production is sold to the tourist trade, which accepts the rustic quality of the wine.

SKILLOGALEE B–B Est 1970 $11.75–15.50 R 3, 48, 55, 69, 126 CLARE V

Off Hughes Park Road, Sevenhill via Clare, SA 5453 (088) 43 4311 or (088) 43 4343
Open 7 days 10–5 **Production** 8000 cases
Winemakers Dave Palmer, Stephen John (Contract)
Principal Wines Ries, LH Ries, Traminer, Shir, Cabernets, fortifieds.

Summary David and Diana Palmer purchased Skillogalee from the George family several years ago and have capitalised to the full on the exceptional fruit quality of the Skillogalee vineyards. The winery also has a well patronised lunchtime restaurant.

Recommended Wines 1992 Rhine Riesling (solid, soft, toasty/honeyed style, quite forward in its development; drink now). 1992 Traminer (clean, crisp and correct with delicately spicy fruit, and a pleasingly dry finish; drink now). 1991 Cabernet Sauvignon Franc Malbec (fresh, lively, minty fruit and slightly raw oak yet to integrate and settle down; needs time; to 1999).

SNOWY RIVER WINERY NR Est 1984 $10–20 ML SD STHN HIGHLANDS

Berriedale, NSW 2628 (064) 56 5041 fax (064) 56 5005
Open 7 days 10–5 **Production** 4000 cases
Winemaker Geoff Carter
Principal Wines Chard, Chab, Ries, Muller, Siegerrebe, Noble Ries, Eiswein Ries, Snowy Red, Cab Mer, Pinot Mer, Cab Sauv, fortifieds.

Summary Claims the only Eiswein to have been made in Australia, picked on 8 June 1990 after a frost of -8° Celsius. Also makes a Trocken Beeren Auslese (sic) picked mid-May from the vineyard situated on the banks of the Snowy River, one hour from Mount Kosciusko. One suspects many of the wines are purchased from other makers.

• SOMERSET CROSSING NR Est 1969 $5.40–10.80 CD SD CENTRAL GOULBURN
1 Emily Street, Seymour, Vic 3660 (03) 457 5440
Open 7 days 10–5 **Production** 1500 cases
Winemaker David Traeger (Contract)
Principal Wines Ries, Chard, Sauv Bl, Shir, Cab Mer, fortifieds.
Summary The acquisition of Somerset Crossing by John and Adele Ubaldi in 1991 will hopefully see an improvement in the early uncertain quality of the wines. What is described as a 'charming, rustic, casual restaurant' with a vine-covered courtyard for outside eating is open daily.

SORRENBERG NR Est 1986 $12–17 CD 175 NE VIC
Alma Road, Beechworth, Vic 3747 (057) 28 2278
Open W'ends 1–5 **Production** 1000 cases
Winemaker Barry Morey
Principal Wines Chard, Sauv Bl Sem, Ries, Gamay, Cab Sauv, Cab Franc Mer.
Summary Barry and Jan Morey made their first wines in 1989 from the 2.5 hectare vineyard situated on the outskirts of Beechworth. They are still learning the winemaking craft.

SPRING VALE BA–A Est 1986 $18 CD 149, 173 EAST COAST, TAS
Spring Vale, Swansea, Tas 7190 (002) 57 8208 fax (002) 57 8598
Open W'ends & hols 10–5 **Production** 850 cases
Winemaker Andrew Hood (Contract)
Principal Wines Chard, Pinot.
Summary Rodney Lyne has progressively established 1.2 hectares of Pinot Noir and 0.8 hectares of Chardonnay (not all in bearing) in the uniquely favoured climate of Tasmania's east coast, and right from the outset has produced wonderfully rich and generous Pinot Noir well worth the search.
Recommended Wine 1991 Pinot Noir (voluptuous, smooth, sweet, plum and dark cherry fruit with velvety richness; to 1995).

STAFFORD RIDGE A–BA Est 1982 $12–19.50 ML 178 ADELAIDE HILLS
2 Gilpin Lane, Mitcham, SA 5062 (residence only) (08) 272 2105 fax (08) 271 0177
Open Sun 11–4 c/o Mount Lofty House **Production** 3000 cases
Winemaker Geoff Weaver
Principal Wines Ries, Chard, Sauv Bl, Cab Mer.
Summary Stafford Ridge is now the full-time business of former Hardy Group chief winemaker Geoff Weaver. He draws upon a little under 10 hectares of vineyard established between 1982 and 1988; for the time being, at least, the physical winemaking is carried out by Geoff Weaver at Petaluma.
Recommended Wines 1992 Sauvignon Blanc (classic tropical gooseberry fruit, clean, crisp and fresh; drink now). 1990 Chardonnay (smooth, now showing significant honeyed bottle-developed characters; hints of cool climate citrus also evident; drink now).

STANTON & KILLEEN B–B Est 1875 $11.50–16.60 R 55, 317 NE VIC
Murray Valley Highway, Rutherglen, Vic 3685 (060) 32 9457
fax (060) 32 8018
Open Mon–Sat 9–5, Sun 10–5 **Production** 8000 cases
Winemaker Chris Killeen
Principal Wines Chard, Moodemere Cab Shir Durif, Shir, numerous Ports, Muscats and Tokay.
Summary A traditional maker of smooth, rich reds, some very good vintage ports and attractive, fruity Muscats and Tokays.
Recommended Wine Liqueur Tokay (light, fresh, very clear tea leaf varietal aroma and flavour; cleansing finish).

STEINS CB–B Est 1976 $7.50–12.50 CD SD MUDGEE
Sandal Park Estate, Pipeclay Lane, Mudgee, NSW 2850
(063) 73 3991 fax (063) 73 3709
Open 7 days 10–4 **Production** 5000 cases
Winemaker Robert Stein
Principal Wines Sem, Chard, Chab, Tram, Shiraz, Claret, Port.
Summary The sweeping panorama from the winery is its own reward, but wines such as the quite delicious 1991 Shiraz are another reason to visit this little-known winery.
Recommended Wine 1991 Shiraz (spotlessly clean, dense, ripe dark berry and cherry fruits intermingling with hints of spice, finishing with soft tannins; to 2005).

ST FRANCIS CB–B Est 1869 $6.90–19.90 CD 11 STHN VALES
Bridge Street, Old Reynella, SA 5161 (08) 381 1925
fax (08) 322 0921
Open 7 days 9.30–4.30 **Production** 9000 cases
Winemakers Various Contract
Principal Wines Sparkl, Chab, Chard, Sem, Fumé, Ries, Fronti, Shir, Cab Sauv.
Summary A full blown tourist facility and convention centre with a thriving cellar door sales facility offering wines purchased in bulk from other makers (usually bottled or cleanskins). Thanks to the skill and contacts of its consultants the average quality is good, especially at the price.
Recommended Wines 1991 Late Harvest Frontignan (intense, spicy, grapy aromas showing perfect varietal definition; on the palate gently sweet fruit balanced by acidity; drink now).

ST GREGORY'S NR Est 1983 $10.50 ML SD WESTERN VIC
Bringalbert South Road, Bringalbert Sth via Apsley, Vic 3319
(055) 86 5225
Open By appointment **Production** 200 cases
Winemaker Gregory Flynn
Principal Wines Port (in various styles).
Summary A strictly weekend hobby of port enthusiast Greg Flynn.

ST HALLETT A–A Est 1944 $7.90–27.50 R 87, 88, 89, 101, 119, 139, 173, 226 BAROSSA V
St Hallett's Road, Tanunda, SA 5352 (085) 63 2319 fax (085) 63 2901
Open Mon–Sat 10–5, Sun 10–4 **Production** 15 000 cases

Winemakers Stuart Blackwell, Peter Gambetta

Principal Wines Poacher's Blend Sem, Chard, Sauv Bl, Cab Mer, Old Block Shir, Barossa Shir, Port.

Best Vintages W '87, '89, '90, '91, '92 R '86, '88, '90, '91, '92

Summary One of the true-blue Aussie success stories, with its Old Block Shiraz gaining super-cult status in markets as far away and as unlikely as Ireland and Paris; it is no exaggeration to say the entire production could be sold in London. It has driven the development of the Barossa Valley Shiraz and Poacher's Blend Semillon, which are cleverly crafted additions to the portfolio.

Recommended Wines 1990 Old Block Shiraz (spotlessly clean, vibrant spicy/minty/berry fruit bouquet, with wonderfully harmonious and elegant flavours, augmented by sensitively handled spicy American oak; so delicious now, hard to see why it should be cellared, but it will hold to 2000). 1991 Barossa Shiraz (fresh, soft, dark cherry fruit with pronounced vanilla, coconut and cinnamon oak; a la mode; to 1996). 1992 Poacher's Blend Semillon (light, crisp apple flavours in no-frills seafood style; drink now).

ST HUBERTS BA–BA Est 1966 $8.90–25.40 R 48, 86–90 YARRA V
Maroondah Highway, Coldstream, Vic 3770 (03) 739 1421
fax (03) 739 1070

Open Mon–Fri 9–5, w'ends 10.30–5.30 **Production** 40 000 cases

Winemaker Greg Traught

Principal Wines Chard, Classic Dry White, Pinot, Cab Mer, Cab Sauv; Rowan is the second label and provides much of the volume.

Best Vintages W '82, '84, '90, '91, '92 R '82, '88, '90, '91, '92

Summary The changes have come thick and fast at St Huberts, which is now part of the Rothbury Estate group and has former Rothbury red winemaker Greg Traught in charge. Traught literally worked miracles with the Rothbury red wines after his appointment in 1989, and it will be more than interesting to watch developments at St Huberts.

Recommended Wines 1990 Cabernet Sauvignon (extremely rich, full and concentrated with sweet dark berry and minty fruit; almost chewy texture; to 2005). 1992 Chardonnay (finely balanced melon and fig fruit with subtle oak, less opulent than preceding vintages and all the better for that; to 1997). 1992 Rowan Chardonnay (light, scented, citrus melon fruit, crisp and fresh; low oak input; may well cellar surprisingly well; to 1996). 1990 Rowan Cabernet Sauvignon (solid, chewy, ripe and fleshy wine with gently gamey overtones and soft tannins; to 1996).

ST LEONARDS B–B Est 1860 $8.90–25 CD 81 NE VIC
Wahgunyah, Vic 3687 (060) 33 1004 fax (060) 33 3636

Open Mon–Sat 9–5, Sun 10–4 **Production** 8000 cases

Winemaker Terry Barnett

Principal Wines Sem, Chard, Sauv Bl, Chenin, Rosé, Pinot, Cab Franc Mer, Cab Sauv.

Best Vintages W '85, '87, '88, '89 R '82, '86, '88, '90

Summary An old favourite, producing always-interesting wines cleverly marketed through an active mailing list and singularly attractive cellar door at the historic winery on the banks of the Murray.

Recommended Wine 1989 Chardonnay (smooth, buttery fruit

with bacony/toasty/oaky bottle developed characters with alcohol sweetness on the palate balanced by good acidity; ready now but will hold).

•ST MARYS VINEYARD NR Est 1986 $14–22.50 CD 72
COONAWARRA
V & A Lane, via Coonawarra, SA 5277 (087) 36 6070
fax (087) 36 6045
Open 7 days 10–4 **Production** 4000 cases
Winemaker Ralph Fowler (Contract)
Principal Wines Chard, Cab Sauv.
Summary The Mulligan and Hooper families established St Marys Vineyard in 1986 on a patch of terra rossa soil 15 kilometres west of the township of Coonawarra and in the proposed Penola appellation district. Only part of the production from the 22 hectare vineyards is made into wine, the remainder of the grapes being sold. Ralph Fowler (Contract) makes the wine at Leconfield.
Recommended Wines 1992 Chardonnay (light, crisp with distinct melon and fig flavours and a slightly hard, faintly peppery finish). 1991 Cabernet Sauvignon (firm, slightly astringent wine with firm, fresh red berry fruit and a touch of spicy American oak; to 1997).

ST MATTHIAS B–B Est 1982 13.50–16.95 CD SD TAMAR V
113 Rosevears Drive, Rosevears, Tas 7251 (003) 30 1700
fax (003) 30 1975
Open 7 days 10–5 **Production** 4000 cases
Winemaker Heemskerk (Contract)
Principal Wines Ries, Chard, Pinot, Cab Mer.
Summary A label that is almost certainly going to disappear, following the acquisition of the vineyard by Moorilla Estate. Founder Laurie Wing retained the stock, and will be progressively selling this over the next year or so. In future the grapes will be used in the Moorilla wines.

ST NEOT'S ESTATE NR Est 1981 $15–19 R SD
MORNINGTON P
63 Red Hill-Shoreham Road, Red Hill South, Vic 3937 (059) 89 2023
Open Not **Production** 500 cases
Winemaker Contract
Principal Wines Ries, Sem, Chard, Pinot, Cab Sauv.
Summary The last St Neot's wines tasted in 1990 showed the typical clear varietal fruit flavours one comes to expect from the district.

STEVENS CAMBRAI CA–CB Est 1975 $4.90–20 CD 20, 106
STHN VALES
Hamiltons Road, McLaren Flat, SA 5171 (08) 383 0251
fax (08) 383 0251
Open 7 days 9–5 **Production** 6000 cases
Winemaker Graham Stevens
Principal Wines Chard, Gewurz, Front, Shir, Zinfandel, Cab Sauv, Vintage Port.
Best Vintages W '83, '87, '90, '91, '92 **R** '84, '86, '90, '91, '92
Summary Graham Stevens knows both his own mind and the district very well; a challenging mixture of the exotic and the run of

the mill, the good and the not so good, has typified the table wines, but the Vintage Ports have been of consistently high quality.

Recommended Wines 1990 Shiraz (strong, scented, American oak drives the wine, but the fruit is clean and the style will appeal to many; to 1998). 1985 Vintage Port (rich, full, high toned aroma with rich, dense chocolate fruit; luscious, full bodied and sweet; to 2005).

STONE RIDGE B–B Est 1981 9–15 CD SD GRANITE BELT
Limberlost Road, Glen Aplin, Qld 4381 (076) 83 4211
Open 7 days 10–5 **Production** 1400 cases
Winemakers Jim Lawrie, Anne Kennedy
Principal Wines Chard, Shir, Mt Sterling Dry Red (second label).
Summary Spicy Shiraz is the specialty with many attractive wines appearing since 1987, but Jim Lawrie is also making progress with Chardonnay, doing quite well with that wine in 1992.

STONIERS MERRICKS A–A Est 1978 $15–20 R 12, 139, 186, 318 MORNINGTON P
62 Thompsons Lane, Merricks, Vic 3916 (059) 89 8300
fax (059) 89 8709
Open 7 days 12–5 **Production** 8500 cases
Winemaker Tod Dexter
Principal Wines Chard, Pinot, Cab Sauv; Winery Selection range is second label.
Best Vintages W '86, '88, '90, '91, '92 R '84, '88, '90, '91, '92
Summary Has now overtaken Dromana Estate as Mornington's largest producer (of Mornington-sourced grapes) and set to become known throughout Australia. The Winery Selection range (blended from owner Brian Stonier's own vineyard grapes and from winemaker Tod Dexter's vineyard) offer very good value; the Stoniers Merricks label is for the top wines.
Recommended Wines 1992 Merricks Chardonnay (complex barrel ferment and Burgundian aromas; stylish, intense, long palate with very good fruit and oak in balance; to 1996). 1992 Winery Selection Pinot Noir (fragrant, stylish, high-toned cherry fruit with a nice stemmy cut; drink now). 1991 Merricks Pinot Noir (potent, plummy/strawberry fruit with good structure and weight; intense; to 1994).

SUMMERFIELD BA–A Est 1979 $9–16 CD SD PYRENEES
Moonambel-Stawell Road, Moonambel, Vic 3478 (054) 67 2264
fax (054) 67 2380
Open 7 days 9–6 **Production** 2000 cases
Winemaker Ian Summerfield
Principal Wines Trebbiano Chard, Shir, Cab Sauv.
Best Vintages R '80, '83, '88, '89, '90
Summary A little known producer brought to prominence when former Victorian Agricultural Department winemaker Drew Noon (now of Cassegrain) became involved; since 1988 has produced consistently outstanding rich, clean red wines.
Recommended Wines 1991 Hermitage (exceedingly rich, complex and generous dark currant cassis and plum fruits; soft tannins and subtle American oak; to 2000+). 1991 Cabernet Sauvignon (vibrant peppermint flavours in Central Victorian mode which may be a little too much of a good thing for some palates; soft sweet oak; to 1997).

SUNNYCLIFF WINES C–B Est 1980 $6–8 R 146 NW VIC
Nangiloc Road, Iraak, Vic 3496 (050) 29 1666 fax (050) 24 3316
Open Not **Production** 38 000 cases
Winemaker Mark Zeppel
Principal Wines Chab, Chard, Colomb Chard, Ries, Sauv Bl, Cab
Sauv, Cabernets.
Summary Part of the Rentiers-Katnook group, producing grape
juice, grape concentrate and bulk wine with a small proportion of the
crush released under the Sunnycliff label, and providing wines of
pleasant quality and modest price.

SUTHERLAND B–B Est 1979 $12–14 CD 29 HUNTER V
Deasey's Road, Pokolbin, NSW 2321 (049) 98 7650
fax (049) 98 7603
Open 7 days 10–4 **Production** 8000 cases
Winemaker Neil Sutherland
Principal Wines Chard, Sem, Chenin, Shir, Pinot, Cab Sauv.
Best Vintages W '85, '87, '90, '91 R '88, '89, '90, '91
Summary With substantial and now fully mature vineyards to draw
upon, Sutherland is a more or less consistent producer of generous,
mainstream Hunter whites and reds.
Recommended Wines 1991 Shiraz (clean, rich and sweet dark
fruits with briary aromas, and gently plummy flavours on the palate
with soft tannins). 1990 Semillon (rich, honeyed, full blown buttery
butterscotch flavours; drink now).

TALIJANCICH CA–B Est 1932 $10–68 CD SD SWAN V
121 Hyem Road, Herne Hill, WA 6056 (09) 296 4289
fax (09) 296 4289
Open Sun–Fri 10–5 **Production** 3000 cases
Winemaker James Talijancich
Principal Wines Sem, Verd, Shir, Port, Muscat and other fortifieds.
Summary A fortified-wine specialist that now produces a small
range of table wines, the latter with consultancy advice from 1989,
which happily transformed their quality. The 1961 Muscat remains
supreme at $68 a bottle.

TALLARA B–B Est 1970 $12 CD SD MUDGEE
'Tallara' Cassilis Road, Mudgee, NSW 2850 (063) 72 2408
Open W'ends 9–5 **Production** 300 cases
Winemaker Phillip Shaw
Principal Wines Chard, Cab Sauv.
Summary Leading Sydney chartered accountant Rick Turner's
weekend hobby, with smooth, full flavoured Chardonnay made by
Phillip Shaw at Rosemount. No recent tastings.

TALTARNI BA–BA Est 1972 $7.50–16 R 30, 86, 89, 165, 169,
170, 181, 199, 305 PYRENEES
Taltarni Road, Moonambel, Vic 3478 (054) 67 2218
fax (054) 67 2306
Open 7 days 10–5 **Production** 50 000 cases
Winemaker Dominique Portet
Principal Wines Ries, Fumé, Shir, Cab Sauv, Mer Cab Franc,
Sparkl.
Best Vintages R '82, '84, '88, '90, '91

Summary The red wines are uncompromising in style; tannin usually teeters on the edge of acceptability, and sometimes the second label Reserve de Pyrenees can outperform its betters simply because it is softer. These are, above all else, wines for the long haul.
Recommended Wines 1990 French Syrah (clean, firm, red berry fruit, subtle oak and that typical austere structure, although tannins are well balanced; to 2004). 1992 Sauvignon Blanc (fairly reserved, understated food style, clean and crisp, but tending to neutrality; drink now).

TAMBURLAINE CB–CB Est 1966 $10.50–16 CD 175 HUNTER V

McDonalds Road, Pokolbin, NSW 2321 (049) 98 7570
fax (049) 98 7763
Open 7 days 9.30–5 **Production** 10 000 cases
Winemakers G. Silkman, M. Davidson
Principal Wines Chard, Sem, Verd, Sauv Bl, Rosé, Syrah, Cab Mer, Liqueur Muscat.
Best Vintages '86, '87, '89, '91, '92 **R** '86, '87, '88, '89, '91
Summary One of the longer-established wineries in the Hunter Valley which has established a solid reputation and following. Overall, the red wines are more reliable than the whites.
Recommended Wines 1991 Cabernet Merlot (light, clean, sweet, cedary fruit and oak; to 1995).

TANAMI RED NR Est 1990 $8–9 CD SD STHN VALES

McMurtrie Road, McLaren Vale, SA 5171 (08) 383 0351
Open W'ends & public hols 11–4.45 **Production** 340 cases
Winemaker Les Payne
Principal Wines Shir, Cab Sauv.
Summary No rating, simply because I have not tasted the wines.

TANGLEWOOD DOWNS NR Est 1984 $11–18 R SD

MORNINGTON P
Bulldog Creek Road, Mornington Rural, Vic 3931 (059) 74 3325
Open 7 days Dec–April 12–5, w'ends May–Nov 12–5
Production 1000 cases
Winemaker Ken Bilham
Principal Wines Chard, Tram, Ries, Pinot, Cab Sauv.
Summary Tanglewood Downs hit a high spot with its '91 Chardonnay and '91 Pinot Noir, but missed the target with the '92 Chardonnay and '91 Cabernet.

TARCOOLA NR Est 1971 $8–10 CD SD GEELONG

Spillers Road, Lethbridge, Vic 3332 (052) 81 9245
fax (052) 81 9311
Open 7 days 10–5 **Production** 4000 cases
Winemaker Keith Wood
Principal Wines Ries, Muller, Hilltop Shir, River Flat Shir, Cab Sauv.
Summary After a period of slow decline, Tarcoola was purchased in 1990 by Keith Wood, who is determined to breathe new life into the vineyard and winery. Old, substandard stock has been disposed of and new labels introduced, emphasising those wines made from estate grown grapes.

TARRAHILL ESTATE CB–B Est 1985 $12–13 ML 132 YARRA V
Lot 2 Old Healesville Road, Yarra Glen, Vic 3775 (03) 439 7425
fax (03) 435 9138
Open Not **Production** 1000 cases
Winemaker Ian Hanson
Principal Wines Cab Sauv, Cab Franc.
Summary Dental surgeon Ian Hanson planted his first vines in the
late 1960s close to the junction of the Yarra and Plenty Rivers; in
1983 those plantings were extended (with 3000 vines), and in 1988
the Tarrahill property at Yarra Glen was established with 10 further
acres. The Lower Plenty wines bear the Hanson label; the Yarra Glen
bear the Tarrahill Estate label.
Recommended Wines 1990 Hanson Cabernet Sauvignon (strong
red-purple colour with firm, deep fruit, weighty and briary, with
slightly dry tannins; to 1998). 1991 Hanson Cabernet Sauvignon
(potent briary/cigar box/leafy fruit in consistent vineyard style; to
1997). 1992 Hanson Cabernet Franc (potent, fragrant tobacco leaf
aromas with crisp, gently tart fruit flavours with some red berry notes).

TARRAWARRA A–BA Est 1983 $10–25 R 163, 202, 263
YARRA V
Healesville Road, Yarra Glen, Vic 3775 (059) 62 3311
fax (059) 62 3887
Open Not **Production** 8000 cases
Winemaker David Wollan, Martin Williams
Principal Wines Chard, Pinot; second label is Tunnel Hill, third is
Ryrie.
Best Vintages W '87, '88, '89, '90, '92 R '88, '89, '90, '91, '92
Summary Slowly evolving Chardonnay of great structure and
complexity is the winery specialty; robust Pinot Noir also needs time
and evolves impressively if given it. The second label Tunnel Hill
wines are more accessible when young, and better value for those
who do not wish to wait for the Tarrawarra wines to evolve.
Recommended Wines 1990 Tarrawarra Chardonnay (very
complex, textured and structured wine with very deliberate and very
successful winemaker influences; malolactic fermentation, barrel
fermentation and prolonged lees contact have all left their mark;
needs much time; to 2002). 1991 Tunnel Hill Pinot Noir (quite
stylish, of light to medium weight with fresh, gently spicy fruit and
well balanced oak; to 1996). 1991 Tunnel Hill Chardonnay (fairly
restrained style, with some malolactic influence evident; complex,
structured wine with no lollipop characters whatsoever; to 1997).

TARWIN RIDGE NR Est 1983 $11–14.50 ML SD GIPPSLAND
Whittles Road, Leongatha South, Vic (vineyard only); postal PO Box
498, Leongatha, Vic 3953 phone and fax (056) 643 2311
Open Not **Production** 700 cases
Winemaker Brian Anstee
Principal Wines Fumé, Pinot, Cab Mer; Cherry Tree Creek is
second label.
Summary For the time being Brian Anstee is making his wines at
Nicholson River under the gaze of fellow social worker Ken
Eckersley; the initial releases of '90 Fumé Blanc and '89 Cabernet
Merlot showed promise, particularly the light but fragrant and clean
Cabernet Merlot.

TAYLORS CB–A Est 1972 $8.95–9.95 R 30, 119, 120, 159, 160, 161, 226, 297 CLARE V
Mintaro Road, Auburn, SA 5451 (088) 49 2008 fax (088) 49 2240
Open Mon–Fri 9–5, Sat & pub hols 10–5, Sun 10–4
Production 120 000 cases
Winemaker Andrew Tolley
Principal Wines Chard, Ries, Wh Burg, Chab, Mos, Pinot, Cab Sauv, Herm.
Best Vintages W '84, '87, '89, '91, '92 **R** '84, '86, '89, '91, '92
Summary The Chardonnay and Cabernet Sauvignon are both major brands, each selling in excess of 50 000 cases a year; what is more, not a bottle is exported. The Chardonnay is light bodied and subtle, developing in bottle for five years or more; the Cabernet Sauvignon is deliberately made in a similarly light style, fully ready when released with four years age. The wines sell in such large volumes simply because they are so well priced.
Recommended Wine 1990 Hermitage (clean, smooth, soft fruit with a gentle touch of American oak; fault free, but does not show a great deal of varietal character or verve; drink now).

TEMPLE BRUER CB–B Est 1981 $7–17.50 CD 43, 115, 207 LANGHORNE CREEK
Milang Road, Strathalbyn, SA 5255 (085) 37 0203
Open 7 days 10.30–4.30 **Production** NFP
Winemaker David Bruer
Principal Wines Chab, Ries, Sparkl Burg, Cab Mer, Rosé, Shir Malb.
Summary Unusual, sappy rather vegetal Cabernet Merlot (the '88 a gold medal winner in 1991), some excellent Eden Valley-sourced Riesling, a velvety Sparkling Burgundy and good botrytis Riesling are among the eclectic range of wines on offer.

TERRACE VALE CB–B Est 1971 $11–14 CD 172 HUNTER V
Deasey's Lane, Pokolbin, NSW 2321 (049) 98 7517
fax (049) 98 7814
Open 7 days 10–4 **Production** 7000 cases
Winemaker Alain Le Prince
Principal Wines Sem, Chard, Gewurz, Sparkl, Shir, Pinot, Cab Sauv, Herm, Port.
Best Vintages W '81, '84, '87, '89, '91 R '81, '83, '88, '89, '91
Summary Every now and then Terrace Vale bobs up with a lovely wine such as the 1989 Cabernet Sauvignon Bin 7; normally, the white wines are better, solid and often slow developing.

T'GALLANT BA–B Est 1990 $13–14 R 120 MORNINGTON P
237 Myers Road, Bittern, Vic 3918 phone and fax (059) 89 2203
Open Summer w'ends by appointment 10–5
Production 4000 cases
Winemakers Kathleen Quealy, Kevin McCarthy (Contract)
Principal Wines Chard, Holystone, Pinot Gris.
Summary Consultant winemakers Kathleen Quealy and Kevin McCarthy have specialised in unwooded Chardonnay for their own label sourced from low yielding, relatively mature vineyards, adding Holystone, a unique, unwooded Pinot Noir-Chardonnay table wine blend, in 1991. Wine quality has been consistently good.

Recommended Wines 1992 Chardonnay (crisp, firm melon and fig fruit with good weight and length). 1991 Pinot Gris (smoky, peachy aroma and fruit flavour; slightly hard finish; interesting wine for the student).

THALGARA ESTATE NR Est 1985 $12.50–15 CD SD HUNTER V
DeBeyers Road, Pokolbin, NSW 2321 phone and fax (049) 98 7717
Open 7 days 10–5 **Production** 1500 cases
Winemaker Steve Lamb
Principal Wines Chard, Sem Chard, Shir, Shir Cab.
Summary No wines tasted recently; the 1988 red wines were rather oaky, but had plenty of flavour.

THISTLE HILL B–B Est 1976 $9–13 CD SD MUDGEE
McDonalds Road, Mudgee, NSW 2850 (063) 73 3546
Open 7 days 9–5 **Production** 4000 cases
Winemaker David Robertson
Principal Wines Ries, Chard, Pinot, Cab Sauv.
Summary David and Leslie Robertson produce supremely honest wines, always full of flavour and appropriately reflecting the climate and terroir. Some may be a little short on finesse, but never on character.
Recommended Wines 1990 Cabernet Sauvignon (solid fruit bouquet with gentle earthy overtones; on the palate clean, firm, red fruit flavours with balanced tannins and good structure; to 1998). 1992 Riesling (voluminous pastille and peach fruit aroma and flavour, apparently botrytis influenced; drink now). 1992 Chardonnay (some smoky barrel ferment influence with solid, sweet fruit tending to tropical; smooth and supple palate; some oak; drink now).

THOMAS NR Est 1976 $15.95 ML SD SW COASTAL
23–24 Crowd Road, Gelorup, WA 6230 (097) 95 7925
Open By appointment **Production** 600 cases
Winemaker Gill Thomas
Principal Wines Pinot, Cab Sauv.
Summary I have not tasted the elegant wines of Bunbury pharmacist Gill Thomas for several years; they are only sold to a local clientele.

THOMAS FERN HILL ESTATE CB–CB Est 1975 $4.50–25
CD 20, 48, 95, 145 STHN VALES
Ingoldby Road, McLaren Flat, SA 5171 (08) 383 0167
fax (08) 383 0107
Open Mon–Fri 10–5, w'ends 12–5 **Production** 4500 cases
Winemaker Wayne Thomas
Principal Wines Brut, Chard, Sauv Bl, Cab Sauv, Shir, Port.
Summary Some very good wines, some not so good, the latter slightly surprising given Wayne Thomas's considerable district experience. A fleshy, soft '91 Sauvignon Blanc and rather oaky '90 Shiraz showed the winery to best advantage. No recent tastings.

TILBA VALLEY NR Est 1978 $9.50–13.50 CD SD SOUTH
COAST
Glen Eden Vineyard, Corunna Lake via Tilba, NSW 2546
(044) 73 7308
Open 7 days 10–5 **Production** 1400 cases

Winemaker Barry Field
Principal Wines Chard, Tram Ries, Sem, Cab Sauv, Cab Herm.
Summary A strongly tourist-oriented operation, with no recent tastings.

TIM ADAMS BA–A Est 1985 $9.50–14 R 12, 17, 34, 178 CLARE V

Warenda Road, Clare, SA 5453 phone and fax (088) 42 2429
Open 7 days 11–5 **Production** 9500 cases
Winemaker Tim Adams
Principal Wines Ries, Sem, Botrytis Sem, Shir, Cabernet.
Best Vintages W '88, '89, '90, '91, '92 **R** '88, '89, '90, '91, '92
Summary Tim and Pam Adams have built a first-class business since Tim Adams left his position as winemaker at Leasingham in 1985. Nine local growers provide the grapes for the enterprise, which has consistently produced wines of exceptional depth of flavour.
Recommended Wines 1991 Aberfeldy Shiraz (extremely sweet, voluptuous berry aromas; berry and eucalypt mint flavours with pronounced tannins; massive wine; to 2005). 1992 Semillon (rich, full flavoured sweet semillon fruit with vanillin oak; forward commercial style offering immediate enjoyment). 1992 Rhine Riesling (strong lime juice-accented wine with rich, full flavoured palate; again, drink now).

TIM KNAPPSTEIN BA–BA Est 1976 $11.25–19.95 R 110, 165, 181, 255 CLARE V

2 Pioneer Avenue, Clare, SA 5453 (088) 42 2600
fax (088) 42 3831
Open Mon–Fri 9–5, Sat 10–5, Sun 11–4 **Production** 35 000 cases
Winemakers Tim Knappstein, Tim Wardell
Principal Wines Ries, Gewurz, Chard, Fumé, Sem, Pinot, Cab Mer, Cab Sauv.
Best Vintages W '82, '85, '88, '90, '92 R '84, '86, '88, '90, '91
Summary While Tim Knappstein has long been regarded as one of Australia's foremost makers of Rhine Riesling and a very good red winemaker there have been significant changes for the better in the past few years. The 17 hectare Adelaide Hills Lenswood vineyards are now in commercial production, and the winery became part of the publicly held Petaluma group in late 1992. One can only imagine that even better things are in store for the future.
Recommended Wines 1991 Lenswood Pinot Noir (an exceptionally stylish, sappy wine, gloriously Burgundian on the palate; quite outstanding; drink now). 1992 Rhine Riesling (clean, lime and toast fruit; surprisingly full and soft on the palate; early developing vintage). 1992 Sauvignon Blanc (clean, crisp, relatively subdued fruit, but good mouthfeel and acidity; a blend of Clare and Lenswood grapes; to 1994).

TINGLE-WOOD A–A Est 1976 $10–12 SD GRT SOUTHERN

Glenrowan Road, Denmark, WA 6333 (098) 40 9218
fax (098) 48 1954
Open 7 days 9–5 **Production** 950 cases
Winemaker John Wade (Contract)
Principal Wines Ries, LH Ries, Cab Shir.
Summary This remote, forest-encircled vineyard has produced some quite lovely wines for owner Bob Wood, with trophy winning

wines from both 1990 and 1991. Sadly no grapes were picked in 1992 owing to seasonal conditions.

Recommended Wines 1991 Rhine Riesling (powerful, concentrated bouquet with classic toast and kerosene characters; great depth and length to the flavour with tight lime juice and again a touch of that so-called kerosene character of powerful Riesling; to 2000). 1990 Rhine Riesling (fresh, crisp, elegant and amazingly youthful; fine feel to the finish which is remarkably long; to 2000).

TINLINS NR Est 1977 $2–4 CD SD STHN VALES
Kangarilla Road, McLaren Flat, SA 5171 (08) 323 8649
Open Mon–Fri 8–5, w'ends 8–4.30
Production 320 000 case equivalent
Winemaker Stephen Bennett
Principal Wines Generic table, fortified and flavoured wines sold in bottle, in flagons, 6 litre casks and 25 litre kegs for as little as $1 a litre.
Summary A staggeringly large direct sale operation relying on strong cellar and sales driven by prices that disappeared 20 years ago.

TISDALL CB–B Est 1979 $6.25–10.50 R 42, 127, 161, 171, 181, 278 NTH GOULBURN R
Cornelia Creek Road, Echuca, Vic 3564 (054) 82 1911
fax (054) 82 2516
Open Mon–Fri 9–5, w'ends 10–5 **Production** 60 000 cases
Winemaker Toni Stockhausen
Principal Wines Dry Wh, Chard Sem, Sauv Bl Sem, Chard, Dry Red, Shir Cab, Cab Sauv, Cab Mer, Sparkl.
Summary Following its acquisition by Mildara Blass in July 1993, and the earlier departure of long-term winemaker Jeff Clarke to join Montana in New Zealand, Tisdall is bound to change. The red wines have always been reliable and good value, the white wines much less so, and it will be interesting to see how the latter shape up under the new regime.
Recommended Wine 1990 Cabernet Merlot (clean, fresh wine of medium weight showing red berry mint and herbaceous fruit flavours; quite well structured; to 1997).

TIZZANA NR Est 1887 $5.50–16.50 CD SD SYDNEY DISTRICT
Tizzana Road, Ebenezer, NSW 2756 (045) 79 1150
fax (045) 79 1216
Open W'ends & hols 12–6 **Production** 200 cases
Winemaker Peter Auld
Principal Wines Estate grown and made Shir, Cab Sauv, Port; 'cleanskin' wines under Tizzana Selection label.
Summary The only estate wines tasted (several years ago) were not good, but the historic stone winery is most certainly worth a visit, and a wide selection of Tizzana Selection wines from other makers gives a broad choice.

TOLLANA BA–BA Est 1888 $4.60–12.60 R 124, 191, 287 BAROSSA V
Tanunda Road, Nuriootpa, SA 5355 (085) 62 0389
fax (085) 62 2494
Open Mon–Sat 10–5, Sun 12–4 **Production** NFP

Winemaker Neville Falkenburg

Principal Wines Ries, Botrytis Ries, Chard, Sem, Sauv Bl, Eden Valley Herm, Cab Sauv TR222.

Best Vintages W '82, '84, '87, '90, '91 **R** '82, '86, '88, '90, '91

Summary Another pawn on the SABH chessboard, and before that on the Penfold chessboard. Over the years Tollana has produced some of the many underrated wines to be found on the Australian market.

Recommended Wines 1992 Sauvignon Blanc (exceptionally stylish wine with sweet tropical gooseberry fruit which is rich and complemented by pronounced but not overwhelming spicy oak; great mouthfeel and total flavour; to 1995). 1990 Botrytis Riesling (powerful, complex wine that is so rich one might almost think there is oak present; very strong luscious mandarin/raisiny fruit, with the botrytis having altered the varietal character, but certainly added to the impact of the wine; drink now). 1992 Chardonnay (cleverly made, but rather oaky style that will appeal to some more than others; some citrus fruit; drink now). 1992 Rhine Riesling (potent lime and passionfruit aroma and flavour, with considerable depth; now to 1997).

TOLLEY WINES PTY LTD B–BA Est 1892 $7.65–15 R 69, 87, 88, 173, 283 BAROSSA V
30 Barracks Road, Hope Valley, SA 5090 (08) 264 2255 fax (08) 263 7485

Open Mon–Sat 9–5 **Production** 150 000 cases

Winemaker Christopher Tolley, Diana Heinrich

Principal Wines Chard, Champ, Sauv Bl, Wh Burg, Colomb Sem, Ries, Ausl Ries, Gewurz, Spat Muscat, Cab Sauv, Pinot; Cellar Reserve is the cheaper, Pedare Range the premium line.

Best Vintages W '81, '82, '87, '91, '92 **R** '83, '86, '88, '89, '91

Summary A large family owned and operated winery, known for the sheer consistency of the quality of its wines; the prices are no less appealing. Its particular forte over the years has been the somewhat unfashionable Gewurztraminer, which has the added virtue of ageing surprisingly well. Oak-matured Semillon and Chardonnay can also rise above their station with a few years bottle-age.

Recommended Wines 1992 Chardonnay (tangy fruit and complex, well integrated oak on the bouquet; seductively balanced and flavoured, with most attractive fig and melon fruit; now to 1995). 1992 Gewurztraminer (elegant, crisp, gently spicy traminer; no phenolic hardness; can be cellared). 1990 Cabernet Sauvignon (concentrated and intense, with dark briary/ berry fruit; strong structure and good tannins; to 2000).

TORRESAN'S HAPPY VALLEY NR Est 1972 $6–13 CD SD STHN VALES
Manning Road, Flagstaff Hill, SA 5159 (082) 70 2500

Open Mon–Sat 8–5 **Production** 13 000 cases

Winemaker Michael Torresan, John Torresan

Principal Wines Ries, Sem, Cab Shir, Cab Sauv, fortifieds.

Summary A substantial cellar door trade and local clientele accounts for most sales of mature but uninspiring wines.

TRENTHAM ESTATE BA–A Est 1986 $7.50–12.50 CD 33, 178, 225 MURRAY R
Sturt Highway, Trentham Cliffs, NSW 2738 (050) 24 8747
fax (050) 24 8800
Open Mon–Fri 9–5, w'ends 10–5 **Production** 15 000 cases
Winemaker Anthony Murphy
Principal Wines Chard, Sauv Bl Fumé, Colomb Chard, Chab, Ries, Pinot, Cab Sauv.
Best Vintages W '87, '89, '90, '91, '92 R '87, '88, '89, '91, '92
Summary Remarkably consistent tasting notes across all wine styles from all vintages since 1989 attest to the expertise of ex-Mildara winemaker Tony Murphy, now making the Trentham wines from his family vineyards. Indeed, Trentham seems to be going from strength to strength with each suceeding vintage. The winery restaurant is also recommended.
Recommended Wines 1992 Chardonnay (sophisicated and elegant wine with peachy/creamy fruit and very well handled oak with light vanilla bean flavours; commercial, perhaps, but excellent winemaking; drink now). 1992 Colombard Chardonnay Chablis (highly scented fragrant fruit salad aroma and flavour, as fresh and as clean as one could hope for; drink now). 1991 Cabernet Merlot (clean, fresh with light mint, sap and red berry flavours; appropriately minimal oak influence; to 1995).

•TUCK'S RIDGE B–A Est 1993 $9.95–13.95 R 1
MORNINGTON P
37 Red Hill–Shoreham Road, Red Hill South, Vic 3937
(059) 74 3933 fax (059) 74 4714
Open 7 days 11–5 **Production** 10 000 cases
Winemaker Contract
Principal Wines Ries, Chard, Pinot, Cab Sauv.
Summary Tuck's Ridge did not appear on the market until July 1993, but under the direction of chief executive Ian Home (formerly of Yellowglen), left no doubt about its intentions of emulating the rapid market penetration achieved by Scotchmans Hill and Yarra Ridge. A little under two hectares of vines were first planted in 1987; since that time plantings have been increased to 25 hectares, making it the largest vineyard on the Mornington Peninsula, with production forecast to grow to 20 000 cases by 1995.
Recommended Wines 1992 Rhine Riesling (clean lime aromas and flavours, with more concentration and weight than one often finds in this region; to 1995). 1992 Chardonnay (a strongly styled wine with a pronounced malolactic influence giving nutty/buttery characters throughout; drink now). 1992 Pinot Noir (aromatic strawberry fruit, with just a hint of oak; perhaps a fraction stemmy for the fruit weight; drink now).

TUERONG ESTATE NR Est 1984 $15 CD SD MORNINGTON P
Mornington-Flinders Road, Red Hill, Vic 3937 (059) 89 2129
Open W'ends 12–5 **Production** 300 cases
Winemaker Peter Cumming
Principal Wines Chard, Meth Champ 'Morning Star', Cab Sauv.
Summary A most unusual operation, which is in reality a family Italian-style restaurant at which the wine is principally sold and

erved, and which offers something totally different on the Mornington Peninsula.

TULLOCH CB–B Est 1895 $9–12.60 R 124 HUNTER V
De Beyers Road, Pokolbin, NSW 2321 (049) 98 7580
fax (049) 98 7682
Open Mon–Fri 9–4.30, w'ends 10–4.30 **Production** 20 000 cases
Winemaker Jay Tulloch
Principal Wines Ranging upwards from J. Y. Chab, Sem, Chard, Verd, Herm to Hector of Glen Hermitage as premium release; however, brand structure under review and likely to change.
Best Vintages W '83, '86, '87, '91, '92 R '83, '86, '87, '89, '91
Summary A once-great name and reputation which suffered enormously under multiple ownership changes, with a complete loss of identity and direction. In production terms at least it has found its feet, for it's now the centre of winemaking activities in the Hunter Valley for the Lindeman, Tulloch and Hungerford Hill brands.
Recommended Wines 1992 Limited Release Chardonnay (exceedingly complex but very strong barrel ferment oak characters drive the wine; for oak afficionados). 1991 Limited Release Chardonnay (a wine in almost identical style that some will hate and some will love; very forward in its development, looking for all the world like a classic aged Semillon of 20 years standing).

TYRRELL'S A–A Est 1858 $6–25 R 103, 172, 181, 182, 210, 228 HUNTER V
Broke Road, Pokolbin, NSW 2321 (049) 98 7509 fax (049) 98 7723
Open 7 Days 9–5 **Production** 500 000 cases
Winemaker Murray Tyrrell
Principal Wines A very large range starting at the bottom with Long Flat Red and White, then the commercial Old Winery series (Chard, Sem, Sauv Bl, Herm, Cab Mer) and thence to the premium vat wines (notably Vat 1 Sem, Vat 47 Chard and vats 5, 7, 8, 9, 10 and 11 all Herm).
Best Vintages W '86, '89, '91, '92, '93 R '83, '85, '87, '91
Summary A quite extraordinary family winery, it has grown up from an insignificant base in 1960 to become one of the most influential mid-sized companies, successfully competing with wines running all the way from cheap, volume-driven Long Flat White up to the super-premium Vat 47 Chardonnay, which challenges the Petaluma and Roxburgh Chardonnays for the title of Australia's best. There is a similar range of price and style with the red wines, but in recent years Tyrrell has barely faltered within the parameters of price and style.
Recommended Wines 1992 Vat 47 Chardonnay (fine, complex barrel ferment aromas with scented, citrus fruit; very stylish palate with length and finesse; has undoubted development potential; to 1996). 1992 Old Winery Chardonnay (strong, bacony charred oak is just a little on the heavy side, but there is good fruit and the style will have great appeal to many palates; to 1995). 1992 Semillon Vat 4 (crisp, clean, some grassy notes, but well balanced; good mouthfeel and varietal character; to 1998). 1990 Futures Hermitage (rich and full, with pepper and spice overtones to dark fruits; firm tannins; to 2005). 1991 Old Winery Cabernet Merlot (very clean and well made wine with soft red berry fruit, good length and mouthfeel, and neatly judged acidity; to 1998).

VASSE FELIX BA–BA Est 1967 $9.80–29 R 140–144, 251
MARGARET R
Cnr Caves Road and Harmans Road South, Cowaramup, WA 6284
(097) 55 5242 fax (097) 55 5425
Open 7 days 10–4.30 **Production** 22 000 cases
Winemakers D. Gregg, C. Otto
Principal Wines Chard, Verd, Noble Ries, Classic Dry White,
Shir, Classic Dry Red, Herm, Cab Sauv.
Best Vintages W '85, '87, '88, '90, '92 R '83, '85, '88, '90, '91
Summary Long regarded as one of the foremost wineries in the
region, founded by Dr Tom Cullity but now owned by Heytesbury
Holdings Pty Ltd, the investment company of the Holmes à Courts.
Much of its reputation was founded on its elegant Cabernets, but
these days the range is much broader.
Recommended Wines 1992 Noble Riesling (intense, long, pure
lime juice flavours; wonderful finish; botrytis Riesling at its best; to
1995). 1992 Classic Dry White (fresh, aromatic tropical fruit aromas;
melon, citrus and tropical fruit flavours with excellent mouthfeel and
plenty of weight; drink now).

VERITAS CA–CB Est 1955 $7–10 CD 67, 264 BAROSSA V
94 Langmeil Road, Tanunda, SA 5352 (085) 63 2330
Open Mon–Fri 9–5, w'ends 11–5 **Production** 7500 cases
Winemaker Rolf Binder
Principal Wines Ries, Sem Sauv Bl, Tramino, Leanyka, Cab
Franc Mer, Cab Sauv, Shir Cab, Bikaver Bull's Blood, Heysen
Vineyard Shir, fortifieds.
Best Vintages W '84, '88, '90, '91, '92 R '80, '84, '88, '90, '91
Summary The Hungarian influence is obvious in the naming of
some of the wines, but Australian technology is paramount in shaping
the generally very good quality. The red wines can be superb, with
fresh fruit and excellent oak handling exemplified by the 1989
Heysen Vineyard Shiraz, with echoes of the Rhone Valley in its
gamey/spicy complexity.

VICARYS CB–A Est 1923 $3.80–18 CD SD SYDNEY DISTRICT
Northern Road, Luddenham, NSW 2745 (047) 73 4161
fax (047) 73 4411
Open Mon–Fri 9–6, w'ends 11.30–5.30 **Production** 3000 cases
Winemaker Chris Niccol
Principal Wines Chard, Sem, Ries, Gewurz, Fumé, Cab Sauv,
Shir, Cab Mer, Mer, Sparkl, fortifieds.
Best Vintages W '84, '86, '88, '89, '93 R '84, '85, '87, '89
Summary Vicary's justifiably claims to be the Sydney region's
oldest continuously operating winery, having been established in a
very attractive large stone shearing shed built around 1890. Most of
the wines come from other parts of Australia, but the winery does
draw upon four hectares of estate Traminer and two hectares of
Chardonnay for those wines, and has produced some very good wines
of all styles over the years.

VINTINA ESTATE NR Est 1985 $10–15 CD SD MORNINGTON P
1282 Nepean Highway, Mt Eliza, Vic 3930 (03) 787 8166
fax (03) 775 2035
Open W'ends & hols 9–5 **Production** 500 cases

Winemaker K. McCarthy

Principal Wines Chard, Sem, Cab Sauv, Pinot.

Summary The initial releases of Vintina (the only wines tasted to date) were mediocre. With competent contract winemaking improvement can be expected. However, no recent tastings.

VIRGIN HILLS A–A Est 1968 $25 R 20, 48, 69 MACEDON

Salisbury Road, Lauriston West via Kyneton, Vic 3444 (054) 23 9169 fax (054) 23 9324

Open By appointment **Production** 2500 cases

Winemaker Mark Sheppard

Principal Wines A single Cab Sauv Shir Mer blend called Virgin Hills; occasional limited Reserve release.

Best Vintages R '82, '83, '88, '91, '92

Summary The Macedon region is not normally a kind host to the Shiraz or the Cabernet Sauvignon family, but in the warmer vintages in particular Virgin Hills produces one of Australia's great red wines. Very quietly, winemaker Mark Sheppard has moved to sulphur-free red winemaking, adding yet a further dimension of interest to this fascinating winery.

Recommended Wines 1991 Virgin Hills (full, complex red- and blackcurrant fruits with subtle, harmonious oak; a riper style with no spice characters; of very high quality). 1990 Reserve Virgin Hills (fresh, elegant and fragrant with strong spicy notes from the Shiraz component; good acidity; low tannins; very long in the mouth; longevity uncertain given the absence of sulphur dioxide). 1990 Virgin Hills (very similar wine, although the spicy Shiraz component is more obvious).

VOYAGER ESTATE NR Est 1978 $12–14 ML 102, 248 MARGARET R

Lot 1 Gnarawary Road, Margaret River, WA 6285 phone and fax (097) 57 6358

Open Not **Production** 5600 cases

Winemaker Stuart Pym

Principal Wines Chard, Chenin, Sem, Sauv Bl, Cab Sauv.

Summary Formerly Freycinet Estate, renamed after its purchase (in May 1991) from Western Australian viticulturist Peter Gherardi. New owner Michael Wright planted an additional 10 hectares in 1993, and plans an additional 5 hectares of vineyard between 1995 and 1998. Production has already been doubled and will increase further (to a total of 20 000 cases) with a new, state-of-the-art winery under construction in 1993.

Recommended Wine 1992 Chardonnay (rather oaky but very stylish with abundant textured fig and melon fruit to carry the French oak; long, full finish; now to 1995).

WA DE LOCK VINEYARDS NR Est 1987 $10.80–13.50 CD SD EAST GIPPSLAND

Stratford Road, Maffra, Vic (051) 47 3244 fax (051) 43 1421

Open Thurs–Tues 10–5 **Production** 850 cases

Winemaker Graeme Little

Principal Wines Ries, Chard, Sauv Bl, Pinot Blanc, Pinot, Cab Mer.

Summary The initial plantings of Pinot Noir, Cabernet Sauvignon and Sauvignon Blanc in 1987 have been progressively expanded, with Chardonnay being added and five hectares now under vine. Grape intake has been supplemented by purchases of Riesling, Merlot and Cabernet Franc grown at Maffra. Quality (and style) has been erratic, with resinous oak affecting some of the wines.

Recommended Wines 1992 Pinot Noir (clean, light, strawberry cherry aromas replicated on the palate, with pleasant if slightly simple strawberry/cherry fruit and good acidity; drink now). 1991 Cabernet Merlot (attractive sweet cassis and raspberry fruit aromas; softly ripe fruit on the mid palate softening on the finish; to 1995).

WALKERSHIRE NR Est 1984 $11.50–13.50 CD SD GOULBURN V

Rushworth Road, Bailieston, Vic 3608 (057) 94 9257

Open 7 days 10–6 **Production** NFP

Winemaker John Walker

Principal Wines Shir Cab, Port.

Summary Bearded Yorkshireman John Walker fills his tiny tasting room with his presence, and does likewise in far grander venues. His wines match his personality: they are monumental, indeed fearsome. The best are very good although more recent tastings have disappointed; because it is some years since my last encounter I feel it unfair to give a rating.

WANDIN VALLEY ESTATE NR Est 1973 $9.50–18 CD 104 HUNTER V

Talga Road, Allandale, NSW 2321 (049) 30 7317
fax (049) 30 7814

Open 7 days 10–5 **Production** 3500 cases

Winemaker Geoff Broadfield

Principal Wines Meth Champ, Chard, Sauv Bl, Ruby Cab, Cab Sauv, Shir, Pinot.

Summary The former Millstone vineyard now owned by the producer of *A Country Practice*, who has acquired the services of Allanmere winemaker Geoff Broadfield. The winery enjoyed incredible success at the 1992 Hunter Valley Wine Show, winning numerous gold medals, a testament to the skills of Geoff Broadfield.

Recommended Wines 1991 Cabernet Sauvignon (clean, slightly minty fruit with lemony/vanillin oak; on the palate, plenty of flavour, with soft fruit; to 1996). 1992 Chardonnay (discrete, underplayed style with some apparent malolactic influence; citrus and mint flavours on the palate; to 1995).

WANINGA BA–BA Est 1989 $9–11 CD SD CLARE V

Hughes Park Road, Sevenhill via Clare, SA 5453 (088) 42 2555

Open W'ends & hols 10–5 **Production** 1400 cases

Winemakers Tim Adams, Jeffrey Grosset (Contract)

Principal Wines Ries, Chenin, Chard, Shir, Cab Sauv.

Summary The large vineyards owned by Waninga were established in 1974, but it was not until 1989 that a portion of the grapes were withheld from sale and vinified for the owners. Since that time, Waninga has produced some quite lovely wines, having wisely opted for very competent contract winemaking.

Recommended Wines 1991 Shiraz (rich, sweet, complex, minty fruit with hints of spice; well balanced oak; long, luscious finish; to 2005). 1991 Cabernet Sauvignon (strong, fresh, youthful cassis/red berry fruit with soft tannins; a few rough edges still to settle down, but should do so with time; to 2005).

WANTIRNA ESTATE NR Est 1963 $18 ML SD YARRA V

Bushy Park Lane, Wantirna South, Vic 3152 (03) 801 2367
fax (03) 887 0225

Open Sat 2–5; closed Mar–Apr **Production** 700 cases

Winemaker Reg Egan

Principal Wines Chard, Pinot, Cab Mer.

Summary Owner/winemaker Reg Egan does not believe in any form of comparative tastings or assessments, and even less in winery or wine ratings.

WARDS GATEWAY CELLARS C–B Est 1979 $7.50–9 CD SD BAROSSA V

Barossa Valley Highway, Lyndoch, SA 5351 (085) 24 4138

Open 7 days 9–5.30 **Production** 5000 cases

Winemaker Ray Ward (plus Contract makers)

Principal Wines Ries, Chablis, Fronti, Fumé, Shir, Cab Sauv, Port.

Best Vintages W '81, '85, '87, '91, '92 R '81, '84, '86, '90, '92

Summary The very old vines surrounding the winery produce the best wines, which are made without frills or new oak and sold without ostentation.

WARRABILLA NR Est 1986 $14–25 ML SD NE VIC

Indigo Valley, Rutherglen (vineyard); postal PO Box 41, Rutherglen, Vic 3685 (0603) 35 1233

Open Not **Production** 800 cases

Winemaker Andrew Smith

Principal Wines Shir, Cab Mer, Shir, Pinot, Touriga Vintage Port, Sparkl.

Summary Former All Saints winemaker Andrew Sutherland-Smith has leased a small winery at Corowa to make the Warrabilla wines from a vineyard developed by himself and Carol Smith in the Indigo Valley. The Smiths hope to establish a cellar door outlet by the end of 1993, building on the success of their trophy winning Shiraz wines from 1990 and 1991.

Recommended Wines 1990 Shiraz (clean, solid, sweet red berry fruit with pronounced but well integrated vanillin American oak; soft tannins; to 1997). 1991 Touriga Vintage Port (impenetrable colour, dense, youthful bouquet; potent dark currant, dark chocolate and pervasive tannins; to 2010).

WARRAMATE CB–CB Est 1970 $13–19 CD SD YARRA V

4 Maddens Lane, Gruyere, Vic 3770 (059) 64 9219

Open W'ends & hols 10–6 **Production** 900 cases

Winemaker Jack Church

Principal Wines Ries, Shir, Cab Sauv.

Summary Excellent red wines made in 1988 (with consultancy advice from Kathleen Quealy) showed what this high quality, mature, non-irrigated vineyard can produce. Subsequent vintages have been disappointing.

•WARREN VINEYARD, THE NR Est 1985 $12–14 ML SD GRT SOUTHERN

Brockman Street, Pemberton, WA phone and fax (097) 76 1115

Open By appointment **Production** 1000 cases

Winemaker Virginia Willcock

Principal Wines Chard, Cab Sauv, Cab Mer, Mer, Cab Blanc.

Summary The 1.4 hectare vineyard was established in 1985, and is one of the smallest in the Pemberton region, coming to public notice when its 1991 Cabernet Sauvignon won the award for the Best Red Table Wine from the Pemberton Region at the 1992 SGIO Western Australia Winemakers Exhibition. The wine in question shows very cool growing conditions, being a little leafy and astringent, but with pleasant overall flavour.

WARRENMANG CB–B Est 1974 $5–17 CD SD PYRENEES
Mountain Creek Road, Moonambel, Vic 3478 (054) 67 2233
fax (054) 67 2309
Open 7 days 9–5 **Production** 4000 cases
Winemaker Roland Kaval
Principal Wines Chard, LH Tram, Cab Sauv, Shir, Grand Pyrenees, Port.
Summary Warrenmang is now the focus of a superb accommodation and restaurant complex created by former restaurateur Luigi Bazzani and wife Athalie, which is in much demand as a conference centre as well as for weekend tourism.
Recommended Wines 1991 Shiraz (dense red-purple in colour, hugely concentrated on both bouquet and palate; a massive wine needing 30 years at least to soften, but does have clean fruit as a starting point). 1992 Late Harvest Traminer (soft, slightly broad lime juice and spice flavours, with a soft finish).

WATER WHEEL B–B Est 1972 $8–15 CD 139, 188 BENDIGO
Bridgewater-on-Loddon, Bridgewater, Vic 3516 (054) 37 3060 fax
(054) 37 3082
Open Mon–Sat 9–5, Sun 12–5 **Production** 7500 cases
Winemaker Peter Cumming
Principal Wines Chard, Ries, Sauv Bl, Pinot, Shir, Cab Sauv; grapes from other districts under premium Wing Fields label.
Summary Peter Cumming gained great respect as a winemaker during his four year stint with Hickinbotham Winemakers, and his 1989 purchase of Water Wheel was greeted with enthusiasm by followers of his wines.
Recommended Wines 1992 Water Wheel Chardonnay (complex, buttery, biscuity, malolactic influence gives the wine structural complexity, with considerable weight and intensity; fruit rather than oak driven; to 1996). 1991 Water Wheel Shiraz (quite strong American oak supports red berry fruit of medium weight; vanillin caramel flavours come again on the finish; to 1997). 1991 Water Wheel Cabernet Sauvignon (fresh, relatively light but bright fruit with pronounced charry/chippy oak; modern, early drinking style).

WATTLEY CREEK WINES NR Est 1990 $13–20 R 33, 48
STHN TAS
Fleurtys Lane, Flowerpot, Tas 7054 (002) 67 4604
fax (002) 67 4828
Open 7 days at Woodbridge Hotel, Woodbridge 7162
Production 500 cases
Winemaker Leigh Gawith
Principal Wines Muller, Chard, Pinot, Cab blend.
Summary Leigh Gawith established St Patricks at Pipers Brook in

1983, but sold the vineyard to Pipers Brook Winery in 1990 and has now relocated in the extreme south of Tasmania at Flowerpot. The wines presently being sold are a mixture from his previous location and his new venture. He is also making wines on a contract basis for three other embryonic makers: Roland View, Tunnel Hill and Polley Estate.

Recommended Wines 1991 Wattley Creek Pinot Noir (strongly stylised wine with tobacco, spice and plum fruit, showing farmyard-derived carbonic maceration characters).

WEIN VALLEY ESTATES NR Est 1985 $2.95–7.95 CD SD RIVERLAND

Nixon Road, Monash, SA 5342 (085) 83 5255 fax (085) 83 5444

Open Mon–Fri 9–4.30, Sat 11–3 **Production** 550 000 cases

Winemaker Otto Konig

Principal Wines The usual array of generic table, fortified and flavoured wines, with premium varietals under the Langhill Estate label.

Summary A major producer of bulk and packaged wine; much is sold to other makers for blending or repackaging. The quality basically reflects the price, although the label design and packaging is quite beautiful.

WELLINGTON WINES B–B Est 1990 $13.30–16.60.95 R SD 258 HUON V

34 Cornwall Street, Rose Bay, Tas 7015 (002) 62 4385
fax (002) 62 4390

Open By appointment **Production** 900 cases

Winemaker Andrew Hood

Principal Wines Chard, Pinot, Easy Cab.

Summary Consultant winemaker Andrew Hood (ex-Charles Sturt University) and wife Jenny purchase grapes from various vineyards and vinify these at Stoney Domaine A winery. The aim is to produce wines for early to medium term consumption, showing distinctive varietal and regional fruit flavours with minimal oak interference.

Recommended Wines 1991 Chardonnay (tight, crisp, slightly herbaceous style; not heavy, but quite intense; pleasing acidity lengthens the palate). 1992 Easy Cabernet (Chinon-like with strong herbaceous notes to both bouquet and palate; within the parameters of its style, very attractive).

WENDOUREE CELLARS A–A Est 1895 $12–15 CD SD CLARE V

Wendouree Road, Clare, SA 5453 (088) 42 2896

Open Mon–Sat 10–4.30 **Production** 2100 cases

Winemaker Tony Brady

Principal Wines Shir Malb, Shir Mataro, Shir, Cab Malb, Cab Sauv, Muscat of Alexandria.

Best Vintages R '83, '86, '89, '90, '91

Summary The iron fist in a velvet glove best describes these extraordinary wines. They are fashioned with passion and yet precision from the very old vineyard with its unique terroir by Tony and Lita Brady, who rightly see themselves as custodians of a priceless treasure.

Recommended Wine 1990 Cabernet Malbec (deep, concentrated, sweet fruit bouquet; massively concentrated deep, dark fruited and tannic palate; in archetypal Wendouree style).

WEST END CA–BA Est 1945 $4.50–9.50 CD SD MIA
12/83 Brayne Road, Griffith, NSW 2680 (069) 62 2868
fax (069) 62 1725
Open 7 days 9–4 **Production** 12 000 cases
Winemaker W. Calabria
Principal Wines Chard, Sem, Chab, Tram Ries, Ries, Pinot, Herm, Cab Sauv, Muscat, Port.
Summary The '82, '84 and '89 Cabernet Sauvignons have each won a gold medal at national wine shows, the '89 at Canberra (in 1990), which is a remarkable achievement in itself for a little-known Riverina winery.

WESTERING NR Est 1980 $8–12 ML SD CANBERRA
Federal Highway, Collector, NSW 2581 (06) 295 8075
Open Not **Production** 300 cases
Winemaker Captain G. P. Hood
Principal Wines Ries, Chard, Shir, Cab Sauv.
Summary Has made some lovely Chardonnay; the wines are snapped up by a loyal local clientele.

•WESTERNPORT ESTATE NR Est 1981 $12.50 CD SD
SOUTH GIPPSLAND
St Helier Road, The Gurdies, Vic 3984 (059) 97 6208
Open 7 days 10–5 **Production** 550 cases
Winemaker Frank Henry Cutler
Principal Wines Southern Late Riesling (dry not sweet), Southern Dry Red (Shir Cab).
Summary The only winery in the south-west Gippsland region, established on the slopes of The Gurdies hills overlooking Westernport Bay and French Island. Plantings of the 4.5 hectare vineyard commenced in 1981, but no fruit was harvested in 1991 owing to bird attack. A winery has been partially completed, and it is intended to increase the vineyards to 25 hectares and ultimately build a restaurant on site.
Recommended Wines Non Vintage Western Dry Red (an interesting non vintage wine with strong, spicy fruit (no doubt Shiraz) that is very clean and has plenty of depth and weight; to 1997).

WESTFIELD B–B Est 1922 $9.80–28 CD 109, 155, 220 SWAN V
Cnr Memorial Avenue & Great Northern Highway, Baskerville, WA 6056 (09) 296 4356
Open 7 days 10–5.30 **Production** 3000 cases
Winemaker John Kosovich
Principal Wines Verd, Chard, Chenin, Sem, Ries, Mer, Cab Sauv, Shir, Port.
Summary Consistent producer of a surprisingly elegant and complex Chardonnay; the other wines are more variable, but from time to time has made attractive Verdelho and excellent Cabernet Sauvignon.

WICKHAM HILL C–B $8.50–30 R 122 MIA
22 Jensen Road, Griffith, NSW 2680 (069) 64 2121
fax (069) 62 7121
Open Not **Production** NFP
Winemaker David Morris
Principal Wines Colomb Sem, Ries, Spat Lexia, Shir.
Summary A brand of Orlando with its grape sources and winery

based in the Murrumbidgee Irrigation Area. The wines are basically of cask quality sold in bottles, but do use the Orlando discipline and production skills.

WIGNALLS BA–BA Est 1982 $11.60–18.70 CD 155, 157, 173, 182, 188, 202, 320 GRT SOUTHERN
Chester Pass Road (Highway 1), Albany, WA 6330 phone and fax (098) 41 2848
Open Mon–Sat 10–4, Sun 12–4 **Production** 6000 cases
Winemaker John Wade (Contract)
Principal Wines Chard, Sauv Bl, Fronti, Pinot, Cab Sauv, Port.
Best Vintages W '85, '86, '90, '91, '92 R '87, '88, '90, '91, '92
Summary Noted producer of Pinot Noir; the wines invariably show extremely well when tasted from barrel and when first bottled. However, they tend to age fairly quickly, and some have shown signs of instability in bottle, a problem that is being addressed by contract winemaker John Wade and owner Bill Wignall.
Recommended Wines 1991 Pinot Noir (very distinctive wine with obvious whole bunch/carbonic maceration influence; quite stalky and sappy; style is good, but a little more sweet fruit would have helped; drink now).

• **WILD DUCK CREEK ESTATE** NR Est 1980 $8.25–12 ML SD BENDIGO
Spring Flat Road, Heathcote, Vic 3523 (054) 33 2934
Open By appointment **Production** 700 cases
Winemaker David Anderson
Principal Wines Shir, Cabernet, Mer Cab Franc.
Summary The first release of Wild Duck Creek Estate from the 1991 vintage marks the end of 12 years of effort by David and Diana Anderson, who commenced planting the 4.5 hectare vineyard in 1980, made their first tiny quantities of wine in 1986, the first commercial quantities of wine in 1991, and built their winery and cellar door facility in 1993. The rich, concentrated yet smooth 1992 vintage reds won a gold and two silver medals at the Victorian Wine Show, auguring well for the future.

WILDWOOD NR Est 1983 $11–23 CD 55, 225 MACEDON
St John's Lane, Wildwood, Bulla, Vic 3428 (03) 307 1118
fax (03) 331 1590
Open 7 days 10–4 **Production** 2000 cases
Winemakers Dr Wayne Stott, Peter Dredge
Principal Wines Chard, Sem, Pinot, Cabs, Shir.
Summary Wildwood is situated at the southernmost part of the Macedon region, just 4 kilometres past Melbourne airport. The vineyard and cellar door are situated at an altitude of 130m in the Oaklands Valley, which provides unexpected views back to Port Phillip Bay and the Melbourne skyline. Plastic surgeon Wayne Stott has taken what is very much a part-time activity rather more seriously than most by undertaking (and completing) the wine science degree at Charles Sturt University. Early vintages showed handling problems, but quality is now very much better.
Recommended Wines 1990 Cabernets (solid, dense minty aromas with some charred oak; on the palate, complex, full bodied wine with a wide array of fruit flavours, a hint of gaminess, and firm

tannins; to 1999). 1990 Pinot Noir (intense, fragrant and tangy Burgundian aromas which are extremely appealing; however, the fruit on the palate is starting to fade a little; drink now).

WILLESPIE BA–BA Est 1976 $11–17.50 CD 33, 207, 315
MARGARET R
Harmans Mill Road, Willyabrup via Cowaramup, WA 6284 phone and fax (097) 55 6210
Open 7 days 10–5 **Production** 4000 cases
Winemaker Michael Lemmes
Principal Wines Ries, Sem, Verd, Sauv Bl, Cab Sauv, Mer, Port.
Best Vintages W '85, '87, '90, '91 R '85, '87, '88, '89
Summary Willespie has produced many attractive white wines over the years, typically in brisk, herbaceous Margaret River style, but its new plantings of Merlot suggest a bright future for this variety once the wine becomes commercially available.
Recommended Wines 1993 Sauvignon Blanc (showed quite striking, rich, sweet, concentrated tropical/gooseberry fruit early in its life; very good potential). 1993 Verdelho (likewise showing exceptional concentration and richness of flavour early in its life). 1990 Semillon (crisp, herbaceous and tangy, still remarkably fresh and undeveloped; to 1997). 1991 Merlot (very elegant and stylish, with fresh, clean, varietal fruit tinged with appropriate sappiness; not for commercial release).

WILLOW BEND NR Est 1990 $12.50 ML SD BAROSSA V
Lyndoch Valley Road, Lyndoch, SA 5351 phone and fax (085) 24 4169; postal PO Box 107, Lyndoch, SA 5351
Open Not **Production** 500 cases
Winemaker Wayne Dutschke
Principal Wines Chard, Dry Red blend.
Summary Wayne Dutschke has had ten years of winemaking experience with major wine companies in South Australia, Victoria and New South Wales, but has returned to South Australia to join his uncle Ken Semmler, a leading grape grower in the Barossa Valley and now in the Adelaide Hills.

• WILLOW CREEEK VINEYARD NR Est 1989 SD
MORNINGTON P
166 Balnarring Road, Merricks North, Vic 3926 (059) 89 7367
Open 7 days 11–5 **Production** 2000 cases
Winemaker Kevin McCarthy
Principal Wines Chard, Cab Mer, Cab Sauv.
Summary Yet another significant entrant in the fast expanding Mornington Peninsula area, with 15 hectares of vines planted to Cabernet Sauvignon, Chardonnay and Pinot Noir. The cellar door sales area boasts picnic areas, barbeque facilities, trout fishing and bocce; lunches are served every day and dinners by appointment.

WILLOWS, THE CB–B Est 1989 $7.50–13 CD 167 BAROSSA V
Light Pass Road, Light Pass, Barossa Valley, SA 5355 (085) 62 1080 fax (085) 62 3447
Open 7 days 10.30–4.30 **Production** 4000 cases
Winemakers Peter & Michael Scholz
Principal Wines Ries, Sem, Pinot, Shir, Cab Sauv.
Summary The Scholz family have been grape growers for

generations. Current generation winemakers Peter and Michael Scholz could not resist the temptation to make smooth, well balanced and flavoursome wines under their own label.

WILSON VINEYARD CA–B Est 1974 $9.50–14 CD 115, 188 CLARE V
Polish Hill River, Sevenhill via Clare, SA 5453 (088) 43 4310
Open Mon–Fri 12–4.30, w'ends 10–4.30 **Production** 2800 cases
Winemaker John Wilson
Principal Wines Ries, Chard, Cab Sauv, Pinot, Hippocrene Sparkl Burg.
Best Vintages W '85, '86, '88, '89, '91 R '81, '84, '86, '88, '91
Summary Dr John Wilson is a tireless ambassador for the Clare Valley and for wine (and its beneficial effect on health) in general. His wines are made using techniques and philosophies garnered early in his wine career, and are often idiosyncratic.
Recommended Wines 1992 Rhine Riesling (intensely flavoured wine with a long, powerful palate; the most recent in a line of distinguished Rieslings; to 1998). 1990 Cabernet Sauvignon (though only of light to medium body, a wine of quite intense flavour with elegantly austere varietal character, and both length and harmonious mouthfeel; now to 2000).

WILTON ESTATE CB–B Est 1977 $5.95–14.95 R 55, 63, 80, 185, 207 MIA
Whitton Stock Route, Yenda, NSW 2681 (069) 68 1303
fax (069) 68 1328
Open Not **Production** 60 000 cases
Winemaker Adrian Sheridan
Principal Wines Sem Sauv Bl, Chard, Botrytis Sem, Marsanne, Cab Mer, Cab Sauv, Heathcote Shir; Hidden Valley is the second label.
Summary The former St Peters distillery has been transformed into a table wine producer, drawing grapes and wine from various parts of southern Australia and New South Wales for its dry table wines, but having outstanding success with its Botrytis Semillon from locally grown fruit.
Recommended Wines 1991 Botrytis Semillon (already deep gold in colour with very strong and rich botrytis influence together with charred oak; a massive wine with powerful fruit and complex oak handling; drink now). 1991 Cabernet Sauvignon (strong, potent, gravelly earthy aromas leading on to a stylish, youthful palate with clean red berry fruits and soft tannins; to 2000). 1991 Hidden Valley Cabernet Shiraz Merlot (fresh, light, redcurrant fruit aromas; slightly dusty oak evident on the palate and some pleasant leafy notes; cool climate style).

WINCHELSEA ESTATE CB–CB Est 1984 $13–19 R SD GEELONG
Winchelsea, Vic 3241 (vineyard only)
Open Not **Production** NFP
Winemaker Bailey Carrodus (Contract)
Principal Wines Ries, Chard, Shir.
Summary Owned by Melbourne retailer Nick Chlebnikowski, and the wines are sold only through the Nick's chain of stores. Vibrantly peppery Shiraz has been the best of the wines by far.

WINEWOOD NR Est 1984 $10–12 CD SD GRANITE BELT
Sundown Road, Ballandean, Qld 4382 phone and
fax (076) 84 1187
Open W'ends 9–5 **Production** 600 cases
Winemaker Ian Davis
Principal Wines Sem, Chard, Cab Mer Franc, Shir, Mars.
Summary A weekend and holiday activity for schoolteacher Ian
Davis and town planning wife Jeanette; the tiny winery is a model of
neatness and precision planning. The Rhone-style Shiraz Marsanne
blend shows that Ian Davis has high aspirations. (Viognier is on the
way, too.)

WIRRA WIRRA B–B Est 1969 $7.99–15.40 R 120, 165, 178,
191, 233 STHN VALES
McMurtrie Road, McLaren Vale, SA 5171 (08) 323 8414
fax (08) 323 8596
Open Mon–Sat 10–5, Sun 11–5 **Production** 40 000 cases
Winemaker Benjamin Riggs
Principal Wines The Cousins Sparkl, Ries, LP Ries, Sauv Bl,
Chard, Wood Matured Sem Sauv Bl, The Angelus Cab Sauv, Pinot,
Church Block Cab Shir Mer, RWS Shir, Port.
Best Vintages W '82, '86, '89, '91, '92 R '80, '82, '86, '90, '91
Summary Long respected for the consistency of its white wines,
which are of unfailing style. 1989 marked the resurgence of its red
wines, carried on with a vengeance with the 1991 Angelus Cabernet
Sauvignon which won the trophy for Best Wine at the 1993 Sydney
International Wine Show.
Recommended Wines 1991 The Angelus Cabernet Sauvignon
(of light to medium weight, with very clean, elegant and balanced
fruit and oak; flavours of both mint and red berry and fine, supple
tannins; of the highest class; to 2005). 1991 Chardonnay (beautifully
balanced and harmonious wine that relies on finesse rather than
power for its impact; will develop nicely in bottle; to 1995). 1992
Sauvignon Blanc (pristine, herbaceous, seafood style, crisp and
cleansing and spotlessly clean; finishes dry; drink now).

WOLF BLASS BA–B Est 1966 $9.20–19 R 110 BAROSSA V
Bilyara Vineyards, Sturt Hwy, Nuriootpa, SA 5355 (08) 236 0888
fax (085) 62 2156
Open 7 days 9–5 **Production** 250 000 cases
Winemakers John Glaetzer (Red), Chris Hatcher (White)
Principal Wines White wines under White, Yellow, Green and
Gold labels, with emphasis on Ries and blended Classic Dry White;
red wines under Red, Yellow, Brown, Grey and Black labels with
emphasis on Cab Sauv, Shir and blends of these. Also sparkl and
fortified wines.
Best Vintages W '80, '86, '87, '90, '91 R '80, '82, '86, '90, '91
Summary Now merged with Mildara, but the brands will
undoubtedly be kept separate. The belief is the merger will hasten
the style changes already in the pipeline at Wolf Blass, and in
particular a scaling back on the extreme reliance on massive usage of
American oak in the wood-matured whites and all of the red wines.
Recommended Wines 1992 Traminer Riesling (fragrant, spicy
and flowery, with excellent Traminer varietal fruit showing through;
neither oily nor sweet). 1992 Gold Label Riesling (toasty, flowery

aromatic and spicy bouquet, with high toned toasty lime fruit). 1989 Classic Shiraz (highly aromatic and full flavoured, with very pronounced American oak; in mainstream Blass style; to 1995).

WOODLANDS NR Est 1973 $18–22 R 162 MARGARET R
Cnr Caves & Metricup Roads, Willyabrup via Cowaramup, WA 6284
(09) 274 6155 fax (09) 274 6421
Open W'ends by appointment **Production** 1000 cases
Winemaker David Watson
Principal Wines Chard, Pinot, Cab Sauv, Cab Mer Malbec.
Summary Burst on the scene with some superlative Cabernet Sauvignons early on, but has not managed to maintain the momentum; the difficulties of weekend winemaking from a Perth base have not helped. A Pinot in a Rosé style is the most recent addition to the line.

WOODONGA HILL NR Est 1986 $8–14 CD SD HILLTOPS
Cowra Road, Young, NSW 2594 (063) 82 2972
Open 7 days 9–5 **Production** 2400 cases
Winemaker Jill Lindsay
Principal Wines Ries, Hock, Chard, Gewurz, Shir, Cab Sauv.
Summary Oxidation, possibly at bottling, has been and continues to be a major problem that Jill Lindsay is trying to overcome.

WOODSTOCK BA–B Est 1974 $6.50–20 CD 1, 101, 120, 204, 229 STHN VALES
Douglas Gully Road, McLaren Flat, SA 5171 (08) 383 0156
fax (08) 383 0437
Open Mon–Fri 9–5, w'ends 12–5 **Production** 15 000 cases
Winemaker Scott Collett
Principal Wines Ries, Sem, Chard, Sauv Bl, Botrytis, Shir, Cab Sauv, Tawny Port.
Best Vintages W '84, '85, '86, '89, '92 R '82, '84, '86, '89, '91
Summary One of the stalwarts of McLaren Vale, producing archetypal full bodied red wines year in, year out, and showing versatility with spectacular botrytis sweet whites and high quality (14 year old) Tawny Port.
Recommended Wines Tawny Port (excellent tawny with its age evident all the way through from the colour to the nutty, dry finish following a rich, flavoursome mid palate). 1990 Shiraz (solid, clean, dark berry/briary/dark chocolate fruit, rounded off with soft tannins; to 2000). 1989 Cabernet Sauvignon (solid, ripe, not especially varietal and with quite pronounced vanillin American oak; to 1999).

WOODY NOOK NR Est 1982 $8.50–13.50 CD 176
MARGARET R
Metricup Road, Busselton, WA 6280 (097) 55 7547
fax (097) 55 5464
Open 7 days 10–4.30 **Production** 3000 cases
Winemaker Neil Gallagher
Principal Wines Sem, LH Sem, Sauv Bl, Sem Sauv Bl, Chenin, Mer, Cab Sauv; Nooky Delight (fortified).
Summary Neil and Linda Gallagher — with help from consultant John Smith — are learning winemaking the hard way: by experience. Much of the wine is sold through the small on-site restaurant in the pretty, forested property which inspired the somewhat twee name.

Recommended Wines 1992 Cabernet Sauvignon (solid, sweet, blackcurrant fruit with good weight and concentration, pleasantly moderate tannins; to 2005). 1990 Cabernet Sauvignon (shows rather more American oak influence than the '92, but has the same generous fruit; received the Trophy for Best WA Dry Red in the 1991 Perth Royal Show).

WRIGHTS NR Est 1973 $12–25 CD 176, 288 MARGARET R
Harmans South Road, Cowaramup, WA 6284 (097) 55 5314
fax (097) 55 5459
Open 7 days 10–4.30 **Production** 2500 cases
Winemaker Henry Wright
Principal Wines Sem Ries, White Herm, Herm Cab, LP Shir, Vintage and White Port.
Summary The red wines of 1988 were the best for some years, but the '89s slipped back again. I have not tasted any wines since 1989.

WYANGA PARK NR Est 1970 $9–15 CD 14 GIPPSLAND
Baades Road, Lakes Entrance, Vic 3909 (051) 55 1508
fax (087) 55 1443
Open Mon–Sat 9–5, Sun 10–5 **Production** 4000 cases
Winemaker Andrew Smith
Principal Wines Ries, Tram, Chard, Sem, Sauv Bl, Crouchen, Shir, Pinot, Cab Sauv.
Summary A striking, complex, long wood-aged 1991 Semillon from the MIA and a leafy, herbaceous, cool climate 1990 Cabernet Sauvignon from local grapes are the best wines in a collection of diverse provenance directed at the tourist trade. Winery cruises up the north arm of the Gippsland Lake to Wyanga Park are scheduled four days a week throughout the entire year.

WYNDHAM ESTATE CB–B Est 1828 $7.95–13.95 R 122, 199, 211, 220 HUNTER V
Dalwood Road, Branxton, NSW 2335 (049) 38 3444
fax (049) 38 3422
Open Mon–Fri 9.30–5, w'ends 10–4 **Production** NFP
Winemaker John Baruzzi
Principal Wines A full range of premium varietal wines released under various Bin numbers or descriptive labels, but all emphasising the Wyndham name.
Best Vintages W '81, '86, '89, '91, '93 R '83, '86, '87, '91, '93
Summary An absolutely reliable producer of keenly priced mid-range table wines that are smoothly and precisely aimed at those who enjoy wine but don't wish to become over-involved in its mystery and intrigue. Every now and then it comes up with a wine of surprising quality, although there does seem to be some variation between different batch bottlings.
Recommended Wine 1992 Show Reserve Verdelho (interesting fruit salad aroma flavour, tinged with a hint of cinnamon; finishes a little short but nonetheless a good example of the variety; drink now).

WYNNS A–A Est 1891 $6–27 R 124, 195, 287 COONAWARRA
Memorial Drive, Coonawarra, SA 5263 (087) 36 3266
fax (087) 36 3202
Open 7 days 10–4 **Production** 190 000 cases

Winemaker Peter Douglas

Principal Wines Ries, Chard, Herm, Cab Herm, Pinot, Cab Sauv, Michael Herm and John Riddoch Cab Sauv, Ovens Valley Burg.

Best Vintages W '82, '85, '87, '91, '92 R '82, '86, '88, '90, '91

Summary The immense production has in no way prevented Wynns from producing excellent wines covering the full price spectrum from the bargain basement Riesling and Hermitage through to the deluxe John Riddoch Cabernet Sauvignon and the newly introduced Michael Hermitage. In years such as 1990 and 1991 Wynns offers extraordinary value for money.

Recommended Wines 1990 Cabernet Sauvignon (complex, sweet fruit with a hint of gamey regional character and subtle oak on the bouquet; outstanding weight, structure and balance on the palate, concentrated but not overly so, with dark berry fruits and fine tannins; to 2015). 1990 John Riddoch Cabernet Sauvignon (massively rich and concentrated wine showing very sweet fruit and sumptuous oak; like very young Grange, not really drinkable yet; to 2020). 1990 Michael Hermitage (of similar weight and style to the John Riddoch with lush minty/eucalypt/berry flavours; scented oak; soft, mouthfilling tannins; needs many years; to 2020). 1991 Hermitage (fresh, well balanced, vibrant, red berry and cherry fruit, tinged with pepper and spice; soft tannins; minimal oak influence; to 1998). 1990 Ovens Valley Burgundy (rich, dense, chewy, sweet fruit with very good tannin structure; extraordinary depth for a wine at its price; to 2010). 1992 Rhine Riesling (fresh, youthful, crisp and toasty; in very different style to earlier vintages; almost Clare-like in its dry, toasty fruit, with good length; to 1997).

YALUMBA BA–BA Est 1863 $7–15.40 R 140–144, 191, 206, 325 BAROSSA V

Eden Valley Road, Angaston, SA 5353 (085) 64 2423
fax (085) 64 2549

Open Mon–Fri 8.30–5, Sat 12–5, Sun 12–4

Production 850 000 cases

Winemaker Brian Walsh

Principal Wines Under the Yalumba label (in ascending order) Kingston Mission, Oxford Landing range, Galway Herm and Christobels Dry White, Family Selection range and Signature Collection. Separate brand identities for Hill Smith Estate, Pewsey Vale and Heggies, with strong emphasis on key varietals Ries, Chard, Sem and Cab Sauv. Angas Brut is a leader in the sparkling wine market.

Best Vintages W '84, '87, '90, '91, '92 R '76, '87, '88, '90, '91, '92

Summary Family owned and run by Robert Hill-Smith; much of its prosperity in recent years has turned on the great success of Angas Brut in export markets, but the company has always had a commitment to quality and shown great vision in its selection of vineyard sites and brands. More recently Oxford Landing has been a major success, with Chardonnay representing great value for money and perceived as such in the United States, but the Riesling also appeals.

Recommended Wines 1991 Signature Chardonnay (rich, complex and strongly oaked, but has the fruit to support its stylish, intense flavours; to 1994). 1990 Signature Show Reserve Cabernet Sauvignon (superbly structured and textured wine with firm,

blackcurrant fruit and perfectly handled gently spicy oak; to 2005).
1992 Kingston Mission Reserve Chardonnay (big, fleshy, mouthfilling
wine with sophisticated oak handling and tangy fruit). Galway Pipe
Port (benefits from obvious barrel age; concentrated liqueur style
Port with masses of flavour and character).

YARRA BURN NR Est 1976 $10–20 R 32, 264 YARRA V
Settlement Road, Yarra Junction, Vic 3797 (059) 67 1428
fax (059) 67 1146
Open 7 days 10–6 **Production** 10 500 cases
Winemaker David Fyffe
Principal Wines Sem, Chard, Sparkl Pinot, Pinot, Cab Sauv.
Best Vintages W '83, '86, '88, '90 R '84, '86, '88, '90
Summary Chris and David Fyffe are now firmly in control at Yarra
Burn after a prolonged period of financial uncertainty. The bluestone
restaurant and cellar door sales area are an important feature in the
Yarra Valley, with the restaurant strongly recommended.

YARRA EDGE NR Est 1984 $13.50 ML SD YARRA V
Lot 3 Edward Road, Lilydale, Vic 3140 (03) 735 3473
fax (03) 735 4853; postal PO Box 711, Lilydale, Vic 3140
Open By appointment **Production** 1200 cases
Winemaker Michael Zitzlaff (Contract)
Principal Wines Chard, Cabernets.
Summary The Bingerman family has made an auspicious entry,
releasing two quite beautiful wines from the 1990 vintage: a clean,
soft, berry/plum Cabernet with a touch of vanillin oak, and an
outstanding Chardonnay with smooth, melon/peach fruit, subtle oak
and length. The 1991 Chardonnay, tasted from barrel, is every bit as
good. The 1991 Chardonnay fulfilled its early promise, and safely
made the transition to bottle from barrel.

YARRA RIDGE BA–A Est 1983 $13.95–14.95 R 34, 86–88
YARRA V
Glenview Road, Yarra Glen, Vic 3755 (03) 730 1022
fax (03) 730 1131
Open W'ends & hols 10–5.30 **Production** 50 000 cases
Winemaker Rob Dolan
Principal Wines Chard, Sauv Bl, Botrytis Sem, Pinot, Cab Sauv.
Best Vintages W '88, '89, '91, '92 R '88, '89, '90, '91, '92
Summary Has risen from obscurity to prominence through a
mixture of good winemaking, keen pricing and aggressive marketing.
The Sauvignon Blanc has become something of a cult wine since its
debut in 1989 (when outstanding) but in truth the other wines in the
portfolio are every bit as good.
Recommended Wines 1992 Chardonnay (a quite extraordinary
wine with its fragrant Sauvignon Blanc-like grapefruit and
passionfruit aromas and flavours; contrary to what one might expect,
these did not diminish as the wine aged through to mid 1993;
seductive, even if unconventional; drink now). 1992 Pinot Noir
(bright red-purple colour with fresh plummy fruit in a fully ripe style,
bordering on the edge of jamminess but impressing with its flavour;
drink now). 1991 Cabernet Sauvignon (full dark berry fruit with some
gamey/meaty overtones, with ripe, sweet mulberry and blackcurrant
flavours; to 1998).

YARRA YERING A–A Est 1969 $20–35 R 115, 258 YARRA V
Briarty Road, Coldstream, Vic 3770 (059) 64 9267 fax (059) 64 9239
Open Sat & public hols 10–5, Sun 12–5 while stocks available
Production 5000 cases
Winemakers Bailey Carrodus, Peter Wilson
Principal Wines Dry White No. 1 (Sauv Sem), Chard, Pinot, Dry
Red No. 1 (Bordeaux-blend), Dry Red No. 2 (Rhone blend), Mer,
Underhill Shir.
Best Vintages R '80, '81, '86, '89, '90, '91
Summary Dr Bailey Carrodus makes extremely powerful,
occasional idiosyncratic, wines from his 25-year-old, low yielding,
unirrigated vineyards. Both red and white wines have an exceptional
depth of flavour and richness, although my preference for what I
believe to be the great red wines is well known.
Recommended Wines 1991 Dry Red No. 1 (dense colour;
extremely concentrated ripe fruit with complex aromas of tobacco,
plum and cherry, and a long, quite luscious finish; to 2005). 1991
No. 2 Dry Red (dense colour; richly concentrated fruit with
liquorice/gamey/spicy characters in wholly individual style; to 2005).
1991 Underhill Shiraz (highly stylised wine, ripe and concentrated
with gamey, liquorice and dark chocolate characters; little or no spice;
subtle tannins; to 2002).

YELLOWGLEN B–B Est 1975 $15.50–26 R 110 BENDIGO
White's Road, Smythesdale, Vic 3551 (053) 42 8617
fax (053) 33 7102
Open 7 days 9–5 **Production** 220 000 cases
Winemaker Jeffrey Wilkinson
Principal Wines Brut non-vintage, Brut Cremant, Brut Rosé,
Cuvee Victoria vintage; also recently introduced Lassetter range.
Summary Generally reckoned to be the most profitable sparkling
winemaker in Australia (wholly owned by Mildara), producing wines
that clearly please the public palate though not always mine. Over
the last three years, however, quality has improved significantly.
Recommended Wine 1990 Brut (crisp, clean, quite perfumed
fruit with Chardonnay predominant; on the palate citrus-tinged, clean
fruit with well balanced acidity, and not overly sweet).

• YERING STATION NR Est 1988 $9.95–12.95 CD SD YARRA V
Melba Highway, Yering, Vic 3770 (03) 730 1107
fax (03) 739 0135
Open W'ends 10–5, w'days by appointment **Production** 2000 cases
Winemaker St Huberts (Contract)
Principal Wines Chard, Pinot, Cab Sauv under Yering Station;
Unwooded Chard, Pinot under Neuchatel Settlement label.
Summary The family of leading Sydney merchant banker Jim
Dominguez have re-established Yering Station on the site of the first
vineyard to be planted in the Yarra Valley in the 1840s. While the
wine is presently made at St Huberts under contract, the historic
brick winery has been restored as a barrel maturation area and
luxurious sales and tasting facility. Well worth a visit.

YERINGBERG A–A Est 1862 $14–20 ML 21, 149, 231 YARRA V
Maroondah Highway, Coldstream, Vic 3770 (03) 739 1453
fax (03) 739 0048

Open By appointment **Production** 1400 cases
Winemaker Guill De Pury
Principal Wines Chard, Marsanne, Roussane, Pinot, Yeringberg (a Bordeaux-blend).
Best Vintages W '85, '86, '88, '90, '91 R '81, '86, '88, '90, '91
Summary Makes wines for the next millennium from the low yielding vines re-established on the heart of what was one of the most famous (and much larger) vineyards of the nineteenth century. The red wines have a velvety generosity of flavour that is rarely encountered yet never lose varietal character, while the Marsanne takes students of history back to Yeringberg's fame in the nineteenth century, and Roussane is a unique offering.
Recommended Wines 1991 Yeringberg Dry Red (strong red-purple colour with very clean, rich, sweet berry fruit and subtle oak; excellent palate with ripe but not overripe fruit and high quality French oak; to 2005). 1991 Marsanne (firm, clean but not particularly aromatic bouquet, with faint citrus and honeysuckle aromas; quite full and round texture, finishing slightly short; no oak influence; to 1997).

• YUNGARRA ESTATE NR Est 1988 $10–12 CD SD

MARGARET RIVER
Yungarra Drive, Dunsborough, WA 6281 (097) 55 2153
fax (097) 55 2310
Open Thurs–Tues 10–4.30 **Production** 1450 cases
Winemaker Erland Happ (Contract)
Principal Wines Sem Sauv Bl, Chenin Verd, Quartet Wh blend, Rosé, Pink Opal Cab blend.
Summary Yungarra Vineyard Estate is a combined tourist lodge and cellar door facility set on a 40 hectare property overlooking Geographe Bay. The 8 hectare vineyard was first planted in 1988, producing its first wines in 1992, contract made by Earland Happ. In the meantime, wines purchased from other makers are being sold through cellar door by owners Gerry and Wendy Atherden.

• ZANTVOORT STUMPY GULLY VINEYARD NR Est 1988 $13 ML SD MORNINGTON P

200 Stumpy Gully Road, Moorooduc, Vic 3933 phone and fax (059) 78 8429
Open First w'end month 12–5 **Production** 1000 cases
Winemaker W. A. Zantvoort
Principal Wines Sauv Bl, Marsanne, Cab Mer, Dab Sauv, Sparkl.
Summary Frank and Wendy Zantvoort have progressively established nine hectares of vineyard planted to Chardonnay, Marsanne, Sauvignon Blanc, Pinot Noir, Cabernet Sauvignon and Merlot, electing to sell 50% of the production to local winemakers and vinifying the remainder.
Recommended Wine 1992 Sauvignon Blanc (strong, tropical, passionfruit aromas and flavours with attractive smoky overtones; good fruit weight and very well made; drink now).

ZEMA ESTATE BA–BA Est 1982 $9–15 CD 101, 115, 184

COONAWARRA
Main Penola-Naracoorte Road, Coonawarra, SA 5263
(087) 36 3219 fax (087) 36 3280

Open 7 days 9–5 **Production** 5000 cases
Winemakers Ken Ward, Matt Zema
Principal Wines Ries, Shir, Cab Sauv.
Best Vintages R '82, '84, '87, '88, '90
Summary Zema is one of the last outposts of hand pruning and hand picking in Coonawarra, the various members of the Zema family tending a 15 hectare vineyard progressively planted between 1982 and 1988 in the heart of Coonawarra's terra rossa soil. Winemaking practices are straightforward; if ever there was an example of great wines being made in the vineyard, this is it.
Recommended Wines 1990 Shiraz (deep colour, with dense, dark berry fruit aromas; full, ripe, cassis berry fruit on the palate with soft tannins; multi gold medal winner; to 2005). 1991 Cabernet Sauvignon (rich, ripe and dense cassis berry fruit with a touch of astringency to the bouquet; masses of red fruit, dark chocolate and blackcurrant flavours, with subtle oak; to 2000).

ZUBER ESTATE CB–CB Est 1971 $10 CD 117 BENDIGO
Northern Highway, Heathcote, Vic 3523 (054) 33 2142
Open 7 days 9–6 **Production** 800 cases
Winemaker A. Zuber
Principal Wines Shir.
Summary A somewhat erratic winery that is capable of producing the style of Shiraz for which Bendigo is famous but does not always do so.

NEW ZEALAND WINERIES

AKARANGI NR Est 1988 $8.50–15 CD SD HAWKE'S BAY
River Road, Havelock North (06) 877 8228
Open W'ends & pub hols 10–5 **Production** 350 cases
Winemaker Morton Osborne
Principal Wines Sauv Bl, Chard, Chen Bl, Muller Thurgau, Cab Sauv.
Summary Former contract grape growers now making and selling tiny quantities cellar door and through one or two local shops.

ALLAN SCOTT WINES NR Est 1990 $12–19 CD 217, 264 MARLBOROUGH
Jacksons Road, RD 3, Blenheim (03) 572 9054 fax (03) 572 9053
Open 7 days 10–4.30 **Production** 12 000 cases
Winemaker Allan Scott
Principal Wines Ries, Autumn Ries, Sauv Bl, Chard; Mount Riley Classic Red is second label.
Summary Eight hectares each of Sauvignon Blanc, Riesling and Chardonnay mean all the front line wines are estate grown. Highly regarded wines have emanated since the first release, no surprise given Allan Scott's career as Corban's chief viticulturist for many years, not to mention his involvement in the establishment of Cloudy Bay. A vineyard restaurant also operates seven days a week.

AMBERLEY ESTATE CB–CB Est 1979 $10–18 CD SD CANTERBURY
Reserve Road, RD 1, Amberley (03) 314 8409 fax (03) 314 8562
Open Summer 7 days 11–5, winter w'ends 11–5
Production 25 000 cases
Winemaker Jeremy Prater
Principal Wines Gewurz, Ries, Chard, Sauv Bl, Pinot, Cab Sauv.
Best Vintages W '86, '87, '89, '91
Summary Jeremy Prater learnt winemaking in France, Germany and Switzerland, and obtained a diploma in viticulture and oenology in the latter country — relevant training for the cool Canterbury region. The 1991 Riesling is an aromatic, well made wine that has developed nicely.

ASPEN RIDGE ESTATE NR Est 1968 $8–9.50 CD SD WAIKATO
Waerenga Road, Te Kauwhata (07) 826 3959
Open Mon–Sat 9–6 **Production** 4000 cases
Winemaker Alastair McKissock
Principal Wines Sauv Bl, Ries, Rosé, Cab Mer.
Summary A specialist in unfermented, non-alcoholic sparkling grape juice, a strange niche for a former head of the Te Kauwhata Research Station with a master's degree in oenology from UC Davis to boot.

ATA RANGI A–A Est 1980 $18–25 CD 217, 249 MARTINBOROUGH
Puruatanga Road, Martinborough phone and fax (06) 306 9570
Open Tues–Sun 11–5 **Production** 3000 cases

Winemaker Clive Paton
Principal Wines Chard, Gewurz, Celebre (Cab Mer Shir), Pinot.
Best Vintages W '86, '88, '89, '90, '91 R '86, '88, '89, '90, '91
Summary Consistently ranks among the best wineries in New Zealand, let alone Martinborough. Both the Pinot Noir and Celebre are remarkable for their depth of colour and sweetness of fruit, showing the impact of full physiological ripeness.
Recommended Wines 1991 Pinot Noir (deeply coloured, rich cherry and plum fruit with well integrated oak and fine tannins). 1992 Chardonnay (soft, creamy and nutty with textured barrel ferment and malolactic characters; long finish).

•AWAITI VINEYARDS NR Est 1989 SD WAIKATO
RD2 Awaiti Road, Paeroa (07) 862 3834
Open Mon–Sat 9–5 **Production** N/A
Winemaker Nick Chan
Principal Wines Chenin, Cab Sauv.
Summary Cliff and Judith Pett have been producing grapes from their three hectare vineyard since 1978, selling to others, but in 1989 commenced to vinify part of the estate production. It is sold principally through cellar door, with a little through local shops.

BABICH B–B Est 1916 $7.25–22.50 CD 11, 210, 244
HENDERSON
Babich Road, Henderson (09) 833 7859 fax (09) 833 9929
Open Mon–Sat 9–5.30, Sun 11.30–5 **Production** NFP
Winemaker Joe Babich
Principal Wines Irongate Chard, Hawkes Bay Chard, East Coast Chard, Stopbank Chard, Marlborough Sauv Bl, Hawkes Bay Sauv Bl, Sem Chard, Fumé Vert.
Best Vintages W '86, '87, '89, '91, '92 R '85, '87, '89, '90, '91
Summary Upholds the reputation it gained in the 1960s, but has moved with the times in radically changing its fruit sources and wine styles. Given volume of production, quality is admirably consistent.
Recommended Wines 1991 Marlborough Sauvignon Blanc (firm, clean, direct with typical Marlborough herbaceous fruit and crisp acidity; drink now). 1992 Stopbank Chardonnay (fresh, lively fruit with citrus overtones; oak subtle and restrained; crisp, dry finish; to 1995)

•BAZZARD ESTATE NR Est 1991 SD KUMEU
RD2 Awa Road, Kumeu (09) 412 8486
Open By appointment **Production** 1500 cases
Winemaker Charles Bazzard
Principal Wines Muller Gewurz, Pinot.
Summary The 1991 vintage produced two very attractive wines that were largely sold in the United Kingdom; vineyard problems meant very little wine was made in 1992.

BENFIELD & DELAMERE NR Est 1987 $30 R SD
MARTINBOROUGH
Cambridge Road, Martinborough phone and fax (06) 306 9926
Open By appointment **Production** 350 cases
WINEMAKERS Bill Benfield, Sue Delamere
Principal Wines 'Martinborough' a single Cab Sauv Mer Cab Franc blend.

Summary Wellington architect Bill Benfield and partner librarian Sue Delamere have single-mindedly set about re-creating Bordeaux, with an ultra high density, very low trellissed vineyard and utilising 'conservative' techniques of the kind favoured by the Bordelaise. Appropriately, both the 1990 and 1991 vintages are strongly European in style.

Recommended Wines 1991 Cabernet Sauvignon Merlot Franc (intense aromas and flavours of medium weight with some leafy characters, but enough red berry fruit to gain high points; gold medal winner at 1992 Air New Zealand Wine Show).

• **BLACK RIDGE** NR Est 1987 SD CENTRAL OTAGO
Controys Road, Earnscleugh, Alexandra (03) 449 2059
Open Mon–Sat 9.30–5 **Production** 600 cases
Winemaker Contract
Principal Wines Ries, Chard, Gewurz, Pinot.
Summary The formidable, rocky vineyard site at Black Ridge is legendary even in New Zealand, where toughness is taken for granted. The six hectare vineyard will always be low producing, but all of the wines (initially made by Rudi Bouer at Rippon Vineyards) are clean and correct, including a light, gently spicy 1991 Gewurztraminer).

BLOOMFIELD VINEYARDS NR Est 1981 $18–32 R SD
MARTINBOROUGH
119 Solway Crescent, Masterton (06) 377 5505
Open Not **Production** 2200 cases
Winemaker David Bloomfield
Principal Wines Sauv Bl, Pinot, Cab Sauv Mer Cab Franc under both Solway and Bloomfield labels.
Summary Tiny quantities of the wines sold to date have been eagerly snapped up by the local clientele, but wines are now being distributed (sparingly) through Kitchener Wines.

• **BLUE ROCK WINERY** NR Est 1986 $15–24 ML 217
MARTINBOROUGH
Dry River Road, Martinborough (06) 306 9353
Open Mon–Sat 10–6 **Production** 2500 cases
Winemaker Jenny Clark
Principal Wines Chard, Sauv Bl, Ries, Magenta, Pinot, Cab Sauv, Cab Franc.
Summary One of the newest of the Martinborough wineries with seven hectares of estate vineyards, a winery completed in time for the 1993 vintage and a restaurant planned for 1993/94.

BROOKFIELDS VINEYARDS B–B Est 1937 $12.95–24.95
CD SD HAWKE'S BAY
Brookfields Road, Meeanee, Napier (06) 834 4615
fax (06) 834 4622
Open Mon–Sat 9–5, Sun 12–4 **Production** 6000 cases
Winemaker Peter Robertson
Principal Wines Chard, Gewurz, Sauv Bl Fumé, Pinot Gris, Cab.
Best Vintages W '86, '87, '89, '90 R '83, '87, '89, '90
Summary Peter Robertson has worked hard since acquiring Brookfields in 1977, producing grassy Sauvignon Blanc, lightly oaked, understated Chardonnay and — best of all — Cabernet Merlot with

distinct overtones of St Emilion, and blackcurrant-flavoured Reserve Cabernet Sauvignon.

•BROWNLIE BROTHERS NR Est 1991 SD HAWKE'S BAY

Franklin Road, Bayview (06) 836 6250
Open 7 days 9–6 **Production** 650 cases
Winemaker Chris Brownlie
Principal Wines Chard, Sauv Bl, Gewurz, Pinot.
Summary Chris and Jim Brownlie have progressively established 15 hectares of vineyards, selling most of the grapes to other wineries but recently taking the plunge and vinifying a small part of the production for mail order and cellar door sales.

CELLIER LE BRUN B–B Est 1985 $18–42.95 R 217, 259 MARLBOROUGH

Terrace Road, Renwick (03) 572 8859 fax (03) 572 8814
Open 7 days 9–5 **Production** 15 000 cases
Winemaker Daniel le Brun
Principal Wines Meth Champ, Rosé.
Summary French-born and trained (in Champagne) Daniel le Brun has only ever sought to make one wine style: Methode Champenoise. After a few early problems, he is doing better than anyone else in New Zealand (if you put Montana Deutz into a category of its own).
Recommended Wines 1990 Blanc de Blancs (deep yellow colour, strongly styled nutty aroma and fruit with deliberately induced aldehydes; controversial, take it or leave it; gold medal winner 1992 Air New Zealand Wine Show). 1989 Blanc de Noir (salmon pink colour, bright, clean fruit with a touch of strawberry; well balanced with good mouthfeel).

CHARD FARM NR Est 1986 $14.80–16.50 CD SD 155 CENTRAL OTAGO

Gibbston, RD 2, Queenstown phone and fax (03) 442 6110
Open 7 days 11–5 **Production** 3000 cases
Winemaker Rob Hay
Principal Wines Sauv Bl, Ries, Gewurz, Chard, Pinot.
Summary Perched precariously between sheer cliffs and the fast-flowing waters of the Kawarau River, Chard Farm is a tribute to the vision and courage of Rob and Gregory Hay. At a latitude of 45°S viticulture will never be easy, but Chard Farm has made every post a winner to date.
Recommended Wines 1992 Sauvignon Blanc (concentrated herbaceous fruit with pronounced, spicy oak; drink now). 1991 Pinot Noir (tangy, sappy with good weight and length; drink now).

CHIFNEY NR Est 1980 $11–25 CD SD MARTINBOROUGH

Huangarua Road, Martinborough phone and fax (06) 306 9495
Open 7 days 9–6 **Production** 1200 cases
Winemaker Stan Chifney
Principal Wines Chard, Chenin, Rosé, Cab Sauv; Garden of Eden white and red are second label wines.
Summary A retirement hobby that became rather more when the 1986 Cabernet Sauvignon won a gold medal at the 1988 Auckland Easter Show; I have tasted that wine, but none more recently and hence do not give a rating. Stan Chifney intends increasing

production to 2800 cases by 1996, and will take a rather higher profile than hitherto.

• CLEARVIEW ESTATE NR Est 1989 $10–25 CD SD
HASTINGS
RD 2 Clifton Road, Te Awanga (06) 875 0150
Open Thurs–Mon 10–6 summer, w'ends 10–5 winter
Production 1200 cases
Winemaker Tim Turvey
Principal Wines Chard, Sauv Bl, Fumé, Rosé, Cabernet.
Summary Clearview Estate is situated on a site first planted by Anthony Vidal in 1916; it has been replanted since 1988 with Chardonnay, Sauvignon, Cabernet Franc and Merlot, with grapes also coming from a neighbouring vineyard. Alfresco lunches are served throughout the summer months.

C. J. PASK NR Est 1985 $7–19 CD SD 264, 271 HAWKE'S BAY
Omahu Road, Hastings (06) 879 7906 fax (06) 879 6428
Open Mon–Sat 9–5, Sun 10–4 **Production** 18 000 cases
Winemaker Kate Radburnd
Principal Wines Chard, Ries, Sauv Bl, Pinot, Cab Sauv, Cab Mer.
Best Vintages W '86, '89, '90, '91, '92 **R** '86, '87, '89, '90, '91
Summary Ex-cropduster pilot C. J. Pask became one of the most highly regarded grape growers in Hawke's Bay; his coup in securing former Vidal winemaker Kate Radburnd (nee Marris) has paid the expected dividends. Production has increased rapidly, while the 1991 Reserve Merlot won a gold medal at the 1992 Air New Zealand Wine Show. The 1992 Sauvignon Blanc has also received praise for its complex melon and stone fruit flavours.

CLOUDY BAY A–A Est 1985 $A15–21 R 30, 66, 158, 169, 170, 182, 198, 219, 284 MARLBOROUGH
Jacksons Road, Blenheim (03) 572 8914 fax (03) 572 8065
Open 7 days 10–4.30 **Production** 45 000 cases
Winemaker Kevin Judd
Principal Wines Sauv Bl, Chard, Pinot, Cab Mer.
Best Vintages W '85, '86, '89, '91, '92 **R** '86, '88, '89, '90, '91
Summary The other arm of Cape Mentelle, masterminded by David Hohnen and realised by Kevin Judd, his trusted lieutenant from day one. A marketing tour de force it became a world recognised brand in only a few years, but the wine quality and style should not be underestimated: quite simply Hohnen and Judd took New Zealand Sauvignon Blanc from curiosity to respectability.
Recommended Wines 1992 Sauvignon Blanc (intense, pungent, complex gooseberry/grassy fruit with crisp, long and dry finish; drink now). 1991 Chardonnay (complex, stylish, barrel ferment oak handling to wonderful citrus, melon and fig fruit; to 1997). 1989 Pinot Noir (extremely stylish eye opener with sappy notes balanced against dark cherry; near-perfect silky finish; drink now).

COLLARDS A–A Est 1910 $5.50–25.10 CD SD 231, 327
HENDERSON
303 Lincoln Road, Henderson, Auckland 8 (09) 838 8341
fax (09) 837 5840
Open Mon–Sat 9–5.30, Sun 11–5 **Production** 17 000 cases

Winemaker Bruce Collard, Geoff Collard

Principal Wines Chard (Rothesay, Gisborne, Hawke's Bay & Marlborough), Chenin, Sauv Bl (Rothesay and Martinborough), Ries, Wh Burg, Gewurz, Claret, Cab Mer.

Best Vintages W '86, '87, '89, '91, '92 **R** '83, '86, '87, '89, '90

Summary Fastidious winemaking evidences itself in all of the Collards wines, although it is the white wines that (deservedly) win most praise and show success.

Recommended Wines 1992 Marlborough Sauvignon Blanc (fragrant, hightoned, passionfruit-tinged bouquet with strong, crisp, herbal/capsicum fruit in mainstream Marlborough style; drink now). 1992 Riesling (very clean, fresh, fragrant, lime-accented wine with typical low phenolics; to 1996). 1991 Yates Vineyard Chardonnay (lifted, tropical/lemony fruit with high toned, slightly botrytis-influenced flavours; drink now). 1991 Rothesay Vineyard Reserve Chardonnay (crisp, citrus-accented wine with an impressively long finish; to 1995).

•CONDERS BEND BA–BA Est 1991 $12.90–19.95 R SD NELSON

23 Birdling Close, Richmond phone and fax (03) 544 6909

Open Not **Production** 3000 cases

Winemaker Craig Gass

Principal Wines Chard, Sauv Bl, Ries.

Summary Craig Gass, together with wife Jane, has had 20 years experience in the industry encompassing stints with George Fistonich in the early days of Villa Maria, and overseas, including Coldstream Hills. More recently he has worked with John Belsham's major contract winemaking operation. All of the grapes for Conders Bend are in fact sourced in Marlborough and made at Belsham's Vinotech winery.

Recommended Wines 1991 Chardonnay (medium to full yellow-green in colour, with smooth fig and melon fruit, subtle oak and a long finish with pronounced but pleasing acidity; to 1996). 1991 Riesling (lots of botrytis influenced aroma and flavour; lime, citrus and honey run through a weighty palate with good mouthfeel; to 1995). 1992 Sauvignon Blanc (direct herbal/capsicum/asparagus aromas and flavours with dry, crisp finish).

COOKS BA–BA Est 1969 $7.60–20.78 R SD 236 HENDERSON

Great North Road, Henderson (09) 837 3390 fax (09) 836 0005

Open Mon–Sat 9–5

Production 7000 tonnes (450 000 case equivalent)

Winemaker Kerry Hitchcock

Principal Wines Top of the range is Winemakers Res Chard, Sauv Bl, Cab Sauv, LH Sauv Sem; Longridge Chard, Fumé Bl, Gewurz, Cab Mer; Discovery Collection Chard, Sauv Bl, Cab Sauv.

Best Vintages W '83, '86, '89, '91 **R** '83, '86, '89, '91

Summary The quality of the Cooks' wines is exemplary given the large volume that are produced, and not infrequently reach great heights. The Winemakers Reserve series usually deserve the name.

Recommended Wines 1992 Longridge Sauvignon Blanc (clean, well balanced, fruit-driven wine with length and power, yet not aggressive and showing nicely ripened fruit; drink now). 1989 Winemakers Reserve Cabernet Sauvignon (classic, dusty Cabernet in relatively lean, austere style; very good, although the 1990 is better still; to 1997).

COOPER'S CREEK BA–BA Est 1980 $9–23.50 CD 82, 163, 208, 217, 247 HUAPAI
State Highway 16, Huapai (09) 412 8560 fax (09) 412 8375
Open Mon–Fri 9–5.30, w'ends 11–5.30 **Production** 30 000 cases
Winemaker Kim Crawford
Principal Wines Ries, Gewurz, Sauv Bl, Coopers Dry, Fumé, Chard, Cab Sauv, Cab Mer; Swamp Road Chard is prestige wine.
Best Vintages W '83, '86, '89, '90, '91, '92
Summary Stylish makers of very good white wines and adequate, if unexciting, reds. Achieved great feats with the difficult 1992 vintage.
Recommended Wines 1992 Swamp Road Chardonnay (stylish grapefruit/melon fruit aromas; elegant, long palate with good acidity balanced by a touch of sweet barrel ferment oak). 1992 Fumé Blanc (a quite outstanding wine with lovely pure fruit, great concentration and luscious ripeness; a cross between the New World and Sancerre). 1992 Sauvignon Blanc (very crisp, spotlessly clean, direct fruit flavours with some grassy notes, but not excessively so; very long finish).

CORBANS BA–A Est 1902 $3.26–20.78 R SD 214, 236, 327 HENDERSON
Great North Road, Henderson (09) 837 3390 fax (09) 836 0005
Open Mon–Sat 9–6 **Production** 750 000 cases plus 3 million casks
Winemaker Kerry Hitchcock
Principal Wines Stoneleigh Chard, Ries, Sauv Bl, Cab Sauv (premium range); Gewurz, Chard, Fumé, Cab Mer (Private Bin range); others under generic or varietal names.
Best Vintages W '81, '83, '89, '90, '91 R '81, '83, '84, '89, '91
Summary New Zealand's second largest wine group (it also owns Cooks and Robard and Butler) making a complete range of wines under a plethora of brand names (St Arnaud, Montel, Velluto, Liebestraum, Seven Oaks) from vineyards in all parts of New Zealand. In recent years the wines have gone from strength to strength, with some quite brilliant wines coming from Marlborough.
Recommended Wines 1992 CB Chardonnay (very well balanced, stylish tangy fruit with smoky/bacony oak; soft, clean and fleshy in the mouth; to 1995). 1991 CB Merlot (spotlessly clean, beautifully ripened fruit with subtle oak and perfectly ripened fruit flavours; despite the luscious fruit, has great elegance; to 1998). 1991 CB Merlot Cabernet Sauvignon (fragrant minty/leafy aromas, but with sophisticated, high-toned American oak coming through on the palate to marry with sweet berry fruit; not quite in the class of the Merlot, but a top wine nonetheless; to 1997).

CRAB FARM NR Est 1989 $10–17 CD SD HAWKE'S BAY
125 Main Road, Bay View, Hawke's Bay (06) 836 6678
Open 7 days 10–5 **Production** 3000 cases
Winemaker Hamish Jardine
Principal Wines Gewurz, Sauv Bl, Pinot, Merlot, Cab Sauv.
Summary Hamish Jardine has worked at both Chateau Reynella and Matawhero; the family vineyards were planted in 1980 and are now mature, so given the equable Hawke's Bay climate there is no

reason why the wines should not succeed. A spicily oaked barrel sample of 1991 Chardonnay looked promising.

•CROSSROADS WINE COMPANY NR Est 1990 SD
HAWKE'S BAY

SH 50, Korokipo Road, Fernhill, Napier (06) 835 4538
Open 7 days 9–6 **Production** 3800 cases
Winemaker Malcom Reeves
Principal Wines Gewurz, Ries, Chard, Sauv Bl, Cab Sauv.
Summary A partnership between Malcolm Reeves, wine journalist and Massey University lecturer, and computer entrepeneur Lester O'Brien. The first wines, made in 1990, were very well received, both the 1990 Chardonnay and 1991 Riesling winning silver medals at the 1992 Air New Zealand Wine Show.

DE REDCLIFFE ESTATES CB–B Est 1976 $10–21 R SD 250, 298 WAIKATO
Lyons Road, Mangatawhiri Valley, Pokeno, near Auckland
(09) 233 6314 fax (09) 233 6215
Open 7 days 9.30–5 **Production** 152 000 cases
Winemaker Mark Compton
Principal Wines Chard, Ries, Fumé, Sem Chard, White Lady, Coral Reef, Pinot, Cab Mer Franc, Port.
Best Vintages W '87, '89, '91 R '87, '89, '91, '92
Summary The Waikato's answer to the Napa Valley, with the $7 million Hotel du Vin, luxury restaurant, wine tours, lectures, the lot; briefly listed on the Stock Exchange but now Japanese owned. The white wines are by far the best.
Recommended Wine 1991 Fumé Blanc (in the baroque New Zealand style with full, complex, tropical fruit flavours and aromas and minimal oak; drink now).

DELEGAT'S WINE ESTATE BA–BA Est 1947 $12.95–22.50
R SD 146, 210, 251 HENDERSON
Hepburn Road, Henderson (09) 836 0129 fax (09) 836 3282
Open Mon–Fri 9–5, Sat 9–6 **Production** 120 000 cases
Winemaker Brent Marris
Principal Wines Winery Estate label of Chard, Sauv Bl and Cab Mer; top-of-the-range Proprietors Reserve label of Chard, Fumé Bl, Cab Sauv and Mer. Also vineyard-designated Chard from Hawke's Bay, Oyster Bay Chard and Sauv Bl from Marlborough.
Best Vintages W '82, '86, '87, '89, '91 R '82, '86, '89, '90, '91
Summary Delegat's now sources most of its grapes from Hawke's Bay, utilising its own vineyards there and contract growers, but has added the Oyster Bay range from Marlborough to its repertoire. The quality of the wines is seldom less than good, with a number of excellent wines under the Proprietors Reserve label.
Recommended Wines 1992 Hawke's Bay Sauvignon Blanc (complex, smoky, gooseberry fruit with plenty of style, depth and bite; drink now). 1991 Oyster Bay Sauvignon Blanc (developing nicely in bottle, quite full bodied by normal Marlborough standards, with very good vinosity and length; drink now). 1991 Proprietors Reserve Merlot (fresh, bright fruit with mint and cherry aromas and flavours with fine-grained tannins, good acidity and balance; to 1996).

1991 Proprietors Reserve Cabernet Sauvignon (strongly influenced by lemony vanillin American oak; for those who like that style; to 1997).

DRY RIVER A–A Est 1979 $16–22.90 ML 217
MARTINBOROUGH
Puruatanga Road, Martinborough phone and fax (06) 306 9388
Open Not **Production** 2200 cases
Winemaker Neil McCallum
Principal Wines Chard, Gewurz, Ries, Sauv Bl, Fumé, Pinot Gris, Pinot.
Best Vintages W '84, '87, '89, '90, '92 R '89, '90, '91, '92
Summary Winemaker/owner Neil McCallum is a research scientist with a doctorate from Oxford University, with winemaking very much a part-time occupation. He has justifiably gained an international reputation for the exceptional quality of his wines, which he jealously guards and protects. Each is made in tiny quantities, and sells out immediately on release. Says Dr McCallum disarmingly: 'We are unable to send wine samples to international critics'. Despite this, one or two Dry River wines do occasionally pass my palate; I only wish more did so.
Recommended Wines 1991 Botrytis Bunch Selection Gewurztraminer (an extraordinary, classic wine showing utterly exceptional spice and lychee varietal fruit which has in no way been modified by the botrytis; it has equally exceptional length and finesse; to 1997).

ESK VALLEY ESTATE BA–BA Est 1933 $4.95–31 CD SD 201, 320 HAWKE'S BAY
Main Road, Bay View, Napier (06) 836 6411 fax (06) 836 6413
Open 7 days 10–6 **Production** 20 000 cases
Winemaker Grant Edmonds
Principal Wines Chard, Ries, Sauv Bl, Muller, Cab Sauv, Cab Mer.
Best Vintages W '86, '89, '90, '91, '92 R '85, '87, '89, '90, '91
Summary The little brother in the Villa Maria-Vidal family and, in typical brash, small boy fashion has on a number of occasions upstaged the others. The 1992 Reserve Botrytis Bunch Selection Riesling, 1991 Reserve Merlot Cabernet, 1990 Reserve Merlot and 1990 Reserve Merlot Cabernet are all extremely good wines, but the Chardonnays in recent years have been consistently disappointing by comparison.

•ESKDALE WINEGROWERS NR Est 1973 SD HAWKE'S BAY
Main Road, Eskdale (06) 836 6302
Open Mon–Sat 9–5 **Production** Under 1000 cases
Winemaker Kim Salonius
Principal Wines Gewurz, Chard, Cab.
Summary Having gained winemaking experience at McWilliams, Canadian-born Kim Salonius and family have established a tiny 2 hectare estate operation, making wines in very small quantities sold cellar door which have gained a strong reputation for consistency of quality.

FORREST ESTATE B–B Est 1989 $12–22 CD SD 258
MARLBOROUGH
Blicks Road, Renwick, Marlborough (03) 572 9084
fax (03) 572 8915
Open Mon–Sun 12–5 **Production** 3000 cases
Winemaker John Forrest
Principal Wines Chard, Sem, Sauv Bl, Botrytis Sauv Bl Sem, Cab Rosé, Mer.
Summary Former biochemist and genetic engineer John Forrest has had considerable success since his first vintage in 1990, relying initially on purchased grapes but with a four hectare vineyard now planted. Wine quality has been remarkably consistent right across the range, perhaps reflecting John Forrest's strong grounding in chemistry.
Recommended Wines 1992 Sauvignon Blanc (highly fragrant and floral with hints of passionfruit on the aroma, and a clean, fresh, direct wine on the palate with good balance of fruit flavours; very well made; drink now).

FRENCH FARM NR Est 1991 217, 258 CANTERBURY
French Farm Valley Road, Akaroa (03) 304 5784 fax (03) 304 5785
Open 7 days 10–6 **Production** 5500 cases
Winemaker Tony Bish
Principal Wines Fumé Bl, Ries, Sauv Bl, Cab Sauv Cab Franc, Rosé.
Summary The name of the enterprise drives from the fact that French immigrants planted vines at Akaroa (one hour's drive south of Christchurch) as early as 1840. The luxurious tasting facilities include a restaurant open every day for lunch, with superb views back across the bay. Winemaker/owner Tony Bish graduated with a wine science degree from Charles Sturt University, and is making wines of a consistently good standard.

• **GATEHOUSE WINES** NR Est 1989 SD CANTERBURY
RD6 Jowers Road, Christchurch (03) 342 9682
Open Mon–Sat Nov–Feb, Sat Mar–Oct 10–5 **Production** NFP
Winemaker Peter Gatehouse
Principal Wines Chard, Gewurz, Ries, Pinot, Mer, Cab Sauv.
Summary The Gatehouse family made their first wines in 1989 from estate plantings commenced in the early 1980s. The initial release was under the Maciriry label although the wines will henceforth be released under the Gatehouse label, and it is planned to increase production through the purchase of additional grapes from contract growers.

GIBBSTON VALLEY CB–CB Est 1989 $12–25 CD SD 258
CENTRAL OTAGO
Gibbston RD1, Queenstown (03) 442 6910 fax (03) 442 6909
Open Mon–Fri 10–6, Sun 12–6 **Production** 7000 cases
Winemaker Grant Taylor
Principal Wines Sauv Bl, Ries, Gewurz, Pinot Gris, Pinot all estate grown; Southern Selection is cheaper range of non estate wines purchased or blended.
Best Vintages W '87, '89, '90, '91 R '89, '90
Summary A highly professional and attractive winery, restaurant

and cellar door sales facility situated near Queenstown that has been an outstanding success since the day it opened. Viticulture poses special problems, and both varietal selection, choice and style will inevitably take time. However, a neat, modern production facility and a succession of very competent winemakers has pushed Gibbston Valley firmly down the road to success. The 1992 Southern Selection Riesling, 1992 Estate Pinot Gris, 1991 Southern Selection Chardonnay and 1991 Estate Reserve Pinot Noir are all good wines.

Recommended Wine 1992 Southern Selection Sauvignon Blanc (smooth, intense with beautifully ripened gooseberry and tropical fruit aromas and flavours; wonderful balance and mouthfeel; richly deserved its 1992 New Zealand Wine Show gold medal).

GIESEN BA–BA Est 1981 $7–30 CD 219 CANTERBURY
Burnham School Road, RD5, Christchurch phone and
fax (03) 347 6729
Open Mon–Sat 10–5 **Production** 25 000 cases
Winemaker Marcel Giesen, Rudi Bauer
Principal Wines Ries, Burnham Road LH Ries, School Road Chard, Sauv Bl, Chab, Muller, Ehrenfelser, Gewurz, Cab Sauv. Top wines under Reserve label.
Best Vintages W '85, '87, '89, '90, '91 R '86, '89, '91
Summary Determination, skill and marketing flair have seen Giesen grow from obscurity to one of the largest family owned and run wineries in New Zealand. Given the Giesens' Rhine Valley origins it is not surprising they have done so well with aromatic, non-wooded white wines, but the 1991 Burnham School Road Reserve Chardonnay extends the range of high quality wines.

GLADSTONE BA–BA Est 1985 $15–17 CD SD
MARTINBOROUGH
Gladstone Road, Gladstone, Waipara phone and fax (06) 379 8563
Open 7 days 10–5 **Production** 1500 cases
Winemaker Dennis Roberts
Principal Wines Ries, Sauv Bl, Cab Sauv Fr Mer.
Summary Dennis Roberts has taken early retirement from a professional career to concentrate on his childhood love of vineyards and wines. A handsome winery presides over an immaculate vineyard situated roughly halfway between Martinborough and Masterton on alluvial soils laid down by the nearby Ruamahanga River. The label design, incidentally, is a model of elegance and simplicity.

Recommended Wine 1992 Sauvignon Blanc (an outstanding wine with superb varietal fruit in the gooseberry spectrum with a delicate touch of spicy, barrel ferment oak, and quite lovely weight and mouthfeel; to 1995).

GLENMARK B–B Est 1981 $8.50–27 CD SD CANTERBURY
State Highway 1, Waipara phone and fax (03) 314 6828
Open 7 days 11–6 **Production** 2000 cases
Winemaker Kym Rayner
Principal Wines Weka Plains Ries, Ries, Gewurz, Waipara White, Waipara Red, Pinot, Port.
Best Vintages W '87, '89, '90, '91 R '86, '88, '89, '90, '91
Summary A consistent medal winner in earlier years, Glenmark hit a golden patch in 1992, winning gold medals at the 1992 International

Wine Challenge in London for its 1990 Sauvignon Blanc and 1990 Chardonnay, following it with a gold medal for its Waipara Red at the Air New Zealand Wine Show. This performance will help focus attention on the Waipara sub-district of Canterbury.

GLOVER'S VINEYARD B–B Est 1984 $11–18 ML SD
NELSON
Gardner Valley Road, Upper Moutere (03) 543 2698
Open 7 days 10–6 **Production** 1200 cases
Winemaker David Glover

Principal Wines Sauv Bl, Ries, LH Ries, Pinot, Cab Sauv.

Summary David Glover studied winemaking and viticulture at Charles Sturt University in southern New South Wales during a 17-year stay in Australia. He returned with wife Penny to establish their own vineyard in 1984, struggling with birds and other predators before producing their first wines in 1989. The quality of the white wines, in particular, has been exemplary.

Recommended Wines 1992 Sauvignon Blanc (crisp, bright, clean, herbaceous/gooseberry fruit in classic seafood style; very competent winemaking). 1992 Late Harvest Riesling (bright green yellow in colour, with good balance and intensity; long finish with good acidity).

GOLDWATER ESTATE NR Est 1978 $17–35 CD 256
WAIHEKE ISLAND
Causeway Road, Putiki Bay (09) 372 7493 fax (09) 372 6827
Open Summer 7 days 10–4 **Production** 10 500 cases
Winemaker Kim Goldwater

Principal Wines Marlborough, Chard and Sauv Bl; Cab Mer (Waiheke Island).

Best Vintages '87, '89, '90, '91, '92 R '85, '87, '89, '90, '91

Summary Goldwater Estate has established a formidable reputation for the quality of its wines, which sell in impressive volumes given their relatively high prices. Dr Richard Smart has been retained as viticultural consultant for the Waiheke Island red wines, while 4500 cases of Marlborough Chardonnay and 1500 cases of Marlborough Sauvignon Blanc have helped propel sales to their present level.

GRAPE REPUBLIC NR Est 1985 $10–26 R SD WELLINGTON
State Highway One, Te Horo phone and fax (06) 364 3284
Open 7 days 10–5 **Production** 1250 cases
Winemaker Alastair Pain

Principal Wines Chard, Sauv Bl, Ries, Rosé, Gewurz, Cab Sauv, selection of fruit wines.

Summary A marketing and promotion tour-de-force using direct mail and wine club techniques, with a vast array of flavoured wines and smaller quantities of more expensive table wines that are distinctly austere. Alastair Pain says this is the European style he is aiming for. I am not so sure, although the 1990 Druid Hill Cabernet Sauvignon is a good wine. A winery cafe opened for business in 1993.

GROVE MILL BA–B Est 1988 $15.95–69.95 R 217, 261, 281
MARLBOROUGH
1 Dodson Street, Blenheim (03) 578 9190 fax (03) 578 9085
Open 7 days 9–5 **Production** 13 500 cases
Winemaker David Pearce

Principal Wines Under the Grove Mill Grosvenor label Sauv Bl, Chard, Ries, Cab Sauv; under the Gold Label Lansdowne Chard, Blackbirch Cab and Drylands Botrytised Sauv Bl.

Best Vintages W '88, '89, '90 R '89, '90

Summary Burst on the scene with a superb '89 Chardonnay, and has shown little or no signs of slackening the pace, reaping medals (including golds) virtually at will at the 1992 Air New Zealand Wine Show. The wines have been slightly less successful in Australian show tastings, but have still performed impressively across the range.

Recommended Wines 1992 Marlborough Chardonnay (intriguing wine with satin-smooth peach aromas and a voluptuous palate that is reminiscent of Viognier; presumably some botrytis influence, but very well made). 1991 Blackbirch Cabernet Sauvignon (quite dense colour with strong and deep herbaceous fruit aromas; the palate too is on the herbaceous side, but has length).

• HERONS FLIGHT NR Est 1987 $24 CD SD NORTHLAND
RD2 Sharp Road, Warkworth (09) 422 7915
Open 7 days 10–6 while stocks last **Production** 800 cases
Winemaker David Hoskins

Principal Wines Barrel fermented Chard; un-oaked Chard; Cab Mer Fr blend.

Summary Herons Flight or Pheonix Flight? Having established a small vineyard in 1987, David Hoskins and Mary Evans have leased the defunct Antipodean Winery, which was the scene of so much marketing hype and excitement in the mid 1980s before disappearing in a bitter family dispute. The first Herons Flight wine (a densely coloured and flavoured Cabernet Sauvignon) was produced from the 1991 vintage; production is expected to peak at 1500 cases.

HIGHFIELD ESTATE NR Est 1990 $10.50–17.50 CD SD 308 MARLBOROUGH
RD2 Brookby Road, Blenheim (03) 572 8592 fax (03) 572 9257
Open Mon–Sat 10–5 **Production** 10 000 cases
Winemaker Tony Hooper

Principal Wines Ries, Chard, Noble LH, Sauv Bl, Mer, Sparkl.

Summary Highfield Estate was purchased by an international partnership in late 1991, the English and Japanese limbs of which are associated with the French Champagne House Drappier, pointing to the addition of a Methode Champenoise sparkling wine to the range of premium varietals.

Recommended Wines 1992 Sauvignon Blanc (crisp, pungent and quite intense green pea/asparagus/herbal aromas and flavours in mainstream Marlborough style). 1992 Chardonnay (scented, high toned citric fruit, a little on the green side, but clean and well made).

HUNTER'S A–A Est 1983 $12.50–18.70 CD 60, 217, 220 MARLBOROUGH
Rapaura Road, Blenheim (03) 572 8489 fax (03) 572 8457
Open 7 days 9.30–4.30 **Production** 37 000 cases
Winemaker Gary Duke

Principal Wines Sauv Bl, Chard, Cab Sauv, Pinot.

Best Vintages W '88, '89, '91 R '87, '88, '89, '91

Summary Hunter's goes from strength to strength, consistently producing flawless wines with tremendous varietal character. Given the quantity and quality of its production, it is a winery of world standing and certainly among the top half dozen in Australasia.

Recommended Wines 1992 Sauvignon Blanc (complex mix of gooseberry and herbal aromas, with almost piercing fruit on the palate, tangy and rich; very long finish; to 1995). 1991 Chardonnay (extremely fragrant and luscious lemon, peach and melon fruit with subtle barrel ferment oak; elegant but intense, of the highest class; to 1998). 1991 Sauvignon Blanc Oak Aged (exceptionally complex, smooth and rich wine with wonderfully ripe Sauvignon Blanc fruit and immaculately balanced and integrated oak; to 1995). 1991 Cabernet Sauvignon (attractive, sweet, red berry fruit aroma and flavour; no vegetal characters; fine, silky tannins; to 1996).

JACKSON ESTATE NR Est 1991 SD 259 MARLBOROUGH
Jacksons Road, Blenheim (05) 69 6547
Open Not **Production** 5000 cases
Winemaker Warwick Stichbury
Principal Wines Sauv Bl, Chard, Ries, Pinot.
Summary Long-term major grape growers John and Warwick Stichbury, with leading viticulturist Richard Bowling in charge, own substantial vineyards in the Marlborough area and have now established their own winery and brand to vinify part of the production, the balance still being sold to others. The 1991 Sauvignon Blanc, 1992 Sauvignon Blanc and 1991 Botrytised Riesling have all won top awards from New Zealand's most respected critics.

KUMEU RIVER B–B Est 1944 $10.50–28 R SD 233 KUMEU
2 Highway 16, Kumeu (09) 412 8415 fax (09) 412 7627
Open Mon–Fri 9–5.30, Sat 11–5.30, Sun 11–4.30
Production 18 000 cases
Winemaker Michael Brajkovich
Principal Wines Chard, Sauv Bl, Mer Cab, Cab Franc, Pinot under three labels: Kumeu River (top), Brajkovich (next) and San Marino (cheapest).
Best Vintages W '85, '87, '89, '91, '92 R '86, '87, '89, '90, '91
Summary The wines of Michael Brajkovich defy conventional classification, simply because the highly trained, highly skilled and highly intelligent Brajkovich does not observe convention in crafting them, preferring instead to follow his own French-influenced instincts and preferences. Not altogether surprisingly, the wines have won high praise overseas.

LANDFALL-REVINGTON C–CB Est 1987 $7–23 CD SD 235 GISBORNE
State Highway 2, Manutuke, Gisborne (06) 862 8577
fax (06) 867 8508
Open Oct–Easter 7 days 9–6 **Production** 5000 cases
Winemaker John Thorpe
Principal Wines Revington Chard, Gewurz; Landfall Muller, Chard, Blush and Gisborne Red.
Summary A fairly complicated joint venture (the brainchild of lawyer/partner Ross Revington) and name changes have kept Australian wine writers on their toes. The Revington label wines come from the four hectare Revington vineyard, the Landfall label wines come partly from its own 4 hectare vineyard, partly from

Revington vineyard and partly from local growers. Landfall wines were previously called Whitecliffs.

LARCOMB BA–BA Est 1985 $8–16 CD SD CANTERBURY
Larcombs Road, RD5, Christchurch (03) 347 8909
Open Nov–Feb, Tues–Sun 9–5 **Production** 2000 cases
Winemaker John Thom
Principal Wines Ries, Gewurz, Pinot Gris, Pinot.
Summary Highly regarded maker of fine, elegant, citrus Rhine Riesling, fleshy, gently oaked Pinot Gris and generous Pinot Noir; the winery restaurant (open from November to February) is extremely popular and contributes substantially to sales.

LIMEBURNERS BAY CA–CB Est 1978 $7–19.75 CD SD KUMEU
112 Hobsonville Road, Hobsonville (09) 416 8844
Open Mon–Sat 9–6 **Production** 3500 cases
Winemaker Alan Laurenson
Principal Wines Muller, Sem Chard, Sauv Bl, Chard, Cab Mer, Cab Sauv.
Best Vintages W '87, '89, '90, '91 R '84, '85, '87, '89
Summary Has rapidly established a reputation for itself as a producer of high class Cabernet Sauvignon, doing especially well with its '84, '87 and '89 wines. Seventy-five per cent of the production is exported, with almost all of the white wines sold in Germany and Denmark.

LINCOLN C–CB Est 1937 $6.95–21.50 CD SD 280 HENDERSON
130 Lincoln Road, Henderson (09) 838 6944 fax (09) 838 6984
Open Mon–Sat 9–6, Sun 11–5 **Production** 38 000 cases
Winemaker Nick Chan
Principal Wines Chard (East Coast and Parklands), Sauv Bl, Ries, Chenin, Muller, Gewurz, Dry Red, Cab, Mer, fortifieds, Sparkl.
Best Vintages W '85, '86, '89, '91, '92 R '83, '86, '89, '91, '92
Summary A former fortified wine specialist that has moved towards table wine production with the aid of a Roseworthy-graduate winemaker and avant-garde labels. Among unconventional but very successful wines are the 1989 barrel fermented Chenin Blanc and the 1990 Ice Wine Gewurztraminer; the 1989 Cabernet Merlot is also pleasantly flavoured and structured.

•LINDEN ESTATE NR Est 1991 $12.80–15.50 CD SD HAWKE'S BAY
Taupo Road, SH2, Eskdale (06) 836 6806
Open 7 days 9–5 **Production** 2200 cases
Winemaker Wim van der Linden
Principal Wines Sauv Bl, Fumé, Chard, Cab Sauv, Cab Mer, Mer Cab, Franc Mer Cab.
Summary This is the project of retired civil engineer and long-term grape grower Wim van der Linden and family, son John being a tutor in viticulture at the Polytechnic in Hawke's Bay. The estate vineyard was replanted in 1989 to 12.5 hectares of premium varieties.

LINTZ ESTATE NR Est 1989 $12–19.50 CD SD
MARTINBOROUGH
Kitchener St, Martinborough (06) 306 9174 fax (06) 306 9237;

postal PO Box 177, Martinborough
Open While stocks last **Production** 2000 cases
Winemaker Chris Lintz
Principal Wines Gewurz, Sauv Bl, Dry White, Pinot, Cab Sauv, Sparkl.
Summary New Zealand-born Chris Lintz comes from a German winemaking family and graduated from Geisenheim. The first stage of the Lintz winery, drawing grapes from the nine hectare vineyard, was completed in 1991, and production is eventually planned to increase to around 13 000 cases. The 1991 Optima Noble Selection (Optima is a German-bred cross) and 1991 Cabernet Merlot have both received high points in New Zealand shows.

LOMBARDI NR Est 1959 $9.25–14.50 R SD HAWKE'S BAY
Te Mata Road, Havelock North (06) 877 7985
Open 7 days 9–5 **Production** 1000 cases
Winemaker Hamish Binns
Principal Wines Hock, Ries Sylv, Sauternes, Pinotage, Sherry, Vermouth, Marsala and flavoured fortifieds.
Summary The Australian Riverland transported to the unlikely environment of Hawke's Bay, with a half-Italian, half-English family concentrating on a kaleidoscopic array of Vermouths and sweet, flavoured fortified wines.

MARTINBOROUGH VINEYARD A–A Est 1980
$9.50–25.50 CD 217, 258, 264 MARTINBOROUGH
Princess Street, Martinborough (06) 306 9955 fax (06) 306 9217
Open 7 days 11–5 **Production** 9000 cases
Winemaker Larry McKenna
Principal Wines Chard, Sauv Bl, Ries, LH Ries, Gewurz, Muller, Pinot, Pinot Gris.
Best Vintages W '86, '88, '89, '91, '92 R '86, '88, '89, '90, '92
Summary Australian-born and trained Larry McKenna has produced the best Pinot Noir to come from New Zealand together with several brilliant Chardonnays. The Pinot Noir goes from strength to strength; after a hugely powerful '89, the elegance, finesse and length of the '90 seemingly put the world class quality of this winery's Pinot Noir beyond question; however, the 1991 Pinot Noir was extremely controversial, amongst other things being declined an export approval.
Recommended Wines 1991 Pinot Noir (a wine that shows technique pushed to its ultimate, and succeeding to 90%; the aroma in particular is complex but undoubtedly has elements of volatility and mercapton, redeemed by the intense underlying fruit and the length and strength of the palate; to 1995). 1992 Sauvignon Blanc (strong varietal flavour, with herbal fruit balanced by a judicious touch of residual sugar; drink now).

MATAWHERO DA–CA Est 1975 $11–24.50 CD 217 GISBORNE
Riverpoint Road, Matawhero (06) 868 8366 fax (06) 867 9856
Open Mon–Sat 9–5 **Production** 10 000 cases
Winemaker Denis Irwin
Principal Wines Gewurz, Chard, Sauv Bl, Chenin, Pinot, Cab Mer.
Summary The wines have always been cast in the mould of

Matawhero's unpredictable founder and owner Denis Irwin: at their best, in the guise of the Gewurztraminer from a good vintage, they are quite superb, racy and powerful; at their worst, they are poor and exhibit marked fermentation problems.

MATUA VALLEY BA–BA Est 1974 $4.70–27.50 CD 140–144, 217, 246 WAIMAUKU

Waikoukou Road, Waimauku (09) 411 8301 fax (09) 411 7982
Open 7 days 9–5 **Production** 120 000 cases
Winemakers Bill Spence, Mark Robertson
Principal Wines A very large range running from generic and varietal white and red table wines at the bottom end of the price scale, then to the Shingle Peak Marlborough range (Sauv Bl, Ries, Chard, Cab Sauv), then on to the premium white and red table wines either under the Reserve, Ararimu or Judd Vineyard labels.
Best Vintages W '81, '84, '89, '91 R '85, '86, '89, '91
Summary One of the undoubted high flyers of the New Zealand wine industry, producing a wide range of wines of quite remarkable consistency of quality. The Shingle Peak label has been particularly successful, while the presentation of the Ararimu Chardonnay and Cabernet Sauvignon sets new standards of excellence for New Zealand.
Recommended Wines 1992 Shingle Peak Sauvignon Blanc (fragrant and seductive passionfruit aroma, with fresh, clean lively and elegant palate; perfect in all respects; to 1994). 1992 Shingle Peak Riesling (full, smooth, Germanic, lime flavours, fleshy and deep; to 1995). 1991 Ararimu Chardonnay (soft, peachy, warm, creamy vanillin fruit and oak; drink now). 1991 Ararimu Cabernet Sauvignon (deeply coloured, with strong, dark chocolate and sweet berry aromas with just a hint of leafiness; sweet oak on the palate balances the herbaceous edges to the full berry fruit; finishes with moderate tannins; to 2000).

• MAZURANS VINEYARD NR Est 1938 SD HENDERSON

225 Lincoln Road, Henderson (09) 838 6945
Open Mon–Sat 9–6 **Production** 1000 cases
Winemaker Rado Hladilo
Principal Wines Sherries and Ports.
Summary A Sherry and Port specialist, still surviving on the reputation built for its wines by George Mazuran, who died in 1980.

MCDONALD WINERY, THE NR Est 1897 SD HAWKE'S BAY

200 Church Road, Taradale (070) 44 2053
Open Mon–Sat 9–5 **Production** NFP
Winemaker Tony Prichard
Principal Wines Chard, Cab Sauv under the Church Road label.
Summary Montana's acquisition of the historic McDonald winery in 1989 and its investment of $2 million on refurbishment followed by the announcement of the Cordier joint venture, together with the acquisition of premium Hawke's Bay vineyards signalled Montana's determination to enter the top end of the market with high quality Chardonnay and Cabernet Sauvignon. Legal squabbles have forced the adoption of the Church Road label for the wines.
Recommended Wine 1991 Cabernet Sauvignon (lively, fragrant,

cool-grown fruit with slight herbal/wintergreen characters offset by sophisticated vanillin oak; to 1998).

MERLEN B–B Est 1989 $12.50–17.50 CD SD 195 MARLBOROUGH
Rapaura Road, Renwick phone and fax (03) 572 9151
Open 7 days 9–5 **Production** 5000 cases
Winemaker Almuth Lorenz
Principal Wines Ries, Gewurz, Sauv Bl, Fumé, Chard, Muller.
Best Vintages W '87, '88, '89, '91, '92
Summary Almuth Lorenz has a strong, indeed overwhelming, personality and makes appropriately strong, rich, vivid white wines with the Chardonnays (high in alcohol, with strong barrel ferment and malolactic characters) leading the way, along with a superb, intense lime juice 1991 Rhine Riesling free from any distracting botrytis or phenolic overtones, and an even better botrytised 1991 Magic Riesling, searingly intense and luscious. All the wines can be enjoyed at the Weingarten Restaurant, open 9 am to 5 pm seven days a week.

MILLS REEF NR Est 1989 $10.50–27.50 R SD 200, 249 BAY OF PLENTY
RD 1 Belk Road, Tauranga (07) 543 0926 fax (07) 543 0728
Open Mon–Fri 9–4.30 **Production** 6000 cases
Winemaker Paddy Preston
Principal Wines Chard, Sauv Bl, Ries, Gewurz, Sparkl.
Summary Mills Reef might only have one neighbour, but it is a powerful one: Morton Estate. Like Morton Estate, all of the grapes are in fact grown in Hawke's Bay and shipped to the winery. The initial releases were of very high quality, but problems with oak volatility has dogged some of the subsequent releases. Perhaps the opening of the new winery and restaurant at Moffat Road, Bethlehem, Tauranga (due to open November 1993) will see a change of fortune.
Recommended Wine 1991 Riesling (full citrus/lime fruit with hints of passionfruit in the bouquet; solidly structured and richly flavoured palate, with a long and powerful finish; a wine of high quality).

MILLTON BA–B Est 1984 $10.85–24.25 CD SD 314 GISBORNE
Papatu Road, Manutuke, Gisborne (06) 862 8680 fax (06) 862 8869
Open Labour w'end–Easter 7 days 10–6 **Production** 10 000 cases
Winemaker James Millton
Principal Wines Chard, Chenin, Sauv Bl Sem, Muller, Ries, Cab Sauv, Mer, usually from separately designated vineyards.
Best Vintages W '86, '89, '90, '91, '92 R '86, '89, '91
Summary The only registered organic vineyards in New Zealand using bio-dynamic methods and banning insecticides and herbicides; winemaking methods are conventional, but seek to limit the use of chemical additives wherever possible. The white wines, particularly botrytised, can be of the highest quality; the germanic, lime-flavoured Opou Vineyard Riesling is almost always outstanding, 1992 being no exception.

MISSION CB–CB Est 1851 $6.95–12.50 CD SD HAWKE'S BAY
Church Road, Taradale (06) 844 2259 fax (06) 844 6023

Open Mon–Sat 8–5 **Production** 40 000 cases

Winemaker Paul Mooney

Principal Wines Chard, Fumé, Gewurz, Muller, Sauv Bl, Sem, Pinot Gris, Cab Sauv.

Best Vintages W '83, '87, '89, '91 R '83, '87, '89, '91

Summary New Zealand's oldest winemaker, owned by the Society of Mary, making honest, basically unpretentious wines at suitably modest prices; the softly rich (if oaky) '89 Cabernet Sauvignon emphasised that one should not dismiss the wines out of hand. The 1991 Fumé Blanc and 1992 Sauvignon Blanc are no less commendable at their price, even if unashamedly commercial in style.

MONTANA A–A Est 1977 $10.95–15.20 R 43, 210 AUCKLAND, GISBORNE & MARLBOROUGH

171 Pilkington Road, Glen Innes, Auckland (09) 570 5549
fax (09) 527 1113

Open 7 days 9.30–5.30

Production 26 000 tonnes (1.65 million case equivalent)

Winemaker John Simes

Principal Wines Sauv Bl, Chard, Ries, Meth Champ, Cab Sauv; brand names include Blenheimer and Wohnsiedler; premium wines include Private Bin and Brancott Estate.

Best Vintages W & R '80, '82, '83, '87, '89, '91

Summary Has a far more dominant position than does SABH through Seppelts-Penfolds-Lindemans in Australia, as it produces 50% of New Zealand's wine. Having parted company with Seagrams many years ago, it is now seeking equity partners and has formed joint ventures with Deutz for sparkling wine making and Cordier with its McDonald winery offshoot. As one might expect the wines are invariably well crafted right across the range, even if most attention falls on its consistently award-winning Marlborough Sauvignon Blanc (a wine which, for once, failed to impress in 1992).

Recommended Wines Cuvee Deutz (complex nutty/yeasty stylish bouquet; a generously flavoured wine with plenty of sweet fruit, with some creamy/caramel flavours which are very attractive). 1991 Brancott Estate Sauvignon Blanc (fragrant gooseberry fruit aromas, tending a little herbaceous on the palate, but does have good length and mouthfeel; drink now). 1990 Ormond Estate Chardonnay (smooth, commercial style with coconut/vanilla oak that is well handled but not entirely appropriate for the variety; drink now).

MORTON ESTATE BA–B Est 1982 $11–23 R 110, 223 WAIKATO

State Highway 2, Kati Kati (07) 552 0795 fax (07) 552 0651

Open 7 days 10.30–5 **Production** 45 000 cases

Winemakers John Hancock, Steve Bird

Principal Wines Chard, Gewurz, Sauv Bl, Pinot Blush, Cab Sauv.

Best Vintages W '83, '85, '86, '89, '91 R '83, '85, '86, '89, '91

Summary A high flyer of the early 1980s, Morton Estate was purchased by Mildara in the late 1980s, although Mildara Blass has since relinquished ownership. The style of wines has always been very positive and, so far as I am concerned, not always successful. However, when the wines succeed, they do so with a vengeance.

Recommended Wines 1991 Black Label Chardonnay (complex, rich, tangy, full blown wine with tremendous power and impact in both bouquet and palate; intense and long finish, with the fruit carrying the richly textured oak; to 1995). 1992 White Label Sauvignon Blanc (pronounced tobacco leaf aromas which border on the extreme; much better on the palate with lively, light and crisp herbal fruit, and most attractive acidity on the finish; drink now). 1991 Black Label Cabernet Merlot (clean, dark berry and cassis bouquet, with elegant cedary/briary notes on the palate, and a cleansing, fresh finish; to 1995).

• MOTEO WINES NR Est 1991 SD HAWKE'S BAY
RD 3 Moteo, Pa Road, Purketapu, Napier (06) 844 9911
Open Not **Production** 10 000 cases
Winemaker Peter Gough
Principal Wines Chard, Sauv Bl, Cab Mer Fr.
Summary Peter Gough is a graduate of Roseworthy College, and worked in the Hunter Valley and Coonawarra before returning to Hawke's Bay. He is also manager and partner of a vineyard partnership that supplies Moteo Wines with its grapes. His experience shows in the 1992 Sauvignon Blanc, a wine with strong oak and rich fruit.

• MUIRLEA RISE NR Est 1991 SD MARTINBOROUGH
50 Princess Street, Martinborough (06) 306 9332
Open Not **Production** 800 cases
Winemaker Willy Brown
Principal Wines Pinot, Shir, Cab, Port.
Summary Former Auckland wine distributor Willy Brown has established a 1.9 hectare vineyard. The first wine released, a 1991 Pinot Noir, has been a consistent show award winner and is another affirmation of the suitability of the Martinborough region for Pinot Noir.

NAUTILUS BA–BA Est 1986 $15–19 R 140–144, 192, 219, 251, 255 AUCKLAND
Bucks Road, Renwick, Marlborough (09) 366 1356
fax (09) 366 1357
Open Mon–Sat 9–5 **Production** 12 000 cases
Winemaker Alan Hoey
Principal Wines Sauv Bl, Chard, Cab Sauv, Cab Mer, Sparkl.
Summary Nautilus is ultimately owned by Yalumba of Australia; the wines are made by Yalumba winemaker Alan Hoey at Matua Valley from Hawke's Bay Sauvignon Blanc and Marlborough Chardonnay. The wines have been consistently good.
Recommended Wines 1991 Chardonnay (high toned, aromatic, cool-grown melon fruit with appropriately subtle oak, and no mould or excessive skin contact characters). 1992 Hawke's Bay Sauvignon Blanc (soft citrus/tropical fruit in pleasant, easy commercial style; drink now). 1992 Marlborough Sauvignon Blanc (rather subdued, slightly hard bouquet, but much better palate, with bite and grip; well made, but shows the limitations of the vintage; drink now). 1990 Cabernet Merlot (bright colour; essentially driven in both and aroma terms by spicy American oak; to 1997).

NEUDORF A–A Est 1978 $13.90–26 CD 64, 217, 258 NELSON
Neudorf Road, Upper Moutere (03) 543 2643 fax (03) 543 2955

Open 7 days 10–5 Nov–Apr **Production** 4000 cases
Winemaker Tim Finn
Principal Wines Chard, Sauv Bl, Ries, Pinot.
Best Vintages W '87, '89, '90, '91, '92 **R** '82, '85, '86, '90, '92
Summary Tim Finn has produced some of Australasia's most stunningly complex and rich Chardonnays, with the 1989 and 1991 wines outstanding in any class. But his skills do not stop there, spanning all varieties which are consistently of show medal standard.
Recommended Wines 1991 Chardonnay (very complex, with strong malolactic influence and a powerful, textured and structured palate; to 1995). 1992 Sauvignon Blanc (crisp, clean, firm, direct style with asparagus and herb flavours; what you see is what you get; drink now).

NGATARAWA BA–B Est 1981 $11–25 CD SD 317 HAWKE'S BAY
Ngatarawa Road, Bridge Pa, Hastings (06) 879 7603
fax (06) 879 6675
Open 7 days 11–5 **Production** 10 000 cases
Winemaker Alwyn Corban
Principal Wines Chard, Sauv Bl, Ries, Botrytis Ries, Cab Mer, fortifieds.
Best Vintages W '87, '89, '90, '91, '92 **R** '85, '86, '89, '90, '91
Summary Alwyn Corban is a highly qualified and highly intelligent winemaker from a famous New Zealand wine family who has elected to grow vines organically and make wines that sometimes (but certainly not always) fall outside the mainstream. Challenging and interesting, and not to be taken lightly.
Recommended Wines 1992 Stables Sauvignon Blanc (unusually ripe and sweet gooseberry fruit, luscious and mouthfilling; gives the impression of some sweetness on the back palate, and would be even better if a little drier; drink now). 1992 Penny Noble Harvest Riesling (intense lime and honey bouquet, with flavours of peach being added to the mix on the palate; relatively low volatile acidity; to 1998). 1991 Alwyn Chardonnay (strongly oak influenced with a nutty/buttery textured palate; ever so slightly cloying, but very clean; to 1995).

NOBILO CB–CB Est 1943 $8–34 R 48, 65, 211, 217, 228
AUCKLAND
Station Road, Huapai (09) 412 9148 fax (09) 412 7124
Open Mon–Fri 9–5 **Production** 280 000 cases
Winemaker Nick Nobilo Jnr
Principal Wines Gewurz, Chard, Sauv Bl, Muller, Pinot, Pinotage, Cab Sauv variously sourced from Gisborne, Hawke's Bay and Marlborough.
Best Vintages W '81, '83, '85, '89, '91 **R** '81, '83, '85, '87, '89
Summary One of the more energetic and effective wine marketers, with production heavily focused on white wines sourced from Gisborne, Hawke's Bay and Marlborough. It would be fair to say, however, that wine quality has more often than not lagged behind that of its major competitors.
Recommended Wines 1992 Marlborough Sauvignon Blanc (ultra herbal style, clean and direct, but tending to slight bitterness on the finish; drink now). 1991 Reserve Chardonnay (reasonably successful and quite complex oak evident on both bouquet and palate; fairly soft fruit; early developing style).

•**OHINEMURI ESTATE** NR Est 1989 SD WAIKATO
Moresby St, Karangahake (07) 862 8874
Open 7 days 10–6 **Production** NFP
Winemaker Horst Hillerich
Principal Wines Chard, Chenin, Gewurz, Ries, Sauv Bl, Pinotage, Cab Sauv.
Summary German-born, trained and qualified winemaker Horst Hillerich came to New Zealand in 1987, first working at Totara before establishing Ohinemuri Estate. Hillerich and his wife plan to open a restaurant at the newly constructed winery in the Karangahake Gorge.

•**OKAHU ESTATE** NR Est 1989 SD NORTHLAND
Okahu Road, Kaitaia, Northland (09) 408 0888 fax (09) 408 0890
Open Not **Production** 300 cases
Winemaker Monty Knight
Principal Wines Chard, Muller, Pinot, Pinot Blush, Dry Red.
Summary The initial release of 1989 90 Mile Red, a blend of Cabernet Sauvignon, Pinotage and Pinot Noir from estate grown grapes, signals the location of Okahu Estate at the bottom end of the 90 mile beach. The other wines are made from grapes purchased from other regions.

OMIHI HILLS NR Est 1984 $15–23 ML SD 322 CANTERBURY
Reeces Road, Omihi, North Canterbury (vineyard); postal 5 Paulus Terrace, Christchurch 2 (03) 337 1763 fax (03) 379 8638
Open Not **Production** 2500 cases
Winemaker Danny Schuster
Principal Wines Pinot Blanc, Pinot.
Summary Austrian-born, German-trained Danny Schuster is arguably better known as a viticultural consultant in the Napa Valley than he is as a winemaker in New Zealand. This, despite the fact that he achieved lasting recognition for the Pinot Noirs he made at St Helena in the early 1980s, and despite his ongoing abiding interest in Pinot Noir, with a major (as yet unpublished) book on the subject to his credit. It is thus the final irony that he has consistently produced better Pinot Blanc than Pinot Noir since establishing the Omihi Hills label.

PACIFIC CB–BA Est 1936 $7.10–14 CD SD HENDERSON
90 McLeod Road, Henderson (09) 836 9578
Open Mon–Sat 9–6 **Production** 12 000 cases
Winemaker Steve Tubic
Principal Wines Chard, Sauv Bl, Gewurz, Ries, Muller, Cab Sauv, Sherry, Port, the best under the Reserve label. Also large quantities of coolers, casks (Chatenberg, Bernhoffen).
Best Vintages W '86, '89, '90 R '86, '87, '89, '90
Summary A very large winery with its 12 000 case production of premium wines dwarfed by its 1000 tonne crush but, nonetheless, gaining both recognition and respect in the wake of recent consistent show success.

PALLISER ESTATE A–BA EST 1989 $16–24 CD 219, 288 MARTINBOROUGH
Kitchener Street, Martinborough (06) 306 9109 fax (06) 306 9946
Open 7 days 10–6 **Production** 10 000 cases
Winemaker Allan Johnson

Principal Wines Chard, Sauv Bl, Ries, Pinot.

Summary A fast-rising, high profile, no expense spared winery that is bound to raise public awareness of the Martinborough region still further. The wines are expensive but are of excellent quality across the full spectrum of style, with the 1992 Late Harvest Riesling, 1992 Riesling and 1992 Sauvignon Blanc all winning gold medals at the 1992 Air New Zealand Wine Show.

Recommended Wines 1992 Sauvignon Blanc (superbly weighted and ripened fruit with intense gooseberry, melon and gently herbal notes; very clean). 1991 Chardonnay (strong, complex fruit with high toned citrus aromas; strong fruit flavour, though it does cloy slightly).

PARKER METHODE CHAMPENOISE NR Est 1987 SD GISBORNE
91 Banks Street, Gisborne phone and fax (06) 867 6967
Open 7 days 9.30–6 **Production** 1000 cases
Winemaker Phil Parker
Principal Wines Dry Flint; Classical Brut; Rosé Brut; Light Red.
Summary A new and highly rated Methode Champenoise specialist that has caused much interest and comment. Has not entered the show ring and I have not tasted the wines. The winery also has a restaurant open for lunch and dinner every day of the week.

PELORUS NR Est 1983 $8–18.50 CD SD NELSON
Patons Road, Richmond, Nelson phone and fax (03) 542 3868
Open Dec–Mar, Mon–Sat 10–5 **Production** 600 cases
Winemaker Andrew Greenhough
Principal Wines Ries, Gewurz, Chard, Muller, Dry White, Pinot, Cab Sauv.
Summary Until recently called Ranzau; the new owners Andrew Greenhough and Jennifer Wheeler plan to rationalise and expand production, concentrating on premium varieties. The wines produced to date have been of modest quality. The winery does not make and is in no way connected with the Pelorus Methode Champenoise of Cloudy Bay.

PENINSULA ESTATE NR Est 1986 219, 258 WAIHEKE ISLAND
52A Korora Road, Oneroa, Waiheke Island phone and fax (09) 72 7866
Open Not **Production** 800 cases
Winemaker Doug Hamilton
Principal Wines In the tradition of Waiheke Island a single Bordeaux blend of Cab Sauv, Mer, Cab Franc and Malbec.
Summary The only wine comes from a two hectare estate vineyard situated on a peninsula overlooking Oneroa Bay. Owners Doug and Anne Hamilton were inspired to plant grapes by the Goldwaters, and have learnt their winemaking on Waiheke Island, trading engineering skills for winemaking expertise. The '89 red was an inspired start, redolent of high toned cassis berry fruit and sweet oak, followed by a firmer and less exotic '90, well balanced and with a cellaring future.

PIERRE ESTATE NR Est 1969 $13.95–19 ML SD WAIKANAE
Elizabeth Street, Waikanae (04) 293 4604; postal 326 Lambton Quay, Wellington

Open Not **Production** NFP
Winemaker Peter Heginbotham
Principal Wines Blanc du Noir (Pinot Noir), Cab Sauv.
Summary Waikanae is situated on the coast north of Wellington; the wines are estate grown, made and produced in the 'Chateau' and underground cellars completed in 1991. I have not tasted the wines.

PLEASANT VALLEY CB–BA Est 1902 $5.95–14.95 CD SD HENDERSON
322 Henderson Valley Road, Henderson (09) 838 8857
fax (09) 838 8456
Open Mon–Sat 9–6, Sun 11–6 **Production** 3000 cases
Winemaker Stephan Yelas
Principal Wines Fumé, Muller, Wh Burg, Gewurz, Pinot, Cab Sauv, Port under Pleasant Valley label; Sem, Ries, Cab Mer under premium Yelas Estate label.
Summary A former moribund fortified winemaker, revitalised since 1984 and helped further by the arrival of Roseworthy graduate Peter Evans in 1988. Table wine quality has improved in leaps and bounds, with clean, well made wines available at low prices. The old Sherries (particularly Oloroso) are among the best, if not the best, in New Zealand.

RIPPON A–B Est 1975 $11.50–28.50 CD 249 CENTRAL OTAGO
Mt Aspiring Road, Lake Wanaka phone and fax (03) 443 8084
Open 7 days 10.30–5.30 **Production** 2500 cases
Winemaker Rudolf Bauer (former)
Principal Wines Chard, Ries, Sauv Bl, Gewurz, Dry White, Pinot, Gamay, Osteiner, Rosé.
Summary Owners Rolf and Lois Mills took the slow road between 1976 and 1989 but, buoyed by their very considerable success in 1989 and 1990, are doubling the vineyard to 8 hectares and planning a new lakeside winery for 1993. Their confidence is fully justified, for the Rieslings and Chardonnays made in 1989 and 1990 have abundant flavour and varietal character, while the 1991 wines are the best yet.
Recommended Wine 1990 Pinot Noir (deeply coloured and flavoured, with fully ripened, velvety, plummy fruit; very good wine; drink now).

•RIVERSIDE WINES NR Est 1989 $10–18 CD SD HAWKE'S BAY
Dartmoor Road, Puketapu, Napier (06) 844 4942
Open Thurs–Sun 10.30–5 summer **Production** 1650 cases
Winemakers Rachel Cadwallader, Nick Sage (Consultant)
Principal Wines Chard, Cab Rosé, Cab Mer.
Summary Ian and Rachel Cadwallader have established 14 hectares of vines, which are coming progressively into production. The wine is made on site in the small winery above the Dartmoor Valley.

ROBARD & BUTLER A–A Est 1972 $7.22–16.84 R 219a HENDERSON
426–448 Great North Road, Henderson, Auckland (09) 837 3390
Open Mon–Sat 9–6 **Production** NFP
Winemakers Kerry Hitchcock, Alan McCorkindale
Principal Wines Chab, Gisborne Chard, Marlborough Fumé Bl,

Pinot, Hawke's Bay Cab Mer, Amberly Ries, Marlborough Ries and other intermittent releases.

Summary Strictly a brand, owned by Corbans, from or through which it acquires its wines. However, it has always limited itself to top class wines, sourced not only from New Zealand but from Australia and even France (the house brand Champagne). Some quite outstanding wines appear under the Robard & Butler label from time to time.

Recommended Wines 1991 Marlborough Pinot Noir (an absolutely outstanding wine, wonderful length and intensity on the palate with spotlessly clean strawberry plum fruit and very good oak handling - yet for all that, not the least bit heavy). 1991 Fumé Blanc (extremely complex, rich, textured wine with multifaceted flavours, just a fraction heavy; more Californian than New Zealand in style; drink now).

RONGOPAI CA–B Est 1985 $12–28 CD SD 234 WAIKATO
71 Waerenga Road, Te Kauwhata (08) 826 3981 fax (08) 826 3462
Open Mon–Sat 9–5, Sun 11–4 **Production** 7300 cases
Winemaker Tom van Dam
Principal Wines Muller, Gewurz, Ries, Botrytis Ries, Chard, Botrytised Chard, Sauv Bl, Syrah, Cab Mer, Mer.
Best Vintages W '86, '87, '89, '90, '91 R '87, '89, '91
Summary The highly trained research scientist partners of Rongopai make an eclectic range of wines, of which the best (and most consistent) are the botrytis styles; others vary disconcertingly in terms of both style and quality.

RUBY BAY NR Est 1976 $10.50–15.80 CD 217 NELSON
Korepo Road, RD 1, Upper Moutere, Nelson (03) 540 2825
Open 7 days 10–6 **Production** 650 cases
Winemaker David Moore
Principal Wines Chard, Sauv Bl, Ries, Gewurz, Pinot, Cab Sauv, Pinot Rosé.
Summary The beautifully sited former Korepo winery, purchased by the Moore family in 1989, is well known for its restaurant; wine quality in recent times has been disconcertingly variable.

SACRED HILL NR Est 1986 $15–20 CD SD HAWKE'S BAY
Dartmoor Road, RD 6, Napier (06) 844 2576
Open By appointment **Production** 3800 cases
Winemaker Mark Mason
Principal Wines Chard, Fumé, Sauv Bl, Gewurz, Pinot Noir; released under Sacred Hill, Dartmoor and Whitecliffs labels.
Best Vintages W '87, '89, '90, '91 R '87, '89, '90, '91
Summary A relative newcomer, which initially impressed with opulent, oaky Fumé Blanc, intense, tangy Sauvignon Blanc, spicy-lime Gewurztraminer and a strikingly sweet, honeyed Chardonnay. However, more recent offerings have not been of the same standard.

ST GEORGE ESTATE NR Est 1985 $8.50–17.50 CD 267 HAWKE'S BAY
St Georges Road South, Hastings phone and fax (06) 877 5356
Open 7 days 9–4 **Production** 2500 cases
Winemaker Michael Bennett

Principal Wines Chard, Sauv Bl, Ries, Gewurz, Cheval Blanc, Rosé, Cab Mer, Petit Syrah, Muscat.

Summary When I saw Cheval Blanc I imagined there was a misprint in the cellar door/mail list brochure. Not so; it is a blend of Rhine Riesling, Sauvignon Blanc and Muscat, which may or may not amuse the owners of Cheval Blanc in St Emilion. Such irrelevancies to one side, former Te Mata Estate winemaker Michael Bennett (1980–84) produces a range of well regarded wines that I, for some obscure reason, have not tasted. They may be purchased by the glass at the winery's well patronised restaurant.

ST HELENA CB–CB Est 1978 $7.50–16 CD 264 CANTERBURY
Coutts Island RD, Christchurch phone and fax (03) 323 8202
Open Mon–Sat 10–5, Sun 12–5 **Production** 8000 cases
Winemaker Peter Evans
Principal Wines Muller, Ries, Pinot Gris, Pinot Blanc, Chard, Pinot.
Best Vintages W '82, '84, '85, '86, '89 R '82, '85, '86, '89, '91
Summary Whether in its moments of success or otherwise, controversy has never been far from St Helena's door. After a spectacular debut for its Pinot Noir in 1982, there has been a roller coaster ride since with more downs than ups. However, the 1991 Chardonnay and 1991 Pinot Noir are sound, well made wines.

ST JEROME B–B Est 1968 $7.50–22.50 CD SD 258 HENDERSON
219 Metcalfe Road, Henderson phone and fax (09) 833 6205
Open Mon–Sat 9–6, Sun 12–5 **Production** 5000 cases
Winemakers Davorin Ozich, Miro Ozich
Principal Wines Ries, Sauv Bl, Chard, Chablis, Gewurz, Cab Mer, Port.
Summary Originally called Nova, then Ozich and now St Jerome, the concentrated, complex and long-lived Cabernet Merlot made from 1986 to 1990 inclusive has exceptional consistency (and quality). This wine is a tribute to the potential of the Auckland area and to winemaker Davorin Ozich's practical winemaking experience gained at Chateau Margaux and Chateau Cos d'Estournel (in Bordeaux), and to his theoretical knowledge gained from a Master of Science degree from Auckland University. In 1992 St Jerome was offering to buy back its 1986 Cabernet Sauvignon for $NZ100 a bottle, an astute move reminiscent of the Antipodean marketing initiatives.

ST NESBIT A–A Est 1980 $24–28.30 CD 264 SOUTH AUCKLAND
Hingaia Road, RD 1 Papakura (09) 298 5057 fax (09) 377 6956
Open Not **Production** 700 cases
Winemaker Dr Tony Molloy QC
Principal Wines Cab Sauv, Cab Franc, Mer, Malb, Petit Verdot.
Best Vintages R '84, '87, '89, '90, '91
Summary Tony Molloy is a leading tax lawyer with a weekend passion; his Bordeaux blend is revered in New Zealand and very well regarded elsewhere. A vertical tasting of the '84 to '89 vintages in late 1990 showed wines in varying style, with the '84 and '87 the best, the '89 very ripe, perhaps too ripe. As at March 1993 neither the '90 nor '91 vintages had been bottled, with the '88 the most recently released thanks to a policy that holds the wine back for five years before sale.

SAVIDGE ESTATES NR Est 1969 $10.50–16.45 R SD
GISBORNE
Solander Street, Gisborne (06) 867 6995 fax (06) 867 8357
Open Not **Production** 6000 cases
Winemaker Corbans (Contract)
Principal Wines Chenin, Chard, Sauv Bl, Cab Mer.
Summary The Savidge family are large landholders in the Gisborne district, producing prime beef and lamb as well as 1000 tonnes of grapes a year from their Tolaga Bay vineyards. The grapes have been sold to Corbans for many years; now around 5% is made by Corbans for Savidge Estates (initially marketed as Venture Vineyards) and is sold both in New Zealand and the United Kingdom.

SEIBEL WINES NR Est 1988 SD HENDERSON
24 Kakariki Avenue, Mount Eden, Auckland (09) 638 8463
Open Not **Production** 1500 cases
Winemaker Norbert Seibel
Principal Wines Chard, Sauv Bl, Gewurz, Ries (from dry to select Noble LH), Chenin, Cab Sauv, Cab Mer.
Summary After seven years with Corbans, German-born and trained (at Geisenheim) Norbert Seibel has established his own brand, using the wineries of others to produce the wines. An unusual Blanc de Noir Blush from 1990 showed distinct and inappropriate botrytis influences; the 1989 Chardonnay was of European style, and really not acceptable by conventional Australasian standards.

SEIFRIED ESTATE BA–BA Est 1973 $8.40–28 R SD 249
NELSON
Sunrise Valley Road, Upper Moutere 7152, Nelson (03) 543 2795
Open Mon–Sat 9–5 **Production** 33 000 cases
Winemaker Saralinda MacMillan
Principal Wines Ries, Gewurz, Muller, Chard, Sauv Bl, Beeren, Pinot, Cab Sauv.
Summary With 40 hectares of vineyards established progressively between 1973 and 1988, and a production in excess of 250 000 litres, Seifried Estate is by far the largest of the Nelson wineries. The production is heavily biased towards white wines, which are of wholly admirable consistency of style and quality. The 1992 Muller Thurgau, 1991 Chardonnay and 1992 Beerenauslesen Rhine Riesling are particularly fine examples.

SELAKS BA–A Est 1934 $5–14 CD SD 64, 200, 201, 233 KUMEU
Cnr Highway 16 and Old North Road, Kumeu (09) 412 8609
fax (09) 412 7524
Open Mon–Fri 9–5 Sat 10–5.30, Sun 11–4 **Production** 35 000 cases
Winemaker Darryl Woolley
Principal Wines Sauv Bl, Sauv Bl Sem, Ries, Chard, Meth Champ, Cab Sauv, Mer.
Best Vintages W '82, '83, '85, '87, '91 R '83, '85, '87, '89, '90, '91
Summary With Montana, first brought Sauvignon Blanc to the attention of overseas markets, especially Australia. Its Sauvignon Blanc and Sauvignon Semillon blends continue to be its forte, always good, sometimes outstanding.

Recommended Wines 1991 Sauvignon Blanc (a wine which shows that well made examples can develop complexity with bottle age, showing strong citrus and herbal fruit with length to the finish, although it is starting to dry out ever so slightly; to 1994). 1992 Sauvignon Blanc Semillon (slightly smoky, sweaty aromas but with classic asparagus, green pepper and gooseberry fruit flavours; to 1994). 1992 Sauvignon Blanc (fragrant, tropical passionfruit aromas showing highly protective winemaking; still needing to open up).

SHERWOOD ESTATE NR Est 1987 SD CANTERBURY
Cnr Weedons Ross & Johnson Roads, West Melton, Christchurch (03) 347 9060 fax (03) 366 7069
Open 7 days 11–5 **Production** 1000 cases
Winemaker Dayne Sherwood
Principal Wines Muller, Ries, Sauv Bl, Chard, Pinot, Mer.
Summary Sherwood Estate produced its first wines in 1990; situated close to Christchurch (15 minutes' drive), it also offers a garden setting tasting room with snacks and lunches available in the Vineyard Bar throughout summer.

• SILVERSTREAM VINEYARDS NR Est 1990 SD
CANTERBURY
Giles Road, Clarkville, Kaiapoi (03) 327 5678
Open By appointment **Production** 700 cases
Winemaker Peter Todd
Principal Wines Chard, Pinot.
Summary One of the newest of the Canterbury wineries, situated on the Waimakari Plains north of Christchurch.

SOLJANS CB–BA Est 1937 $7.40–18.50 CD SD HENDERSON
263 Lincoln Road, Henderson (09) 838 8365 fax (09) 838 8366
Open Mon–Sat 9–6, Sun 11–5 **Production** 8000 cases
Winemaker Tony Soljan
Principal Wines Muller, Chard, Gewurz, Sauv Bl, Cab Sauv, Pinotage, many fortifieds.
Best Vintages W '85, '86, '89, '90, '91 R '84, '86, '89, '91, '92
Summary Well made wines sold at very modest prices which deserve a wider audience.

• STONECROFT VINEYARD NR Est 1987 217 HAWKE'S BAY
RD 5 Mere Road, Hastings (06) 879 9610
Open W'ends & public hols 11–5 **Production** NFP
Winemaker Dr Alan Limmer
Principal Wines Chard, Sauv Bl, Gewurz, Cab Sauv.
Summary Analytical chemist Dr Alan Limmer produces very full bodied, rich and ripe wines from his three hectare vineyard situated on free draining, gravelly soils which promote early ripening.

STONYRIDGE A–A Est 1982 $27 ML SD 249 WAIHEKE ISLAND
80 Onetangi Road, Waiheke Island phone and fax (09) 372 8822
Open Fri–Sun 1.30–5 **Production** 1000 cases
Winemaker Stephen White
Principal Wines 'Larose' Cabernets, 'Airfield' Cabernets.
Best Vintages R '87, '89, '90, '91, '93
Summary The winery that justifies the hype about Waiheke Island;

the '87 was a quite lovely wine, balanced, fine and cedary, the '89 even better, with tremendous concentration of rich, sweet fruit, good tannins and again some of those hallmark cedary/briary aromas. Respected New Zealand critic Bob Cambell regards the 1991 as even better, classing it as 'Waiheke's most impressive red made to date'.

TARAMEA C–CB Est 1987 $10–15 CD SD CENTRAL OTAGO
Speargrass Flat Road RD 1, Queenstown (03) 442 1453
Open Sat 1–6 Nov–March **Production** 250 cases
Winemaker Michael Wolter
Principal Wines Gewurz, Muller, Pinot Gris.
Summary Small quantities of wines of modest quality that are free of winemaking faults and invariably sell out before the next release.

TE KAIRANGA CB–CB Est 1984 $12.80–17.80 CD 293 MARTINBOROUGH
Martins Road, Martinborough (06) 306 9122 fax (06) 306 9322
Open Mon–Sat 10–5, Sun 11–5 **Production** 10 000 cases
Winemaker Chris Buring
Principal Wines Gewurz, Chard, Sauv Bl, Classic Wh, Chenin, Pinot, Durif, Cab Sauv.
Summary One of the largest of the Martinborough wineries and, it must be said, one that has been disappointing over the years. However, winemaker Chris Buring has certainly lifted quality significantly with the 1991 and 1992 vintage wines, suggesting that even better things may be in store.
Recommended Wines 1991 Cabernet Sauvignon (fresh, fragrant, clean, red berry fruit with green olive and slightly stemmy notes in the background which do not detract; well made; crisp, clean finish; to 1998). 1991 Reserve Chardonnay (high toned, tangy, citrus/melon fruit with subtle oak; to 1996). 1991 Reserve Pinot Noir (fragrant aroma with strong spicy background; fresh, crisp, peppery/spicy wine on the palate, lacking ripe varietal fruit, but otherwise well made; drink now).

TE MATA ESTATE A–A Est 1896 $10.70–31.40 CD 19, 217, 272 HAWKE'S BAY
Te Mata Road, Havelock North (06) 877 4399 fax (06) 877 4397
Open Mon–Sat 9–5, Sun 11–4 **Production** 16 000 cases
Winemaker Peter Cowley
Principal Wines Elston Chard, Castle Hill and Cape Crest Sauv Bl, Awatea and Coleraine Cab Mer.
Best Vintages W '82, '85, '89, '90, '91 R '82, '83, '85, '89, '91
Summary In the eyes of many, New Zealand's foremost producer of Cabernet Merlot, notwithstanding the consistency of the show success of the Vidal/Villa Maria group. The wines of Te Mata are made in a different style, restrained and elegant but always packed with fine fruit. Nor should the consistently stylish and varietally correct white wines be ignored; these too are of the highest quality.
Recommended Wines 1991 Coleraine Cabernet Merlot (clean, ripe, dark berry fruits with a nice touch of Cabernet-induced astringency, leading to ripe, dark berry and plum fruit flavours on the palate, with good tannins and subtle oak; to 2008). 1991 Awatea Cabernet Merlot (smooth, clean, dark berry fruit aromas with some mineral overtones; slightly lighter and more fruity than the Coleraine,

even though the alcohol is higher; hints of mint add complexity; to 2005).

TE WHARE RA CA–B Est 1979 $11–17 CD SD MARLBOROUGH
Anglesea Street, Renwick, Marlborough (03) 572 8581
Open 7 days 9–5 **Production** 2500 cases
Winemaker Allen Hogan
Principal Wines Chard, Fumé, Gewurz, Ries, Botrytis, Cab Mer.
Best Vintages W '86, '87, '89, '91 R '86, '87, '88, '89, '91
Summary Best known for intermittent superb releases of botrytised wines, made variously from Riesling, Muller Thurgau, Traminer and Sauvignon Blanc. However, the 1990 Cabernet Merlot showed Hogan is able to produce excellent wines across the full range of style.

TOTARA B–BA Est 1950 $7–12 R SD WAIKATO
Main Road, Thames (07) 86 6798 fax (07) 868 8729
Open Mon–Sat 9–5.30 **Production** 10 000 cases
Winemaker Gilbert Chan
Principal Wines Gewurz, Chard, Fumé, Chenin, Muller, Rosé, Cab Sauv; Private Bin wines are top of the range; also casks and proprietary wines including Fu Gai and City of Sails.
Summary A substantial operation which, however, has had its share of problems, leading to a decision to remove all its vineyards in 1986 under the Vine-Pull scheme; it now relies on local growers to provide the grapes for its wines. The '90 Reserve Chardonnay (with potent, charred oak and high toned, botrytis-enriched fruit) and the standard Chardonnay of the same year were both good wines in their youth, but have developed wonderfully in bottle, the Reserve sweeping all before it at the 1992 Air New Zealand Wine Show. The 1991 Cabernet Sauvignon is yet another feather in a resurgent Totara's cap.

VAVASOUR AB–A Est 1986 $10.80–27.75 CD 218, 288 MARLBOROUGH
Redwood Pass Road, Awatere Valley (03) 575 7481
fax (03) 575 7240
Open Mon–Sat 10–5 **Production** 8500 cases
Winemaker Glenn Thomas
Principal Wines Reserve range of Chardonnay, Sauvignon and Cab Sauv Cab Franc; Dashwood is second label for Chard, Sauv Bl and Cab Sauv.
Summary A high profile newcomer that has quickly fulfilled the expectations held for it. The drier, slightly warmer climate of the Awatere Valley and the unique river terrace stony soils on which the 12.5 hectare vineyard is established are producing grapes of great intensity of flavour, which are in turn being skilfully handled in the winery. Both the 1990 and 1991 white wines had unusual intensity and length of flavour, while the 1990 Reserve Cabernet Sauvignon/Cabernet Franc has the quality of the very best Hawke's Bay reds, with intense colour, potent red berry/cassis fruit and good tannin structure. The 1992 white wines, however, showed the limitations of the vintage.

VICTORY NR Est 1968 $6–8 CD SD NELSON
Main Road South, Stoke (03) 547 6391

Open 7 days 9–5 **Production** 500 cases
Winemaker Rod Neill
Principal Wines Chasselas, Seibel, Cab Sauv, Gamay Beaujolais.
Summary A part-time occupation for orchardist Rod Neill.

VIDAL BA–A Est 1905 $5.50–13.50 R SD 201, 249 HAWKE'S
BAY
913 St Aubyns Street East, Hastings (06) 876 9662
fax (06) 876 5312
Open 7 days 11–9 **Production** 35 000 cases
Winemaker Elise Montgomery
Principal Wines Chard, Fumé, Gewurz, Muller, Cab Sauv, Cab
Mer, Sparkl, under Private Bin and Reserve Bin labels.
Best Vintages W '85, '86, '89, '90, '91 **R** '83, '87, '89, '90, '91
Summary Together with Te Mata, Villa Maria and Esk Valley,
consistently produces New Zealand's finest red wines; they have
ripeness, richness and balance, a far cry from the reds of bygone
years. The all-conquering '89 vintage reds were followed by wines of
similar style and quality in 1990, underlining the reputation of the
winery. However, the white wines are very ordinary, with insensitive
use of what often seems to be indifferent oak.
Recommended Wines 1990 Reserve Cabernet Sauvignon (an
elegant, fragrant wine with red berry fruit strongly influenced by
charred oak and some barrel ferment characters; to 1998). 1990
Reserve Cabernet Merlot (potent, intense, leafy wine with some
green tannins; strong Merlot influence; to 1996).

• **VILAGRAD WINES** NR Est 1922 SD WAIKATO
RD2 Rukuhia Road, Ohaupo (07) 825 2893
Open Tues–Sat 10–6 **Production** 2000 cases
Winemaker Peter Nooyen
Principal Wines Chard, Sauv Bl, Muller, Ries, Cab Sauv.
Summary A low profile operation making wines of modest but
consistently acceptable quality that age surprisingly well.

VILLA MARIA A–A Est 1961 $6.90–13.50 R SD 257
AUCKLAND
5 Kirkbridge Road, Mangere, Auckland (09) 275 6119
fax (09) 275 6618
Open 7 days 10–6 **Production** 100 000 cases
Winemaker Grant Edmonds
Principal Wines Gewurz, Sauv Bl, Muller, Chard, Cab Sauv, Cab
Mer under Private Bin, Estate and Reserve Bin labels.
Best Vintages W '86, '89, '90, '91, '92 **R** '85, '87, '89, '90, '91
Summary Villa Maria is the star all-round performer in its corporate
group. The Cabernet Sauvignon and Cabernet Merlot are in the same
ripe, lush style as those of its stablemates, but whereas they falter
with their white wines, Villa Maria does not. There is a plethora of
labels to contend with, and it is true that the Estate Reserve and
Estate Cellar Selection wines are usually better than the Private Bin
range, but that only goes to prove that occasionally there is honesty in
labelling.
Recommended Wines 1992 Estate Cellar Selection Sauvignon
Blanc (strong, powerful, rich and concentrated wine, bordering on
aggressive but redeemed by its length of flavour; quite forward and

developed). 1991 Estate Cellar Selection Chardonnay (intense, cool climate citrus/grapefruit aroma and flavour, piercing in its purity and length; to 1997). 1991 Private Bin Rhine Riesling (rich, lime juice aromas with most attractive high flavoured lime fruit on the palate, with no phenolic thickness or roughness; to 1995). 1992 Private Bin Rhine Riesling (spicy, toasty wine with soft, lime fruit flavours; early developing). 1990 Reserve Cabernet Merlot (solid, ripe and sweet red berry fruit with gently earthy overtones adding complexity).

VOSS ESTATE NR Est 1988 $16–20 CD SD MARTINBOROUGH
Puruatanga Road, Martinborough (06) 306 9668
Open 7 days 11–6 **Production** 800 cases
Winemaker Gary Voss
Principal Wines Chard, Pinot, Cab Sauv Cab Franc, Mer.
Summary Voss Estate has been established by Annette Atkins and Gary Voss; the latter spent a year studying winemaking in Australia before working for New Zealand wineries in both Auckland and Martinborough. Estate grown wines will come on-stream from the 1992 vintage, in the meantime being supplemented by Hawke's Bay grapes. The two wines on sale in 1993 — 1992 Chardonnay and 1992 Merlot — were made from Hawke's Bay fruit; both won silver medals at the 1992 Air New Zealand Wine Show.

• WAIMARAMA ESTATE NR Est 1988 $24.50 CD 217
HAWKE'S BAY
Waimarama Road, Havelock North (06) 877 6794
fax (06) 877 6789
Open Not **Production** 950 cases
Winemaker Nick Sage
Principal Wines Cab Sauv, Cab Mer, Dessert Cab.
Summary An exciting newcomer that had already gathered much critical attention and praise before its two entries in the 1992 Air New Zealand Wine Show received a top gold medal (1991 Cabernet Merlot) and strong silver medal (1991 Cabernet Sauvignon) respectively. It would seem that this vineyard, situated on a north facing slope at the foot of Te Mata peak, may well be one of the stars of the Hawke's Bay region in the years to come.

WAIPARA SPRINGS NR Est 1990 $13–21 SD 318
CANTERBURY
Waipara Springs Vineyard, RD 3, Amberley (03) 314 6777
Open 7 days 10–7 **Production** 5500 cases
Winemaker Mark A. Rattray
Principal Wines Sauv Bl, Chard, Ries, Pinot.
Summary The newly established venture (although the vineyards were planted earlier) of ex-St Helena winemaker Mark Rattray. The 1992 Sauvignon Blanc is a very good wine, underlining the suitability of the Canterbury Plains for both this variety and Chardonnay.

• WAIRAU RIVER WINES NR Est 1978 $11.90–21.50 CD
168, 201, 294 MARLBOROUGH
Cnr Rapaura Road & State Highway 6, Blenheim phone and fax (03) 572 8584
Open 7 days 9–5 **Production** 10 000 cases
Winemaker John Belsham (Contract)

Principal Wines Sauv Bl, Chard.

Summary Phil and Chris Rose have been long-term grape growers in the Marlborough region, having established a 60 hectare vineyard progressively since 1978. The first wines were made under the Wairau River label in 1991 by contract winemaker John Belsham, and both the 1991 and 1992 vintages are of exemplary quality, particularly the pungent, tropical-accented Sauvignon Blanc.

WAITAKERE ROAD VINEYARD NR Est 1986
$10.50–17.50 CD SD KUMEU
Waitakere Road, Kumeu (09) 412 7256
Open Sat 12–6 **Production** 3000 cases
Winemaker Tim Harris
Principal Wines Uppercase Red, Harrier Rise Red.
Summary The project of Auckland lawyer and wine writer Tim Harris, who purchased half of the vineyard in 1986 and the balance (with 15-year-old Cabernet Sauvignon planted) in 1988. Uppercase Red is a Beaujolais-style light bodied wine made from a blend of Cabernet Sauvignon, Cabernet Franc and Merlot, with high yielding vines; Harrier Rise is a much more concentrated Cabernet from lower yielding vines, providing a strong style contrast.

WEST BROOK CB–CB Est 1937 $7–15.50 CD SD HENDERSON
34 Awaroa Road, Henderson phone and fax (09) 838 8746
Open Mon–Sat 9–6, Sun 12–5 **Production** 7000 cases
Winemaker Anthony Ivicevich
Principal Wines Sauv Bl, Sauv Bl Sem, Chard, Sem, Chenin, Gewurz Ries, Cab Sauv, Cab Mer.
Summary Unpretentious producer of wines of reliable quality, seldom aspiring to greatness but — with the white wines in particular — capable of a very pleasant surprise from time to time; the Rhine Riesling and Sauvignon Blanc have done particularly well. Among recent releases, the 1990 Sauvignon Blanc Semillon and 1990 Traminer have stood out.

•WILLIAM HILL WINERY NR Est 1982 SD CENTRAL OTAGO
Dunstan Road, Alexandra (03) 448 8436
Open By appointment **Production** 200 cases
Winemaker Rippon Vineyards (Contract)
Principal Wines Gewurz, Chard, Sauv Bl, Pinot, Cab Sauv.
Summary Notwithstanding that Willaim Hill Vineyards extend to three hectares, production has remained at miniscule levels and almost all of the wines are sold by mail order and through selected local outlets.

DISTRIBUTORS

Australian Distributors

1 Alan Nelson
PO Box 231
Kew East Vic 3102
(03) 859 8402

2 Alexander & Paterson
600 Dawson St
Brunswick Vic 3057
(03) 380 6199

3 Allied Vintners
PO Box 96
Erindale ACT 2903
(06) 291 7361

4 Andrew Waterman Wholesales
3 Clark St
Wayville SA 5034
(08) 271 4858

5 Angoves Pty Ltd
Cnr Queen & Marion St
Auburn NSW 2144
(02) 649 6044

6 Angoves Pty Ltd
30 Bellrick St
Acacia Ridge Qld 4110
(07) 345 2344

7 Angoves Pty Ltd
1320 North East Rd
Tea Tree Gully SA 5091
(09) 264 2366

8 Angoves Pty Ltd
14 Bingley St
Howrah Tas 7018
(002) 47 1196

9 Angoves Pty Ltd
PO Box 547
Mulgrave Vic 3170
(03) 561 6111

10 Angoves Pty Ltd
325 Treasure Rd
Welshpool WA 6106
(09) 353 1900

11 Appellation Wines & Spirits
9 Woodvale Close
St Ives NSW 2075
(02) 449 5548

12 Aria Wine Co.
PO Box R417
Royal Exchange NSW 2000
(02) 314 5730

13 Arrowfield Wines Pty Ltd
3/19–21 Bourke Rd
Alexandria NSW 2015
(02) 698 8033

14 Australian Prestige Wines
3a Moorfield Ave
Hunters Hill NSW 2110
(02) 955 2711

15 Australian Prestige Wines
PO Box 325
Northcote Vic 3070
(03) 481 3582

16 B & J Distributors
PO Box 3862
Winnellie NT 0820

17 Badge Mullen & Assoc.
23 Fircroft Way
Hamersley WA 6022

18 Ballyellis Fine Wines
9 Cumbrae Pl
Kambah ACT 2902
(06) 296 1837

19 Balmain Liquor Supplies
263 Darling St
Balmain NSW 2041
(02) 810 7277

20 Barrique Fine Wines
PO Box 34
Stones Corner Qld 4120
(07) 808 3322

21 Brisbane Gourmet Pty Ltd
2/97 Macquarie St
St Lucia Qld 4067
(07) 371 8703

22 BRL Hardy Wine Co.
104 Bay St
East Botany NSW 2019
(02) 666 5855

23 BRL Hardy Wine Co.
43 Murray St
Bowen Hills Qld 4006
(07) 52 7933

24 BRL Hardy Wine Co.
Reynell Rd
Reynella SA 5161
(08) 381 2266

25 BRL Hardy Wine Co.
25 McDonald's Lane
Mulgrave Vic 3170
(03) 561 1332

26 BRL Hardy Wine Co.
Dale Rd
Middle Swan WA 6056
(09) 274 5100

27 Broadway Liquor Distributors
Pty Ltd
151 Glebe Point Rd
Glebe NSW 2037
(02) 660 3908

28 Broken Bay Liquor Distributors
PO Box 32
Woy Woy NSW 2256
(043) 43 1550

29 Busby Wine Co.
PO Box 433
Wahroonga NSW 2076
(02) 989 8280

30 Caon Tucker Classic Wines
11 Kings Court
Adelaide SA 5000
(08) 211 7599

31 Capital Fine Wines
PO Box 7
Barker Centre ACT 2603
(06) 239 6968

32 Carlton Special Beverages Co.
PO Box 318
Mt Waverly Vic 3149
(03) 565 7177

33 Carol-Ann Classic Wines
PO Box 1065
Potts Point NSW 2011
(02) 356 2007

34 Chace Agencies
PO Box 227
Hindmarsh SA 5007
(08) 346 9555

35 Chancellors Wines & Spirits
GPO Box 88a
Hobart Tas 7001
(002) 23 6377

36 Chateau Yaldara Pty Ltd
PO Box 383
Homebush Bay NSW 2140
(02) 748 1258

37 Chateau Yaldara Pty Ltd
PO Box 188
Black Rock Vic 3193
(03) 589 5900

38 Chateau Yaldara Pty Ltd
6 Elmton Court
Duncraig WA 6023
(09) 447 7388

39 Chittering Estate
14 Neil St
Osborne Park WA 6017
(09) 242 1150

40 Classical Wines of Australia
313A Homer St
Earlwood NSW 2206
(02) 558 8588

41 Combined Wines & Spirit
Merchants
Lot 5 Sheridan Close
Milperra NSW 2214
(02) 792 3033

42 Concorde Liquor
5 Bennelong Rd
Homebush NSW 2140
(02) 647 2877

43 Concorde Liquor
4 Trade Pl
Vermont Vic 3133
(03) 873 5399

44 Concorde Liquor
87 Holbrooks Rd
Underdale SA 5032
(08) 43 7011

45 Concorde Liquor
836 Boundary Rd
Coopers Plains Qld 4108
(07) 277 8500

46 Country Wine Agencies
Suite 1 106 George St
Port Melbourne Vic 3207

47 Cowra Wines Ltd
PO Box R167
Royal Exchange NSW 2000
(02) 905 0765

48 David Johnson & Assoc.
6 Montpelier Retreat
Battery Point Tas 7004
(002) 24 0653

49 David Ridge
205 Grote St
Adelaide SA 5000
(08) 231 1066

50 De Bono Wine Merchants
116 Queen St
Alexandria NSW 2015
(02) 698 2319

51 De Bortoli Wines Pty Ltd
De Bortoli Rd
Bilbul NSW 2680
(02) 63 5235

52 De Bortoli Wines Pty Ltd
874 Mountain Hwy
Bayswater Vic 3153
(03) 720 3153

53 De Bortoli Wines Pty Ltd
23 Collinsvale St
Rocklea Qld 4106
07) 274 2923

54 Dilaterre
PO Box 60
Essendon Vic 3040
(03) 462 2763

55 Domaine Wine Shippers
PO Box 69
Doncaster East Vic 3109
(03) 894 3888

56 Douglas Lamb Investments P/L
5/63 Elizabeth Bay Rd
Elizabeth Bay NSW 2011
(02) 358 3079

57 Draper Agencies
PO Box 293
Gosford NSW 2256
(018) 22 0000

58 Dural Agencies
8 Caber Close
Dural NSW 2158
(02) 963 1772

59 Elite Wines
21 Allambee Ave
Edwardstown SA 5039

60 Elizabeth Radcliffe
466 Queensberry St
North Melbourne Vic 3051
(03) 328 1564

61 Estate Wines
116 Queen St
Alexandria NSW 2015
(02) 310 1005

62 Evans & Tate
1/36 Salisbury Rd
Rose Bay NSW 2029
(02) 363 4577

63 F. M. Liquor Pty Ltd
2 Pamment St
North Fremantle WA 6159
(09) 430 4815

64 Farmer Bros.
42 Mort St
Canberra ACT 2601
(06) 247 2344

65 Fesq Dorado
PO Box 192
Botany NSW 2019
(02) 316 7400

66 Fesq Dorado
600 Nicholson St
Fitzroy North Vic 3068
(03) 482 4244

67 Festival Wines & Spirits
984 Port Rd
Albert Park SA 5014
(08) 268 8066

68 Fin Vin Agencies Pty Ltd
PO Box 367
Strawberry Hills NSW 2012
(02) 310 2077

69 Fine Wine Wholesalers
PO Box 319
West Perth WA 6005
(09) 227 6877

70 Fiorelli's
131 Anderson St
Cairns Qld 4870
(070) 32 1100

71 Fleurieu Wine Merchants
O'Connell St
North Adelaide SA 5006
(08) 239 1980

72 Flinders Wholesale Wine &
Spirits
3 Wandarri Crt
Cheltenham Vic 3192
(03) 584 5233

73 Geoff White
16 Nagle St
North Turramurra NSW 2074
(02) 449 3848

74 Global Agencies
45 Piccadilly Rd
Salisbury East SA 5109
(08) 258 2906

75 Global Liquor
PO Box 471
Nerang Qld 4211
(075) 96 4146

76 Go Betwine Pty Ltd
12 Cook Rd
Centennial Park NSW 2021
(02) 332 2384

77 Gordon Smith Fine Wines
5 Sexty St
Armadale WA 6112
(09) 497 1464

78 Halloran Manton Pty Ltd
3 Welder Ave
Seven Hills NSW 2147
(02) 624 7244

79 Hanging Rock Winery
Jim Rd
Newham Vic 3442
(054) 27 0542

80 Harry Williams Ltd
24 Essington St
Mitchell ACT 2911
(06) 241 7591

81 Haviland Wine Co.
12 Hopetown Ave
Chatswood NSW 2067
(02) 419 3877

82 Hills International Liquor
4a/6 Boundary Rd
Northmead NSW 2152
(02) 683 2729

83 Hills International Liquor
PO Box 408
Nerang Qld 4211
(075) 78 3900

84 Hollick Wines Pty Ltd
184 Grandview Rd
Rosanna Vic 3084
(03) 459 9856

85 Houghton Wine Co.
Dale Rd
Middle Swan WA 6056
(09) 274 5100

86 Inchcape Liquor Marketing
1834 Princes Hwy
Clayton Vic 3168
(03) 543 2333

87 Inchcape Liquor Marketing
408–426 Victoria Rd
Gladesville NSW 2111
(02) 879 6766

88 Inchcape Liquor Marketing
10 Success St
Acacia Ridge NSW 4110
(07) 277 7600

89 Inchcape Liquor Marketing
16 Aitken Way
Kewdale WA 6105
(09) 353 3737

90 Inchape Liquor Marketing
70–72 Pym St
Dudley Park SA 5008
(08) 344 3577

91 Independent Liquor Distributor
65 Deeds Rd
North Plympton SA 5037
(08) 294 7755

92 Inglewood Wines Pty Ltd
18–20 Cleg St
Artarmon NSW 2064
(02) 436 3022

93 J. Addley
PO Box 7151
East Brisbane Qld 4169

94 J. Burke
63 Tuart Rd
Greenwood 6024 WA
(09) 246 2092

95 J. Harvey Long Wine Co.
7 Ramsey St
Burwood East Vic 3151
(03) 808 6004

96 Jeanette Simpson
9 Gungarra St
Rivett ACT 2611
(06) 288 0917

97 James Richardson Pty Ltd
Gray St
Adelaide SA 5000
(08) 211 8966

98 John Collar
173 Mt Pleasant Rd
Eltham Vic 3095
(03) 439 1071

99 John Parker
45 Piccadilly Rd
Salisbury East SA 5109
(08) 258 2906

100 Kenneth Graham Brokerage
PO Box 479
Woodend Vic 3442
(054) 27 1739

101 La Forgia Wine Agency
4/348 Richmond Rd
Netley SA 5037
(08) 352 1588

102 Lionel Samson & Son
PO Box 80
Fremantle WA 6160
(09) 335 7444

103 Liquid Assets
4 Bowen St
Kensington SA 5068
(08) 364 3229

104 Liquor Distributors
43 Mons St
Condell Park NSW 2200
(02) 794 9555

105 Lofton Agencies
PO Box 286
Newtown NSW 2042
(02) 557 4782

106 McLaren Vale Cellars
PO Box 177
Fyshwick ACT 2609
(06) 280 6329

107 McWilliams Wines Pty Ltd
68 Anzac St
Chullora NSW 2190
(02) 707 1266

108 Metro Wine Distributors
20/3 Abbotsford St
West Leederville WA 6007
(09) 382 2098

109 MGM Wine Distributors
Cabon Crt
Osborne Park WA 6176
(09) 244 3299

110 Mildara Blass Ltd
101 Dundas Pl
Albert Park Vic 3206
(03) 690 9966

111 Miranda Wines Pty Ltd
PO Box 405
Griffith NSW 2680
(069) 62 4033

112 National Liquor Co.
6a/2958 Logan Rd
Underwood Qld 4119
(07) 841 0077

113 National Liquor Co.
210 Bannister Rd
Canning Vale WA 6155
(09) 455 2477

114 National Liquor Co.
26 Giddes St
Mulgrave Vic 3170
(018) 34 9502

115 National Wine Merchants
185 Sturt St
Adelaide SA 5000
(08) 231 1066

116 Negociants Australia
205 Grote St
Adelaide SA 5000
(08) 231 1066

117 Nicks Wine Merchants
13 Swanston St
Melbourne Vic 3000
(03) 650 3056

118 Norman Zerbe
PO Box 4843
Cairns Qld 4870
(070) 51 5544

119 Northern Australian Liquor
Distribution
PO Box 39498
Winnellie NT 0821
(089) 84 4622

120 Oak Barrel Wines
24 Barrier St
Fyshwick ACT 2609
(06) 280 6371

121 Oakwood Wines
2/7 Olive Grove
Keysborough Vic 3173
(03) 798 6278

122 Orlando Wyndham
33 Exeter Terrace
Devon Park SA 5008
(08) 208 2444

123 Pat Dilling
7/57 Raleigh St
Carlisle WA 6101
(018) 94 9188

124 Penfold Wine Group
634 Princes Highway
Tempe NSW 2044
(02) 559 1466

124a Peter Bourne Wine
Emporium
127 Bayswater Rd
Rushcutters Bay NSW 2011
(02) 361 4885

125 Pinnacle Wine Merchants
PO Box 332
Brighton Le Sands NSW 2216
(02) 567 5443

126 Porter & Co.
PO Box 351
Kingswood SA 5062
(08) 373 3010

127 Queensland Fine Wines
PO Box 535
Mt Gravatt Qld 4122
(07) 849 6896

128 Queensland Liquor Distributor
PMB 20
Archerfield Qld 4108

129 Regional Liquor Agencies
5 Theresa St
Norwood SA 55067
(08) 363 0733

130 Regional Wines Pty Ltd
PO Box 4
Darlinghurst NSW 2010
(02) 858 5818

131 Remy Australie Pty Ltd
484 Victoria Rd
Gladesville NSW 2111
(02) 816 5000

132 RHL Wine Consultants
11 Bridge St
Port Melbourne Vic 3207
(03) 645 3778

133 Richard Mackie Fine Wines
155 Stephen Terrace
Walkerville SA 5081
(08) 269 1162

134 Roger Brown Wine Agencies
82 Grosevnor St
Wahroonga NSW 2076
(02) 489 3139

135 Rosemount Estates Pty Ltd
18 Herbert St
Artarmon NSW 2064
(02) 906 2613

136 Rosemount Estates Pty Ltd
14 Campbells St
Bowen Hills Qld 4006
(07) 252 2795

137 Rosemount Estates Pty Ltd
2 River St
South Yarra Vic 3141
(03) 826 1327

138 Rosemount Estates Pty Ltd
252 Cambridge St
Wembley WA 6014
(09) 388 3154

139 Rutherglen Wine Co.
67–69 Thistlethwaite St
South Melbourne Vic 3205
(03) 646 6666

140 S. Smith & Son Pty Ltd
PO Box 10
Angaston SA 5353
(085) 64 2423

141 S. Smith & Son Pty Ltd
30–32 Skarrat St
North Auburn NSW 2144
(02) 648 4511

142 S. Smith & Son Pty Ltd
13 Shoebury St
Rocklea Qld 4106
(07) 892 5022

143 S. Smith & Son Pty Ltd
109 Hyde St
Footscray Vic 3011
(03) 689 1122

144 S. Smith & Son Pty Ltd
114 Radium St
Welshpool WA 6106
(09) 451 9822

145 S & V Wine Merchants
11/47 OG Rd
Klemzig SA 5087
(08) 369 1113

146 Saltram Wine Estates
10 Jasmine St
Botany NSW 2019
(02) 316 7129

147 Seabrooks
347 Victoria St
Brunswick Vic 3056
(03) 388 0400

148 Seagram Australia Pty Ltd
PO Box 171
Botany NSW 2019
(02) 659 3999

149 Select Vineyards
35 Market St
South Melbourne Vic 3205
(03) 696 0200

150 Selwyn Wines
26–28 Coolgardie St
West Perth WA 6005
(09) 481 2355

151 South Australia Liquor
75 Hardys Rd
Underdale SA 5032
(08) 352 5611

152 Stuart Mellington
16 Clonaig St
East Brighton Vic 3187
(03) 596 5344

153 Suntory (Aust) Pty Ltd
PO Box 1838
Woden ACT 2606
(06) 231 9887

154 Suntory (Aust) Pty Ltd
PO Box 171
Roseberry NSW 2018
(02) 698 9200

155 Sutherland Cellars
371 Flinders St
Melbourne Vic 3000
(03) 629 5296

156 Swift & Moore
8 Egerton St
Silverwater NSW 2141
(02) 647 1599

157 Tallerman Wine & Spirits
Unit 5 Bayland Ave
Coopers Plains Qld 4108
(07) 875 1980

158 Tasmanian Fine Wine
Distributors
124 Davey St
Hobart Tas 7000
(002) 34 5211

159 Taylors Wines Pty Ltd
1–3 Charles St
Petersham NSW 2049
(02) 560 2122

160 Taylors Wines Pty Ltd
1 Yarra Pl
South Melbourne Vic 3205
(03) 696 2066

161 Taylors Wines Pty Ltd
67 Bellrick St
Acacia Ridge Qld 4110
(07) 344 3022

162 The Fine Wine Specialist
PO Box 192
Botany NSW 2019
(02) 316 7400

163 The Wine Company
4/56 Smith St
Springvale Vic 3171
(03) 562 3900

164 Tierce Select Wines
PO Box 1173
Carlton Vic 3053
(03) 419 4477

165 Tim Seats Pty Ltd
PO Box 39613
Winellie NT 0821
(089) 81 2418

166 Tisdall Wines
114–118 Miller St
West Melbourne Vic 3003
(03) 339 8788

167 Tootells Wine & Spirits
45 Plantation Ave
Brighton East Vic 3187
(03) 592 4853

168 Trimex Pty Ltd
213 Botany Rd
Waterloo NSW 2017
(02) 698 5155

169 Tucker & Co.
11 Roseberry Ave
Roseberry NSW 2018
(02) 662 2725

170 Tucker & Co.
1/26 Bailey St
West End Qld 4101
(07) 844 2381

171 Tucker & Co.
87 Knutsford Ave
Rivervale WA 6103
(09) 277 1100

172 Tyrrell's Vineyards
Broke Rd
Pokolbin NSW 2320
(008) 04 5501

173 Vaughans Wines & Spirits
PO Box 984
Launceston Tas 7250
(003) 34 3244

174 Victorian Wine Consultants
34 Millton St
West Melbourne Vic 3003
(03) 328 3033

175 Victuals Pty Ltd
113 Ferrar St
South Melbourne Vic 3205
(03) 696 1250

176 Vinimpex
PO Box 414
Bassendean WA 6054
(09) 377 4699

177 Vintners Wine Company
1/350 Military Rd
Cremorne NSW 2090
(02) 904 1999

178 Vintners Wine Company
176 Rathmines Rd
Hawthorn East Vic 3123
(03) 813 1879

179 Virginia Liquor
1908 Sandgate Rd
Virginia Qld 4010

180 Western Australia Liquor
Distributors
1/14 Keegan St
O'Connor WA 6163
(09) 314 1811

181 Webster Wine & Spirits
9 Patrick St
Hobart Tas 7000
(002) 38 0200

182 West Coast Wine Cellars
94 Thompsons Rd
North Fremantle WA 6159
(09) 335 3869

183 Western Wine Agency
4 Judd St
South Perth WA 6151

184 Westwood Wine Agencies
6 Wharton St
Surrey Hills Vic 3127
(03) 836 7341

185 Wine 2000
11 Eurella St
Kenmore Qld 4069
(07) 378 0210

186 Wine Partners
94 Moray St
New Farm Qld 4005

187 Yarra Valley Wine Consultants
176 Rathmines Rd
Hawthorn East Vic 3123
(03) 813 1879

188 Young & Rashleigh Wine
Merchants
3/19–21 Bourke Rd
Alexandria NSW 2015
(02) 310 3233

Canadian Distributors

189 Arvin Inc
739 Rue St Pierre
Terrebonne Quebec J6W 1E1

190 Ascona Agents
5881 Beresford St
Burnaby BC V5J 1K1

191 Australvin
1967 Baile St
Montreal Quebec H3H 1P6

192 Charton & Hobbs Inc.
408/5080 Timberlea Blvd
Mississauga Ontario L4W 4M2

193 Du Chasse Wines & Spirits
58 Fairview Blvd
Toronto Ontario M4K 1L9

194 Dumont Vins & Spiriteux
175 Chemin Marieville
Rougemont Quebec J0L 1M0

195 Featherstone & Co.
5945 Kathleen Ave
Burnaby BC M4P 2E5

196 Gilbey Canada
400 Kipling Ave
Toronto Ontario M8V 3L2

197 Gladstone & Company Wine
Imports
6650 Vine St
Vancouver BC V6P 5N5

198 Grady Wine Marketing
3134 East 20th Ave
Vancouver BC V5M 2V5

199 Inniskillin Wines
RR 1 Niagara Parkway
Niagara-on-the-Lake Ontario
L0S 1J0

200 J Cipelli Wines & Spirits
Unit 6
109 Woodbine Downs Blvd
Etobicoke Ontario M9W 6Y1

201 John F. Kelly & Assoc.
3057 West 44th Ave
Vancouver BC V6N 3K5

202 John Hanna & Sons
14 Park Lane Circle
Richmond Hill Ontario L4C 6S8

203 Labatt International Brands
Suite 600
6711 Mississauga Rd
Mississauga Ontario L5W 2W3

204 Lifford Agencies
Suite 502
1155 Yonge St
Toronto Ontario M4T 1W2

205 Lorac Wine Inc.
204 Old Forest Hill Rd
Toronto Ontario M6C 2G9

206 Mark Anthony Group
1290 Homer St
Vancouver BC V6B 265

207 Michel Reichart Agencies Inc.
5th Floor, 468 Queen St East
Toronto Ontario M5A 1T7

208 Noble Estates Wines & Spirits
3875 Keele St
North York Ontario M3J 1N6

209 Pacific Wine & Spirits
Suite 007–11523
100 Avenue
Edmonton Alberta T5K 0J8

210 Remy Canada
Suite 703, 2345 Yonge St
Toronto Ontario M4P 2E5

211 Saverio Schiralli Agencies
642 The Queensway
Toronto Ontario M8Y 1K5

212 Select Wine Merchants
PO Box 2005
Vancouver BC V6B 3P8

213 Termes Agencies
1108 Eyremount Dr
West Vancouver BC V7S 2C1

214 The Delf Group
13120 Delf Pl
Richmond BC V6V 2A2

215 Torion Trading
PO Box 844
Bradford Ontario L3Z 2B3

216 Totally Awesome Wine
Company
104–5562 Balsam St
Vancouver BC V6M 4B7

New Zealand Distributors

217 Eurowine
PO Box 12559
Thornton Wellington
(04) 499 1734

218 Kitchener Wines
6 Heather St
Parnell Auckland

219 Negociants NZ
130-138 St Georges Bay Rd
Parnell Auckland
(09) 366 1356

219a New Zealand Wine & Spirits
Cnr Springs & East Tamaki Rds
East Tamaki Auckland
(09) 274 2500

United Kingdom Distributors

220 A. H. Wines
Back St
West Camel Nr Yeovil
Somerset BA22 7QB
(0935) 850 1167

221 A. L. Vose & Co.
Town House
Main St
Grange-over-Sands LA11 6DY
(05395) 33328

222 Alex Finlater & Co.
77 Abbey Rd
London NW8 OAE
(071) 624 7311

223 Alliance Wine Co.
Bridge of Weir
Renfrewshire
Scotland PO11 35A
(0505) 61 3215

224 Anthony Byrne Fine Wines P/L
88 High St
Ramsey Cambridgeshire PE17
1BS
(0487) 81 4555

225 Australian Estates
31 Hitchin St
Baldcock Herts AL5 1RH

226 Australian Wine Centre
50 The Strand
London WC2N 5LW

227 Australian Wineries Ltd
20 Craddocks Pde
Ashstead Surrey KT21 1QJ
(037) 227 4065

228 Averys of Bristol Ltd
7 Park St
Bristol BS1 5NG
(0272) 21 4141

229 Barwell & Jones
24 Fore St
Ispwich Suffolk IP4 IJU
(0473) 23 2322

230 Berkmann Wine Cellars
12 Brewery Rd
London N7 9NH
(071) 609 0018

231 Bibendum Wine Ltd
113 Regents Park Rd
London NW1 8UR
(071) 722 5577

232 Booze Brothers
11 Beechway
Wilmslow Cheshire SK9 6LB
(0625) 50 2383

233 Boxford Wine Co.
Butchers Land
Colchester Essex CO6 5EA
(0787) 21 0187

234 Broad Street Wine Co.
Wharf St
Warwick CV34 5LB
(0926) 49 3951

235 Bywater & Broderick
7 Main St
Nether Poppeton
York YO2 6H5

236 Caxton Tower Wines
4 Harlequin Ave
Brentford Middlesex TW8
9EW
(081) 758 4500

237 Charles Mitchell Wines
Thames Trading Centre
Woodrow Way
Manchester M30 6BP
(061) 775 1626

238 Charles Taylor Wines Ltd
64 Alexandra Rd
Epsom Surrey KT17 4B7
(0372) 72 8330

239 Chennell & Armstrong Ltd
Manor Lane
Shipton Rd
York YO3 6TX
(0904) 64 7991

240 Christopher Piper Wines Ltd
1 Silver St
Ottery St Mary
Devon EX11 1DB
(0404) 81 4139

241 Corney & Barrow Ltd
13 Helmet Row
London EC1V 3QJ
(071) 251 4051

242 Crestview Wines Ltd
205b Old Dover Rd
Canterbury Kent
(0227) 76 691

243 D & D Wines Ltd
Adams Court
Knutsford Cheshire WA16 6BA
(0565) 65 0952

244 Deinhard & Co.
95 Southwark St
London SE1 OJF
(071) 262 1111

245 Domaines Direct
29 Wilmington Sq
London WC1X 0EG
(071) 837 1142

246 Domaines Drouhin & Assoc.
7 Old Park Ln
London W17 3LJ
(071) 499 6292

247 Ehrmanns Wine Shippers
29 Corsica St
London N51 JT

248 Fields Wine Merchants
55 Sloane Ave
Chelsea London SW3 3DH
(071) 589 5753

249 Fine Wines of New Zealand
PO Box 476
London NW5 2NZ
(071) 482 0093

250 Francis Stickney Fine Wines
1 The Village
North End Way
London NW3 7HA
(081) 201 9096

251 Geoffrey Roberts Agencies
430 High Rd
London MW10 2HA
(081) 451 880

252 Gleblands
Vincents Lane
Dorking Surrey RH4 342

253 Granby Wines
28 Granby Ave
Harpenden Herts AL5 5QR

254 Grants of St James
56a Packhorse Rd
Bucks SL9 3EF

255 Griersons
430 High Rd
London NW10 2HA
(081) 459 8011

256 Hallgarten Wines
Dallow Rd
Luton Beds LU1 1UR
(0582) 22 538

257 Hatch Mansfield Agencies
Guildford Business Park
Guildford
Surrey GU1 5AD
(0483) 64861

258 Haughton Fine Wines
Chorley
Nantwich Cheshire CW5 8JR
(0270) 74 537

259 Hedley Wright & Co.
10–11 Twyford Centre
London Rd
Bishops Stortford Herts
(0279) 50 6512

260 Heyman Bros Ltd
130 Ebury St
London SW1
(071) 730 0324

261 John E. Fells & Sons
Fells House
Birbreck Grove
London W3 7QD
(081) 749 3661

262 Justerni & Brooks
61 St James St
London SW1
(071) 493 8271

263 Lawlers
88/92 South St
Dorking Surrey RH4 2EZ
(0306) 88 4412

264 Lay & Wheeler
John Lay House
95 Gosbecks Rd
Colchester Essex C01 1JA
(0206) 76 4446

265 Maisons Marques et Domaines
Ltd
4 College Mews
St Annes Hill
London SW18 2SJ
(081) 871 3955

266 Malcolm Desborough
21 George St
St Albans Herts AL3 4ES
(0727) 34 314

267 Marchant Wine Cellars
Marchant Rise
Northian
Rye East Sussex

268 Margaret Francis
The Manor House
120 Kingston Rd
Wimbeldon SW1 9ILY
(081) 542 8101

269 Mayor Sworder & Co. Ltd
21 Duke St Hill
London SE1 2SW
(071) 407 5111

270 McKinley Vintners
50 Lanercost Rd
London SW2 3DN
(081) 671 7219

271 Merchant Vintners
Red Duster House
101 York St
Hull HU2 0QX
(0482) 29 443

272 Michael Druitt Agency
135–142 New Kent Rd
London SE1 6TU
(071) 493 5412

273 Michael Morgan Ltd
Thames House
18 Park St
London SE1 9EL
(071) 407 3466

274 Millex Wines
3 The Gables
Whitchurch Hants RG28 7NH
(025) 689 2623

275 Milton Sandford
PO Box 3
Twyford Reading
Berkshire RG10 NUG
(0734) 34 5251

276 Moet et Chandon Ltd
13 Grosevnor Cres
London SW1X 7EE
(071) 235 9411

277 Montana Wines Ltd
Telegraph St
Shipston-on-Stour
Warwickshire CU36 4AF
(0608) 63 025

278 Mount Helen Wines
April Cottage
Anvil Rd
Pimperne Blandford Forum
Dorset DT11 8UQ

279 Negociants UK
64a High St
Harfenden Herts AL5 2SP
(0582) 46 2859

280 Neville Cox Wines
44 Hunts Hill
Glemsford
Suffolk CO10 7RP
(0787) 28 0187

281 New World Wines
31 Hitchin St
Baldock
Herts SG7 6AQ

282 Oddbins Ltd
31 Weir Rd
Wimbeldon
London
(081) 944 4400

283 O.W. Loeb & Co. Ltd
64 Southwark Bridge Rd
London SE1 0AS
(071) 928 7750

284 Paragon Vintners Ltd
91 Park St
London W1Y 4AX
(071) 491 0623

285 Pattisons Wines
Charlecote Mill House
Hampton Lucy
Warwickshire

286 Peel Estate
2 Onslow Rd
Walton-on-Thames
Surrey KT12 5BB

287 Penfolds PWG Vintners
12 King St
Richmond Surrey TW9 1ND
(081) 332 6600

288 Peter Diplock Ltd
William Blake House
Warshire St
London W1
(071) 734 2099

289 Peter Lehmann (UK) Ltd
Godmersham Park
Godmersham, Nr Canterbury
Kent CT4 7DT
(0227) 731 1353

290 Peter Watts Wines
Wisdoms Barn Colne Rd
Coggeshall Essex CO6 1TD
(0376) 561130

291 Pol Roger Ltd
Lanark House New St
Ledbury Herts HR8 2DX
(0531) 61 11

292 Rainbow Wines
Appledore Rd
Tenterden Kent TN30 7BE
(0580) 763327

293 Rawlings Voigt
144–152 Bermondsey St
London SE1 3T
(071) 403 9269

294 Reid Wines
The Mill
Marsh Lane
Hallatrow Nr Bristol BS18 SEB
(0761) 45 2645

295 Remy & Assoc.
The Malthouse
45 New St
Henly-on-Thames
Oxon RG9 2BP
(0491) 41 0777

296 Ren Vic Wines Ltd
2 School Cottages
North Royston
Herts SG8 0S4

297 Richards Walford
Manor House
Pickworth
Stamford Lines PE9 4DJ
(0780) 41 0242

298 Rodney Densem Wines
Stapley Bank
Nantwich
Cheshire CW5 7JW
(0270) 62 3665

299 Rosemount Estates Pty Ltd
Hatchlands
East Clandon
Guildford Surrey GU4 790
(0483) 21 1466

300 Rutherglen Agencies
22 Oxford Rd
Denham
Middx UB9 RDQ

301 Ryecroft Vineyards Pty Ltd
c/o Hatchlands
East Clandon
Guildford Surrey GU4 790
(0483) 21 1717

302 Stevens Garnier Ltd
3/5 Hythe Bridge St
Oxford OX1 2EW

303 Stratford Wine Merchants
High St
Cookham-on-Thames
Berks SL6 9SQ
(0628) 81 0606

304 T & W Wines
51 King St
Thetford Norfolk IP24 2AU
(0842) 76 5646

305 Taltarni
PO Box 2040
Boxford Sudbury
Suffolk CO10 5DY
(0787) 21 1411

306 Tanners Wines
26 Wyle Cop
Shrewsbury
Shropshire SY1 1XD
(0743) 23 2400

307 Terry Platt Wine Merchant
Ferndale Rd
Llandudno Junction
Gwynedd LL31 9NT
(0492) 59 2971

308 The Chigwell Wine Cellar
181 High Rd
Chigwell Essex 1G7 6NU

309 The Hanwood Group Ltd
41–43 High St
Lutterworth
Leicestershire LE17 4AY
(0455) 55 6161

310 The Wine Treasury
143 Edbury St
London SW1W 9QN
(071) 730 6774

311 Tony Lamont Consulting
8 Cardain House
Gregories Rd
Beaconsfield
Buckinghamshire HP9 1HG
(0494) 67 8971

312 Unifare Ltd
Oslo Crt
Pr Albert Rd
St Johns Wood NW8 7EN

313 Villeneuve Wines
27 Northgate
Peebles EH45 8RX
(0721) 22 500

314 Vinceremos Wines
65 Raglan Rd
Leeds LS2 9DZ
(0532) 43 1691

315 Viniceros (Cornwall Wine
Merchants)
Chapel Rd
Tuckingmill Camborne
Cornwall TR14 8QY
(0209) 71 5765

316 Vintage Roots
Shephards Farm
Wargrave Rd
Berks RG10 8DT
(0734) 40 1222

317 Walter S. Seigal Ltd
50 Battersea Park Rd
London SW11 4JP
(071) 627 2720

318 Waterloo Wine Co.
6 Vineyard Borough
London SE1 1QI
(071) 403 7967

319 Waverly Vintners Ltd
PO Box 22
Creiff Rd
Perth PH1 25L
Scotland
(0738) 29 621

320 Whittaker Wines
35 Chatsworth Rd
High Lane
Stockport Cheshire SK6 8DA
(0663) 64 497

321 Whiclar & Gordon
Gleblands
Vincents Lane
Dorking Surrey RH4 342
(0306) 88 5711

322 Windrush Wines Ltd
The Barracks
Cecily Hill
Cirencester
Gloucester GL7 2EF
(0285) 65 0466

323 Wine Cellars
153–155 Wandsworth High St
London SW18 4JB

324 Wine Raks
21 Springfield Rd
Aberdeen Scotland AB1 7RJ
(0224) 31 1460

325 Winesource
393 Ham Green
Holt Trowbridge
Wilts BA14 6PX
(0225) 78 3007

326 Yalumba
64a High St
Harpenden Herts AL5 25P